THE EXPERIMENTAL

EXERCISE OF FREEDOM

THE EXPERIMENTAL EXERCISE OF FREEDOM

LYGIA CLARK
GEGO
MATHIAS GOERITZ
HÉLIO OITICICA
MIRA SCHENDEL

ORGANIZED BY Rina Carvajal and Alma Ruiz

WITH ESSAYS BY
Rina Carvajal
Catherine David
Suely Rolnik
Alma Ruiz
Sônia Salzstein
Osvaldo Sánchez

EDITED BY Susan Martin and Alma Ruiz

THE MUSEUM OF CONTEMPORARY ART, LOS ANGELES

This publication accompanies the exhibition "**THE EXPERIMENTAL EXERCISE OF FREEDOM: LYGIA CLARK, GEGO, MATHIAS GOERITZ, HÉLIO OITICICA, AND MIRA SCHENDEL**," organized by Rina Carvajal and Alma Ruiz and presented at The Museum of Contemporary Art, Los Angeles.

October 17, 1999–January 23, 2000

"**THE EXPERIMENTAL EXERCISE OF FREEDOM: LYGIA CLARK, GEGO, MATHIAS GOERITZ, HÉLIO OITICICA, AND MIRA SCHENDEL**" is made possible in part by generous support from The Andy Warhol Foundation for the Visual Arts, Inc.; Catharine and Jeffrey Soros; Richard Shapiro; the Lampadia Foundation; the Los Angeles County Arts Commission; the Brazilian Embassy; and Pacific Bell.

The exhibition catalogue is made possible in part by generous support from Colección Patricia Phelps de Cisneros, Caracas.

EDITORS: Susan Martin and Alma Ruiz
COPY EDITORS: John Alan Farmer and Sherri Schottlaender
PHOTO RESEARCH: Susana Smith Bautista
DESIGNER: Rebeca Méndez, Rebeca Méndez Communication Design
ASSOCIATE DESIGNER: Lesley Tucker
Printed and bound in Ostfildern, Germany, by Cantz

THE MUSEUM OF CONTEMPORARY ART, LOS ANGELES
250 South Grand Avenue, Los Angeles, California 90012
TEL 213.621.2766
FAX 213.620.8674
www.moca-la.org

Library of Congress Cataloging-in-Publication Data
Rina Carvajal and Alma Ruiz
The Experimental Exercise of Freedom: Lygia Clark, Gego, Mathias Goeritz, Hélio Oiticica and Mira Schendel/Rina Carvajal and Alma Ruiz; with essays by Rina Carvajal, Catherine David, Suely Rolnik, Alma Ruiz, Sônia Salzstein, Osvaldo Sánchez.

p. cm.

Exhibition presented at The Museum of Contemporary Art, Los Angeles, 17 October 1999–23 January 2000.
Includes bibliographical references.

ISBN 0-914357-64-6

I. Exhibitions. 2. I.
II. Museum of Contemporary Art (Los Angeles, Calif.)
III. Title.

CONTENTS

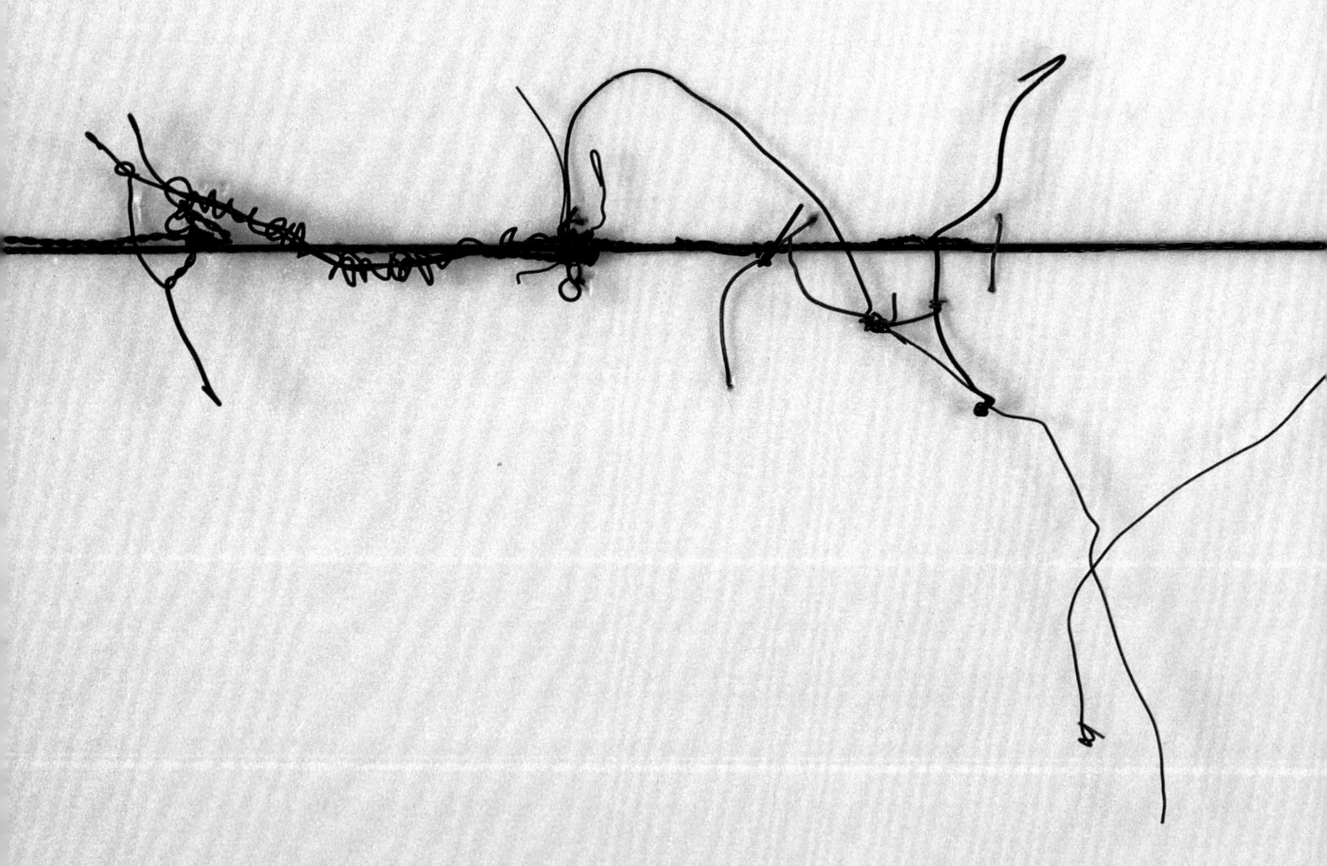

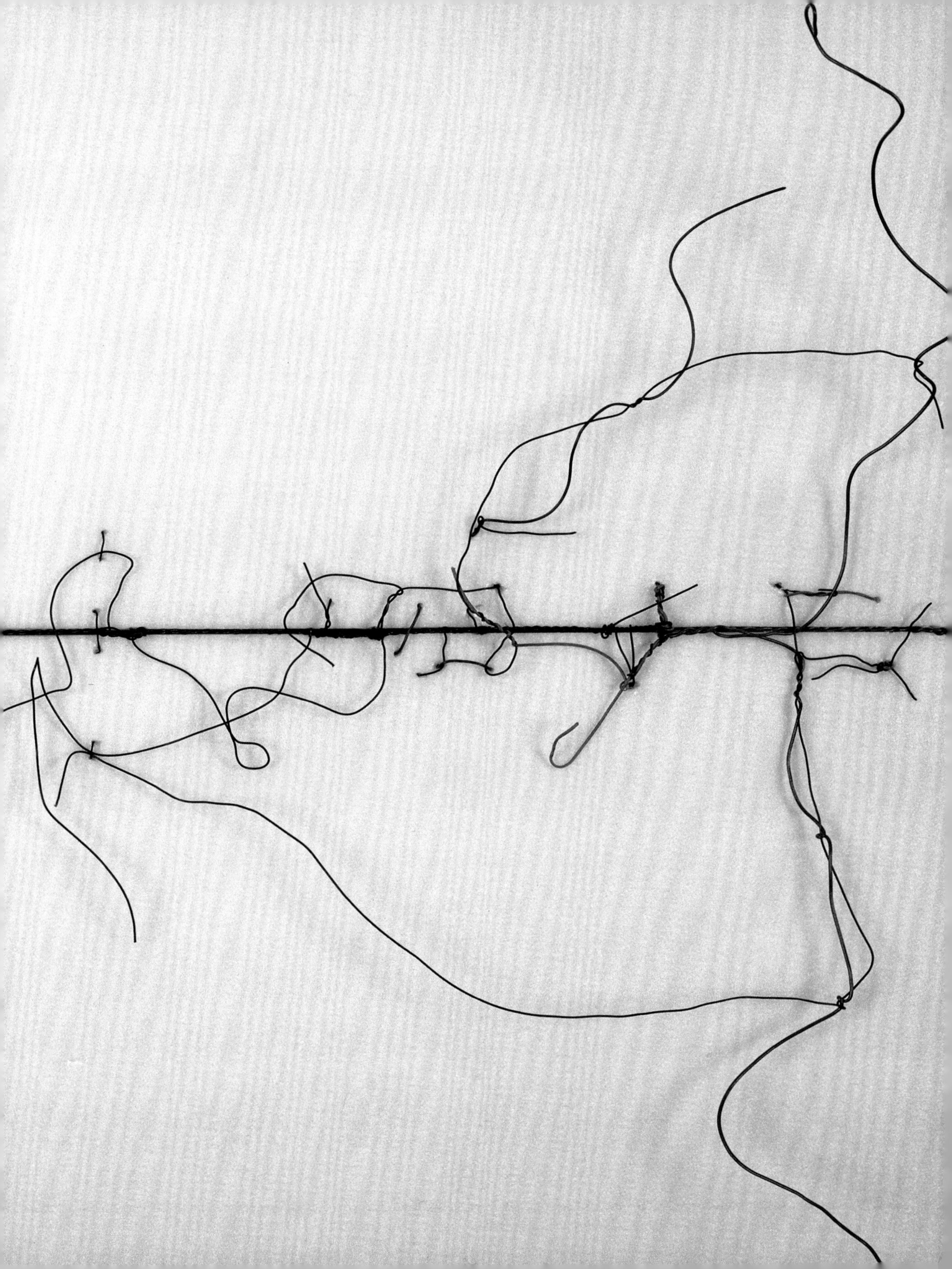

FOREWORD

"The Experimental Exercise of Freedom: Lygia Clark, Gego, Mathias Goeritz, Hélio Oiticica, and Mira Schendel" focuses its attention on a period in post-war Latin America marked by great artistic experimentation and cultural dynamism. In a broad range of work, each of these artists exemplifies the largely unexplored and unacknowledged notions of avant-gardism in the region. Significantly, this exhibition represents the continuing fulfillment of MOCA's commitment to bringing contemporary art from Latin America to Los Angeles and Southern California and joins other successful exhibitions of Latin American artists such as Brazilian Rosângela Rennó ("Cicatriz," 1996), Cuban Kcho ("Todo Cambia," 1997), and Cuban-American Ana Mendieta ("Ana Mendieta," 1998).

Begun during Richard Koshalek's tenure as MOCA Director and due in great part to his discerning vision of the museum as an international art center, the exhibition seeks to remap the history of twentieth-century art by expanding upon commonly acknowledged artistic developments in Latin America, and captures a specific moment of change, largely brought about by global upheaval. It reflects upon issues such as the complicated relationship between Latin America's past and present, as well as the cultural, social, and artistic bonds that connect the region to Europe, and the continent's capacity to assimilate European and indigenous cultures and transform them into a unique and original hybrid closer to New World realities. Organized with great intelligence and sensitivity by MOCA Assistant Curator Alma Ruiz and Ahmanson Curatorial Fellow Rina Carvajal, "The Experimental Exercise of Freedom" will be a revelation to many.

This exhibition would not have been possible without the generosity and kindness of collectors and funders. We are very thankful to all the collectors

PRECEDING PAGES: GEGO ***Untitled: Drawing without Paper 85/2*** 1985

for enthusiastically embracing the project's scope and intention, and in particular to the artists' families who, as executors of estates, made everything possible to facilitate their inclusion. As we embarked on a fundraising campaign, we did so with apprehension and caution, for unfamiliar names and places do not necessarily get people's attention. To our surprise, the response to this exhibition has been extraordinary. On behalf of the museum staff and the Board of Trustees, we would like to express our sincere appreciation to the individuals and institutions who readily responded with funding for the exhibition: The Andy Warhol Foundation for the Visual Arts, Inc.; Catharine and Jeffrey Soros; Richard Shapiro; the Lampadia Foundation; the Los Angeles County Arts Commission; Colección Patricia Phelps de Cisneros, Caracas; the Brazilian Embassy; and Pacific Bell.

The entire Board of Trustees embraced this project. We are especially grateful to them, particularly to Chair Audrey M. Irmas, President Gilbert B. Friesen, and Vice Chairs Ruth Bloom, Robert C. Davidson Jr., and Clifford J. Einstein for their singular vision and unwavering support.

We are extremely proud to present "The Experimental Exercise of Freedom" and its accompanying publication, and I look forward to working together with the staff to build the museum's successful exhibitions program and to leading the institution into a challenging new era.

Jeremy Strick
Director

FOREWORD

ACKNOWLEDGMENTS

As curators of "The Experimental Exercise of Freedom: Lygia Clark, Gego, Mathias Goeritz, Hélio Oiticica, and Mira Schendel," we feel very fortunate to have been able to bring this project to fruition. The experience has been intellectually challenging and rewarding. We are indebted to The Museum of Contemporary Art for opening its doors to this exhibition.

The first person we would like to thank is Richard Koshalek, former director of The Museum of Contemporary Art. He supported the project from the beginning, and he worked closely with us through every phase of the exhibition and publication development. He was also a constant source of sympathetic encouragement during the many difficult moments. No less supportive has been Jeremy Strick, MOCA's current director. In the short time that he has been at the museum, Jeremy has demonstrated an enormous interest in this project; he encouraged us to organize a symposium, and he has facilitated ways for the exhibition and related programs to reach the largest possible audience.

We would like to express our deepest appreciation to all the artists' families for their collaboration. For MATHIAS GOERITZ: Ferruccio Asta, Daniel Goeritz, and Ida Rodríguez Prampolini. For GEGO: the Gego Foundation. We received full support from the Foundation through Gego's daughter, Barbara Gunz, and her granddaughter, Ester Crespín. Midway through the exhibition's development, Josefina Manrique became the Foundation's contact person, and she graciously and efficiently worked with us, expediently fulfilling our numerous requests, facilitating close contact with local collectors, and overseeing crating and shipping arrangements for all Venezuelan loans. For LYGIA CLARK: Alvaro Edwards Clark, Eduardo Lins Clark Ribeiro, and Elisabeth Clark. For HÉLIO OITICICA: the Projeto Hélio Oiticica through Cesar

Oiticica Sr., Claudio Oiticica, and Cesar Oiticica Jr. As director of the Projeto Hélio Oiticica, Cesar Oiticica Jr. worked closely with us to enable the successful presentation of *Eden*. For MIRA SCHENDEL: her daughter, Ada Schendel, who generously gave of her time and knowledge. She lent key works to the exhibition and played a major role in contacting other collectors on our behalf. In addition to the artists' families, we would also like to express our gratitude to the following collectors: Ricard Takeshi Akagawa; Aracy Amaral; Guy Brett; Brondesbury Holdings Ltd.; Colección acervo del patrimonio artístico y cultural de la Facultad de Arquitectura, UNAM; Colección Banco Mercantil; Colección Ignacio y Valentina Oberto; Colección Patricia Phelps de Cisneros; Helen Escobedo; Fundación Polar; Guilherme and Israel Issar Furmanovich; Boris and Yolanda Gerson and Manuel González; Monica Gutglass; Philip Henríquez; Museo de Barquisimeto; Museu de Arte Contemporânea de Campinas "José Pancetti"; Rodrigo Naves; José Resende; Seka Severin; Pedro Tassinari Filho; Universidad Central de Venezuela; and the collectors who wish to remain anonymous. We would not have been able to realize this exhibition without their participation and their generosity.

For their crucial involvement in the various aspects of the exhibition, we would like to acknowledge and express our sincerest thanks to the following MOCA staff: Assistant Director Kathleen Bartels for expertly and collegially guiding us through a web of administrative matters; Chief Curator Paul Schimmel for lending his extensive experience in curatorial matters; Chief Operating Officer Jack Wiant for working with us on all aspects of the exhibition budget; Director of Development Erica Clark, working with Grants Officer Jillian Spaak and Grants Associate Jackie Kersh, for their successful funding campaign; Director of Education Kim Kanatani, Associate Director of Education Toby Tannenbaum, and Adults Program Coordinator Caroline Blackburn, for facilitating through surrounding educational programs the understanding and appreciation of the ideas and artworks presented in the exhibition; Exhibitions Production Manager John Bowsher, Exhibitions

Production Associate Zazu Faure, Chief Exhibition Technician Jang Park, Media Arts Technical Manager David Bradshaw, and all of the preparators, for the invaluable knowledge and professionalism they brought to the exhibition's complex installation; Associate Registrar Portland McCormick, for her expert handling of loans and for her unflinching resolve to make the crating and shipping of all artwork as safe and expedient as possible; Director of Marketing and Public Relations Sylvia Hohri, Press Officer Katherine Lee, and the design staff for putting together a superb marketing campaign, for admirably handling press matters, and for creating outstandingly designed materials for the exhibition. Peter Kirby of Media Art Services has worked with MOCA on several exhibitions, and we have grown accustomed to relying on his technical abilities and thoughtful suggestions for much of our audiovisual needs; this exhibition is no exception, and we are thankful to him for his contribut on.

We are indebted to Curatorial Secretaries Deborah Vogel and Ellie Kevorkian, who tirelessly and diligently worked on the exhibition, and to Curatorial Secretary Virginia Edwards, who joined the project team during its last and most delicate phase and whose organizational skills and calm demeanor greatly facilitated bringing the exhibition to a successful completion. It was a pleasure to work with all of them, and we are most grateful for their contributions. Special mention and thanks also go to intern Filipa Oliveira. Filipa's language skills, intelligence, cheerful disposition, and ability to cross cultures made her an indispensable member of the exhibition team; she greatly facilitated communication between the museum and our Latin American collaborators. To the rest of the MOCA staff whose names cannot be mentioned here due to lack of space, we thank you for the pride you take in doing your jobs well and for the spontaneous expressions of support you have so openly demonstrated to us at various times.

This exhibition is accompanied by an extraordinary publication. We are very fortunate to have had the collaboration of authors Catherine David, Suely Rolnik, Sônia Salzstein, and Osvaldo Sánchez; their talent is reflected in the insightful texts they so generously contributed. Our utmost thanks go to editor Susan Martin for her exceptional work in editing the book and bringing it to completion under a rather tight schedule, and to her assistant, Danielle Lesniewski, for skillfully assisting with this project. We also want to express our appreciation to John Alan Farmer in New York and Sherri Schottlaender in Los Angeles for their help in shaping the book's content through their exceptional copyediting skills. In addition, John's knowledge of Latin American art made him an ideal collaborator on the publication. Thanks are also owed to Research Assistant Susana Smith Bautista for gathering all the visual materials for the catalogue, organizing the artists' bibliographies, and assisting in the coordination of various aspects of the symposium; to Rebeca Méndez of Rebeca Méndez Communication Design and her talented staff, in particular Lesley Tucker, for the admirable manner in which they creatively and expertly translated the exhibition's concept into a unique publication design; and to translators Noah Chasin, Bernardine Fajerman, Nicolas Guagnin, Lyn Di Iorio, Clifford Landers, Isabelle Marmasse, Karen Medeiros Schneider, Patience Mohl, and Jason Weiss. We warmly thank them all for their constant adjustments to our schedule in the face of mounting time pressures.

Manuel J. Borja-Villel, former director of the Antoni Tàpies Foundation and current director of the Museum of Contemporary Art, both in Barcelona, deserves a special mention as well as our deepest gratitude. Manuel's scholarly advice throughout the exhibition's organization was of utmost importance. He lent his unwavering support during many of the exhibition's most complex moments and generously gave his time and objective opinions each time he was consulted.

We owe a debt of gratitude to museum colleagues, institutions, artists, collectors, scholars, and friends. In Brazil we would like to thank Luciana Brito, Sandra Brito, Wilson Coutinho, Anna Maria Maiolino, Maria Regina do Nascimento Brito, Adriano Pedrosa, Reynaldo Roels Jr.; in Mexico, Itzel Alba, Ferruccio Asta, Dolores Beistegui de Robles, Bertha Cea Echenique,

Miguel Cervantes, Rita Eder, Cristina Galvez Guzzi, Teodoro González de León, Magdalena Graham, Lily Kassner, Eugenio López, Ana María Rodríguez, Isabel Rodríguez Alonso, and Ana Cecilia Trebiño; in Venezuela, Guillermo Barrios, Jimmy and Leonora Belilty, José Camilo Betancourt, Maitena de Elguezábal, Lisbeth Flores, Harry and Masula Mannil, Luis Pérez Oramas, Rafael Romero D., and Rosa Amelia Sosa. We would also like to thank Andre Arahna Corrêa do Lago in Washington, D.C.; Marian Goodman and Patrick Gavigan in New York; Lynda Bunting and Esthela Provas in Los Angeles; Carolina Ponce de León in San Francisco; María Fernández in Pittsburgh; Arna Ramis, Noemí Cohen, and the Antoni Tàpies Foundation in Barcelona; José Gil in Lisbon; and Gerhard Haupt in Berlin.

Finally, we appreciate the positive reception and crucial support that the funders gave us, and we are deeply grateful for their trust in the exhibition.

Alma Ruiz
Assistant Curator

Rina Carvajal
Ahmanson Curatorial Fellow

ACKNOWLEDGMENTS

I am against any insinuation of a "linear process"; as I see it, the processes are global.[1]

—HÉLIO OITICICA

Alma Ruiz

OPEN UP: AN INTRODUCTION

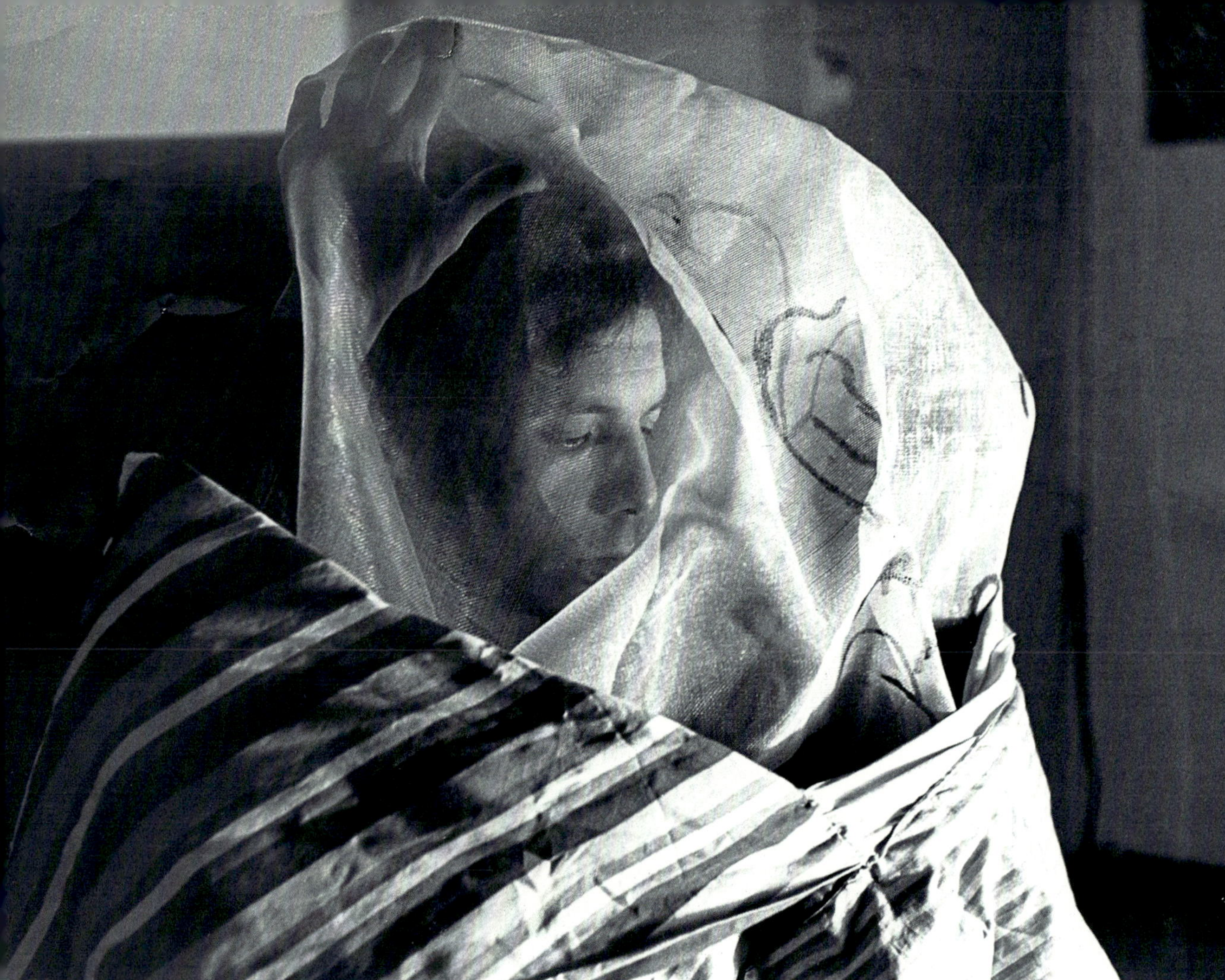

HÉLIO OITICICA: ***Parangolé P19 Cape 15, Gilease: To Gilberto Gil*** 1968

Exhibitions like "The Experimental Exercise of Freedom: Lygia Clark, Gego, Mathias Goeritz, Hélio Oiticica, and Mira Schendel" happen when a series of dynamics converge to create a propitious moment for their realization. Over the last decade, The Museum of Contemporary Art has demonstrated growing interest in and support of Latin American art. This interest has occurred as curators, critics, and scholars have become increasingly aware of the contributions that Latin American artists have made to the history of twentieth–century art. In order to fully recognize these contributions in an international context, however, it is necessary to remap the field of "Latin American art"—a term that transforms a complex web of practices and discourses into a monolithic entity that is often perceived to exist in derivative opposition to "European art." In fact, Latin American art of the twentieth century encompasses a diverse range of artistic, cultural, social, political, and philosophical histories that are intricately interwoven with the histories of European art, as the present exhibition makes visible.

"The Experimental Exercise of Freedom" brings together for the first time a group of artists from Latin America whose reputations have extended beyond national borders, as attested to by the increased interest their work has been receiving from international curators, critics, scholars, collectors, and the museum-going public. Nevertheless, outside of the artists' countries, very few writers have addressed the relationship their work has to hegemonic international artistic practices, especially those that developed simultaneously in Europe and the United States from the 1950s to the mid–1970s, including Minimalism, environmental art, conceptualism, concrete poetry, body art, and performance.

Taking its name from a phrase coined by the Brazilian art critic Mário Pedrosa (1900–1991) to describe the experimental nature of Hélio Oiticica's work and that of a group of artists in Brazil in the 1950s, the exhibition focuses on works and projects by Lygia Clark, Gego, Mathias Goeritz, Hélio Oiticica, and Mira Schendel. It examines the ideas and philosophies that motivated them to abandon traditional art forms such as painting and sculpture for a new aesthetic that connected directly with the cultures in which they lived. With shared roots in the modernist canon—particularly geometric abstraction and constructivism—these five artists developed strongly experimental practices that responded to new aesthetic dimensions and established distinctive and unexplored links with architecture and other mediums. They all believed that it was essential to regard the work of art not simply as an aesthetic object for passive contemplation, but as an experience that called for a new relationship between art, life, and the social. "The experimental exercise of freedom" became an exhortation, an open road for the proposition of new practices or "situations to be lived," and a way of life for some.[2]

The artists in the exhibition assigned great importance to art as a living experience in which the artist, as Oiticica wrote, "understands his/her position not any longer as a creator for contemplation, but as an instigator of creation"[3]; from this perspective, the spectator was no longer considered to be a passive contemplator but an active participant in the production of meaning. The so-called live element defining, in Guy Brett's words, a "significant cross-section of the art of the sixties and seventies, wherever it originated and whatever stylistic category it was eventually consigned to," is one quality that allows greatly dissimilar work to be brought together into a coherent framework.[4] The open-ended possibility for experimentation, coupled with a new kind of collectivism in which artist and spectator unite to complete the work of art, became a cogent proposal around which to organize this exhibition.

It is not accidental that the artists included lived and worked in Mexico, Brazil, and Venezuela—three Latin American countries with strong traditions of modernist art. In the 1920s, Muralism in Mexico and modernism in Brazil originated from attempts to define the national character of these countries and changed the course in which art developed in Latin America. Exerting a strong influence on generations of Latin American artists, both movements led to the creation of alternative tendencies. Although smaller in size and blessed with natural resources essential to global industrialization, Venezuela became an important art center in the 1950s. In search of a national model, Venezuelan artists turned their attention to international movements, especially to geometric abstraction, which at the time answered their needs for an art closely identified with the technological changes taking place in that nation.[5] Occurring in three widely divergent countries, the experimentation freely expressed by the artists in the exhibition evolved out of a need to move beyond established art traditions to create an independent art that functioned outside of their influential sphere.

Bringing together artists of dissimilar backgrounds who were nonetheless operating under similar circumstances, the exhibition seeks to disrupt the traditional paradigms by which Latin American art has been presented internationally. Of the five artists, three were postwar émigrés, and two were Brazilians who lived abroad for extended periods. Mathias Goeritz (1915–1990) and Gego (1912–1994) were born in Germany and grew up in Berlin and Hamburg respectively. Invited by the Universidad de Guadalajara's Escuela de Arquitectura (School of Architecture) to teach courses in art history, Goeritz, accompanied by his wife Marianne Gast, arrived in Guadalajara, Mexico, in 1949; two years later they settled in Mexico City, where Goeritz divided his time as a teacher and artist. Fleeing Nazi Germany in 1939, Gego arrived in Caracas, Venezuela, a year after she had graduated from Stuttgart's prestigious Technische Hochschule (Technical University). Trained in engineering and architecture, she taught in art schools and at the university while pursuing a career as an artist. Like Goeritz and Gego, the Zurich–born Mira Schendel (1919–1988) moved to Brazil to escape the upheaval caused by World War II. After hiding for several years in the former Yugoslavia, she briefly returned to Italy, where her German-Italian mother had raised her. In 1949 she traveled to Brazil, settling in Porto Alegre before permanently relocating to São Paulo. A self-taught artist, Schendel was primarily interested in philosophy, which, along with theology, became the basis for the ideas that eventually lead to a productive experimental period in the 1960s. Goeritz, Gego, and Schendel synthesized their European heritages with

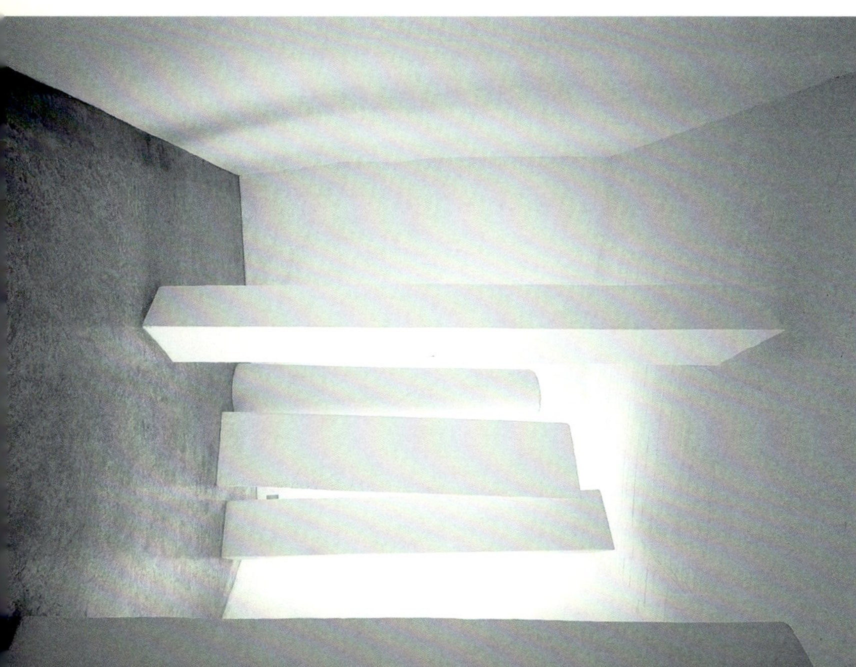

MATHIAS GOERITZ: *Temixco Towers* 1957–58

their experience of Latin American cultures to produce a unique art in which elements of Dada, German Expressionism, geometric abstraction, constructivism, concrete poetry, and European philosophy combined with a newfound freedom peculiar to postwar Latin America.

Brazilian-born Lygia Clark (1920–1988) and Hélio Oiticica (1937–1980) were citizens of Rio de Janeiro, once the country's capital. Born in an affluent milieu that offered them the possibility to devote their lives to art, Clark and Oiticica lived abroad for extended periods of time. Clark studied painting in Paris, where she would eventually spend several years teaching at the Sorbonne. By the time Oiticica traveled abroad, he had already created his most important work. He resided in London following his retrospective at the Whitechapel Gallery in 1969, and he lived in New York from 1970 to 1978.

The significance of these artists' work lies more in the production of an immediacy of experience than on visual effect. Goeritz's experiments with site-specific sculpture and "emotional architecture" (an architecture that elicits feelings or emotions) introduced an art form unknown in Mexico at the time. Gego's perplexing weblike constructions, with their variety of dense and light, large and small, integrate formal qualities with an organic and pulsating notion of space. Schendel's delicate works, more a product of inward analysis than public dialogue, are visually seductive and intellectually challenging. Clark's sensorial and relational objects require interaction, a communion between the object and the viewer achieved through the dissolution of the space that separates them. Oiticica's work is the outcome of acute observations about art's social role and the discovery of popular manifestations like Samba schools and street art. In their explorations, these artists, for the most part, preferred actions that emphasized process while assigning little or no artistic value to the finished product. They held in disregard a market system that equates sales with success. Most importantly, they endeavored to erase the separation between the artist and the spectator by making collective art that aspired to communicate on a large scale. To this day, their most progressive and influential work remains, with few exceptions, neither salable nor collectable. The unorthodox forms and ephemeral materials they chose has made their presentation in the museum environment a curatorial challenge, but paradoxically, the museum has become in some cases the only viable locus of display.

The exhibition has been conceived in five separate sections, with each section devoted to the work of one artist. The section on Goeritz focuses on his emotional architecture and his efforts to establish a tradition of public sculpture. The relationship of sculpture to architecture is explored in great detail in full-scale reproductions of seven towers of varying heights and shapes that Goeritz built in his Temixco studio (1957–58), in a series of miniature towers of varying heights, widths, and shapes (some of which were eventually realized as public sculpture),[6] and through models and photographs of his two most important projects: the Museo Experimental *El Eco* (*The Echo* Experimental Museum, 1953) and the *Torres de Ciudad Satélite* (Towers of Satellite City, 1957–58). By focusing on sculpture, Goeritz attempted to find an identity of his own in an artistic milieu in which the Mexican School—immensely influential in establishing a mode of public painting deeply rooted in the Mexican consciousness—dominated.[7] His experimental ideas, based on the principles of the Bauhaus and German Dada, found fertile ground in the post–World War II political and economic changes taking place in Mexico.[8] Goeritz considered himself fortunate to be living in a city searching for architectural solutions to urban problems.[9]

Gego's incursion into the art world began in 1953. Throughout her career, her work was characterized by the use of metal, through which she explored structural systems joined by linkages of her own invention.[10] The complexity and site-specific nature of Gego's mature work, the *Reticuláreas*, makes their transfer to a museum environment difficult. For this reason, the exhibition centers on her most sculptural works—the *Chorros* (Streams), *Columnas* (Columns), *Troncos* (Trunks), *Mallas cuadradas* (Square Meshes), and a

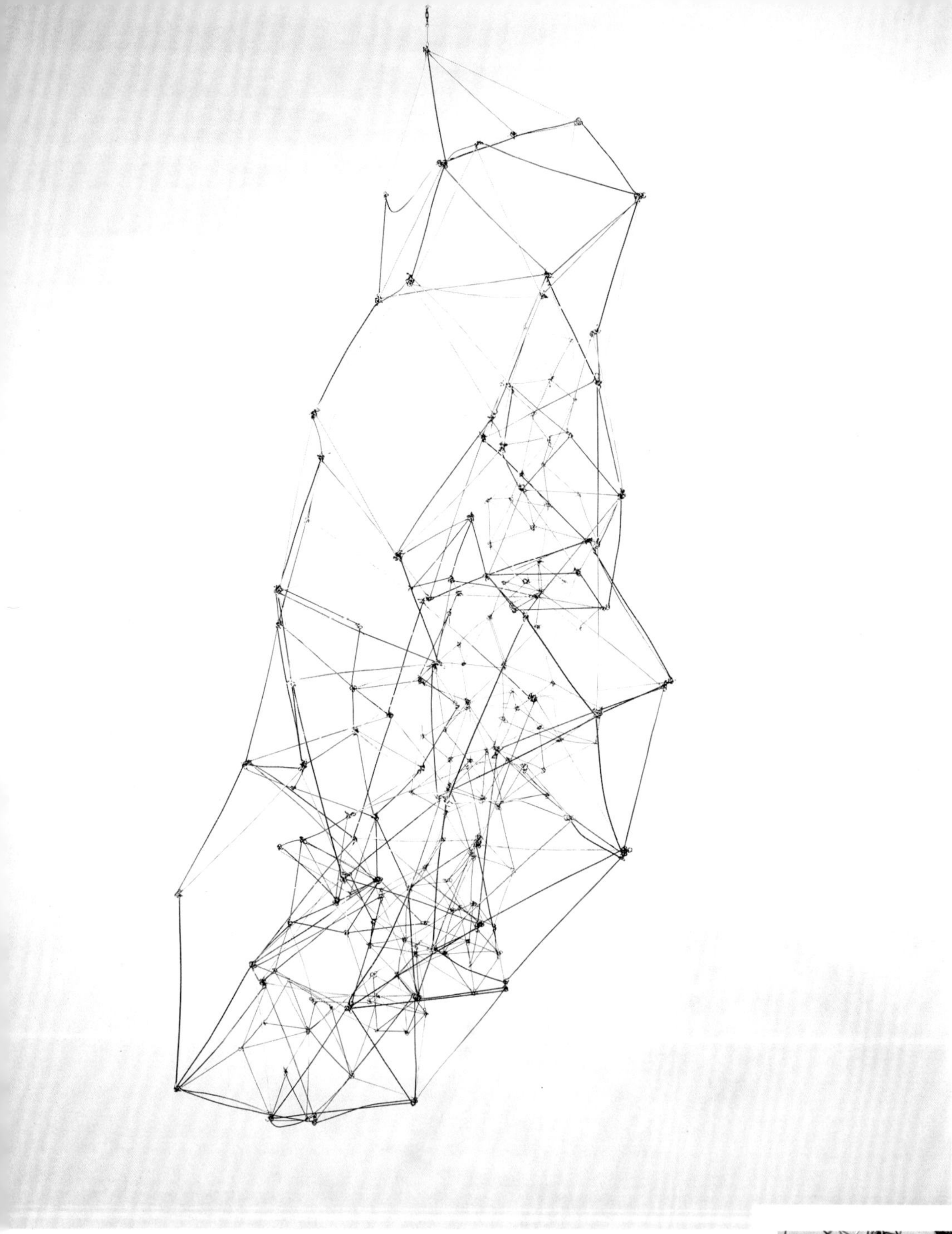

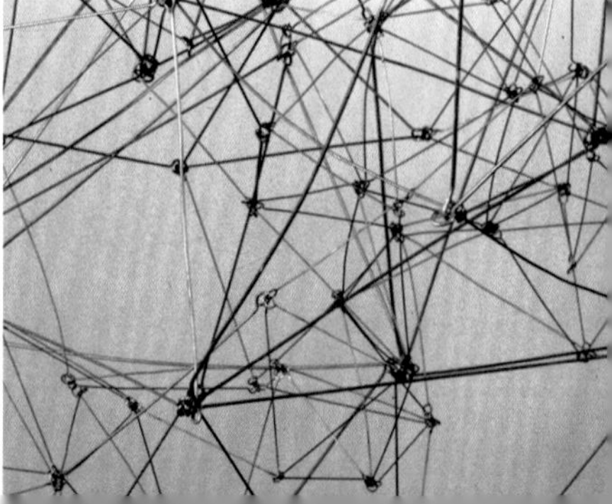

GEGO: ***Chorro*** 1988

series of *Dibujos sin papel* (Drawings without Paper)—which the artist constructed using the same principles. Combining her architectural/engineering background with artistic concerns and aided by systematic research conducted over a long period, Gego found a unique language with which to express the relationship of sculpture to space. By remaining on the fringes of prevailing art movements in Venezuela in the 1950s, she retained her independence and nurtured a highly personal style.[11]

Of all the artists in the exhibition, Mira Schendel is perhaps the one whose work does not easily present an obvious interactivity between the viewer and the object. She created her work in the studio rather than on the streets as collective experiments or public commissions. However, as one observes and experiences it, it becomes evident that the transition into the public dimension takes place when the object is taken away from the wall and brought into the spectator's space. Schendel is represented by a series of works constructed of delicate Japanese rice paper; these mark a temporary deviation from the pictorial form she had initially chosen. Numbering in the thousands, the *Monotipias* (Monotypes, 1962–64) indicate the beginnings of her investigation of language, philosophy, the void, and the ephemeral in a medium other than painting. The *Monotipias* were followed by the *Droguinhas* (Little Nothings, 1966), small works that emphasized (through twisting, knotting, and tying) the handmade quality of the paper. The works that came after—*Trenzinhos* (Little Trains, mid-1960s), *Objetos gráficos* (Graphic Objects, 1967–68), *Discos* (Disks, 1972), and *Toquinhos* (1972)—also partook of this new sensibility. Hung from the ceiling or a corner, these works move into the spectator's space, away from the traditional wall support. Placed at eye level, they afford an intimate view (front and back) of their intricate typographical compositions, enhanced by the light filtering through the opaqueness of the rice paper. To appreciate them in their totality, the spectator must walk around and between them. Through scale (dimensions vary from very small to fairly large), repetition (the multiplicity of letters, numbers, marks, shapes, and materials), and placement (hanging from the ceiling often in a semilinear composition in the middle of the space or very close to but not touching the wall), these works move toward an expressive poetic language that is simultaneously serious and playful.

Lygia Clark is represented in the exhibition by a body of work begun in 1963 which explores the concepts of the disappearance of the author and art as a collective experience. She brought these experiences together under the title *Nostalgia do corpo* (Nostalgia of the Body), a series of works that consist of simple and ephemeral objects. She conceived works such as *Pedra e ar* (Air and Stone), *Máscaras sensoriais* (Sensorial Masks), *Respira comigo* (Breath with Me), *Diálogo de mãos* (Dialogue of Hands), and *Camisa-de-força* (Straightjacket) as "vehicles for a bodily experience," intended to be handled, worn, felt, and played with.[12] Linked with this development was Clark's initiation of group experiences involving friends and students, which, like her individual objects, was intended to "put an individual in touch with themselves," creating a dialogue between the person and his or her inner self.[13] In these collective experiments, individuals were required to participate or

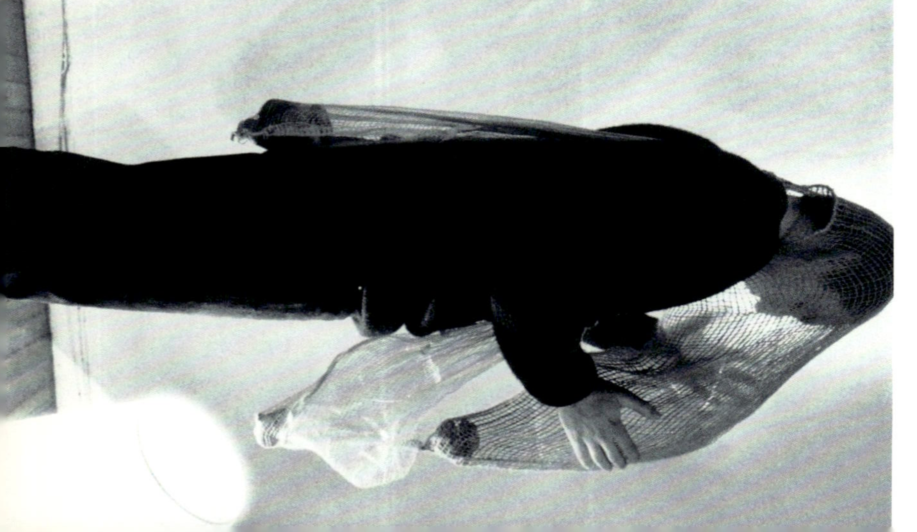

LYGIA CLARK: ***Abyss Mask*** 1968

leave, eliminating both the role of the spectator and that of the author of the work. Also included in the exhibition is an installation entitled *A casa é o corpo. Penetração, ovulação, germinação, expulsão* (The House Is the Body: Penetration, Ovulation, Germination, Expulsion). Originally produced for the 1968 Venice Biennale, this work is a metaphorical journey through a woman's reproductive system. It is the reenactment of a passage all of us took at the beginning of life, with the difference being that this time it is conscious and self-imposed. In an introduction that the critic Yve-Alain Bois, a friend of the artist, wrote to accompany a selection of Clark's writings, he expressed his wish that her work would someday be seen in a North American museum: "Perhaps one day, on this side of the Atlantic, an institution will allow itself to take part in the game."[14] This exhibition, although not a retrospective, is the first one in a North American museum to include a large number of her works.

A year after he created *Tropicália*, a work that resulted from his preoccupation with developing an art that was genuinely "national, tropical and Brazilian," Hélio Oiticica formulated *Eden* for his 1969 retrospective at the Whitechapel Gallery in London.[15] Oiticica described it as "an experimental 'campus,' a kind of *taba* [indigenous encampment], where all human experiments will be allowed. . . . It is a kind of mythical place for feelings, for acting, for making things and constructing one's own interior cosmos."[16] Unlike *Tropicália*, which bursts forth with color, plants, and birds, *Eden* is somber and austere. With the sensory information sharply reduced to modest experiences—walking over sand, hay, and crushed stones; listening to music in the Caetano-Gil tent; resting, reading, or chatting with friends in the nests—*Eden* offers a quiet and meditative environment that realizes Oiticica's desire to connect with the spectator by sharing the experience. "I want the spectator to create his own sensations from it, but without conditioning him to that and the other sensations. The sand, the straw, are only qualitative differences, and the spectator will 'act' upon those areas looking for 'internal meanings' within himself, rather than trying to apprehend external meanings, or sensations."[17]

Taking art from the intellectual plane to the corporeal, and ultimately to a higher level that could be compared to a dream state or ascetic meditation, *Eden* immerses the spectator into the experience of total participation in a work of art.[18] As the visitor spends time in *Eden*, he or she completes the journey from passive spectator to active participant, realizing both Oiticica's and Clark's expectations that the spectator, more than the artist, lends meaning to the object.

In this introduction, I have touched on the work of the artists included in the exhibition. Their accomplishments are addressed in depth in the essays that follow. Rina Carvajal writes about the exhibition in general. She is also the author of the essay on Gego, whose work she reexamines using new scholarship. Osvaldo Sánchez, a Cuban-born, Mexico-based critic and the director of the Museo de Arte Carrillo Gil in Mexico City, traces Goeritz's catalytic activities as artist, architect, teacher, mentor, and collaborator in a country deeply concerned with national identity. The São Paulo–based critic Sônia Salzstein, curator of Schendel's largest exhibition to date, has written an insightful essay on the life experiences and metaphysical investigations that shaped the artist's oeuvre during the 1960s. Suely Rolnik, a psychoanalyst and professor at Catholic University in São Paulo, analyzes Clark's work from 1963 to 1988—her most original and difficult period—during which she embarked on an investigation of practices that united art and life. One of the curators of Oiticica's 1992 retrospective and the director of Documenta X, Catherine David welcomed one more time the opportunity to discuss the work of this significant artist. Rethinking an argument she developed in her essay "The Great Labyrinth,"[19] she examines Oiticica's writings vis-à-vis current scholarship on the artist to explore his role as a cultural critic. She also examines the "aesthetical anthropology" dimension of his work, which, she maintains, "exceeds the area of visual arts."

The field of Latin American art since 1945 is still relatively unknown in the United States. For some of the artists, this is the first time that a North

MIRA SCHENDEL: *Droguinha* 1966

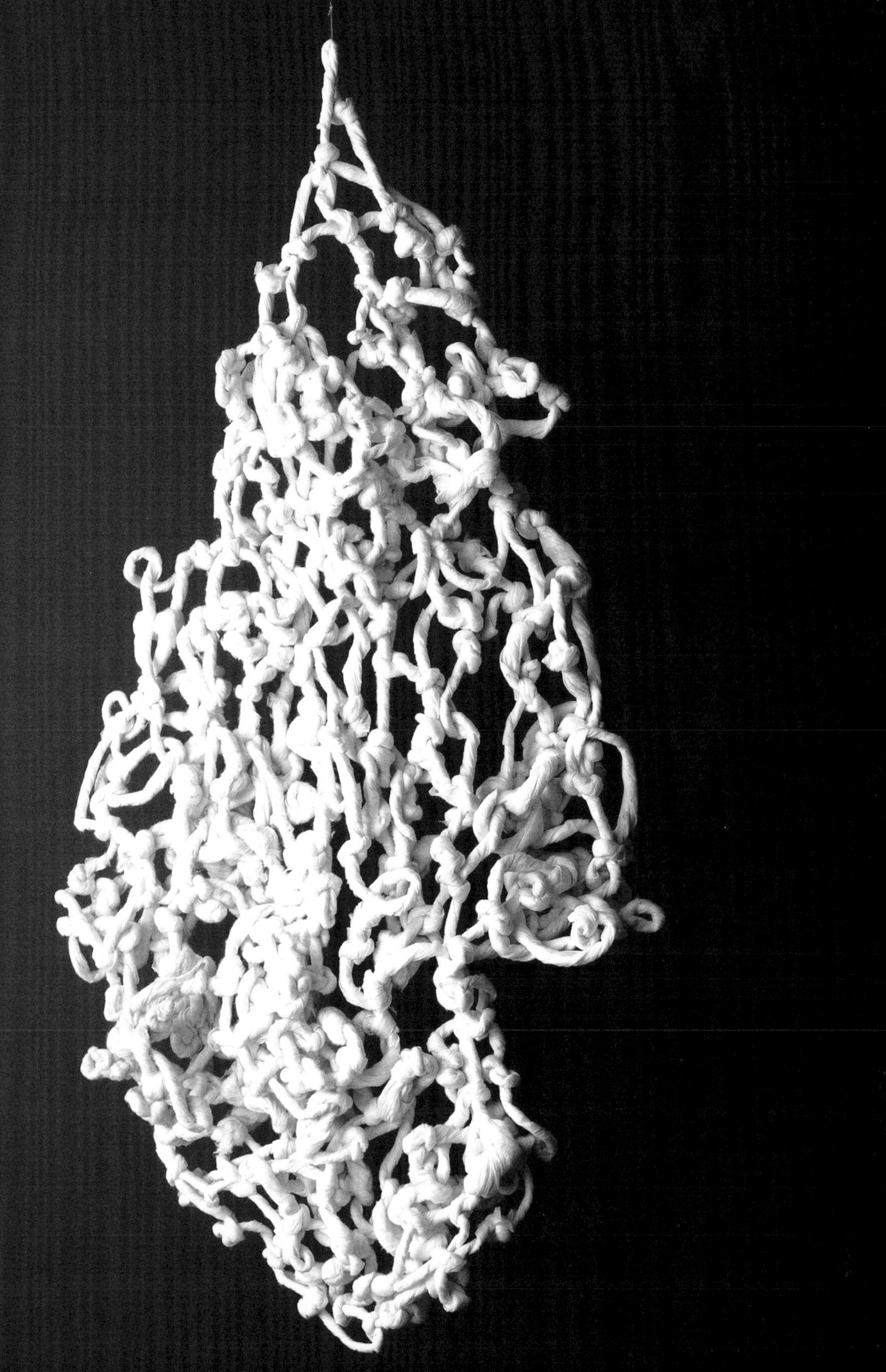

American museum has bestowed so much attention on their work; for others, it is an invaluable opportunity to present yet another dimension. "The Experimental Exercise of Freedom" will present the artists as investigators of new experiences, entrepreneurs, educators, and creators of new experimental conditions. They express what the Brazilian art critic Ferreira Gullar wished for avant-garde art in Latin America—that it "should spring from an analysis of a given country's social and cultural characteristics, never from advanced ideas imported intact from the developed countries to which they properly apply."[20] Finally, we hope that the exhibition will occupy its proper place within the discourse of international art since 1945 and contribute to a more complex understanding of this period.

Notes

I would like to thank Guy Brett for his indirect contribution to this project. His writings on South American artists provided me with a scholarly source on the subject and became a guiding light in developing my thoughts on the exhibition. Many of the ideas that inform the exhibition were first explored by Mr. Brett in his essay "A Radical Leap" in *Art in Latin America: The Modern Era, 1820–1980*, organized by The South Bank Centre, London, 1989.

1 Hélio Oiticica, "Brazil Diarrhea" (1973), in *Hélio Oiticica*, exh. cat. (Paris: Galerie National du Jeu de Paume; Rio de Janeiro: Projeto Hélio Oiticica; Rotterdam: Witte de With, Center for Contemporary Art; Barcelona: Fundació Antoni Tàpies, 1992), 17.

2 Hélio Oiticica, "*subterranean* TROPICÁLIA PROJECTS" (1971), in ibid., 143.

3 Hélio Oiticica, "POSITION AND PROGRAM" (1966), in ibid., 100.

4 Guy Brett, "Life Strategies: Overview and Selection: Buenos Aires/London/Rio de Janeiro/Santiago de Chile, 1960–1980," in *Out of Actions: Between Performance and the Object, 1949–1979*, exh. cat. (Los Angeles: The Museum of Contemporary Art, and New York: Thames and Hudson, 1998), 197.

5 Rina Carvajal, "Gego: Weaving the Margins," in *Inside the Visible: An Elliptical Traverse of Twentieth-Century Art in, of, and from the Feminine*, ed. M. Catherine de Zegher, exh. cat. (Cambridge, Mass.: MIT Press, 1996), 342.

6 *Torres de Automex* (Automex Towers, 1963–64), *La Osa Mayor* (Big Dipper, 1968), and *La pirámide de Mixcoac* (Mixcoac Pyramid, 1969) are some of the many public sculptures that were realized.

7 Jorge Alberto Manrique, "Otras caras del arte mexicano," in *Modernidad y modernizacion en el arte mexicano: 1920–1960* (Mexico City: Instituto Nacional de Bellas Artes, 1991), 132.

8 Ibid., 142.

9 Mario Monteforte Toledo, "Los hacedores," in *Conversaciones con Mathias Goeritz* (Mexico City: Siglo Veintiuno Editores, S.A. de C.V., 1993), 64.

10 Carvajal, 341.

11 Ibid., 342.

12 Yve-Alain Bois, "Nostalgia of the Body: Lygia Clark," *October*, no. 69 (Summer 1994): 86.

13 Guy Brett, "Lygia Clark: Six Cells," in *Lygia Clark*, exh. cat. (Barcelona: Fundació Antoni Tàpies, 1998), 26.

14 Bois, 88.

15 Oiticica, "TROPICÁLIA," in *Hélio Oiticica*, 125.

16 Oiticica, "EDEN" (1969), in ibid., 12.

17 Ibid.

18 Ibid., 13.

19 Catherine David, "The Great Labyrinth," in *Hélio Oiticica*, 248.

20 Marta Traba, "New Blood from the Avant-Garde," in *Art of Latin America: 1900–1980* (Baltimore: The Johns Hopkins University Press, 1994), 54.

THE EXPERIMENTAL EXERCISE OF FREEDOM

Rina Carvajal

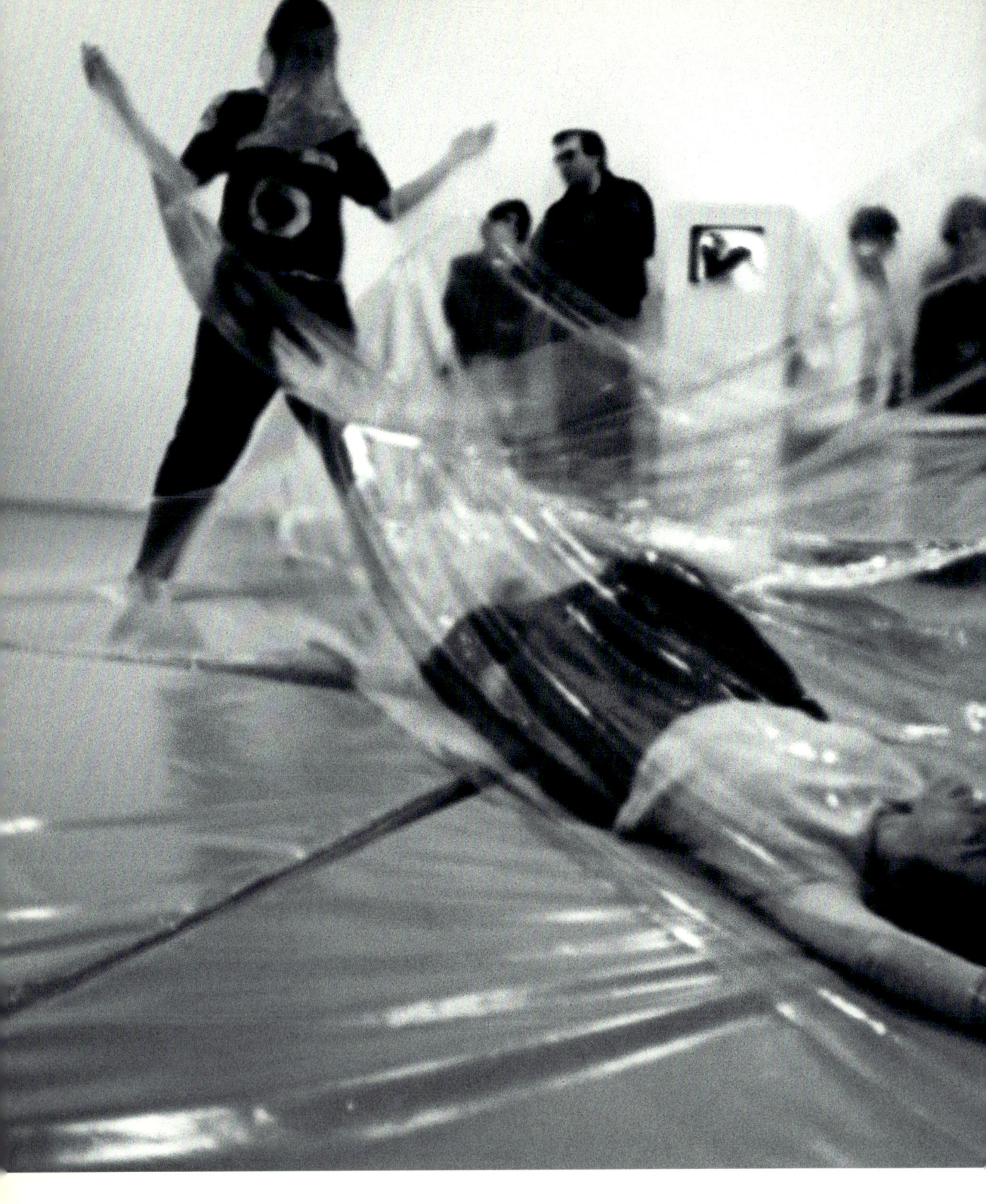

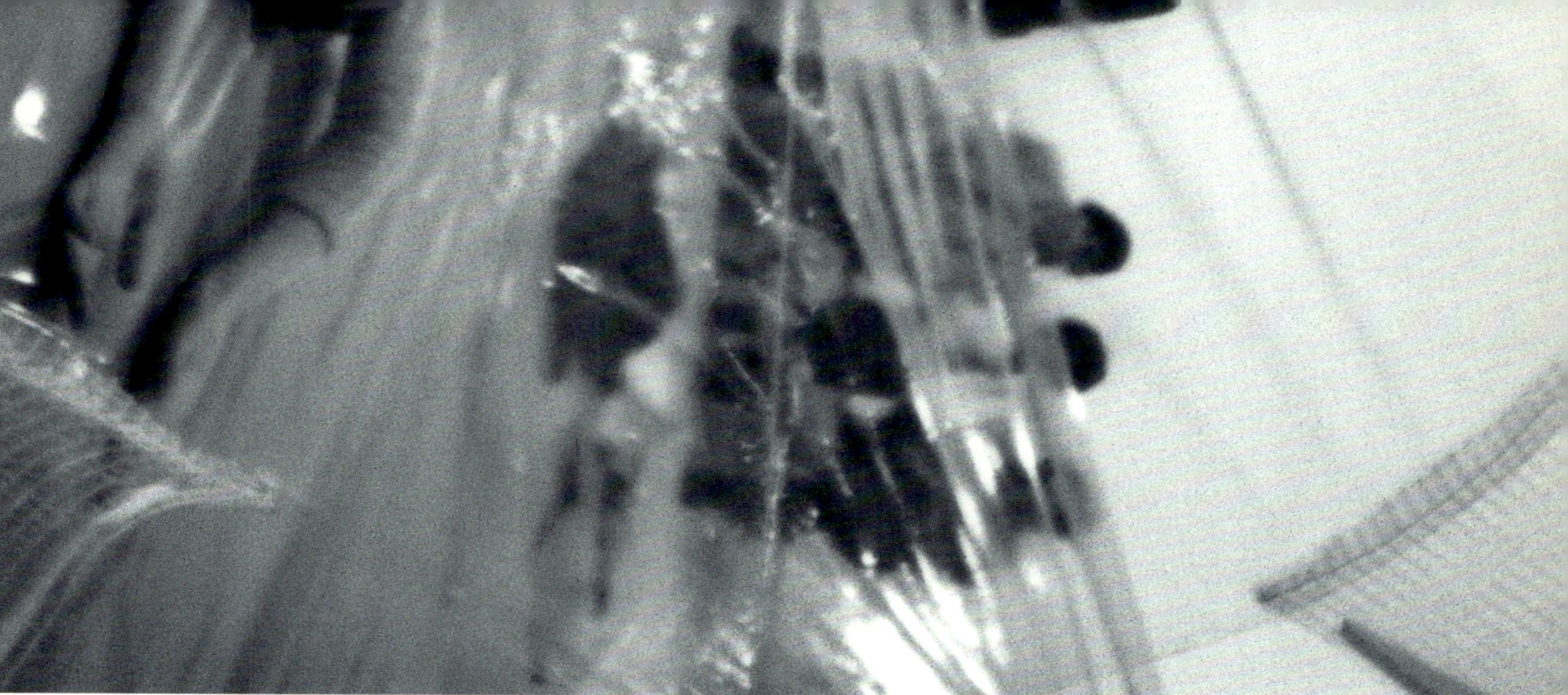

One of the key figures to understand the objectives and formulations of the Brazilian vanguards of the 1960s was the eminent critic and intellectual Mário Pedrosa. The ideas that Pedrosa proposed, though almost always formulated in the context of Brazilian art, concisely express the search for experimentalism shared by the artists of other origins whose works comprise this exhibition. In his 1970 article "La Bienal de cá para lá" (The Bienal from Here to There), Pedrosa coined the phrase that gives the exhibition its title. He used this phrase to describe those artistic practices in Brazil, as well as the rest of the world, which sought to overcome the material consumption of the object, rejected the contingencies of the art market, and privileged experiential and collective practices. These artists conceived the object not as something finished, but as an open proposition—as a situation to be lived or experienced. Their practices represented, above all, "gestures, collective actions, movements in the plane of activity"—practices that reformulated and liberated the aesthetic act so that it could give itself up to completely unfamiliar transactions: to . . . the experimental exercise of freedom."[1]

The experimental practices of the five artists included in the exhibition—Lygia Clark, Gego, Mathias Goeritz, Hélio Oiticica, and Mira Schendel—profoundly questioned and transformed the functionalist programs of the pre–World War II European constructivist vanguards in Latin America between 1950 and 1970. These artists critically and syncretically absorbed and reinvented these languages in original and idiosyncratic terms, investing them with social and cultural dimensions emerging from their countries of origin or adoption.[2] Their mature works emphasized the experimental aspects of artistic practice, which they regarded as a mode of emancipation—a mode of destabilizing and demystifying the aesthetic and commercial value of the traditional art object. They introduced a subjective dimension, privileging the role of the individual and his or her experience, thereby transforming the spectator into a participant in the creation of the work and a subject of his or her own liberation;[3] they also privileged the immanence of the act over any notion of the permanent object. Their practices led to the creation of new forms and new ideas that recuperated the concepts of the object and of space as entities alive and in constant flux—as open and dynamic processes rather than completed or static works. They also valued the void as a space of potentiality and freedom and introduced novel links with architecture and the body. Viewing art as a creative intervention into the space of society and of the individual, these artists sought a practice in which the transcendent dissolved into the experience of things, registering the movements of the body, of sensation, and of thought, thus reaffirming the indissoluble bond between art and everyday life.[4]

The work of these artists grew out of different attitudes toward constructivism—or, rather, toward the dynamic relationship between construction and deconstruction—and a speculative interest in breaking down the limits of objects, of mediums, and of the relationship with the spectator. They moved between categories and mediums, questioning, destabilizing, and often pushing them toward a crisis point. Regardless of obvious correspondences and points of convergence, these artists never comprised a cohesive group, as each pursued a singular path that drew on modes of inquiry, strategies, and directions very different from those of the others.

All of the artists were active during a period in which the Latin American countries where they lived were launching modernization projects. Beginning just after the end of World War II and reaching an apogee in the 1950s and 1960s, these *desarrollista* (developmentalist) projects sought to build modern industrial nation-states modeled after the rational, technocratic order of Western Europe and the United States, which resulted in models of accelerated industrial, urban, and architectural development. Within the cultural sphere, constructivist currents—with their principles of lucidity and reflexivity, their idealization of scientific and technological progress, and their commitment to integrating art and architecture—perfectly suited the *desarrollista* objectives, offering artists a way to deprovincialize and contest long-dominant nationalist and conservative traditions and reshape important aspects of their own local contexts through a dynamic dialogue with progressive elements of international art and culture.

The growth of constructivist languages in Brazil in the 1950s coincided with a period of liberal government, prosperous economic conditions (the country had accumulated significant wealth through the export of raw materials and agricultural products to the Allies during World War II and was welcoming new investments and foreign capital), and the growth of a progressive middle class supporting rapid modernization. This confluence of conditions was embodied in the 1960 inauguration of the new federal capital, Brasília. It was also in this environment that the museums of modern art in São Paulo (1948) and in Rio de Janeiro (1949), as well as the São Paulo Bienal (1951), were founded, establishing the infrastructure that would bring international art to the country.[5] Abstract geometric and concrete art gradually became the new aesthetic, and the integration of painting, sculpture, and architecture was stimulated by the growth of modern architecture and a desire for a social art for the new age.[6] The award given to the Swiss artist Max Bill at the 1951 Bienal confirmed the value put on these tendencies.

In 1952 the *Ruptura* (Rupture) movement, the first formal association of Concrete artists, arose in São Paulo. That very year Haroldo de Campos, Augusto de Campos, and Decio Pignatari, three great poets of Brazilian Concretism, founded *Noigandres*, the magazine of the movement. The mid-1950s witnessed the consolidation of the São Paulo Concrete movement, an interdisciplinary group influenced by the mathematical abstractionism and the rationalist objectivism of Max Bill and of the Ulm Superior School of Form in Germany, of which Bill was a director, and their ideas about scientifically integrating art into industrial society. In Rio de Janeiro, some artists formed Frente (Front) in 1953–54, a group that did not defend a particular stylistic approach but nevertheless played a revitalizing role in Brazilian art, opening the way for the more radical proposals that arose later (many of the future Neoconcrete artists, including Lygia Clark and Hélio Oiticica, were part of this group). The Concrete artists of Rio and of São Paulo established ongoing exchanges until the relationship was broken by the Rio artists' rejection of the dogmatism of their São Paulo counterparts.

The real momentum for Brazilian aesthetic renewal, manifested in the development of constructivist languages and their autonomy from European models, occurred shortly after the break. Reacting to the excessive technicism, formalism, and rationalism of the São Paulo Concretists, who imported foreign models without critically questioning their adaptability to local conditions,[7] artists in Rio formed the Neoconcrete movement, which encompassed both literature and the visual arts. This movement, whose ideas took theoretical form in the manifesto presented in the catalogue for its inaugural exhibition in Rio in 1959, included Clark, Oiticica, Lygia Pape, Amilcar de Castro, Frank Weissman, Reynaldo Jardim, and Theon Spanudis. Mário Pedrosa and the poet Ferreira Gullar also played important roles in the conceptual articulation of the movement. Despite its brief duration (it dissolved in 1961), Neoconcretism represented "the apogee of the constructivist consciousness in Brazil and its explosion."[8] It marked the climactic moment for the singular reinsertion of constructivist ideas into the cultural environment of Brazil. The Neoconcrete artists created experimental proposals that embraced expressiveness and involved the body, the senses, and subjectivity. They also sought to express an "organic" notion of the artwork—to establish a dialogue between art and the public by incorporating the space-time of lived experience and by transposing the object and the pictorial plane into the social space of everyday life.[9] This was the beginning of a process that would later lead artists like Clark and Oiticica to radicalize the role of the spectator, turning him or her into an active participant of their own liberation as an individual, enabling one to make a connection between art and life in one's own existence.[10]

The critical absorption and reelaboration of European modernism achieved by the Neoconcrete artists reactivated the idea and tradition of the *antropofagia* (anthropophagy) of Brazilian culture brilliantly articulated by the poet Oswald de Andrade in the context of the modernist movement of the 1920s, a tradition that inspired and framed the strategies of successive Brazilian vanguards in this century. *Antropofagia* represented a strategy of cultural emancipation and a particular attitude toward history, the European legacy, and hierarchical relationships with other cultures.[11] Artists and writers associated with this mode used metaphors of selective digestion, metabolization, and the transformation of the cultural legacy of the colonizer by means of a syncretic combination of elements derived from both local and foreign contexts.

Lygia Clark, for example, profoundly reformulated European constructivist languages, cannibalizing them and taking them to completely new territories in which she sought to awaken in the spectator a latent sensory energy and open a path for the development of his or her own creativity. From the beginning until the end of her work, her practices, which always sought to reconnect art and life, approached the object as a living entity "migrating from the plane to relief, from relief to space," and from there "to the spectator, the act, the body and from the body to the relationship between bodies to finally address subjectivity."[12] They dissolved the limits between object and subject and sought the disappearance of the author, thereby proposing a new conception of the artist as "a person who induces and channels experiences" and of art as "a ritual without myth."[13] These practices also sought to potentialize the creative possibilities of the individual and transform him or her into an active participant in their own existence, the object of the work thereby becoming "the act of creation."[14] Regarding the body and architecture, Clark proposed an especially original idea: her work "passed from an architecture conceived as body, that is, as a receptacle to be inhabited by man, the body conceived as architecture, as the place of the unique experience, not to be standardized, and remaining open."[15] The last phase of her work is situated on the boundary between art and therapy. One of the possible effects emerging from this frontier is to "recover the critical potential against the dominant mode of subjectivation" in the two fields. Clark believed that by renewing the art field through work with the subjectivity of the spectator, "individuals could re-invent their own existence," making their lives a work of art.[16]

Hélio Oiticica, who always accompanied his work with lucid formulations and who fervently defended the relevance of experimental art, saw artistic work as a series of proposals, as open and incomplete processes, as "situations to be lived" and inserted into social space.[17] Like Clark's, his work was influenced by geometric abstraction and by the quest to rupture traditional notions of the pictorial plane. He was particularly interested in transporting color and form out of the medium of painting, thereby giving them corporeality and structure and integrating them into the space-time of the spectator, who would then live the experience through his or her body and senses. As

HÉLIO OITICICA: Nildo of Mangueira with ***Parangolé P4 Cape 1*** 1964

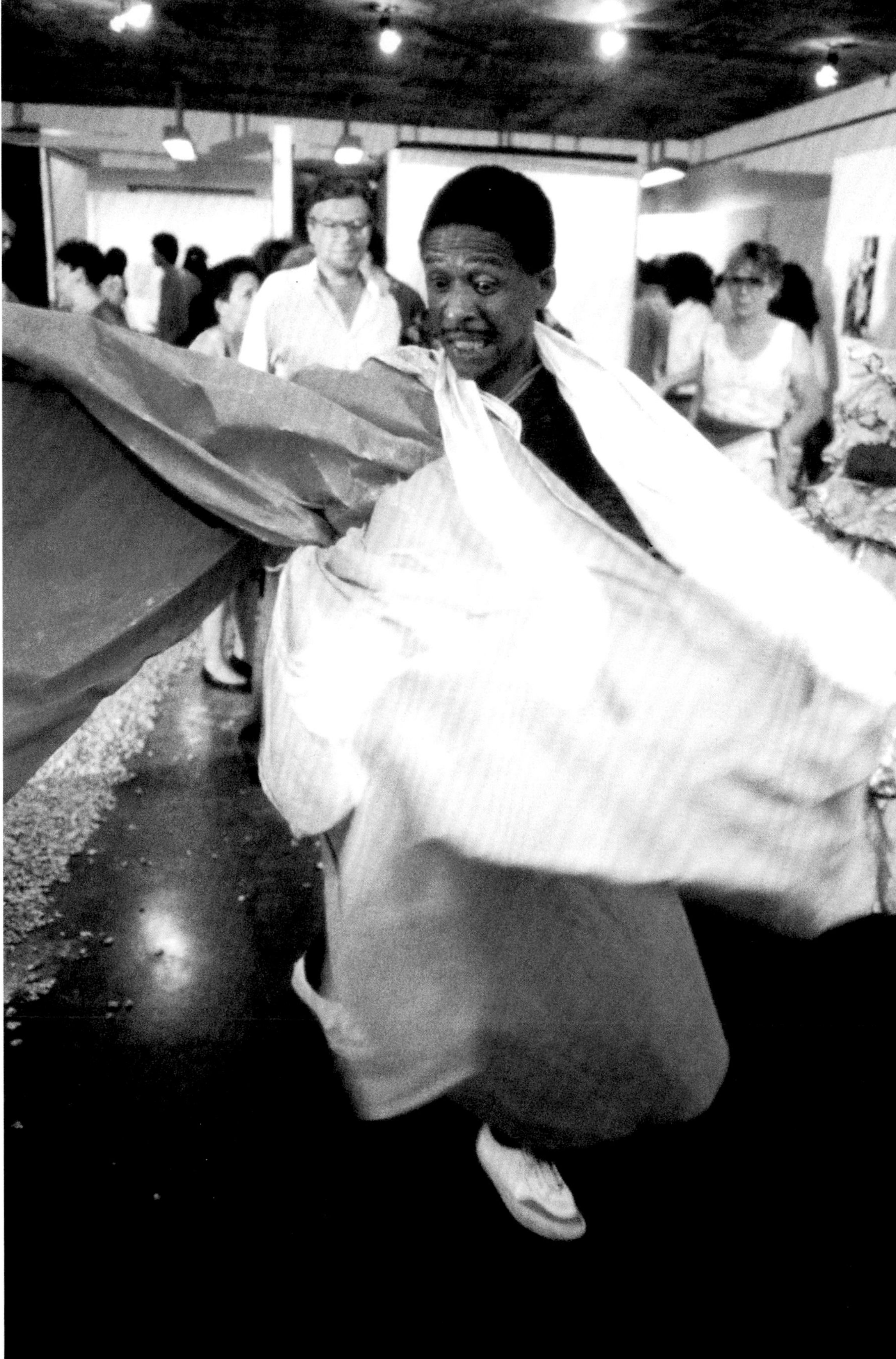

well as sharing a very close friendship, Clark and Oiticica maintained an important, enriching dialogue throughout their careers. They helped one another articulate their ideas and individual formulations, which were registered in the extensive, fertile correspondence they exchanged. Although their practices developed separately and in different directions—Clark focused on subjectivity and the processes of individual subjectivation, whereas Oiticica favored cultural and social intervention in both individual and collective situations—in reality they complemented each other and had similar objectives. They both sought the real integration of art and life and the dissolution of the artist's authorship to give a protagonist's role to the individual, offering him or her the possibility of experiencing art as a fundamental vehicle in the formation of their own subjectivity.[18]

Throughout his work, Oiticica created a versatile and complex series of forms and constructions—*Penetrables*, *Bólides*, and *Parangolés*, among others—which allowed him to touch on and interconnect numerous ideas, areas, and themes that ranged "from the object to the body, to architecture, to 'environmental totalities.'"[19] He questioned and undid many of the formal categories of art by means of these orders, which he intermingled in extremely diverse and original ways, articulating new and radical formulations that simultaneously transformed and reelaborated specific aspects of Brazilian culture, as well as the culture of the international vanguard.[20] The *Penetrables*, which he defined as "mobile frescoes on a human scale," transposed an experience of color, movement, time, and materials to the space of everyday life, inviting the spectator to penetrate them in bodily and sensorial ways in an exploratory journey through different types of spatial elements and materials displaced from their habitual contexts into paradoxical situations. The *Bólides* (in Portuguese: fireballs or nuclei) are colored structures made of elements such as boxes, bottles, bags, booths, nests, beds, and so on, and filled with substances, pigments, and other materials that became activated by the intervention of the spectator. Conceived by Oiticica as "transobjects," or energy-centers, the *Bólides* opened up a wide range of per-

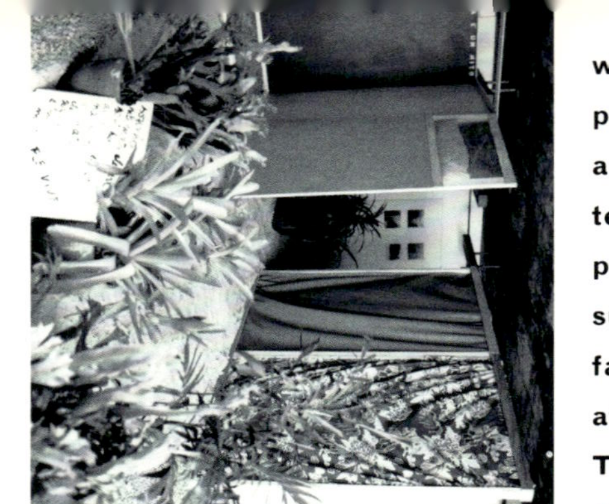

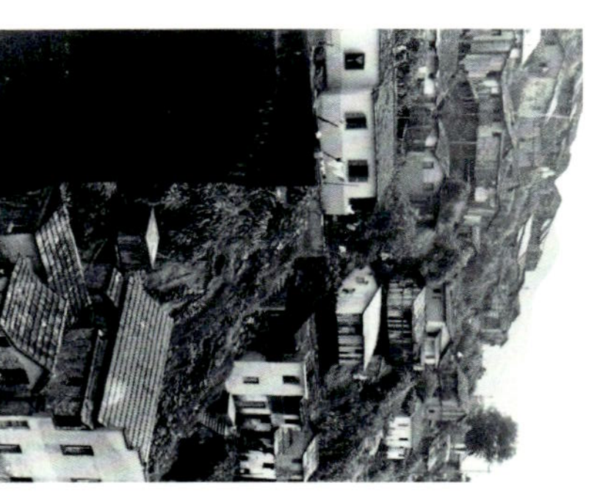

HÉLIO OITICICA: ***Tropicália*** with ***Penetrables PN2 and PN3*** 1967 (LEFT)
The Shantytown on Mangueira Hill, Rio de Janeiro 1965 (RIGHT)

ceptive, sensory, and social experiences. His formulation of the *Parangolés* in 1964 marked, in his own words, a crucial point in his work and defined a specific position in the theoretical development of his experience of "structure-color," creating a "new space-time" for the work in environmental space.[21] In the *Parangolés*, a kind of form-structure-color-architecture-dance-words activated by the participant's body, he sought to appropriate the structure and the constitutive principles of certain objects and situations from everyday life and popular culture, using them to create what he called an "environmental anti-art." Even when a *Parangolé* took the shape or structure of an already existing object or construction—such as a cape, standard, banner, or the architecture of the *favelas* (slums)—it did not refer properly to an object, but rather to an "expressive-creative mode of conduct," "a program, a vision of the world, an ethic."[22] The *Parangolés* incorporated the individual and the environment as a whole, promoting the imaginative-perceptive and corporeal interaction of the subject with his or her social space in a search for what Oiticica called the participant's "state of invention." In works like *Tropicália* (1967)—which would have an important role in the context of Brazilian political and cultural life of the 1960s and 1970s—and of *Tropicalismo*,[23] a movement of which he was a catalyst and which dynamically reactivated the principles of the *antropofagia* tradition, Oiticica sought to "impose an evidently Brazilian image within the actual vanguard context and among manifestations of national art in general."[24] He accomplished this objective with practices that, as Catherine David writes in this volume, proposed an alternative model of intervention into culture which transgressed dominant models of social and historical determinism.

Although Mira Schendel settled in São Paulo during the height of the Concrete movement, she chose to work alone, participating only sporadically in the artistic context of the period. Instead, she opted for a different path, motivated by intense philosophical, metaphysical, and theological interests that led her to establish enriching dialogues with scholars in various fields—dialogues that always played a fundamental role in the articulation of her work.[25] From the beginning, her practice displayed an idiosyncratic attitude toward the constructive (of which deconstruction was an intrinsically dialectical component), forming itself out of an extremely subtle and enigmatic dialogue between opposite yet complementary categories, seeking to express great energy as well as an emptying out, a profound baring of form, from the fundamental essence of language. For Schendel the constructive was never a purely visual or rational problem but rather something invisible and immaterial pertaining to the plane of experience which led back to the transformative, emancipatory potential of the act, of the subject's affirmative gesture in an immanent relationship with the world.[26]

Schendel's most productive and experimental phase began in the mid-1960s, when she created numerous series of works emphasizing an open-ended notion of process and oriented toward the world of action and experience. During this period she focused on the tactile and bodily dimension of the work.[27] Subject-object, body-mind, void-matter relationships also began to dissolve, converging, instead, as reciprocal energies on the same plane. Her work of these years, exceptionally discreet and difficult to apprehend (the content was always oblique), pulsates on an intimate and quotidian scale, in the amplification of the minimal, in the imperceptible yet intense passage of a continuum of perceptions we barely notice but which suddenly reveal to us the forces and the gestures shaping forms and language in the "moment of origin."

In the *Monotipias* (Monotypes, 1964), Schendel undertook a singular exploration of writing and gesture. She produced a sequence of many drawings, registering in their movement the action of gesture and the body.[28] Drawn on very fine, almost transparent, sheets of rice paper stretched over smooth ink-covered surfaces marked on the opposite side, the drawings include linear impressions, textual elements (letters, fragments, phrases), and architectures. The *Droguinhas* (Little Nothings, 1966) are Schendel's most endearing creations. These "little nothings," as she called them, made from rice paper twisted and kneaded into a rope, then woven into knots, forming nets, balls, and braids, sprang from experience itself. With gentle irony they sought to express the ephemeral, the value of the precarious and the instant, in contrast to the ownable and the permanent.[29] The *Droguinhas* were not properly objects, or "something separate from the body," but rather registers, memories of action, the "aggregate of the gestures deposited in them," involving an attitude of self-determination, of the subject remaking him- or herself in the creation and experience of the object.[30] In this way, Schendel introduced a singular relationship with the public sphere. Although the *Droguinhas* are protagonists in an intimate, personal space and are not interactive, they connote, a posteriori, the entrance into a collective dimension, inviting us to discover the potential in action and self-reflection. They presuppose our construction as individuals so that through this process we can later insert ourselves into a social and collective space.[31]

The *Objetos gráficos* (Graphic Objects, 1968) represented Schendel's new attempt to express temporality in her work, this time affirming even more strongly its transparency (and therefore its opacity). In these object-drawings, the rice-paper sheets—printed, written over, covered with drawings or appliquéd letters—are grouped together, pressed between two acrylic plates, suspended from nylon cords and visible from both sides. They establish a reading of simultaneous planes and writings, dissolving the outside-inside, before-after, private-public dichotomies and provoking a circular reading involving the body and the participation of the spectator, who must move around in order to observe them. Taking her exploration of language even further and establishing a rich and complex relationship between poetics, visual imagery, and writing, Schendel sought to capture in these "mental screens"[32] "discourse in the moment of emergence" and "the process of immediate experience lived in all its intensity."[33] In its apparent fragility, simplicity, and lightness, Schendel's work reveals a powerful energy and seems to offer a lesson about existence:[34] it accepts the void but also lightens the burden of life through the pleasure of self-reflective doing, in the encounter with the small things of everyday life, the richness of "being and nothing more."[35]

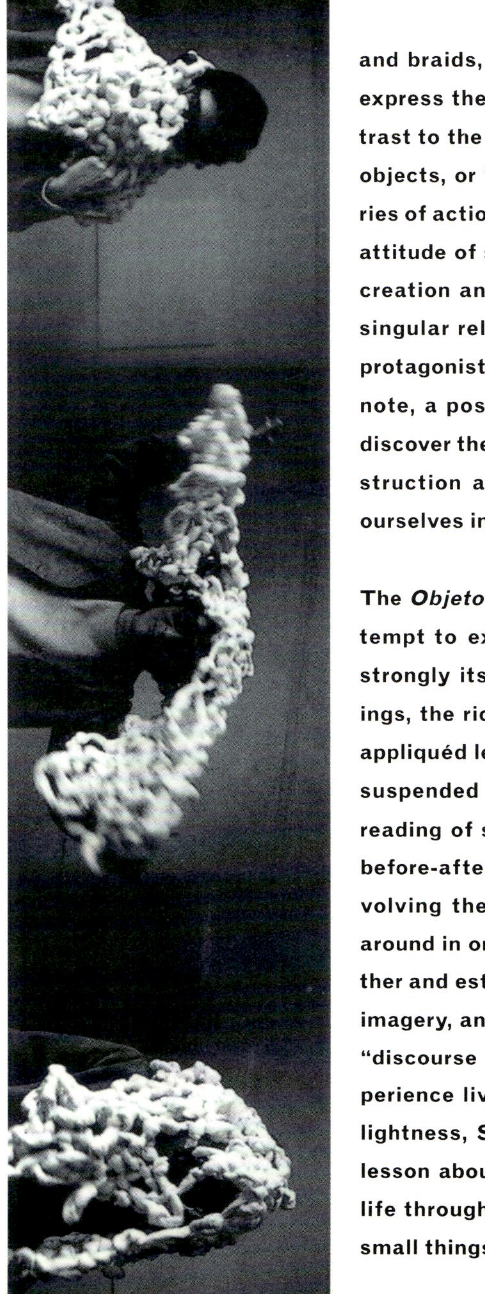

MIRA SCHENDEL: Schendel with ***Droguinha***, London 1966

Gego (Gertrude Goldschmidt) began her artistic activity in Venezuela in the 1950s, in a moment when constructivist tendencies were rapidly integrating into the cultural and social scene, auspiciously fitting into the new development processes and accelerated modernization of the country, then in the midst of an oil boom.[36] These languages, with their proposals to integrate the visual arts and architecture, and animated by a desire to find a model of order that would serve, outside the weight of tradition, to create a new culture open to international ideas and consonant with the new times, became the vanguard project of Venezuelan art. This project was animated by a utopian vision for the construction of a technological and industrialized society that came to represent, in the midst of great contradictions, the progressive aspirations of the government and the political and economic elite.

Gego participated in her own manner in the Venezuelan art world, as Schendel did in the Brazilian, choosing to develop her work independently and at the margins of the abstract-geometric movements. She found a singular way to reinvent a constructivist language, which gradually led her toward experimental paths of subjectivation. Fleeing Nazism, she immigrated to Venezuela in 1939, bringing with her a will to survive, a strong affirmation of life, and a solid education in architecture and engineering—a confluence that led her to develop her work in the fluid passage of two apparently opposite registers: one rational and objective, the other organic and expressive. Her work intuitively marked the dislocation of a constructive order, expressing through the movement of form itself the trace of experience, of the body, and of perception. It also inscribed an architectonic-existential notion of space—the idea of an interiority permanently projecting itself outward.

In sculptures of her mature period, like the *Reticuláreas*, Gego favored notions of process and temporality, emphasizing perceptive and experimental possibilities. She incorporated the idea of the work as an active field in its passage toward planes of subjectivity and flux: the spectator-participant lives the space according to his or her own experience, and the work becomes the means of his or her own subjectivation.

GEGO: ***Reticulárea***, Museo de Bellas Artes, Caracas 1969

While Mexico, too, redefined its political and economic development models throughout the 1950s, entering a new age of modernization, industrialization, foreign investment, and architectural building, its reception of constructivist tendencies was very different from the Venezuelan experience. With a rich pre-Columbian history and strongly rooted local artistic traditions, Mexico was the scene of an outright confrontation between deeply consolidated na-

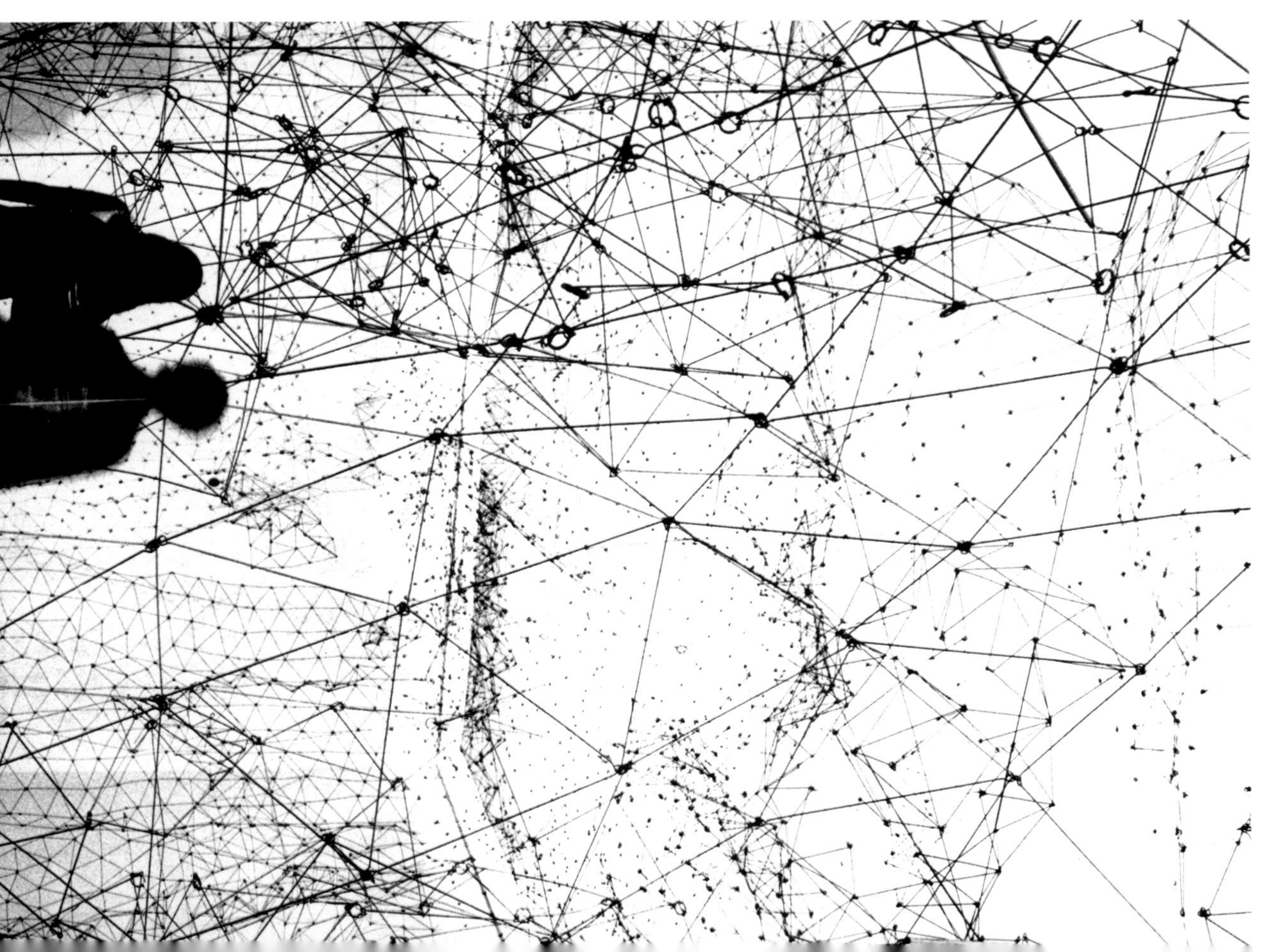

tionalistic tendencies—the Mexican Muralist school, in particular—and others avidly seeking new artistic languages and international ideas. Mathias Goeritz propitiously inserted himself into this context when he arrived in the country in 1949, after a complex detour from Germany through North Africa, Spain, and finally Mexico, where he remained for the rest of his life. Possessing a keen discursive talent and an ample aesthetic and intellectual knowledge, Goeritz quickly introduced himself to the Mexican artistic milieu, proposing new ideas and situations and bringing international art to the country.[37] He adopted a combative posture toward the Muralist school (then at its climactic point of exhaustion and struggle for power), and his provocative, inventive attitude facilitated the creation of new alternatives for experimentalism, constructivist tendencies, and abstraction.

Charismatic and controversial, Goeritz moved easy among mediums and genres. He was a painter, sculptor, critic, concrete poet, cultural activist, and architect, and he often assumed extremely paradoxical positions in his proposals. His attitude toward modernity and the vanguards of international art

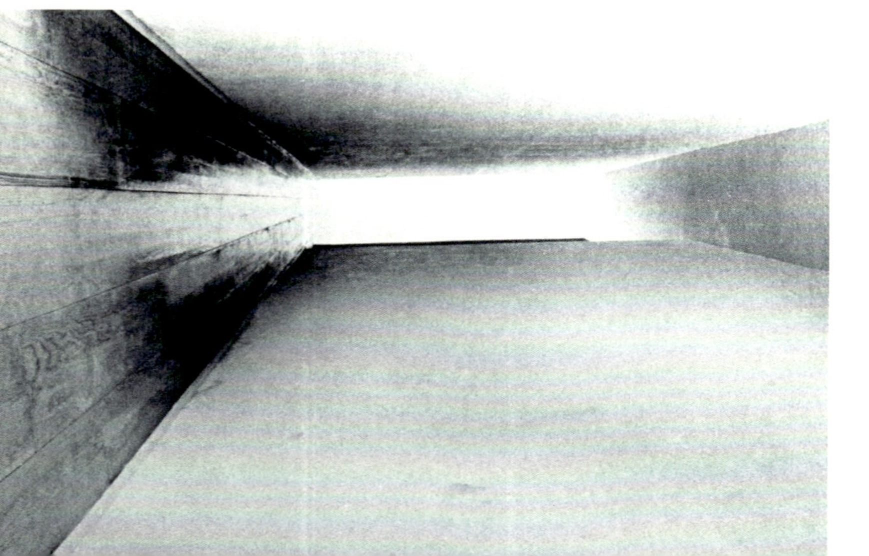

MATHIAS GOERITZ: The Experimental Museum *El Eco* (Detail: Hallway) 1953

was always contradictory. Even though he was ultramodern and the only one at the time in Mexico to foresee the crisis of genres and the passage of the art object into the public sphere in the 1960s, he had a theological perspective and a nostalgia for the organic societies of the past and the collective art they generated, tendencies that often neutralized his radicalism.[38] Motivated by social and ethical inclinations that made him see the creative gesture as a communal good, he sought to erase his artistic authorship.[39] He contradicted, however, his anti-individualist tone with the provocative, confrontational stance that always marked his manifestos and declarations.[40]

Goeritz had a speculative interest in breaking the boundaries between sculpture and architecture, and his great contribution was in the invention of a hybrid genre combining the two and the concept of an "emotional architecture" (an architecture whose principal function is to elicit emotions), formulated in a manifesto with this name published shortly after he inaugurated his Museo Experimental *El Eco* (*The Echo* Experimental Museum) in 1953.[41] Stimulating and productive, the destabilizing effect of his work on Mexican art and architecture introduced important ideas about spatiality and monumentalism, as well as the notion of a personal, architectonic object constantly revealing its possible functions,[42] and the concept of art as an interdisciplinary, open, experimental process. From the beginning, Goeritz found architecture, rather than the visual arts, to be an environment more propitious for his work. Even though he was a pioneer in the latter, his combative attitude toward the Mexican Muralist school forced him into a defensive posture, and he permanently faced the hostility and violent public attacks of Diego Rivera and David Alfaro Siqueiros. Throughout his career, however, he established successful collaborations, essential to the development of his work, with architects and engineers. Particularly important in this respect were his encounters with Luis Barragán and Chucho Reyes, with whom he would work closely for many years.

Goeritz began his most relevant and experimental stage in Mexico with *El Eco*. This project sought to critically counteract the exaggerated rationality of functionalist architecture, then at its height in the country, subordinating it to organic, spiritual, and social values. It was, above all, a neoconstructivist, antifunctional proposition that grew out of the idea of architecture as a sculptural-spatial experiment on a grand scale, whose intention was to provoke psychological emotions and perceptions in the spectator's own encounters with the possibilities of space. In this respect, it introduced a corporeal experience implicated by the body's movement and modes of spatialization. *El Eco* was, in addition, an interdisciplinary experiment that aspired to fuse the arts and to shelter events of an ephemeral character. In describing *El Eco*, critics and others of the period mentioned the strange sense of movement created by the architectonic elements of the interior spaces, noting that "they seemed to have the vitality and qualities of a living organism."[43] Goeritz thought of this structure—its high walls separating it from the exterior and turning in on the completely empty interior space—as "an enormous negative sculpture" and "a modeling of the void." Constructed without exact plans and with subtle asymmetrical dispositions that sought to express the imperceptible irregularity "observed in any living being," its walls, hallway, and entrance were created to be felt as a space and as sculptural elements. Some walls, for example, were wider on one side and thinner on the other; in addition, the hallway descended and converged with the ceiling to form a much wider perspective than, in fact, existed in reality. Imbued with notions of instability, movement, and the organic, all the elements in *El Eco* formed a flexible and dynamic spatial compass that erased the materiality of space and gave shape to new planes of subjectivity.

With the *Torres de Ciudad Satélite* (Towers of Satellite City, 1957), a project carried out in collaboration with Barragán which represented the most important phase of his conception of emotional architecture, Goeritz continued to rupture the limits between sculpture and architecture. In this work, he introduced the idea of a structure visible from a distance and seen from the fluctuating point of view of a spectator traveling in a car at great speed. The proposal—which he viewed as painting, sculpture, and emotional architecture—was also a successful intervention in urban space. It consisted of a group of five monumental geometric structures of great formal simplicity and of various heights (the tallest was 187 feet high) constructed of reinforced and painted concrete. The idea behind the work was "to express a pure gesture, without a trace," to raise, through its vertical and monumental scales, a metaphysical sense of space in the spectator.[44] The result would be, in Goeritz's words, the creation of "at last, a monumental work the sole function of which should be emotion."[45]

The artists in this exhibition proposed, in a continuous metabolic journey, complex and original alternative models of experimentation which syncretically absorbed and reelaborated an already exhausted constructivist vanguard culture. In the process, they revitalized and restated it in completely new terms. Their practices not only dismantled and reinvented traditional artistic categories through the reelaboration of specific aspects of international vanguard culture, as well as their own cultures, but reinserted them into new contexts of expression and subjectivation. In different measures, the presence of the constructive in their work—and its instability—functioned as a vehicle for the liberation of the subject, in which he or she could, through the creative experience, reconstitute his or her own subjectivity and reconnect art and reality. In its incessant movement between territories—from the local to the international, the cultivated to the popular, the intellectual to the corporeal, from art, to the individual, to the environment—the work of these artists reaches beyond metaphor to make present a most radical intervention: the immanence of art and life, the possibility of the experimental exercise of freedom.

Translated by Lyn Di Iorio

Notes

I would like to take this opportunity to thank Richard Koshalek, former director of The Museum of Contemporary Art, Los Angeles, for inviting me, as an Ahmanson Curatorial Fellow, to organize this exhibition, along with Alma Ruiz. The project's concept originated in a seminar I taught at McGill University in Spring 1995 entitled "Constructivist and Neoconstructivist Tendencies in Latin America." I am grateful to my students for their thoughtful responses to my ideas. This exhibition would not have been possible without the invaluable collaboration of my co-curator, to whom I extend my sincere thanks.

1 Mário Pedrosa, "La Bienal de cá para lá" (1970), in Otilia Arantes, ed., *Mário Pedrosa: Política das artes* (São Paulo: Universidade de São Paulo, 1995), 283.

2 Clark and Oiticica were native-born; Schendel, Goeritz, and Gego were postwar émigrés.

3 Hélio Oiticica, "Suprasensory Apparitions," in *Hélio Oiticica* (Paris: Galerie National du Jeu de Paume; Rio de Janeiro: Projeto Hélio Oiticica; Rotterdam: Witte de With, Center for Contemporary Art; Barcelona: Fundació Antoni Tàpies, 1992), 127: "I must insist that the quest here is not for a new 'conditioning' for the participant, but rather the collapsing of any kind of conditioning to seek the freedom of the individual, by means of ever more open propositions . . . this would be what Mário Pedrosa defined prophetically as 'the experimental exercise of freedom.'"

4 For Lygia Clark, for example, it is impossible to achieve the modern utopia of reconnecting art with life if this connection is not also re-formed in the subjectivity of the spectator, so that he or she recuperates the capacity to perceive how the world's objects affect him or her, as well as the potential to create and re-create existence as a function of these affects and not form representations cut off from experience. Conversation with Suely Rolnik, 3 July 1999.

5 In its early years, the works of the artists of the vanguards of the 1920s and 1930s—including Paul Klee, Kasimir Malevich, László Moholy-Nagy, Piet Mondrian, Pablo Picasso, Georges Vantongerloo, the Futurists, the Dadaists, the artists of the de Stijl and Bauhaus movements, as well as artists such as Max Bill and Josef Albers—were shown at the São Paulo Bienal.

6 Aracy Amaral, "Abstract Constructivist Trends in Argentina, Brazil, Venezuela, and Colombia," in *Latin American Artists of the Twentieth Century*, ed. Waldo Rasmussen with Fatima Bercht and Elizabeth Ferrer, exh. cat. (New York: The Museum of Modern Art, 1993), 90.

7 Ronaldo Brito, *Neoconcretismo: Vértice e ruptura do projecto constructivo brasileiro* (Rio de Janeiro: Funarte/Instituto Nacional de Artes Plásticas, 1985), 44.

8 Ibid., 49.

9 Ferreira Gullar, "Da arte concreta a arte neoconcreta," in Aracy Amaral, ed., *Projeto constructivo brasileiro na arte (1950–62)* (São Paulo: Pinacoteca do Estado; Rio de Janeiro: Museu de Arte Moderna, 1977), 112.

10 Suely Rolnik, "Molding a Contemporary Soul: The Empty-Full of Lygia Clark," in this volume, 56–108.

11 For a brilliant analysis of the ideas and cultural strategies that the notion of cultural *antropofagia* involves, see Haroldo de Campos, "De la raison antrophofage," *Lettre International*, no. 20 (Spring 1989), and Suely Rolnik, "Subjetividade antropofágica," in *Arte contemporânea brasileira: Um e/entre outro/s* (São Paulo: Fundação Bienal de São Paulo, 1998).

12 Rolnik, "Molding a Contemporary Soul."

13 Manuel J. Borja-Villel, "Introducción," in *Lygia Clark* (Barcelona: Fundació Antoni Tàpies,1997), 15.

14 Rolnik, "Molding a Contemporary Soul."

15 Borja-Villel, 13.

16 Ibid., 14.

17 Hélio Oiticica, "Subterranean Projects," in *Hélio Oiticica*, 143.

18 *Lygia Clark–Hélio Oiticica: Cartas, 1964–1974*, ed. Luciano Figueiredo (Rio de Janeiro: Editora de UFRJ, 1996).

19 Guy Brett, "Notes on the Writings," in *Hélio Oiticica*, 208.

20 For an analysis of the strategies and contributions of Oiticica's cultural and artistic project, see Catherine David, "Hélio Oiticica: Brazil Experiment," in this volume, 169–201.

21 Hélio Oiticica, "Fundamental Bases for a Definition of the *Parangolé*" (November 1964), in *Hélio Oiticica*, 85–88.

22 "Expressive-creative mode of conduct": Guy Brett, *Transcontinental* (Birmingham: Ikon Gallery, and Manchester: Cornerhouse, 1990); "a program, a vision of the world, an ethic": Frederico Morais, *Pequeno roteiro cronologico das invenções de Hélio Oiticica* (Rio de Janeiro, 1980), cited in ibid.

23 *Tropicalismo* is the last great movement of the Brazilian vanguard. Emerging in the mid-1960s in Brazil as a cultural revision of the critical manifestations that arose after the 1964 military coup, it manifested itself in music, poetry, drama, and the visual arts. *Tropicalismo* represented "a cultural sum with anthropophagite characteristics" (Favaretto) which sought "to affirm in a direct line with modernism, a Brazilian culture original and open to the world but decolonized: *tropicalismo* removes, recycles and assimilates in a spectacular and carnivalesque way the most heterogeneous influences. It . . . sought a language and imagery capable of expressing the plural components and contradictory aspirations of a culture in formation." Catherine David, "The Great Labyrinth," in *Hélio Oiticica*, 249–52, and Celso Favaretto, *Tropicália—alegoria, alegria* (São Paulo: Atelier Editorial, 1996).

24 Hélio Oiticica, "TROPICÁLIA" (4 March 1968), in *Hélio Oiticica*, 124.

25 Schendel studied theology and philosophy (she was particularly interested in phenomenology and certain Eastern philosophical disciplines such as Zen Buddhism) and, at different moments of her life, established fertile dialogues with Dominican clergymen and intellectuals of various kinds. Some of her interlocutors throughout different periods were the physicist Mário Schenberg, the philosophers and semiologists Max Bensen and Elizabeth Walther (Stuttgart University), the poets Theon Spanudis and Haroldo de Campos, the philosopher Jean Gebser (Bern University), and Hermann Schmitz (Kiel University), a phenomenologist who developed a concept about corporeality, of great interest to Schendel.

26 Conversation with Sônia Salzstein, 21 June 1999.

27 Sônia Salzstein, "Mira Schendel: The Immersion of the Body in Thought," in this volume, 202–33.

28 Ibid.

29 In a letter to Guy Brett (1965), Schendel said of the *Droguinhas*: "I started a new work, perhaps more important for myself than any previous one. 'Sculpture' on the same rice paper as the drawings. Something technically primary and very easy. From an occidental point of view, these 'sculptures' (that senseless word!) might be seen under the perspective of a phenomenology of 'being-having.' From an oriental point of view, well, they are related to Zen . . . [My new work] is

in open opposition to the 'permanent' and 'ownable.' Cited in Guy Brett, "Actively the Void," in *No vazio do mundo/Mira Schendel* (São Paulo: Galeria de Arte do Sesi, 1996), 60. In the *Droguinhas*, she also sought to "concretize the problematics of transitoriness," seeing in them the possibilities of an "art that would be ephemeral," of objects that "would be exposed to life" and that "might be made by anybody." Cited in Guy Brett, *Schendel* (New York: Studio Vista, Reinhold Art PaperBook/John Lewis, 1968).

30 Salzstein, "The Immersion of the Body in Thought."

31 Conversation with Sônia Salzstein.

32 Jean-François Chevrier, "The Year 1967," in *From Art Objects to Public Things (Or Variations in the Conquest of Space)* (Barcelona: Fundació Antoni Tàpies, 1997), 207.

33 Referring to this aspect of her work, Schendel said that she waited until language formed itself, that it assume its form on paper, binding itself to others "in a pre-literal discursive writing"; unpublished text.

34 Conversation with Rodrigo Naves, 23 July 1999.

35 Vilém Flusser, unpublished text.

36 For a more detailed description of the historical and art-historical context of constructivist idioms in Venezuela and Gego's work, see my essay "Gego: Outside In, Inside Out," in this volume, 110–35.

37 Goeritz organized several exhibitions of international art in Mexico, including "II Confrontation of Experimental Art" (Galeria Proteo, 1955), which brought artists such as Lucio Fontana, Oyvind Fahlstrom, and Bernhast Schultze (the latter two were members of the Parisian group Phases).

38 Conversation with Cuauhtémoc Medina, 27 March 1999.

39 Frederico Morais, *Mathias Goeritz* (Mexico City: UNAM, 1982), 46.

40 Yve-Alain Bois, "Mathias Goeritz," in *America, Bride of the Sun: 500 Years Latin America and the Low Countries* (Antwerp: Royal Museum of Fine Arts, 1992), 386–88.

41 For a detailed explanation of this idea, see Osvaldo Sánchez, "Mathias Goeritz: The Ministries of Space," in this volume, 136–67.

42 Jorge Alberto Manrique, "Mathias Goeritz, el provocador," in *Los ecos de Mathias Goeritz: Ensayos y testimonios*, ed. Ida Rodríguez Prampolini and Ferruccio Asta (Mexico City: Instituto de Investigaciones Estéticas, UNAM, 1997), 143–49.

43 Lily Kassner, *Mathias Goeritz: Una Biografía* (Mexico: Instituto de Investigaciones Estéticas, UNAM, 1998), 59.

44 Morais, 39.

45 Mathias Goeritz, in Ida Rodríguez Prampolini, "Mi encuentro con Mathias," *Revista de la Escuela Nacional de Artes* (Mexico City) 3, no. 13–14 (1991–92): 68, cited in Osvaldo Sánchez, "Mathias Goeritz: The Ministries of Space," in this volume, 158.

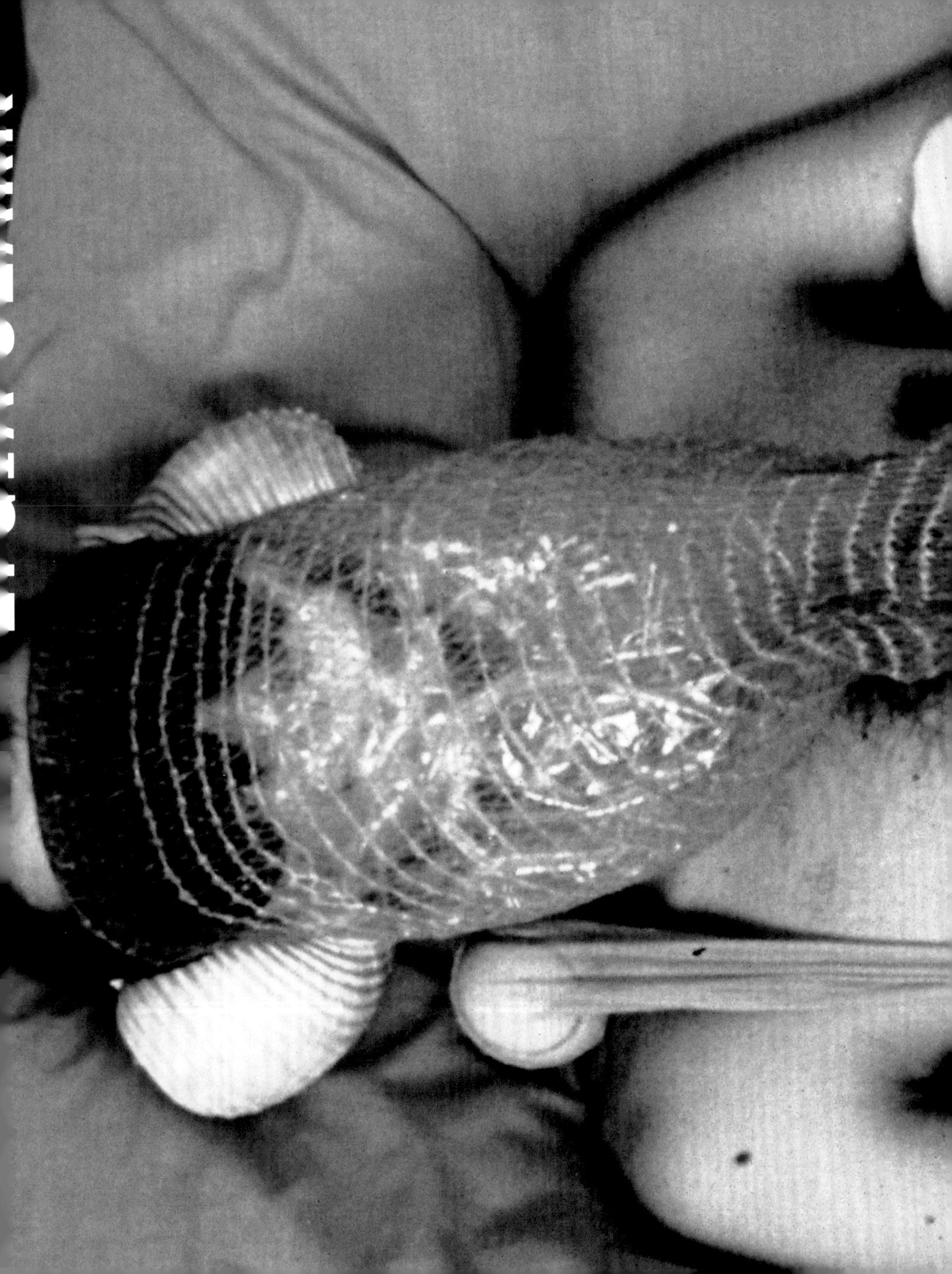

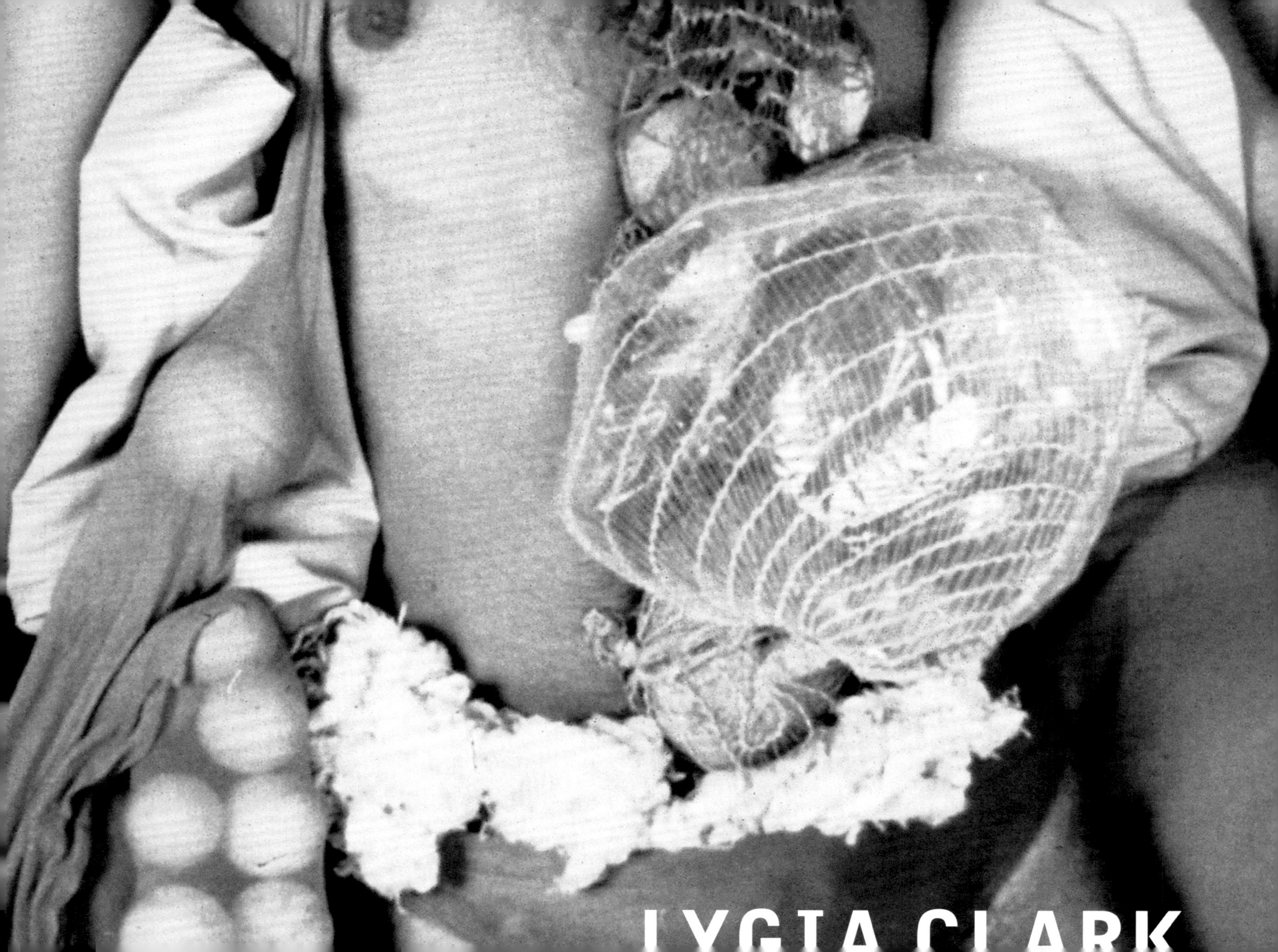
LYGIA CLARK

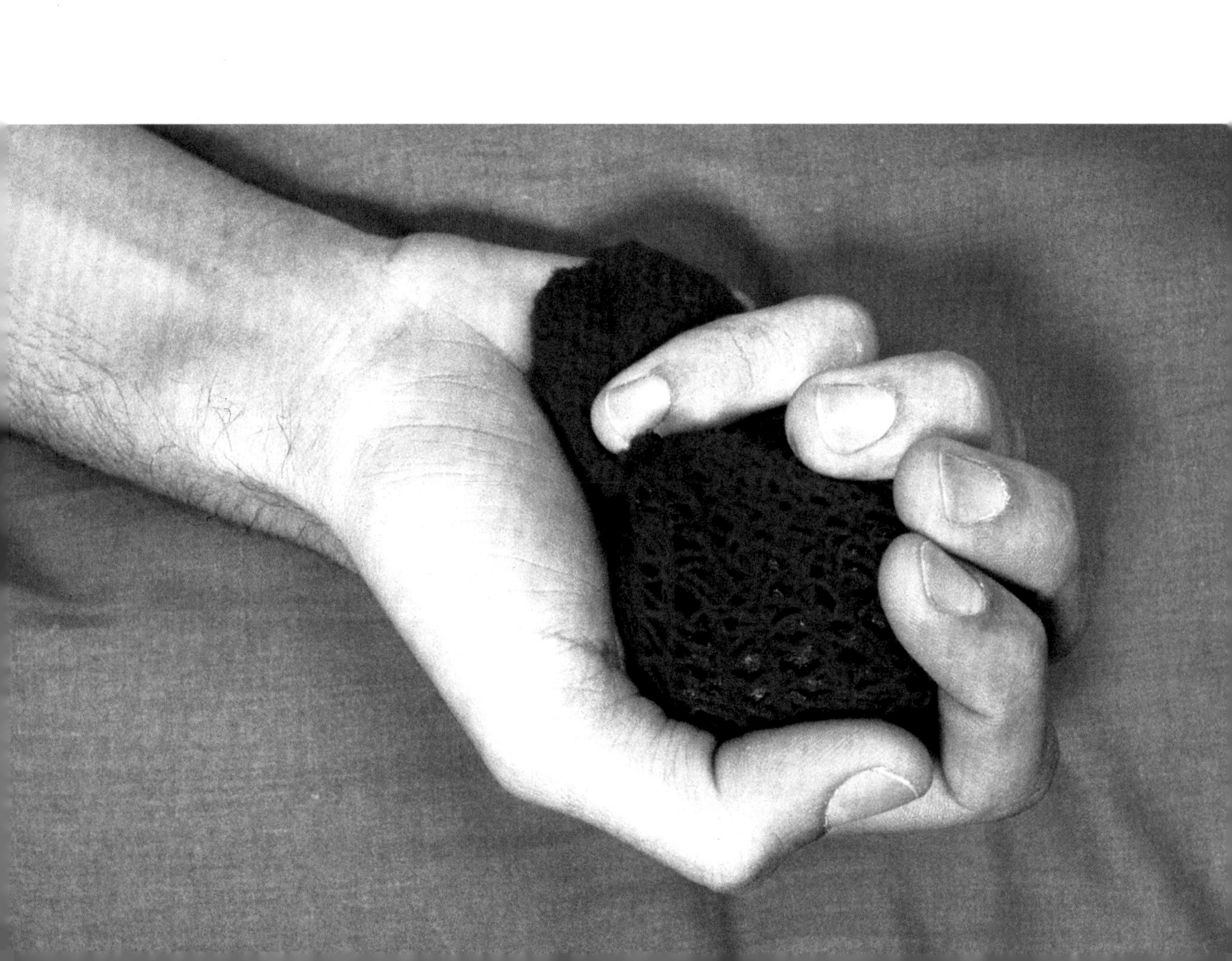

> Literature (cf. art) thus appears as an undertaking of health: not that the writer (cf. the artist) necessarily has a strong constitution . . . but he enjoys a fragile irresistible health, which comes from the fact of having seen and heard things that are too big for him, too strong, unbreathable, whose passing exhausts him, but nevertheless permits him becomings that fat, dominating health would make impossible. . . . What kind of health would be enough to free life wherever it is imprisoned by man and in man?[1]
>
> —GILLES DELEUZE

Molding a Contemporary Soul: The Empty–Full of LYGIA CLARK

Suely Rolnik

Lygia Clark is the name of an existence convulsed by the eruption of an idea that gradually took shape throughout the totality of a unique oeuvre. Elaborated step by step from the 1950s to the 1980s, this idea situated itself on the horizon of one of the most insistent issues facing modern art—the reconnection of art and life—as an original answer with the power to carry this project toward its very limit. This is probably why Brazilian and international culture of that time did not assimilate the artist's work, not even half of it, especially during the period beginning with *Caminhando* (Walking, 1963). Some eleven years after her death, this assimilation is only starting to take shape. From this seminal work emerged a path in which the idea that propelled Clark presented itself in all its radicality and took on a vitality that would remain indefatigable until her final work, *Estruturação do self* (Structuring the Self), produced through her *Objetos relacionais* (Relational Objects, 1976–88). The last of the artist's propositions, this work completed her idea in masterful form, revealing the rigorous coherence of the whole of her oeuvre.

Throughout the century, much imagination has been dedicated to working out strategies to effect the utopia of the reconnection of art and life. Some of these strategies form the specific landscape in which Clark's work carried out its dialogue: liberating the artistic object from its formalist inertia and its mythifying aura by creating "living objects" in which could be glimpsed the forces, the endless process, the vital strength that stirs in everything; mixing materials, images, and even objects taken from daily life with the supposedly noble materials of art; freeing the spectator from his or her soporific inertia, whether by making possible the spectator's active participation in the reception or in the execution of the work or by intensifying his or her faculties of perception and cognition; emancipating the system of art from the inertia established by its mundane elitism or its reduction to a commercial logic by exhibiting or creating in public places or by opening such spaces to other publics; liberating the aesthetic realm from its confinement in a specialized sphere to convert it into a dimension of everyone's existence by making life itself a work of art. In summary, all of these strategies con-

PRECEDING PAGES: ***Structuring of the Self: Relational Objects*** 1976

taminate exhibition spaces, materials, and above all the fictions of art with the world and the social milieu, as well as the life of the ordinary citizen, with art.

In the 1960s, when Clark's work became radicalized, the project of reconnecting art and life, in addition to intensifying artistic practices through experimentation of all kinds, exceeded its boundaries and contaminated social life, becoming a crucial touchstone of the explosive counterculture movement that rocked the period and launched the foundations of an irreversible transformation of the human landscape that even today has not been fully absorbed. Surely we cannot attribute to mere chance the invention of this particular utopia in art, its incorporation by the youth culture in the 1960s, and the resonance between these phenomena. What mobilized these movements, both in art and in society, was the crisis of a certain cartography of human existence that began to make itself known at the end of the nineteenth century and intensified more and more during the next hundred years. A short visit to this landscape will allow us to localize the problematics that Clark worked out in her oeuvre as an unprecedented orientation for the issues of her time.

One of the most interesting aspects of this cartography for the present work is the exile of artistic practice into a specialized domain, which presupposed that a certain plane of the processes of subjectivation would be confined to the experience of the artist. This plane is the "vibrating body," in which contact with the other, human and nonhuman, mobilizes affects as changing as the variable multiplicity that constitutes otherness.[2] The constellation of such affects forms a reality of sensations—corporeal reality—which, though invisible, is no less real than visible reality and its maps. It is the world composing itself over and over, uniquely, in the subjectivity of each person. Wherever the world changes, the sensitive consistency of subjectivity changes as well, inseparably linked: between me and the other, nonparallel becomings of each person are unleashed in an endless process. It is from listening to the vibrating body and its mutations that the artist, disquieted by the conflict between the new reality of sensations and the old references used to orient him- or herself in existence, feels compelled to create a map for the future world which takes form in his or her work, from which it then becomes autonomous. Through the practice of art—a semiotic activity of human experience in its becomings—life affirms itself in its creative eroticism, generating new landscapes of existence.

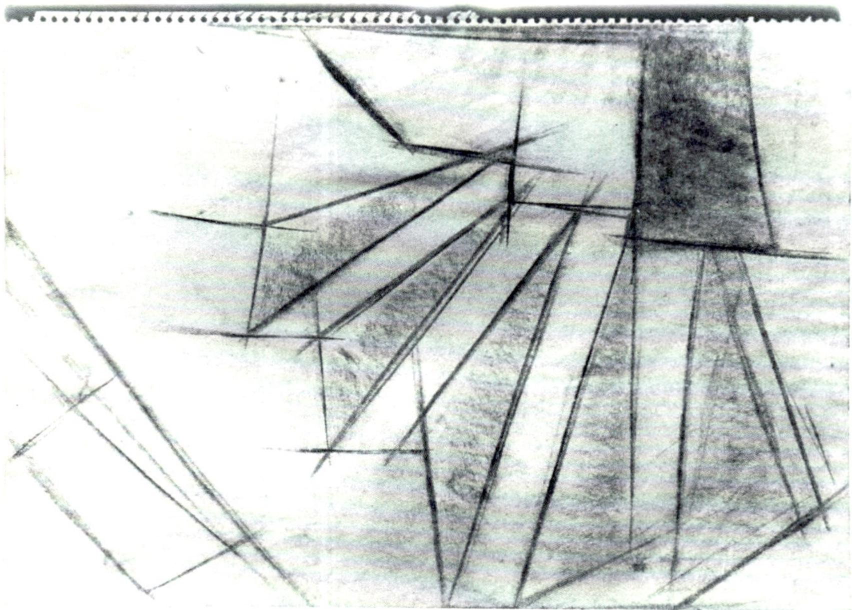

Untitled 1950–51

The reverse side of this plane in the process of the subjectivation of the artist is its anesthetic effects on the rest of social life: the ordinary person, that is, every human being, loses control of this activity—that of creating value and sense to the changes that go on ceaselessly around him or her—and comes to orient him- or herself with passively consumed *a priori* guidelines. What emerges is the figure of the "individual," a self-enclosed entity who extracts his or her feeling of self from an image lived as essence and maintains itself identical to itself, immune to otherness and its turbulent effects.[3] It is the identity principle governing the construction of subjectivity, under the exclusive regime of representation. The transforming power of estrangement engendered by the collapse of existing cartographies and their accompanying figures of subjectivity is sterilized and replaced by fear, fear provoked by the illusory idea that the collapse is that of subjectivity itself in its supposed essence.

This is the model that entered a state of crisis at the end of the nineteenth century, when significant changes in human existence began to emerge—among the most obvious, industrialization and technological development. Subjectivity was confronted with conditions different from the familiarity of the relatively stable world to which human beings had grown accustomed. The mutability of the landscape intensified to the point that it became impossible to silence the estrangement that instability produces in the vibrating body. The identity principle could no longer sustain itself: forced to experience these becomings at point-blank range, without being equipped to absorb them, subjectivity was terrified. The consequences of this terror we already know: the manifestations of the vibrating body were experienced pathologically, mobilizing fantasizing interpretations and the construction of defenses that would constitute a mode of subjectivation that came to be called "neurosis." It was in this context that psychoanalysis arose, through the need to treat the side effects of this dissociation in subjectivity, which at that time stridently evinced their presence through the corpus of hysteria. The fact is, from the moment that the forces operating in the invisible are "seen," where energies are orchestrated in such a way as to create a shelter in the strange and to find a new equilibrium, the intervention of a specialist becomes necessary, one whose function is that of initiating subjectivity into listening to estrangement, in order to interpret it in light of an individual history and reconstitute an identity. Art, as a ghetto of the creative impulse,

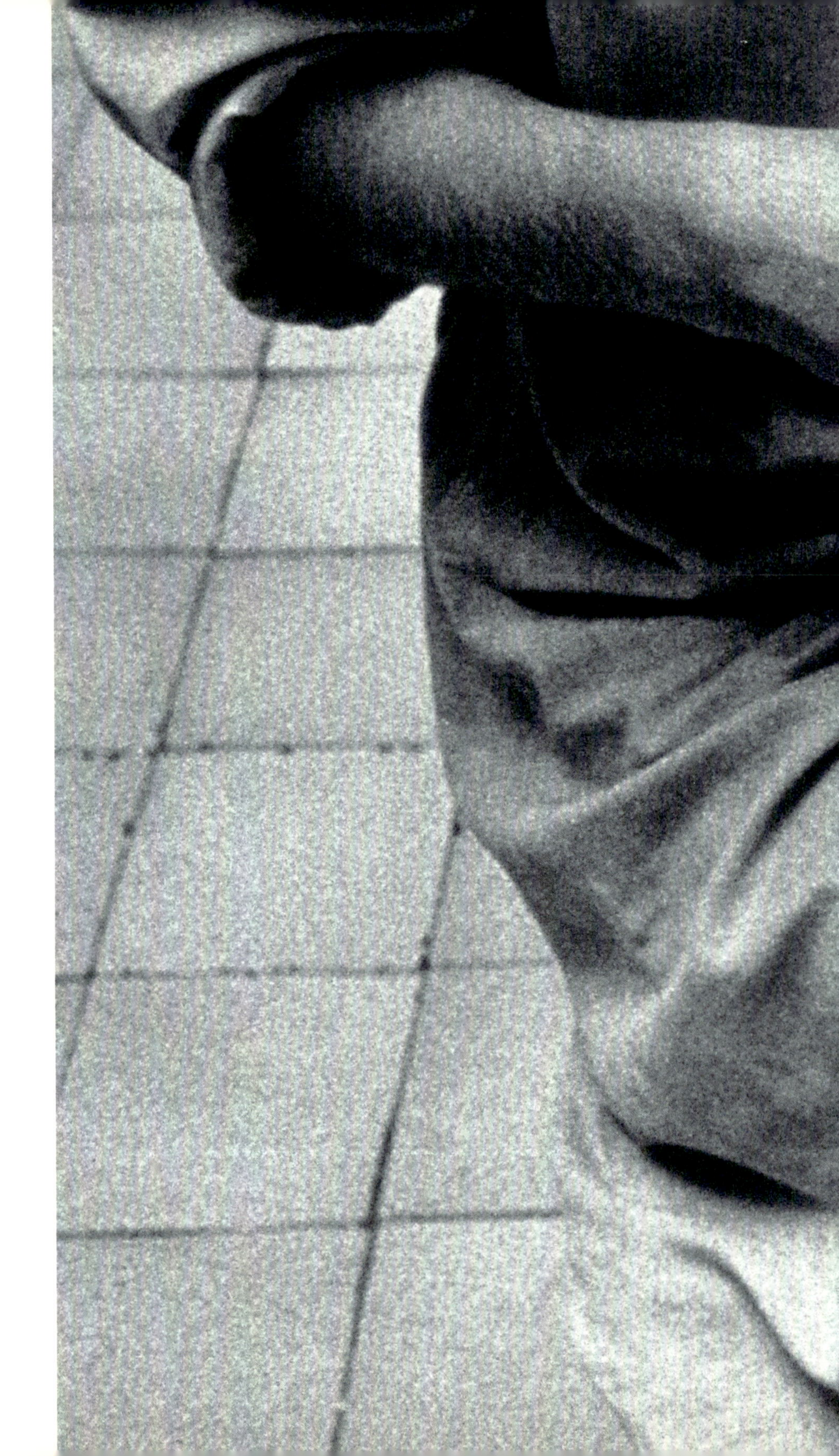

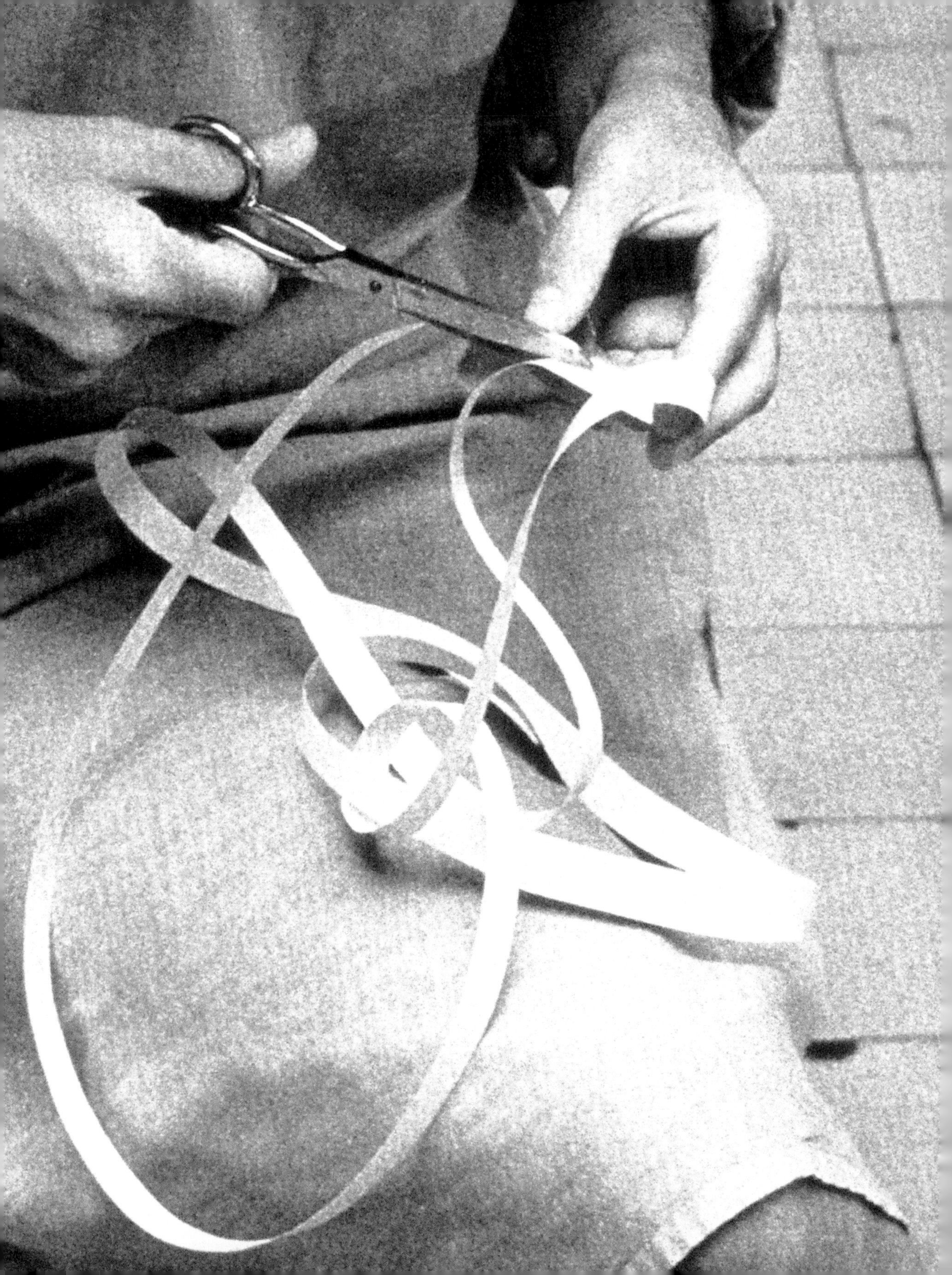

THIS AND PRECEDING PAGES: ***Walking*** 1963

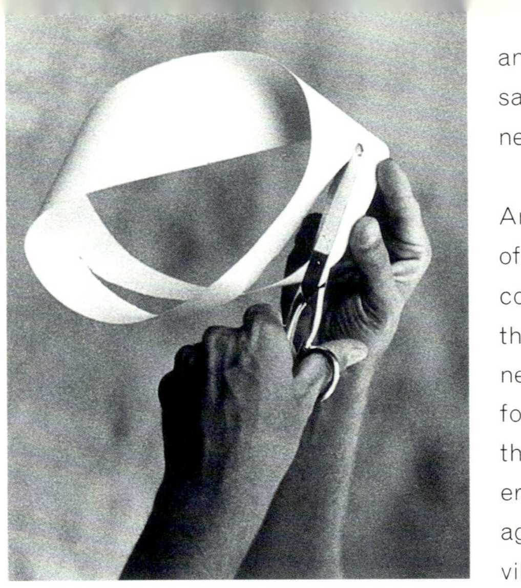

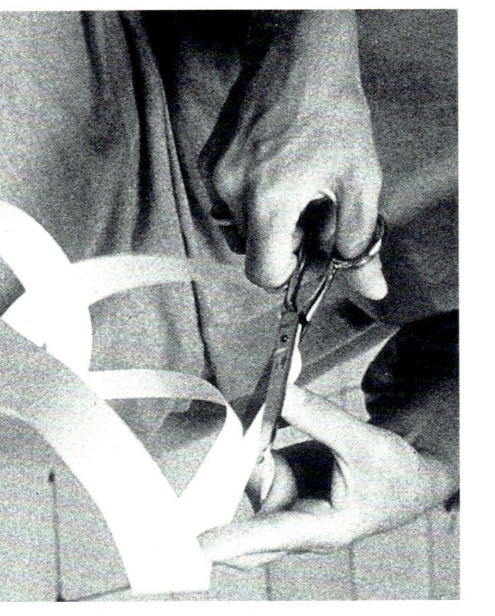

and psychoanalysis, as a medicine of the affects, are the products of the same process. It is in the depths of this process that modern subjectivity—neurotic, oedipal, personalogical—is constituted.

Art, however, since the beginning of the bankruptcy of this model at the end of the nineteenth century, rebelled and began to dream of the utopia of reconnecting itself to life, while society invented the strategy of the neurosis that readapted subjectivity in order to keep it in the same place. It would be necessary for this malaise to reach the level of an intolerable paroxysm before a reaction occurred in the heart of society. This would happen only in the 1960s, with the force of a collective process: the subjectivity of the generation born after the war exploded in an inescapable movement of desire against the culture that separated itself from life, reclaiming access to the vibrating body as a compass for a permanent reinvention of existence.

In Brazil, this process appeared particularly intense, finding a unique expressiveness in the Tropicalist[4] movement and touching a significant portion of youth, in contrast to other Latin American countries where the obstinate political militancy of the period was not accompanied by the same grasp of experimental revolution. Cultural movements of great power and originality emerged in this period. In 1968, the fulcrum of the counterculture movement, Clark moved to Paris, where she stayed until 1976. At the time she wrote: "What I am proposing already exists in numerous groups of young people who integrate the poetic sense into their lives, who live art instead of making it."[5] In the artist's work this was the decade of disruption, which would result in an oeuvre that even today pulsates in its mystery while crying out for interpretation.

Clark's artistic life began in 1947, in her own words, "to survive the crisis"[6] after the birth of her third child. Crisis would be a frequent companion to her work, breaking out in the gestation of each new proposition or following the completion of a work too disconcerting for her to bear, as in the case of *Caminhando*. At these moments, she would write texts of a singular density and turbulent corporeality.[7]

Clark's crises are neither a secondary nor a picturesque piece of information, nor objects of frivolous curiosity about the artist's private life or her "confused personality"; they are, rather, at the very core of her work. They are the experience of that which from early on and until the end of her life she would insistently call the "empty-full," the experience of the vibrating body at the moment in which the exhaustion of a cartography is processed, when the silent incubation of a new reality of feeling is under way, that incubation being the manifestation of the fullness of life in its power of differentiation. The crises were the living of these passages, which in the artist's subjectivity took place like "vulvanic [sic] eruptions," as she wrote in one of her manuscripts.[8]

The beginning of Clark's artistic arc is marked, therefore, by a rebellion against the dissociating of the experience of the empty-full in subjectivity, which may have led her crises to a pathological conclusion. It was as an artist that Clark would set in motion the surpassing of this fate. As she wrote, it was a matter of "receiving perceptions raw, living them, elaborating oneself through the processes, regressing and growing outward, toward the world. Earlier in the projection, the artist sublimated his problems through symbols, figures, or constructed objects."[9] From the beginning, her work was moved by her awareness that the experience of the empty-full must be incorporated for existence to be lived and produced as a work of art. Her inventions in the field of art always overlapped the reinvention of her existence. But this alone would not suffice to distinguish her from several other artists of her time: what sets her apart is that her work was directed toward the incorporation of the empty-full into the subjectivity of the spectator, without whom the plan to connect art with life fails.

I propose to divide Clark's work into two parts, with *Caminhando* being the turning point. The first part (1944–63) unfolds after the end of World War II and the fall of the dictatorship of Getúlio Vargas, which preceded and set the stage for the Brazil of the 1950s, geared toward development and dreaming of integration into modernity under the presidency of Juscelino Kubitschek. This was the time of the construction of Brasília, the new capital and the greatest symbol of this dream, rocking to the sound of the bossa nova. In this context, not only in Brazil but in other countries of Latin America undergoing a similar process, constructivist tendencies reactualized themselves through the resonance of the new local landscape with the context in which those tendencies had appeared in Europe at the end of World War I. That is how *Concretismo* (Concretism) and later *Neoconcretismo* (Neoconcretism) emerged, with Clark figuring as one of the latter's most vigorous proponents. These movements were preceded by the creation of the Museu de Arte Moderna (Museum of Modern Art) in São Paulo in 1948 and in Rio de Janeiro in 1949, the São Paulo Bienal in 1951, and the *Ruptura* (Rupture) movement in 1952.

Four phases may be identified in this first part. The first phase (1947–53)[10] is that of Clark's initiation into artistic practice. The landscape architect Burle Marx would play a central role in this process with his concept of the "organic garden." Clark frequented his studio in Rio beginning in 1947. During her first stay in Paris (1950–51), she also frequented the studio of Fernand Léger, who valorized line in the formulation of space.[11] Although this was a time of apprenticeship, her work already presaged the explorations that would unfold in the later phases—for example, in *Escadas* (Stairs, 1951), which "shed like a set of planes in space," with their "steps of flat planes."[12]

A few years later, Clark prematurely gained the autonomy that would mark her oeuvre. In the following three phases (1954–63), her work found resonance in that of contemporary artists with whom she formed a group in 1959: the *Movimento Neoconcretista* (Neoconcretist Movement), which was dissolved in 1961.[13] However, from the very beginning—as attested to in a letter she wrote in 1959 to Piet Mondrian, who died in 1944[14]—the strong autonomy of Clark's investigation would lead her to question her allegiance to the group. In 1961 she rejected the application of the term *nonobject* to her work (as proposed by the group's ideologue, Ferreira Gullar), and she withdrew. From the group, Clark would conserve her dialogue with Hélio Oiticica, with whom she would maintain a friendship until his untimely death in 1980.[15]

Neoconcretism, a renegade faction of the Concretist movement[16] initiated by the group from Rio, was a reaction to what those artists considered the excessive rationalism of their São Paulo counterparts, who from constructivism had inherited only the outer shell, stripped of its soul, and concentrated on problems of form reduced to formulaic plastic solutions and purely optical explorations. The Rio movement introduced an experimental vein, placing greater emphasis on the existential and affective significance of the work, as well as its expressiveness and uniqueness. The group adopted the notion of the "organic" to denote the life that had its revival in their work, in contradistinction to what they saw as the São Paulo group's lifeless formalism.

However, in order to extract all the richness of the Neoconcretist project, we would have to speak of a nonorganicity of the life that these works reveal, for what they propose is not mimesis or an expression of life in its constituted (organic) forms, but the incarnation, within the work, of life as a creating impulse. What we are dealing with here are two distinct concepts of the notion of life, two types of vitalism worth exploring more carefully, for therein lies the central idea that drove the whole of Clark's work.

The phenomenology of Maurice Merleau-Ponty and Susanne Langer is the philosophy that oriented the thought both of Gullar and Oiticica himself, whose work was always accompanied by the artist's sophisticated theoretical elaboration.[17] A similar influence is equally clear in certain passages from Clark's texts, although she was never a reader of philosophy.[18] However, the idea of life which permeates her work (as well as many of her texts) is difficult to apprehend in all its radicalness if we restrict it to within these perimeters. The concept of vitalism introduced by Gilles Deleuze can help us go further in this reading. Strictly speaking, one cannot talk of vitalism, insofar as phenomenology is concerned, but only of a separation from idealism, in the direction of the world. Phenomenology invokes thought to get close to things (Merleau-Ponty's "being in the world") but still remains something like a subject facing the world's objects, or an intentionality, whether of consciousness or of the body. Merleau-Ponty went beyond the notion of the organic body to develop the idea of the *corps propre* (body proper), already suggested by Edmund Husserl and others. For Merleau-Ponty, the contemplation of a ballerina's dance, for example, is not that of her organic body but of her body proper, taken over by the symbolic form of the music. As for Deleuze, in the spectator's participation we must take into account not only the rapture of the body proper but also a plane of forces, vibrations, and intensities; the author calls these "bodies without organs," which belong not to the ballerina or to the person watching her, but rather occur "between" the two, where becomings are unleashed. Deleuze's notion of life was inspired mostly by Benedict de Spinoza, Friedrich Nietzsche, and Henri Bergson: life as creationism, the permanent genesis of the world, productivity. It is the very plane of absolute immanence. The main idea of this conception of vitalism is that life is the constant resolution of problems in the face of the resistances encountered in its differentiation. This vitalism is distinguished from its evolutionist and mechanistic forms that err in the idea of necessity and finality, thus losing the idea of life's creativity.[19]

Clark's work was to be an obstinate exploration designed to provoke in the subjectivity of the spectator the power to be contaminated by the art object, not only by discovering the life that pulses internally within itself and in relation to space, but also the life that, in contact with the work, manifests itself as a differentiating force of its own subjectivity. Clark attempted to help the spectator reach the level of difference borne by the work in order for that person to dig from his or her own soul the new way of perceiving and feeling which the work summons forth. This would launch the spectator into unforeseeable becomings.

In the last three phases of the first part of the artist's oeuvre, which may be identified as Neoconcretist, certain constructivist principles were retained, such as the choice of objects reduced to their material essence, the importance given to the material's properties, and the perception of structures generated through their action. Such principles, however, were not the artist's goal, but rather the means for a whole constructivism of life itself in its inexhaustible differentiation. Clark's works in this initial moment may be classified as the creation of "living objects" that migrate from the plane into relief, and from relief into space. Although her works in this period are still very close to the propositions of the art of the time, it is already here that her exploration veers in an original direction.

In the plane,[20] several of Clark's discoveries—including the organic line and the breaking of the frame—revitalized geometry and revealed its processual aspects. In the first of those discoveries, she freed line from its supposedly

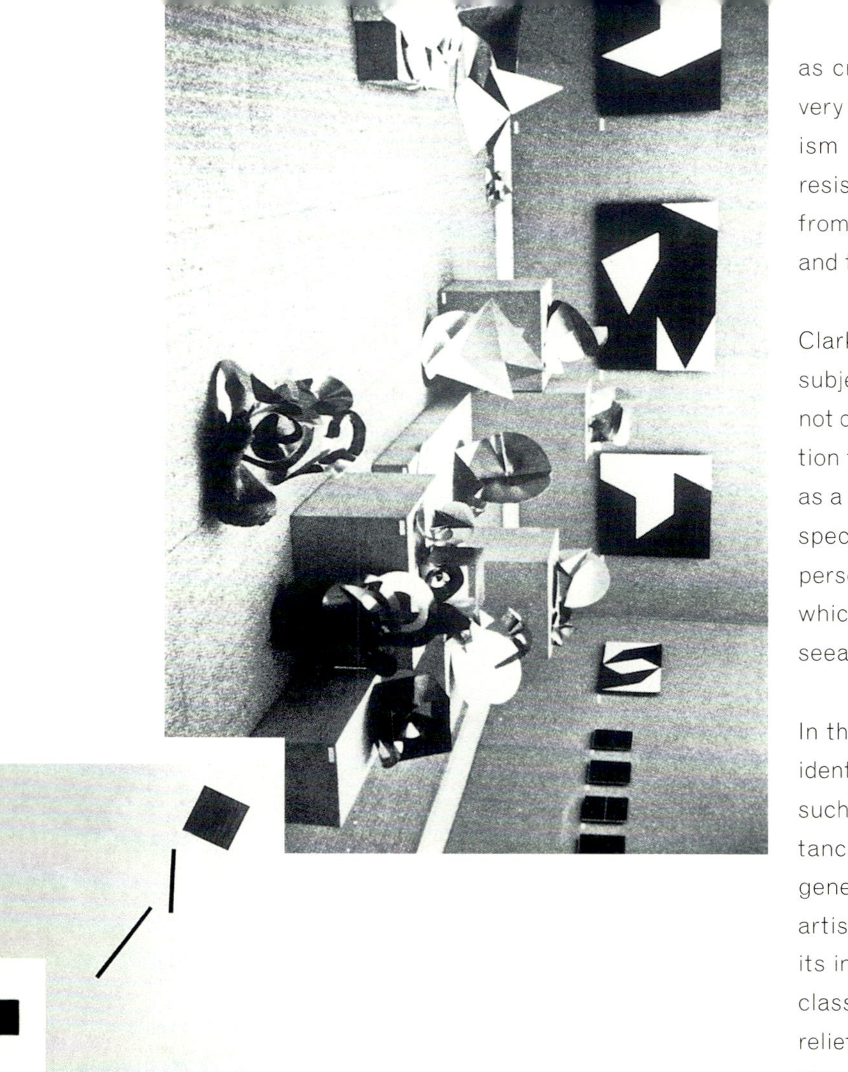

Venice Biennale 1968
Discovery of the Organic Line 1954

inanimate condition, recovering its vitality and transforming space. In the second, she dissolved the neutral zone representing the frame, which, in separating the canvas from the exterior world, buffers the disruptive power of art, as Gullar stated it.[21] Clark succeeded in summoning this power, liberating the plane of transcendence and returning it to immanence.[22] The plane thus recovers its poetic pulse.

With the "discovery" of the organic line, Clark, at this moment, had already extracted three-dimensionality from the two-dimensional plane. The planes are juxtaposed with lines and gaps that make the surface dynamic, as if irrigating it in life-giving sap, causing the work to spill over and contaminate space. We are now on the frontier between painting and sculpture. Then the next step is outlined: in 1959, the plane, pregnant from its fertilization by space, was inflated to become the *Casulo* (Cocoon, 1959–60). Unfolding in three-dimensional articulations, it reveals in the plane the virtual presence of relief. Clark's work went from the juxtaposed or superimposed planes of *Superfícies moduladas* (Modulated Surfaces, 1956–58) to wall-hung constellations in which the plane stood out concretely.[23]

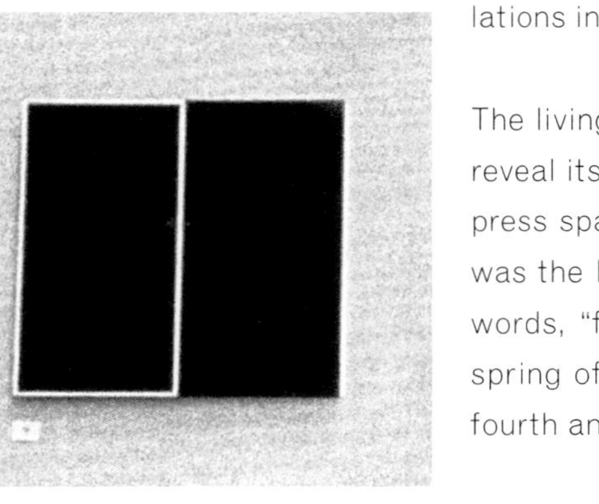

Units (***Units*** 1 and 7) 1958

The living work advanced in its reconquest of the world. The next region to reveal itself processually was space. "In reality, what I wanted to do was express space in and of itself, and not compose within it," Clark wrote.[24] This was the birth of the famous *Bichos* (Beasts, 1960–63), which, in the artist's words, "fell, like real cocoons, from the wall to the floor."[25] Numerous offspring of these *Bichos* would be born between 1960 and 1963, closing the fourth and final part of the first stage of the artist's oeuvre.[26]

The *Bichos* are linked to the constructive project and to the modern tradition in sculpture, which challenged such traditional values as the use of "natural" materials and the solid, immutable volume. But her solutions are unique: the use of precision-cut, polished metal to make objects fabricated in series takes us directly to the technological-industrial milieu to produce the strange effect of revealing the life that pulsates in the most artificial of environments. As for volume, here it is the fleeting effect of the agency of planes, "surface-process." The movements of the hinged metal plates produce volumes in space which seek an ever changing equilibrium. In addition, their movements are not mechanical, characteristic of a supposedly solipsistic existence of the object, for they require the hand of the spectator, giving us this strange sensation of being alive. What begins to dissolve here is the separation between subject and object.

In this final stage of the first part of Clark's oeuvre, immediately prior to *Caminhando*, the artist began to include the spectator in the work, with the vibrating body now more intimately exposed to the body of her vibrating objects. Further, the *Bichos* were originally intended to multiply in number, which would contribute not only to their losing any fetishistic status but also would lead to the propagation of their species in the world, thus contaminating virgin territories of art. We are now in the full beginning of the 1960s, when Clark found resonance in the project of reconnecting art and life not only in the experimentation of many other artists, but also in the movement of desire which was disrupting the social field.

However, her *Bichos* awaited the spectator and could even forego his or her presence, for they maintained the possibility of existing either as inert objects of passive contemplation or as sterile objects resistant to multiplying. They could be stuffed or exhibited in display cases in museums, galleries, or the homes of collectors, without any suspicion that they had once been alive. This was exactly what happened: the manner in which they were appropriated by the art system was such that the dissolution of the boundary between art and life operative in the *Bichos* was interrupted and their proliferation aborted. Taken back to the display case, and therefore to the pedestal, their freedom to live unattached in the world, to benefit from affective intimacy with the largest possible number and variety of others, was pruned away. For this reason, the first part of the artist's work is the best known, with the *Bichos* at its apogee, perhaps because they were the last of Clark's objects capable of being neutralized by the art system and of being consumed as simple, inoffensive objects of art, with their value determined solely by the market. Until the end of the artist's life (and even many years after her death), her works from this period, especially the *Bichos*, would be the ones privileged in countless one-person or group exhibitions and would by the same token constitute the focus of the majority of the studies of her work.[27] I will not go on at length about this first part of the artist's career, for in addition to there being an excellent bibliography available to evaluate it, the focus of this essay is the challenge in understanding the second part, both more mysterious and more extensive (1963–88), without which Clark's oeuvre cannot achieve full intelligibility.

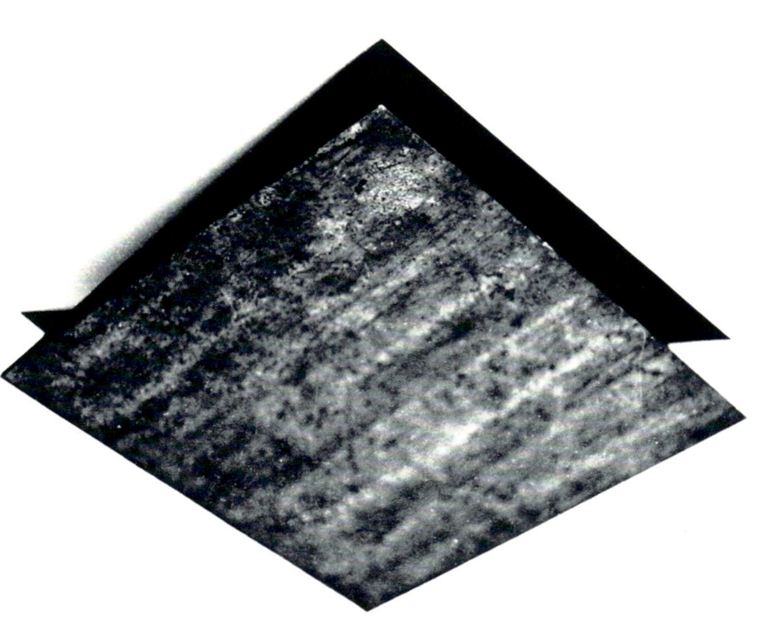

Cocoon 1959

Very early, beginning with *Caminhando*, the questions that would present themselves to Clark were these: To what avail is it to bring to presence in the work the "vision" of the invisible effervescence of life which stirs within and transforms all things, if the spectator lacks the key to this vision? To what avail is it to contaminate the life of the common citizen with art if his or her soul lacks the possibility of affirming in his or her own existence the creative power of life? Without the transformation of this character, the modern project, in its eagerness to reconnect art and life, would not be an effective strategy for meaningful intervention in the culture. In fact, the strategies on whose horizon Clark's work insinuates itself, evoked at the beginning of this text, leave intact on the art scene its characters, with their modes of subjectivation, and therefore the relationship with the invisible dynamics of things remains ghettoized in the artist's subjectivity. The artist continues to be the one who sees life shaking everything, and although he or she makes this vision material so that his or her perception acquires autonomy, this perception remains inert, inaccessible to a subjectivity dissociated from what would allow it to "see." Thus, the proposition goes unrealized. Only the "clothing" of some pieces changes in the interior of the same cartography.

Beginning with *Caminhando* and continuing until the end of her life, Clark's exploration would attempt to go beyond this limit, seeking strategies for awakening the spectator's vibrating body so that, freed from its prison of the visible, it could initiate itself to the experience of the empty-full and accede to the plane of immanence of the world in its mysterious germination. Just as it had moved from the plane to relief and from relief to space, her work would now turn toward the spectator, moving from the act to the body and from the body to the relation between bodies, to finally direct itself to subjectivity by delineating a wholly original trajectory in relation to the propositions of art (not only at that time but in our own as well). At the conclusion of seven stages, this provocative journey of initiation will have revealed to us a new landscape.

The first phase was formed from a single proposition: *Caminhando*, strips of paper, twisted 180 degrees, whose ends are glued together in such a way as to transform them into a Moebius strip, in which front and back become indistinguishable. The work consists simply in offering to the spectator this object and a pair of scissors, with instructions to choose a point at random to begin the cut and avoid hitting the same spot upon each completion of the circuit. The strip simultaneously narrows and lengthens with each successive cycle, until the scissors can no longer avoid the starting point. At this moment, the strip regains its front and back, and the work is concluded.

Here, Clark transfers to the spectator the act of cutting the paper, as she had in her preliminary studies for the creation of the *Bichos* (especially in the final examples of that series, which have no hinges and are made from a single piece). But now the spectator's participation in the work is not limited to reception but achieves realization itself. It is the act of creation which becomes the oeuvre, the work in progress, like life itself. It is in the act that the poetic will be revived. As Clark wrote,

> It is no longer the problem of feeling the poetic through a form. The structure exists there only as a support for the expressive gesture, the cut, and after it is finished, it has nothing to do with the traditional work of art. It is the state of "art without art," for the important thing is the act of doing that has nothing to do with the artist and everything to do with the spectator. By presenting this type of idea, the artist in reality presents this "empty-full" in which all potentialities of the option that comes through the act take place. . . . The act makes contemporary man aware that the poetic is not outside him but within him and that he had always projected it by means of the object called art.[29]

The figure of the spectator begins to deterritorialize itself, at the same time as the art object is no longer reducible to visibility, not even having the possibility to exist in inert passivity, isolated from the one who executes it.

Even if this were only the beginning of a process, Clark foresaw the magnitude of the transformation of the art scene which her proposition heralded; she underwent a crisis, perhaps the most violent of them all, which would torment her for two years. This was a moment in which Brazil itself was also experiencing intense political and cultural movement, probably overly disruptive for the nation's conservative forces. The denouement was the military coup that imposed a dictatorship on the country which would last until 1984, with one general after another occupying the presidency. During her crisis, and mobilized by it, Clark would feel the need to return to the earlier stage of her work to explore it in light of her new discovery.

The second stage (1963–64)[30] was therefore that of Neoconcretism revisited, contaminated by the disturbing presence of *Caminhando*, a retaking of the *Bichos*, which began with *O dentro e o fora* (The Inside Is the Outside, 1963), in which the Moebius strip moved from paper to metal. At the same time, Clark rebaptized one of the *Bichos* she had previously created, giving it the name *O antes é o depois* (The Before Is the After, 1963), as if what came after *Caminhando* now signified the before of the *Bicho* that gave rise to it. Soon afterward came the *Trepantes* (Climbers, 1964), first in stainless steel, later replaced in *Obra mole* (Soft Work, 1964) by rubber, like the pieces found hanging on the walls in mechanical workshops. From *Caminhando* she inherited the use of the cheap, everyday materials that she was never to abandon. Totally malleable, the *Bichos* now supported themselves on any base: a table, the floor, a bookcase, a shoebox, a tree branch—in short, whatever presented itself. And they supported themselves by any means: by twisting, grasping, hanging, spreading about, embracing all within their reach, taking on different shapes as a function of what they embraced and how they embraced it. In the flexibility of the interaction, they sculpt themselves, their manner of becoming dependent on what they encounter. That same year, Clark also made other works, among them *Abrigo poético* (Poetic Shelter, 1964), as if at that moment of disruptive turnabout, the idea motivating her work had been translated into a concept: to overcome the separation between shelter and poetry, to create conditions through which the person who previously had remained in the position of spectator could leave behind various shelters constructed from *a priori* representations, separated from experience, in order to construct shelters, "at-homeness," incarnating what his or her vibrating body would register as a new reality of sensations.

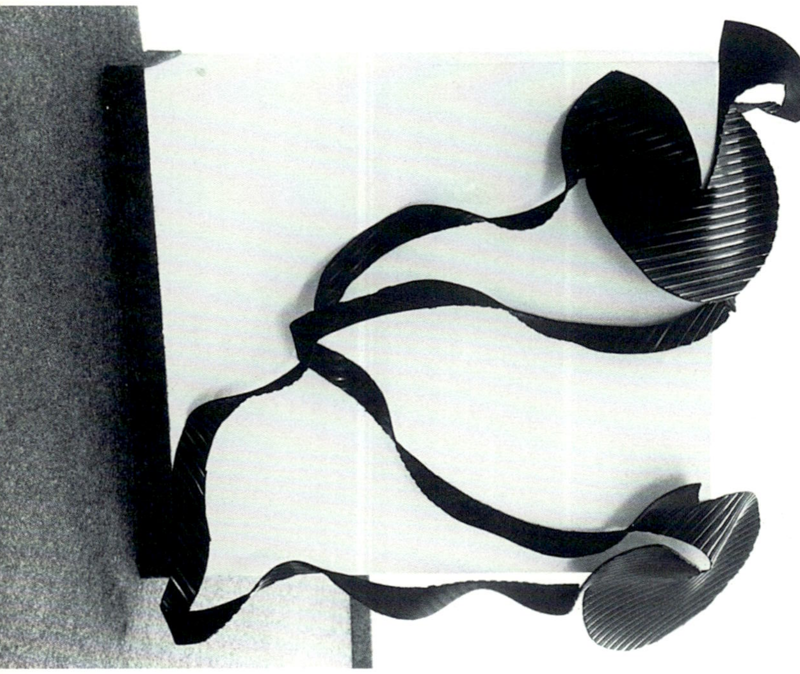

Trepantes 1964

The works from this period were Clark's last attempt at creating "objects of art," which, although they found their completion in the hands of the spectator, could still exist as neutral objects despite being manipulated—or even not manipulated—thus lending themselves to passive contemplation.[31] From this point on, the artist would move forward with her search to reintegrate life and art, and her objects would have no possible existence outside of the experience of those who lived them; abandoned to their own inertia, they lose thought, substance, meaning. That same year (1964), Clark created the *Livro-obra* (Work/Book),[32] where she made explicit the perceptions that had led her to her works until that moment, accomplishing the revision of her oeuvre and offering the spectator the opportunity to retread that same path, as she had already done with the *Bichos,* through *Caminhando*. This constitutes the definitive closure of the first part of her work.

The third stage (1966–69) Clark would call *Nostalgia do corpo* (Longing for the Body).[33] It began with *Pedra e ar* (Stone and Air, 1966), a transmutation that she executed on a small plastic bag sealed with a rubber band that she had been advised to affix to her wrist after breaking it in a car accident in the midst of her great crisis. It was from this object, used to treat her trauma, that she would extract the power to surmount the crisis and return to creativity. The work consisted of a common plastic bag, filled with air and sealed with an ordinary rubber band, on one of whose ends, pointing upward, was placed a pebble. The accompanying instructions were to hold the bag in the palm of one's hand, pressing it with systolic and diastolic movements to make the pebble rise and fall, like the very inhalation-exhalation motions of the life pulse.

In this stage, participation by the spectator took on a new dimension: the work began to move from the act to the sensation that it evoked in the one who touched it. In addition to no longer being reducible to its visibility and possessing no existence in isolation, the work was only achieved in the sensation mobilized in the relationship between it and the person manipulating it. Oiticica proposed translating *Nostalgia do Corpo* as "Longing of the Body," for

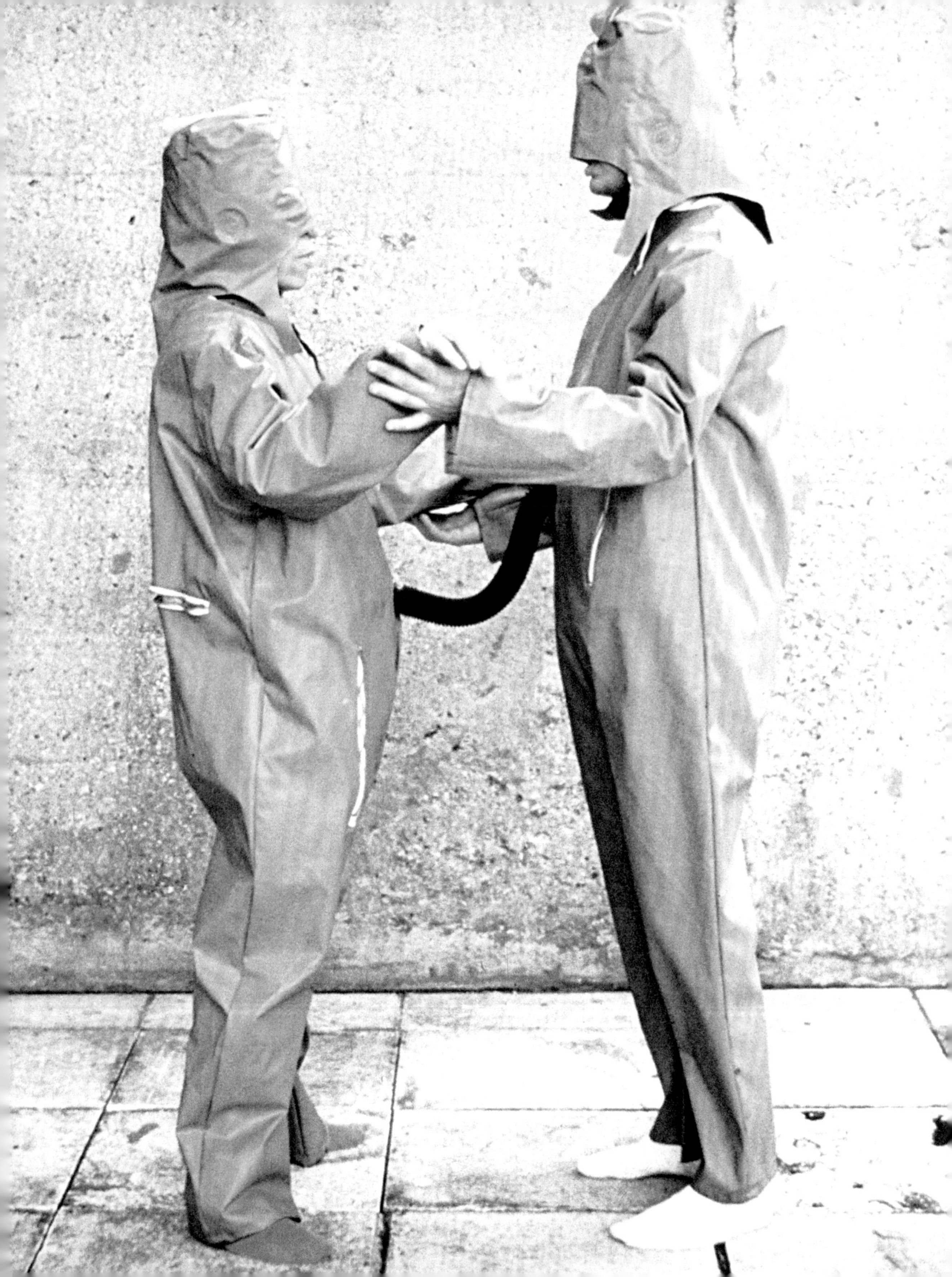

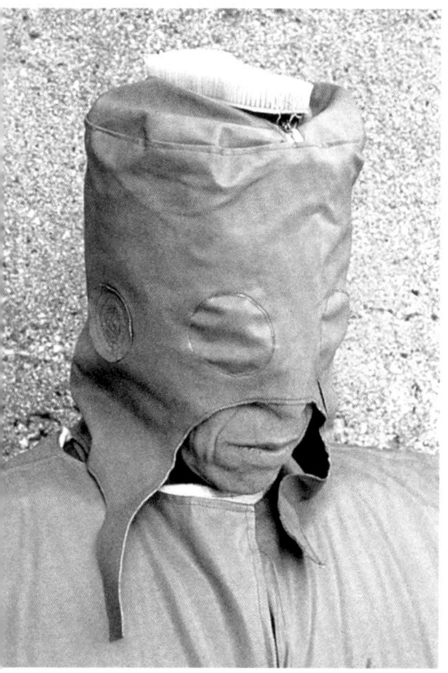

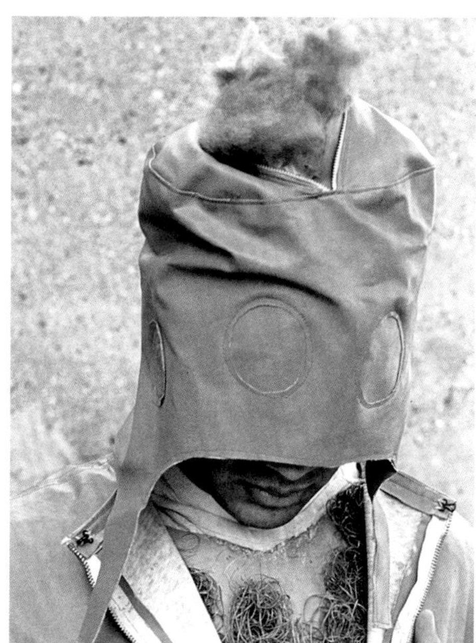

it deals more with the longing for the body than with melancholy nostalgia. One more step was taken toward the dissolution of the figure of the spectator. The evocation of the vibrating body is sketched here, though it is still not essential to the works of this period. Attention is still directed toward the object, which in this proposal continues to be, in Clark's words, "an indispensable means between sensation and the participant."[34] It was necessary to go further. The moment was propitious for such an approach: at this time the counterculture was at its apogee internationally, creating a social landscape that authorized and encouraged her experimental exploration. The subsequent stages would be elaborated while Clark was living in Paris, after 1968, as well as when she took part with Oiticica in the First International Tactile Sculpture Symposium in California—high temple of the counterculture—which reechoed in the artist's soul the resonance of the events of 1968 in Paris.

The fourth stage (1967–69)[35] Clark called *A casa é o corpo* (The House Is the Body). The inaugural work of this period is the *O eu e o tu: Série roupa-corpo-roupa* (The I and the You: Clothing-Body-Clothing Series). Two pairs of overalls made of thick plastic, joined at the navel by a rubber tube of the type used for underwater breathing (the same as in her earlier work *Respire comigo* [Breathe with Me]) with a hood covering the eyes, were to be worn by a man and a woman. The lining was made of various materials (a plastic bag filled with water, loofah, rubber, steel wool, and so on), different in each of the overalls, in order to allow the man a sensation of femininity and the woman a sensation of masculinity (for example, the chest of the woman's overalls was lined with steel wool, suggesting the hairy texture of this area of the male body). Six zippers on different parts of the overalls opened to allow access for each person to touch the inside of the other's body.

The object completely loses its visibility and comes to "dress" the body and integrate itself into it. Blindfolded and with those strange textures covering them, it becomes impossible for the spectators to orient themselves from an

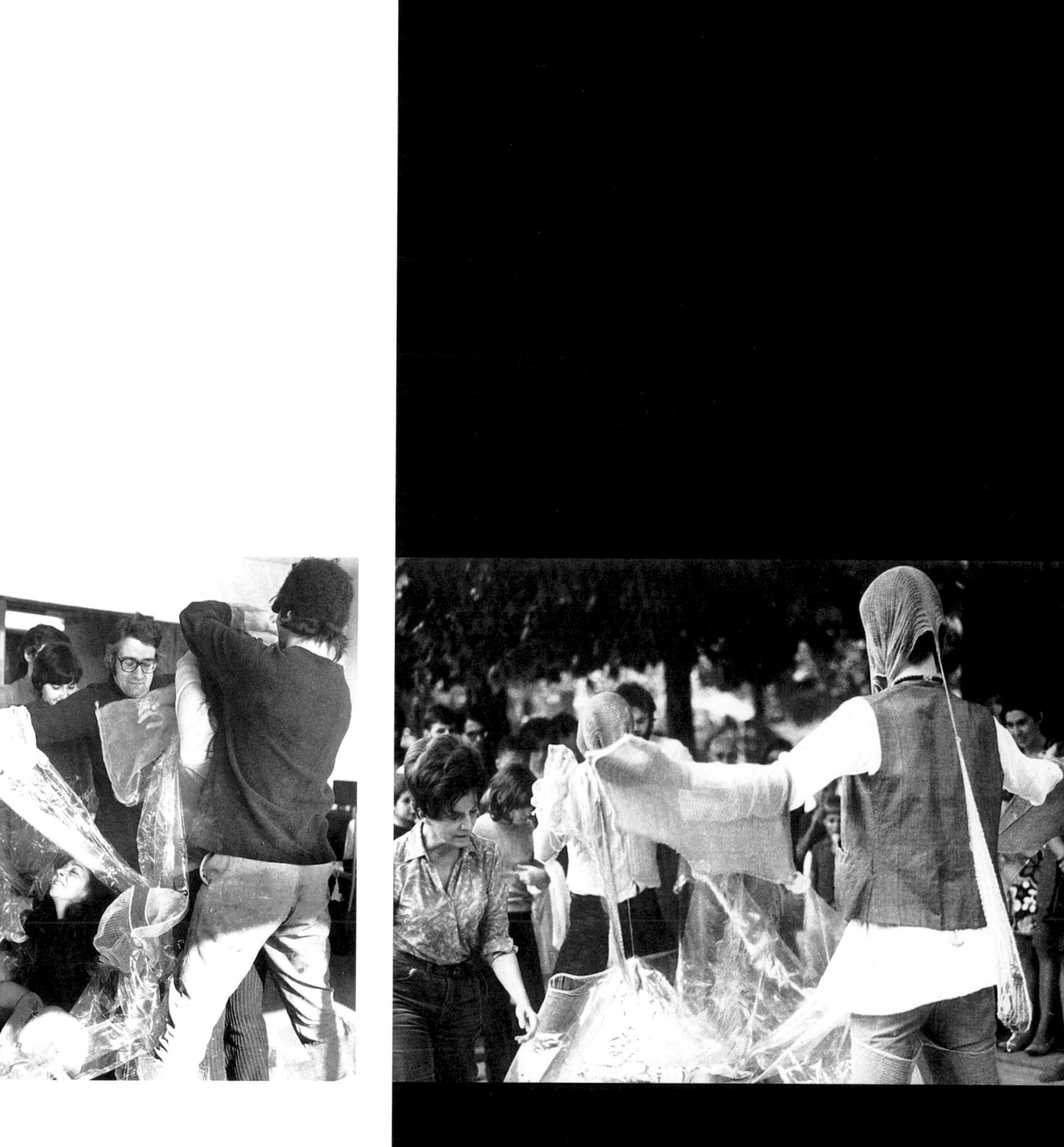

Biological Architectures I and *II* 1969

image of either the object or their own body, dissociated from the sensations mobilized by the exploratory gestures. Any identifying classification, such as gender in the case of this work, is dissolved. The spectator discovers him- or herself as a vibrating body whose consistency varies in accordance with the constellation of sensations evoked by the pieces of the world which affect him or her. It is from these sensations that the spectator will situate him- or herself in the world, making successive shelters. The feeling of being "at home" as a familiarity with the world ceases to stem from a supposed identity, in order to be built and rebuilt in the experience itself: the house is the body. Here, it is the body, in its relation to objects, which becomes poetic again. The territorialization by the spectator and the work in isolation became irreversible.[36] Attention moved entirely away from the object to concentrate on the vibrating body of its wearer. However, even here we have an object and a subject, for "people reencounter their own bodies through the tactile sensations operating in objects external to themselves," Clark wrote.[37]

The following stage (1968–79),[38] which developed in part parallel to the previous one, Clark called *A casa é o corpo* (The House Is the Body). It began with the *Arquitetura biológica: Ovo-mortalha* (Biological Architecture: Egg-shroud, 1968), a large rectangular piece of transparent plastic with nylon or jute bags sewn to its ends, in which two people stick their hands or feet and improvise movements so that each wraps the other in plastic. Later architectures were variations of the first; they would have more plastic, be sewn in different ways, and have additional nylon or jute bags at their ends, permitting participation by a larger number of people.

In the "visible," the work is a flexible structure made from the gestures of the participants in their interaction, aided by minimal materials "completely void of meaning and with no possibility of regaining life except by human support,"[39] a major step. But the work goes beyond this: in the invisible it is "an experience so biological and cellular that it can only be communicated by means equally biological and cellular. From one to two, to three or more, something always emerges out of the other, and it is an extremely intimate communication, from pore to pore, from hair to hair, from sweat to sweat."[40] The work achieves its realization in the pure sensation of the experience captured by the vibrating bodies of the participants. The "colorless transparent plastic is almost like ectoplasm that links the bodies in a nonmaterial way," Clark commented in a letter to Oiticica.[41] It materializes the nonmaterial presence of the vital energy that emanates from the bodies in their encounter, linking everything in a single moving continuum, the immanence. Here it is the interaction between the bodies which becomes poetic again.

No longer do subject and object exist; "The people become the support of the 'work' and the object is incorporated: it disappears;"[42] "man becomes the object of his own sensation,"[43] Clark wrote at this time. Each one is the support of "the living structure of a biological and cellular architecture" in which people and things form "the mesh of an infinite cloth,"[44] agitated by a dynamic of constant differentiation. The work is this biological and cellular architecture between bodies, produced by desire. They are true collective rituals of initiation into the vibrating body.

The participants, already quite distant from the position of spectators, discover themselves as the effect of a collective disposition, from which is defined, in the vibrating body, the consistency of their subjectivity in process.[45] The identity principle has completely dissolved: if in the previous stage creating a sensation of familiarity in the world, an "at-homeness," depended on the effects of things on the vibrating body, an experience lived individually, now creating such a shelter depended on what happened between the bodies in their encounter and of the becomings that this experience mobilized uniquely in the vibrating body of each of them. The body is the house. "It is a poetic shelter where dwelling is equivalent to communication. People's movements construct this habitable cellular shelter, starting from a nucleus that mixes with the others."[46] The reconnecting of shelter and poetry was a qualitative leap forward: "the erotic experienced as 'profane' and art as 'sacred'

FOLLOWING PAGE: ***Abyss Mask*** 1968

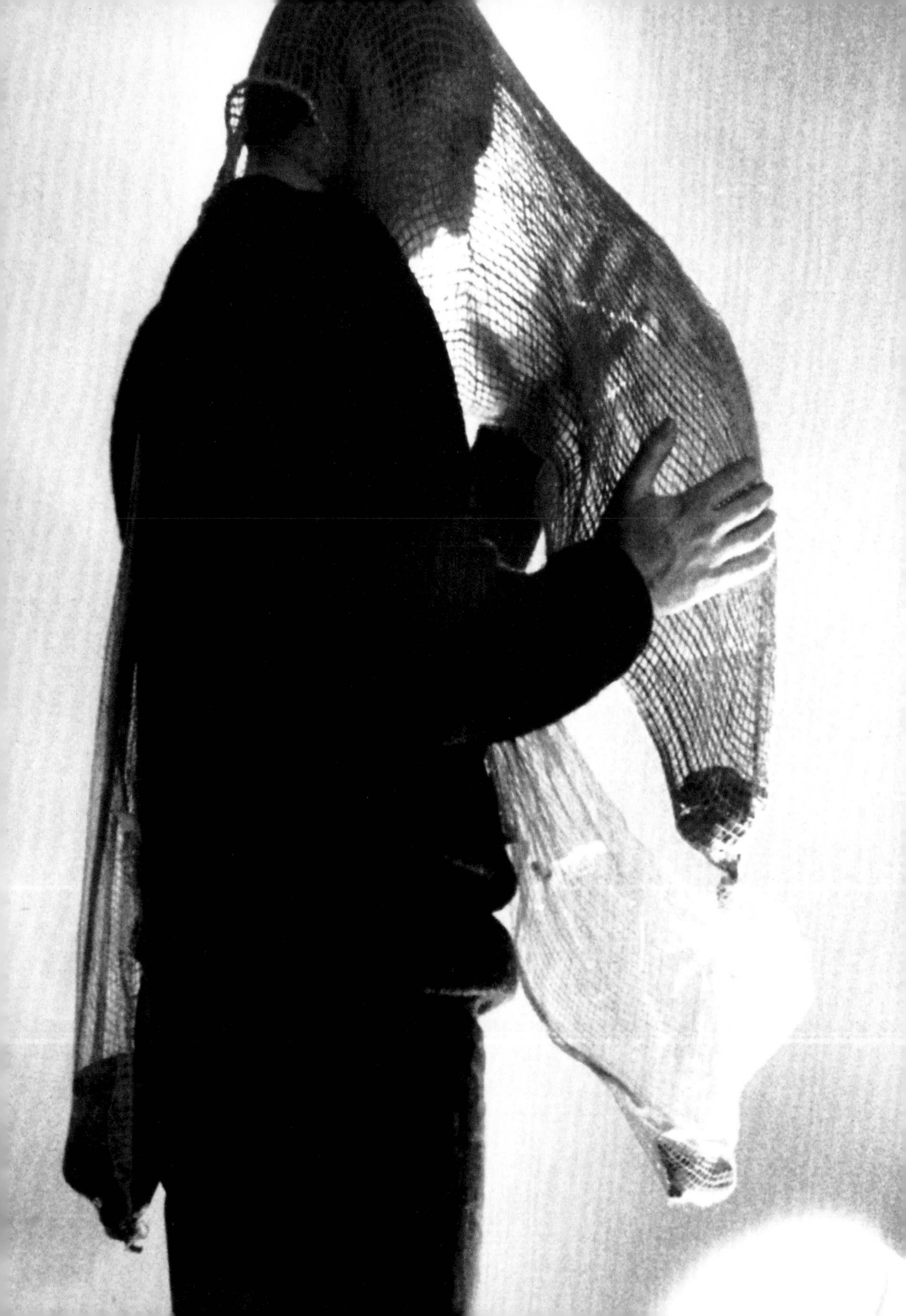

fuse into a unique experience."[47] Art and life mingled to the point that Clark entered a new crisis.

The year 1971 was an interval of silence in the work that Clark called "without formulation." In reality she was formulating the idea of "*Pensamento mudo*" (Mute Thought), which had occurred to her countless times during this period. It referred to the experiencing of the poetic through life rather than through works of art, which provoked in her a mixture of euphoria and fear. Mute thought is the concept of freeing the act of thought from its yoke of representation, to place it fully at the service of the vibrating body and create the bridge to the visible existence: the germination of new states of sensation no longer needs works of art, for now the maps are produced directly from life. It is toward mute thought that Clark's work aims and which would reach fruition in the two stages that followed: *Fantasmática do corpo* (Phantasmatic of the Body) and *Estruturação do self* (Structuring of the Self),

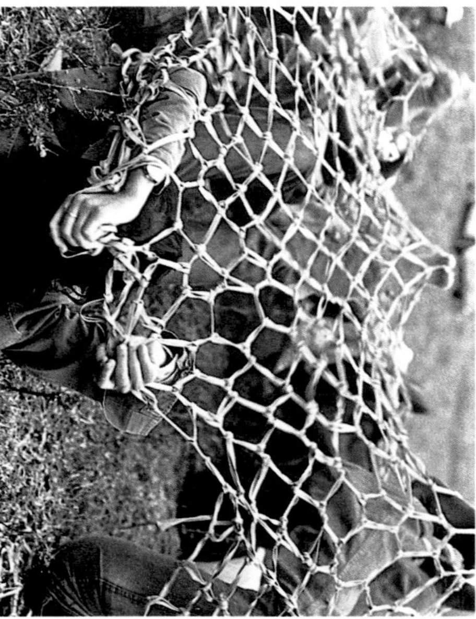

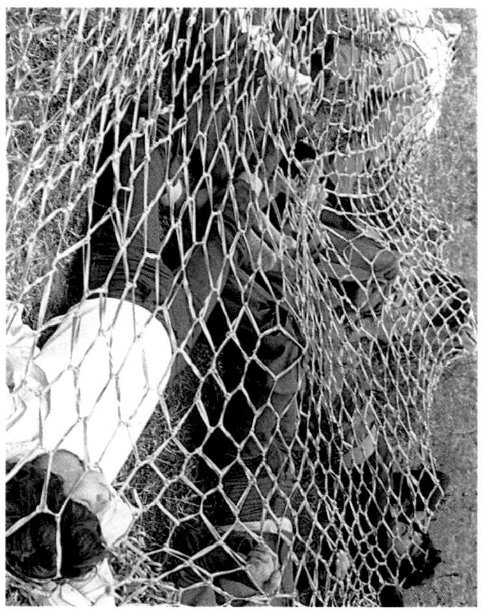

Elastic Net 1973

the latter produced with the help of her *Objetos relacionais*, which bring to a close the initial course suggested by the artist.

That same year, Clark fell ill, quite a common occurrence during her crises, and in January she traveled to Rio to treat a kidney problem. In February she returned to Paris, then back to Brazil in November for an exhibition in São Paulo. In October 1972 she was invited to give a course in gestural communication at the Sorbonne. It was in this context that she would emerge from her crisis, to begin her sixth post-*Caminhando* stage, which she called *Fantasmática do corpo* or *Corpo-coletivo* (Collective-body).[48]

The inaugural work in this stage is *Baba antropofágica* (Anthropophagic Slobber), in which a group of people each received a spool of colored thread which they were instructed to place in their mouths. They sat on the floor around one member of the group, who agreed to lie down with a blindfold

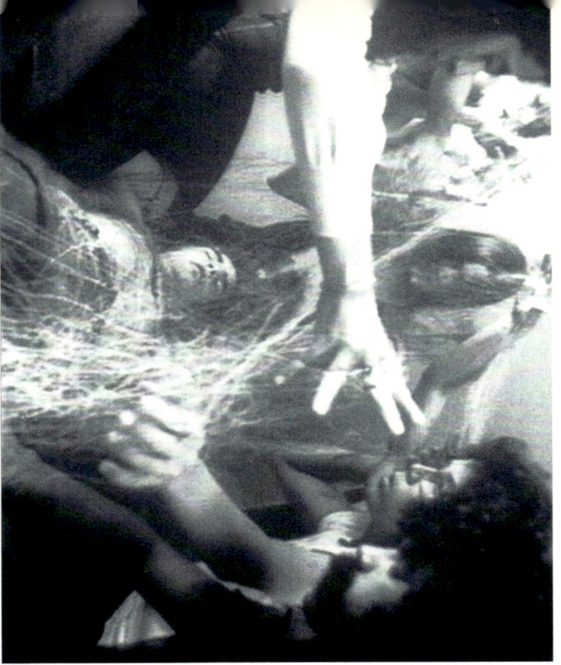

over his or her eyes, then pulled the thread, setting it on the reclining body until the spool was empty. They then stuck their hands into the tangle of saliva-moistened thread, which completely covered the body of the person lying down, and tore it until the web was completely undone. At this point, the blindfold was removed and the members of the group shared their experience verbally. This concluded the work.

In this ritual, bodies affect other bodies until their intertwined emanations form a mold about the affected body. While still damp, the mold is removed, like a placenta from some collective womb from which a new body is born, sculpted by all. Anthropophagically incorporated by the affected body, the emanations acquire autonomy from the bodies in which they originated. A becoming both by the affecter and the affected unleashes itself in this process, which does not happen through identification (each one "becoming like the other") but through contamination (each one "becoming another," without any parallelism between the two). If the tangle is yanked away aggressively, it is because this is the fate of each one's emanations on the body of the other, where the emanations lose themselves, tearing apart an individuality that which was believed to exist. It becomes impossible to remain indifferent to what links the bodies nonmaterially and produces their constant differentiation.[49]

This was the continuation of her works of collective initiation to the vibrating body, in which each participant discovers him- or herself as a "living structure of a biological and cellular architecture." But here, in addition to the work involving an average of sixty people, Clark created two new formulas to realize her project of reconnecting life and art in the spectator's subjectivity: the statements the participants made at the end of the session, should they choose to do so, and the regularity of the sessions, which took place twice a week for three hours per session.

Clark discovered at this time that in order for the vibrating body to consolidate itself in a subjectivity marked by the trauma of this experience, engendering its own repression, the ritual required this continuity in time and the expression of the fantasies produced by the trauma. This occurred because this type of subjectivity constructed its "at-homeness" with solid neurotic defenses based on a generous production of fantasies—veritable ghosts that haunt the experience of the vibrating body and keep it lethargic. Clark called the assemblage of these ghosts the "phantasmatic of the body."[50] To extract the body from its torpor, it is necessary to create the conditions under which, little by little, the fantasies/ghosts, along with their poison, would be "vomited," as she insisted, and the defensive construct would crumble. This depends on an atmosphere of trust established over time, for as the artist wrote, "To get there, one must deinstitutionalize both the body and every concrete relation."[51] Pore-to-pore work, one person at a time, carefully accompanied by his or her confrontation with the empty-full, is an indispensable imperative for the realization of this project. The next step was already delineated: in 1976, when Clark returned to Brazil, she began her sessions of *Estruturação do self* with the *Objetos relacionais*, the last stage of her work.[52]

The collective ritual in regular sessions for as long as necessary, capped by the final testimony in which the phantasmatic is expelled from the body, here transformed itself into a solitary ritual in which the spectator's initiation is completed through the settling of the vibrating body into his or her subjectivity. Working each time with a single "spectator" created a more protected space that afforded greater intimacy and a more radical journey. What was to be structured was a mode of subjectivation in which "at-homeness" was no longer the neurotic ego of the modern subject but a living structure in a process of becoming, engendering itself through impregnation by the world, which Clark called "self." "At the moment in which the subject manipulates it [the *Objeto relacional*], creating relations of 'fulls and empties' through the masses that flow in an unceasing process, identity with his psychotic nucleus unchains itself in the processual identity of molding itself."[53]

Strictly speaking, it would no longer be possible here to speak of identity, for this idea is incompatible with a subjectivity composed of the processual dynamic of molding oneself. It was surely to accommodate this new conception that Clark created the concepts of "relational object" for objective reality and of "structuring of the self" for subjective reality, each of which involves the other: the object reveals itself to be relational—no longer neutral or indifferent—toward a subjectivity structured as self and no longer as identity. Individuality is enclosed in itself, anesthetized to the murmurs of life in its constructivism, to time, to the other, to death. It is the definitive deterritorializing of the subject spectator, of the object of art, and of its de-eroticized relation.

The *Objetos relacionais* are in part new creations that Clark had been making for two years, in which she practiced her *Estruturação do self*, and in part earlier works that, since 1966, had been moving from stage to stage, integrating themselves into new propositions until emerging in a final work, either retaining the same function or reinventing themselves for other uses.[54] One example

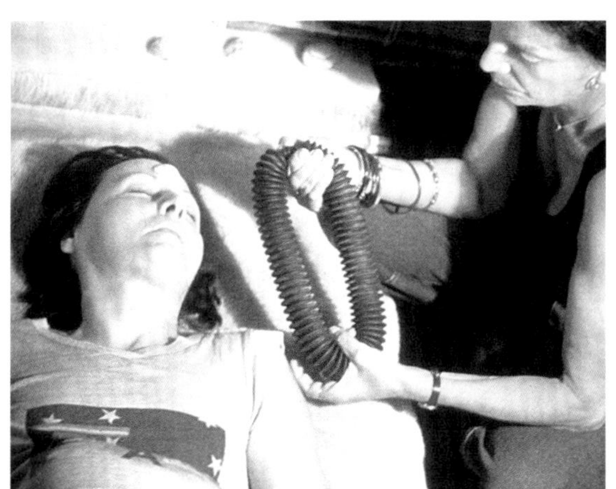

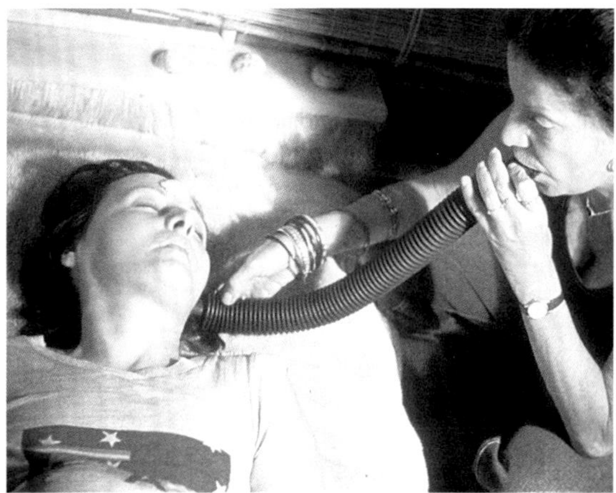

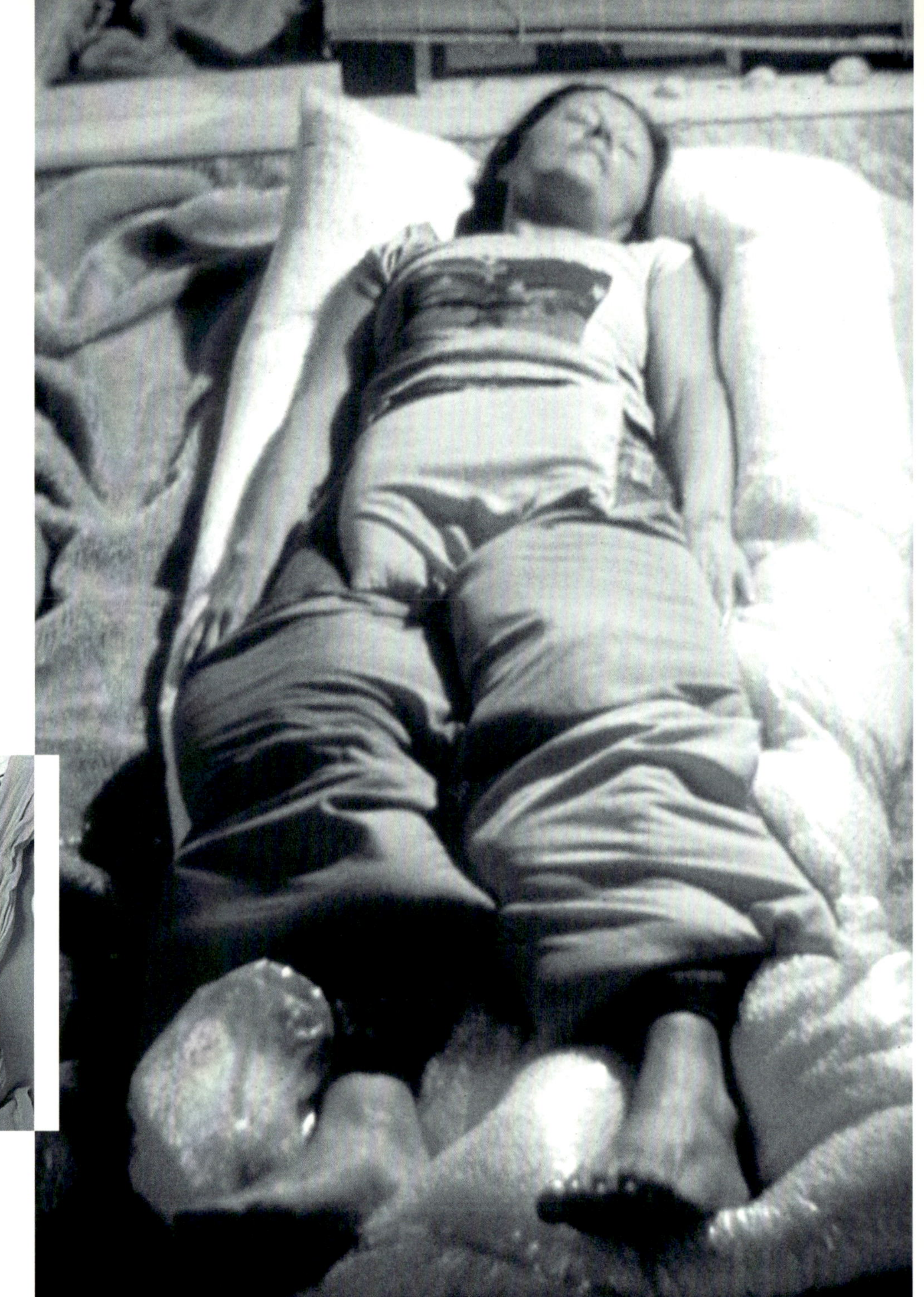

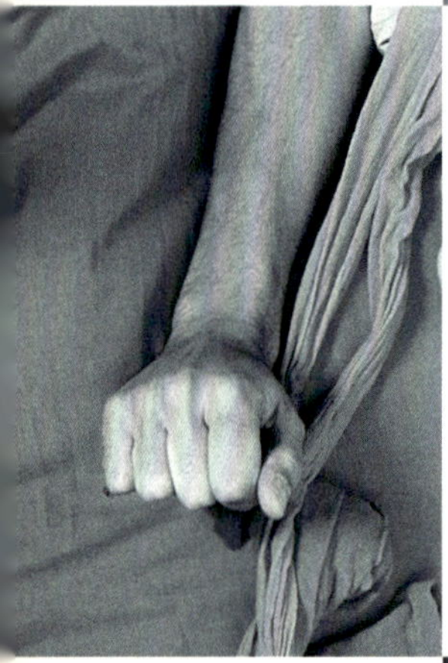

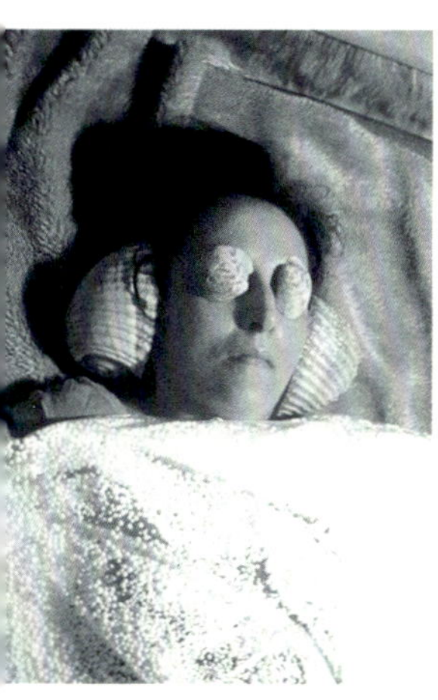

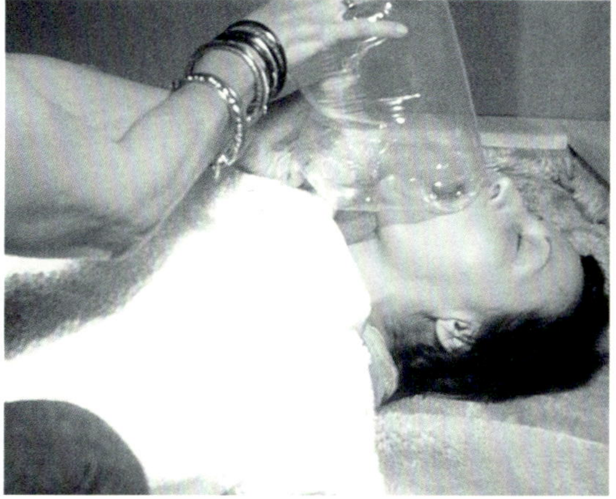

of an object that retained the same function is the stone that the person holds in his closed hand throughout the ritual; it functioned, according to Clark, as "proof of reality." It permitted going to the vibrating body and experiencing the empty-full, preventing the fear of disintegrating by the certainty that there would be a return—without it the experience would become too risky and would succumb to the resistance controlled by fantasies/ghosts. Proof of reality had been used in *Relaxação* (Relaxation, 1974–75), the proposition immediately before *Estruturação do self*, and reappeared as *Objeto relacional*. The banality of the materials in these objects acquired the sense of making this experience an encounter of another order with the things of daily life, contaminated by familiarity with the vital process.

Clark insisted that what these works proposed was a "ritual without myth." In fact, what was ritualized and inscribed on the body during the "sessions"

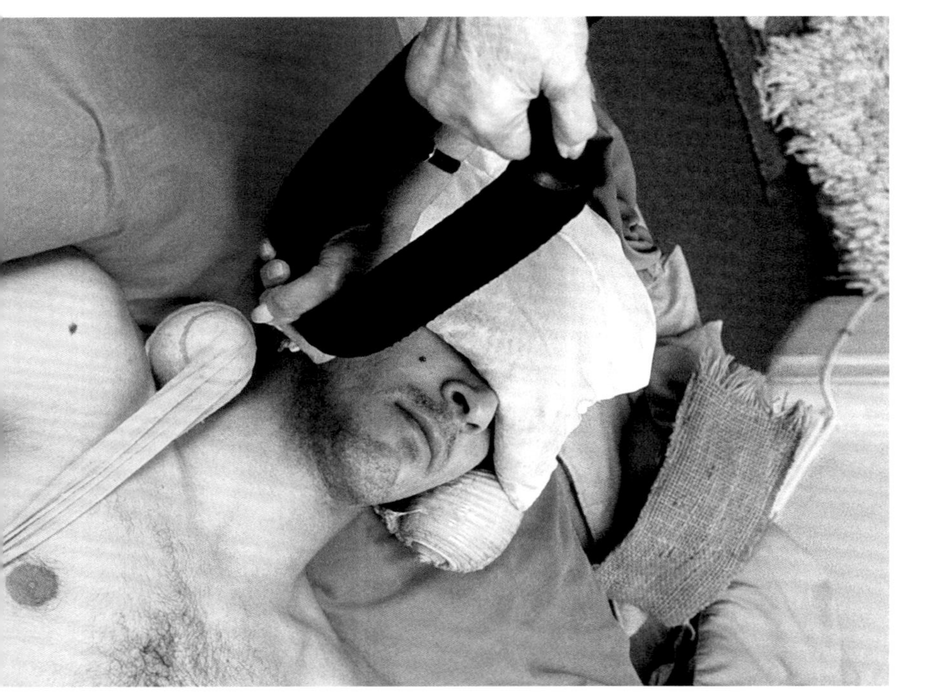

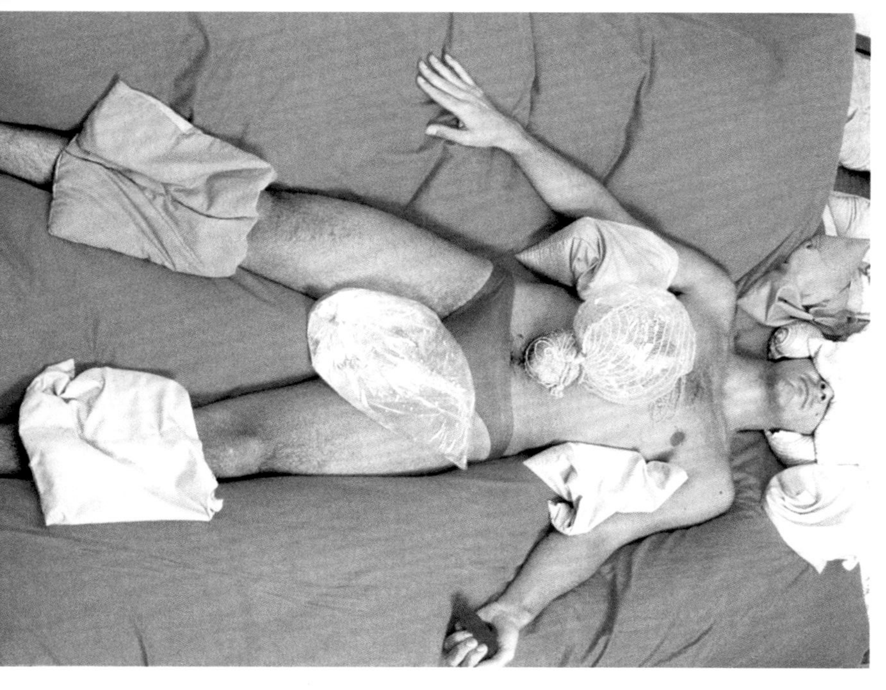

was not an image or sense of the world, of which the artist, since the death of God, would be the demiurge. It is not this transference of myths, exterior to man, which would be recorded, but the power of permanent creation in the sensing of self and of the world, which every person, as a living being, possesses virtually: it is this power that would be reactivated—a tuning of energies to constitute an "at-homeness" within deterritorialization itself, and not in its illusory evasion. It is a ritual for the end of the millennium, when surfing in deterritorialization has become indispensable for the construction of a shelter in the new landscape in which we live, with its rapid technological changes and its globalization that expose the vibrating body to every kind of other and which mix everything into the subjectivity of every inhabitant of the planet. In Clark's words, "The work creates a kind of exercise to develop this expressive sense inside him/her [the spectator]. It would be a kind of prayer added to his full participation in the religious ritual itself. . . . We are the new primitives of a new era and are beginning to revive ritual, the expressive gesture, but now within a concept totally different from all other eras."[55]

The *Estruturação do self* was, and continues to be, the object of an unfortunate misunderstanding in which Clark's final work was displaced from the field of art into that of therapy; Clark herself was partly responsible for this. With this last work Clark termed herself a therapist, but countless times she vehemently denied it, insisting that she had always been on the frontier. She also frequently used psychoanalytic concepts to interpret the experiences of the "clients" who submitted to her proposition of the structuring of the self, or to explain this proposition. This tendency to explain and interpret through the precepts of psychoanalysis was due not only to the strong presence of psychoanalysis in the life of Clark, who went through various analytical processes throughout her career, but also to the strong presence of psychoanalysis at that time in the culture itself (especially in France in the 1970s, where Clark lived for much of the period in which she developed the second part of her work). This phenomenon was replicated in Brazil in the 1980s, when Clark developed part of her *Estruturação do self*. Her proposition being very much in the vanguard, there existed no other theory capable of apprehending it in its radicality; thus she used psychoanalysis, at that time the legitimate theory to refer to work with subjectivity. But psychoanalysts took no interest in the matter, and critics at the time did not follow this turn in Clark's work—and still do not today. Interpreted in the best light, it was accepted that what was being dealt with was therapy and not art, and so it was accorded no further thought.

When, in 1978, Clark asked me to choose as my thesis the final part of her work,[56] her expectation was probably that I would find a way of putting it into theory. Actually, it was the artist herself who best found words to conceptualize her work, intermingling her psychoanalytic reading with moments of lucidity which left very clear the uniqueness of her invention, as well as its consequences. In any case, her comments delayed a greater understanding not only of this final part but also of the totality of her oeuvre, which achieved its full intelligibility only when conceived as part of the proposition to which it led at the end.

My own research into Clark's work, motivated by her request, oriented itself along the lines of the same interpretation. Some years later, when I resumed the research,[57] this reading struck me as not only mistaken but also deleterious to the understanding of the strength and originality of her work. At the time, my perspective was that the issue driving her oeuvre from the outset had been the boundary between art and therapy in her final work, which brought about disruptive effects in both the fields of art and therapy. However, my present resumption of the research for the third time leads me to an even more radical point of view: in reestablishing the link between art and life in the spectator's subjectivity, Clark's proposition surmounts in the work itself the separation between the artistic domain and psychotherapy. She creates a territory situated neither in the sphere of art as a department of social life specializing in semiotic activities, where access to the creative power of life is confined, nor in the sphere of therapy, specialized in treating a subjectivity separated from this power, nor in the border between the two—it is an entirely new territory. As I mentioned at the beginning of this text, the origin of these two phenomena dates historically to the decline of a certain cartography at the end of the nineteenth century. At that time, the cleaving of the aesthetic plane within the subjectivity of the ordinary individual became inoperative, while originating alongside the institutionalization of art as a separate sphere. Concomitantly, therapy was born to treat the pathological effects of this dissociation, and art began to dream of being reconnected to life, a utopia that runs through all of modern art. In inventing a user who ceases to be a spectator, Clark provoked the dissolution of the disjunction of the aesthetic plane in its process of subjectivation and at the same time the liberation of this plane from its confinement in the artist's subjectivity. Art effectively reconnects itself to life, and the existence of psychotherapeutic treatment loses any meaning. From this follows the conclusion that it is impossible to consider that in this work we are on the border between the two domains, for here they cease to exist as such. Nor can it be said that it was a territory that implied the abandonment of art and its replacement by therapy or a fusion of the two.

Why was this not a matter of the "death of art" or "anti-art"? Various artists throughout the twentieth century aired these ideas in their eagerness to surmount the limits of the art of their time in the direction of life. Clark insisted many times on her disagreement with this outlook.[58] Her proposition retains the artist's privilege to incarnate in the work the perception of life that pulsates in things, autonomous from the person. However, this autonomy goes much further in Clark's proposition, insofar as her work has no possible existence outside the experience of the erstwhile spectator. To achieve this intimacy, the artist had to remove herself completely from the art milieu—its institutions, its market, its mode of exhibition and reception—for whoever becomes a part of that milieu can only divest him- or herself of it with great difficulty. In removing the spectator from this milieu, Clark facilitated his or her willingness vis-à-vis the work of transmutation of his/her subjectivity, which begins to operate in *Estruturação do self*. It was for this reason that she opted to show her work not in galleries, museums, and so on, but in universities, in the streets, and finally in her own apartment, where she held the *Objetos relacionais* sessions. For the same reason, the few times that she was given the opportunity to exhibit the second part of her work or speak about it, Clark stipulated the condition that it not be in an art space.

Why was this also not a matter of replacing art with therapy, or using therapy as a form of opposition to art? Because therapy as practiced, as we have seen, was merely the corollary of art as a separate sphere: it created the conditions for listening to the vibrating body, which had become necessary since the end of the nineteenth century, but it integrated them into the experience of the psyche through the interpretation of fantasies/ghosts, looking toward the construction of an individual history in order to reconstitute an identity—the goal of treatment. In Clark's proposition, however, the emphasis was not on the fantasies/ghosts or on their interpretation—in this case, practically nonexistent—much less on the reconstruction of an identity. As we have seen, if there is a story of fantasies/ghosts to be brought to the surface, it is the story of the strategies for obstructing the vibrating body that was constructed in that existence and must by the same token be dismantled and expelled from the scene. The singularity of Clark's proposition lies in creating the conditions for listening to this plane, already linked to the discovery of the life in all things, through the experience of her objects, which reacquire the status of "relational." Thus are overcome both the neutrality to which works of art are submitted and the identity principle that kept subjectivity blind to the pulsation of the life that stirs in all things, resulting in its sterility.

Why was it also not a matter of a boundary or fusion between art and therapy in a kind of conciliatory "holistic" totality? Because the existence of each of these spheres cannot be dissociated from the division of functions that have as their basis the de-eroticizing of human life in its creative force. The re-eroticizing of life at work in Clark's oeuvre establishes the bases for construction of a new territory with another cartography and other characters having nothing more to do with the universe in which such spheres have their raison d'être. To remove oneself from that universe is to remove oneself from any possibility of pacifying the disquiet that life, in its differential quivering, mobilizes in subjectivity, calling it to the permanent task of reinventing itself and its mode of existence, a task that is finished only at death.

With her last work, Clark did not begin making objects for therapeutic ends but, as she explored the therapeutic potential of her proposition, she revealed the vital power of art itself as a semiotic activity when it reintegrates itself with the subjectivity of any person. "Until our era, the artist was only a thermometer in which the new spiritual reality of the future was indicated. There will come a time when everyone will be that thermometer and bring within themselves that future-present."[59] Clark made this future happen in her work.

Rereading from the end to the beginning, Clark's oeuvre in its totality reveals itself as motivated by a single idea that develops rigorously, stage by stage, and to which she sought to provide consistency throughout her trajectory as artist: to awaken the perception of the creative vitality in different areas of human experience. Initially, this perception was mobilized in relation to the plane, to relief, and to space; later, in relation to the act, to the body, and to the encounter of bodies; and, finally, to reach the stage of creating conditions for this perception in the spectator's subjectivity to be possible. To do so, she created specific objects for each of these areas, which after a certain time were accompanied by a ritual. Little by little, it was the world that was illuminated in its process of differentiation, in the "vision" of all and of each one, and not merely the vision of the artist.

With Clark's work was created a territory that did not exist until that moment, in which the modern project to reconnect art and life reached its limit. The proposition to "make living objects, reveal the life in things, their incessant state of process, allow a glimpse of the forces" goes beyond space and touches existence as a whole, giving it a new body, a new universe, a new cartography, new characters. The proposition to "produce an intensification of the faculties of the spectator" is realized concretely by Clark in the very core of the spectator's subjectivity, bringing about its transmutation. In Clark's proposition, the artist effectively abandons his condition of dweller in the ghetto of the poetic plane in the processes of subjectivation and makes a contribution toward activating it in the collective by freeing the user from his or her condition as spectator (of the work of art, but also of life), to initiate him or her to what Mário Pedrosa defined as the "experimental exercise of freedom." Aesthetics is reintroduced to ethics. Life in its creative power thanks.

If we examine the whole of Clark's trajectory, the idea permeating her work reveals itself in all its complexity and all its power to intervene in the culture, a unique map for contemporary experience. It is a powerful reply—incarnate and not merely formal or theoretical—to the impasses confronting subjectivity today, where the construction of territories in which one can feel "at home" is no longer sustainable when it obeys an identity principle. As Clark wrote, "Previously, man had a discovery, a language. He could use it his entire life and thus feel alive. Today, if we crystallize into a language we stop, inexorably. We totally stop expressing. It's necessary to be always catching."[60] In evoking this power in the spectator "to be attracting" the mutations of time that manifest themselves in his or her vibrating body, Clark's work turns him or her into the missing contemporary person, replacing the modern person, that spectator of art and life, who runs the risk of succumbing to the impasses of contemporary experience if he or she persists in the way one has organized one's subjectivity, or worse still, the risk of producing irreparable damage such as the carnage we have witnessed in the name of perpetuating supposed ethnic, religious, and national identities in a world irreversibly invaded by hybridization.

In realizing the modern utopia in her work, Clark exhausted this cartography and prepared the ground for a new dream. To ask whether it makes sense in the present to reactivate her post-*Caminhando* propositions, whether they are still living objects or only documents from the past, means wondering whether the question that this oeuvre introduces is still valid. Although thirty-six years have passed since the disruptive turning point in the artist's trajectory in 1963, we are far from having incorporated into subjectivity the experience of the empty-full, through which poetry and shelter merge in a permanent creation of existence, far from a heterogeneous subjectivity with its structured self, the axis of its unending transmutation.

We are still too modern. When will we join Lygia Clark in her visionary proposition?

Translated by Clifford Landers

Notes

1 Gilles Deleuze, *Critique et clinique* (Paris: Minuit, 1993), 14.

2 The vibrating body is a concept that I developed in my book *Cartografia sentimental: Transformações contemporâneas do desejo* (São Paulo: Estação Liberace, 1989), and which I have been pursuing ever since. It refers to the power of the body to vibrate to the music of the universe, to the composition of affects that play "live" in our subjectivity. Our consistency is made up of these compositions as they create themselves over and over again, inspired by the aspects of which the world affect us. The vibrating body is therefore that which, within us, is both the inside and the outside at the same time, the inside being nothing more than a fleeting combination of the outside.

3 About this, Lygia Clark wrote: "Individuality is the brick with its name written on it. We need urgently to tear down that plaque just as we tore down others with the name of god, love, so that everything in reality can be process and totality"; letter to Hélio Oiticica, 26 October 1968, in Luciano Figueiredo, *Lygia Clark–Hélio Oiticica: Cartas, 1964–1974* (Rio de Janeiro: UFRJ, 1996), 59–60. This book is indispensable for anyone researching the work of these artists.

4 *Tropicália* is a term invented by Oiticica and adopted by the poetic-musical movement led by Caetano Veloso and Gilberto Gil. More than an aesthetic, it imparted an attitude that greatly influenced countercultural thought in Brazil.

5 Lygia Clark, "1969: O corpo é a casa," in *Lygia Clark* (Rio de Janeiro: Funarte, 1980), 27. This text is reprinted with the title "The Body Is the House: Sexuality, Invasion of Individual 'Territory,'" in Manuel J. Borja-Villel, ed., *Lygia Clark* (Barcelona: Fundació Antoni Tàpies, 1997), 248. This catalogue, which accompanied an exhibition organized by the Fundació Antoni Tàpies, is an important source for anyone studying Clark's work because it includes previously unpublished and inaccessible manuscripts, crucial for an understanding of the artist's oeuvre.

6 Lygia Clark, "Pensamento mudo" (Mute Thought), undated manuscript, in Borja-Villel, ed., 270–71.

7 In a lecture on the writing profession and women, Virginia Woolf spoke of two indispensable tasks necessary for a woman to liberate her power of creation. The first: to kill the angel in the house, for the shadow of its wings clogs the investment of desire in the work with guilt. The second: to tell the truth about one's own experiences living in the body of a woman, truths about her passions, for the awareness of what men in their conventionality would say has the power to interrupt this trance and dry up the imagination. As she suggest in her text "Killing the Angel in the House" (1931), Woolf felt that this second task was still to be realized, even in her own work. Clark certainly succeeded in overcoming the second obstacle, less evident and more dangerous. The same can be said of Clark's contemporary, Clarice Lispector, in the field of literature.

8 In the manuscript found in the Lygia Clark Archives of the Museu de Arte Moderna in Rio de Janeiro, the word "vulvanic" is crossed out and replaced by "obsessive," probably by the artist herself. With this revision, the text was included in Borja-Villel, ed., 289–90. In her manuscripts Clark often "corrected" expressions of convulsive intensity probably for fear of being looked on with disfavor by the academic superego embodied by a certain Brazilian intelligentsia, which at moments of fragility had the effect of inhibiting her. It is curious how the revised or deleted passages from her original manuscripts

are precisely those in which she affirms most resoundingly the becoming woman of writing, to which Woolf refers (see note 7). These passages are generally eliminated or replaced by a rationalistic discourse that denies and sidesteps the presence of the body motivating the writing. But the creative force in Clark was always stronger than the inhibitory power of the superego of empty obsequious rhetoric.

9 Lygia Clark, "Da supressão do objeto (anotações)," in Borja-Villel, ed., 264.

10 From this initial phase, among other works, are: *Óleos* (Oils, 1950–51), *Desenhos* (Drawings, 1950–51), *Escada* (Stairs, 1950), *Guaches* (Gouaches, 1950–51), *Sem título* (Untitled, 1952), *Composição* (Composition, 1952–53), and the portraits of her children (series in pencil and charcoal).

11 Paulo Herkenhoff, "A aventura planar de Lygia Clark—de caracóis, escadas e Caminhando," in *Lygia Clark* (São Paulo: Museu de Arte Moderna, 1999), 10–13.

12 Ibid., 9–10.

13 The first Neoconcretist exhibition was held in March 1959 at the Museu de Arte Moderna in Rio de Janeiro and was followed by an exhibition with the same name, held two years later at the Museu de Arte Moderna in São Paulo.

14 See Lygia Clark, "Letter to Mondrian," May 1959, in Borja-Villel, ed., 116.

15 About this fecund exchange, see Figueiredo.

16 The National Exhibition of Concrete Art took place in 1956, followed the same year by the Atelier Abstração.

17 See Hélio Oiticica, *Aspiro ao grande labirinto: Textos de Hélio Oiticica*, ed. Luciano Figueiredo, Lygia Pape, and Waly Salomão (Rio de Janeiro: Editora Rocco, 1986).

18 In an undated manuscript in the Lygia Clark Archive, Clark wrote: "I never had any culture nor did I read anything; any culture I got was from spending time with Mário Pedrosa and Mário Schenberg. They impregnated my ears with all that was interesting and good."

19 Regarding this issue I would like to thank Luis B. L. Orlandi for his collaboration. Regarding the notions of life and vitalism in Gilles Deleuze, in addition to the author's texts dedicated to Nietzsche, Spinoza, and Bergson, see also, among others: *Pourparlers* (Paris: Minuit, 1990), 196, and, in collaboration with Félix Guattari, *Mille Plateaux* (Paris: Minuit, 1980), 512.

20 From this second stage (1954–58) are: *Quebra da moldura* (Breaking the Frame, 1954), *Descoberta da linha orgânica* (Discovery of the Organic Line, 1954), *Interior* (a series of plans, including a scale model, 1955), *Construa você mesmo o seu espaço a viver* (Construct Yourself Your Own Living Space, 1955), *Superficie modulada* (Modulated Surface, series, 1955–58), *Plano em superficie modulada* (Plane in Modulated Surface, series, 1956–58), *Espaço modulado* (Modulated Space, series, 1958), *Unidades* (Units, series, 1958), and *Ovo linear* (Linear Egg, 1958).

21 "Lygia Clark, uma experiência radical (1954–58)," in *Lygia Clark*, 8–9.

22 About this, see Lygia Clark, "A morte do plano," in Borja-Villel, ed., 117.

23 From this third stage (1959–60) are *Ovo contra-relevo* (Counter-Relief Egg, 1959), *Contra-relevo* (Counter-Relief, series, 1959), and *Casulo* (Cocoon, series, 1959–60).

24 Undated and unpublished manuscript in the Lygia Clark Archives.

25 Ibid.

26 *Bichos* is the generic name of this family of sculptures, which received various names,

including *Bicho* (series, 1960–63), *Bicho flor* (Flower Beast, series, 1960–63), *Relógio de Sol* (Sundial, series 1960–63), *Caranguejo* (Crab, series, 1960–63), *Ponta* (End, 1960), *Disfolhado* (Stripped, 1960), *Articulado* (Jointed, 1960), *Articulado duplo* (Double-jointed, 1960), *Invertebrado* (Invertebrate, 1960), *Metamorfose I e II* (Metamorphoses I and II, 1960), *Contrário I e II* (Contrary I and II, 1960), *Vazado I e II* (Emptied I and II, 1960), *Prisma* (1960), *Vegetal* (1960), *Constelação* (Constellation, 1960), *Cidade* (City, 1960), *Bicho planta* (Plant Beast, 1960), *Sobre o redondo* (About the Round, 1960), *Máquina* (Machine, 1962), *Em si* (In Itself, 1962), *Projeto para um planeta* (Plan for a Planet, 1963), *Pancubismo* (Pancubism, 1963), *Arquiteturas fantásticas* (Fantastic Architectures, series, 1963), *Monumento em todas as situações* (Monument in All Situations, 1964), *Crescente gigante* (Gigantic Growing, 1964), and *Bicho de bolso* (Pocket Beast, 1964), as well as *Parafuso sem fim* (Endless Screw), *Pássaro no espaço* (Bird in Space), *Monumento a Descartes* (Monument to Descartes), *Linear*, *Bachiana*, and so on.

27 An excellent bibliography about this period exists, beginning with the work of the critics of the time, Ferreira Gullar and Mário Pedrosa, whose criticism remains vital. Notable among the authors who have dedicated themselves to Clark's work, posthumously, are the Brazilians Ronaldo Brito, Maria Alice Milliet, Ricardo Fabbrini, Paulo Herkenhoff, as well as Guy Brett, Yve-Alain Bois, and Manuel Borja-Villel.

28 In creating the *Bichos*, Clark first explored them on paper.

29 Lygia Clark, undated manuscript, probably from 1963–64, in the Lygia Clark Archives.

30 From this stage are: *O dentro e o fora* (1963), *O antes é o depois* (The Before Is the After, 1963), *Trepante* (1963–65), *Trepante (Obra mole)* (1964), *Abrigo poético* (Poetic Shelter, 1964), *Estruturas de caixas de fósforos* (Matchbox Structures, 1964), and *A casa do poeta* (The Poet's House, 1964).

31 About this stage, Clark wrote: "From 1959 to 1964, including the *Trepantes* in stainless steel and the *Trepantes* in rubber (Soft Work), I extended their structure to the point of exhaustion. I experienced in that period the end of the work of art, of the base on which it expressed itself, the death of metaphysics and of transcendence, discovering the here and now in immanence"; undated manuscript in the Lygia Clark Archives.

32 The *Livro-obra* was written in 1964 and published in 1983 by Luciano Figueiredo and Ana Maria Araújo, in a limited edition of twenty-four.

33 From this stage are: *Pedra e ar* (1966); *Natureza (Estrutura cega)* (Nature [Blind Structure], 1966–67); *Livro sensorial* (Sensory Book, 1966); Ping-pong (1966); *Desenhe com o dedo* (Draw with Your Finger, 1966); *Água e conchas* (Water and Shells, 1966); *Respire comigo* (Breathe with Me, 1966); *Diálogo de mãos* (Dialogue of Hands, 1966); *Diálogo de pés* (*Estrutura viva*) (Dialogue of Feet [Living Structure], 1966); and *Proposições existenciais: Campo de Minas, Cintos-diálogos* (Existential Propositions: Campo de Minas, Dialogue Belts) and the films *Convite à viagem* (Invitation to the Journey), *Filme sensorial* (Sensorial Film), *Western*, and *O homem no centro dos acontecimentos* (Man at the Center of Events, 1967–68).

34 See Lygia Clark, "L'art c'est le corps," *Preuves*, no. 13 (Paris, 1973), in Borja-Villel, ed., 232.

35 From this stage are: *Série roupa-corpo-roupa* (Cloth-Body-Cloth Series, 1967), among which are *O eu e o tu* (The I and the You), *Cesariana* (Caesarian), *Máscara abismo* (Mask Abyss, 1968), *Máscara sensorial* (Sensorial Mask, 1968), *Óculos* (Eyeglasses, 1968), *Diálogo: Óculos* (Dialogue: Eyeglasses, 1968), *A casa é o corpo. Penetração, ovulação, germinação, expulsão* (The House Is the Body. Penetration, Ovulation, Germination, Expulsion, 1968), *Luvas sensoriais* (Sensorial Gloves, 1968), *Casal* (Couple, 1969), and *Camisa-de-força* (Straitjacket, 1969).

36 About a work from this stage Clark wrote: "When he [the man] puts on his head a sensory helmet he isolates himself from the world, after having already situated himself in an entire earlier process in the development of art; in that turning inward he loses contact with reality and finds within himself the whole spectrum of fantastic experiences. It is a way of bringing to him the breath of experience. . . . The man-helmet has the tendency to fall into parts at the moment of the experience. Longing for the body, to behead it and live it in parts in order to later reintegrate it as a living and total organism"; undated manuscript, probably from 1967, in Borja-Villel, ed., 219–20.

37 "L'art c'est le corps" (see note 42), in ibid., 232.

38 From this stage are: *Arquiteturas biológicas* (Biological Architectures, 1968–70), among them: *Ovo mortalha* (Egg Shroud, 1968), *Nascimento I e II* (Birth, 1969), *Estruturas vivas* (Living Structures, 1969); among them the *Diálogos* (Dialogues, 1969).

39 Lygia Clark, "A casa é o corpo: Penetração, ovulação, germinação, expulsão, 1968," in ibid., 232–33. Even in these conditions there are those who insist on returning these objects to the status of work of art, independent of the experience in which they take on their meaning. For example, when *Arquiteturas biológicas* is exhibited without the possibility of experiment, what is shown is the piece of plastic with its jute bags tossed on a table, devoid of life, like the mortal remains of some unrecognizable body.

40 Lygia Clark, letter to Mário Pedrosa dated 22 May 1969, in Borja-Villel, ed., 250.

41 Lygia Clark, letter dated 20 May 1970, in Figueiredo, 154.

42 "L'art c'est le corps," 232.

43 Undated and unpublished manuscript in the Lygia Clark Archives.

44 "A casa é o corpo," 232–33.

45 About this, Clark wrote: "In my so-called 'cheap' works, where each one could make his own object from materials given to him or her, could be found in embryonic form the same characteristic of my new works. But each experience was individual and ran the risk of closing itself, whereas it is now simultaneously individual and collective, since it is not executed without the others' experience, in the heart of the same polynuclear structure" ("1969: O corpo é a casa," in *Lygia Clark*, 37).

46 Ibid., 36.

47 Ibid.

48 From this stage (1972–75) are: *Baba antropofágica* (Anthropophagic Slobber, 1973), *Canibalismo* (Cannibalism, (1973), *Túnel* (Tunnel, 1973), *Viagem* (Journey, 1973), *Rede de elásticos* (Network of Rubber Bands, 1974), *Relaxação* (Relaxation, 1974–75), and *Cabeça coletiva* (Collective Head, 1975).

49 For a detailed analysis of *Baba antropofágica*, see Suely Rolnik, "For a State of Art: The Actuality of Lygia Clark," in *Núcleo Histórico: Antropofagia e histórias de canibalismo*, catalogue of the 24th Bienal de São Paulo (São Paulo: Fundação Bienal de São Paulo, 1998), 462–67.

50 *Fantasma*, which means "ghost," is the Portuguese translation for the Freudian concept of *Phantasie*: the unconscious fantasy that substitutes a repressed memory and becomes a veritable ghost. This knowledge can help us apprehend the meaning of Clark's concept of "Fantasmática do corpo" as the accumulation of fantasies/ghosts mobilized by the bodily experience.

51 Lygia Clark, undated manuscript in Borja-Villel, ed., 301.

52 Clark started *Estruturação do self*, done with the *Objetos relacionais*, beginning in 1976. In 1981, she reduced the number of "clients" and began to transmit the experience so that others could carry it on. In 1984 she partially abandoned the

experiment, stopping totally in February of 1988. In April of that year she died suddenly from a myocardial infarction at the age of sixty-seven.

53 "Objetos relacionais," text written in collaboration with Suely Rolnik, in *Lygia Clark*, 49.

54 The *Objetos relacionais* were many and varied over time. The artist herself described them as follows: "light, light-heavy, and heavy cushions . . . I also work with a large and very thick mattress filled with foam rubber into which the body sinks as if in a mold. I also made another foam-rubber mattress covered with a voile to revitalize the client's body at the end of the session. Besides these objects I use many others: a plastic bag filled with air, a plastic bag filled with water; 'breathe with me'; onion bags with stones inside them; a breathing tube; a flashlight to shine in the eyes and mouth when their eyes are blindfolded; a piece of plastic filled with seeds; loofah; oakum; large seashells to place over the ears; stones at the bottom of a small, empty bag tied with a rubber band at the end, which I manipulate above the patient's body; marbles; tails of rabbits; nylon stockings with shells at one end and stones at the other; nylon stockings with ping-pong balls at one end and tennis balls at the other"; "A propósito do instante," in "Memórias do corpo: O dentro e o fora," unpublished and undated manuscript in the Lygia Clark Archives.

55 Lygia Clark, "Do ritual," manuscript, 1960, in Borja-Villel, ed., 122.

56 Suely Rolnik, "Mémoire du corps," thesis defended in the U.E.R. de Sciences Humaines Cliniques, Université de Paris VII, 1978.

57 The resumption took place in 1994, at the time of the retrospective of the artist at the 22nd São Paulo Bienal. It stemmed from an invitation from the curator, Nelson Aguilar, to consider her oeuvre starting from her final propositions.

58 To cite only one example of text in which Clark deals with this theme: "Art or anti-art? The elaboration of the work of art continues to be very important to my way of thinking. Not only for the artist but also for the spectator. In my proposition is the thought (the element given by me) and the expression (the moment in which the spectator expresses this given thought). There continues, then, to be that which was always important in an artistic expression, except that now those elements are apparently separated because the work of art has lost its uniqueness. . . . To me, the poetical in the communication of the work of art ceased to be achieved through transcendence and comes to be achieved in immanence, which results from the act itself"; undated manuscript, probably 1969, for in the same text Clark refers to the plastic pieces in the *Arquiteturas biológicas*.

59 Lygia Clark, undated manuscript, in Borja-Villel, ed., 156–57.

60 "Lygia Clark: O homem é o centro," interview with Vera Pedrosa, in *Correio da Manhã* (Rio de Janeiro), 30 April 1968, Segundo Caderno, in Borja-Villel, ed., 227–28.

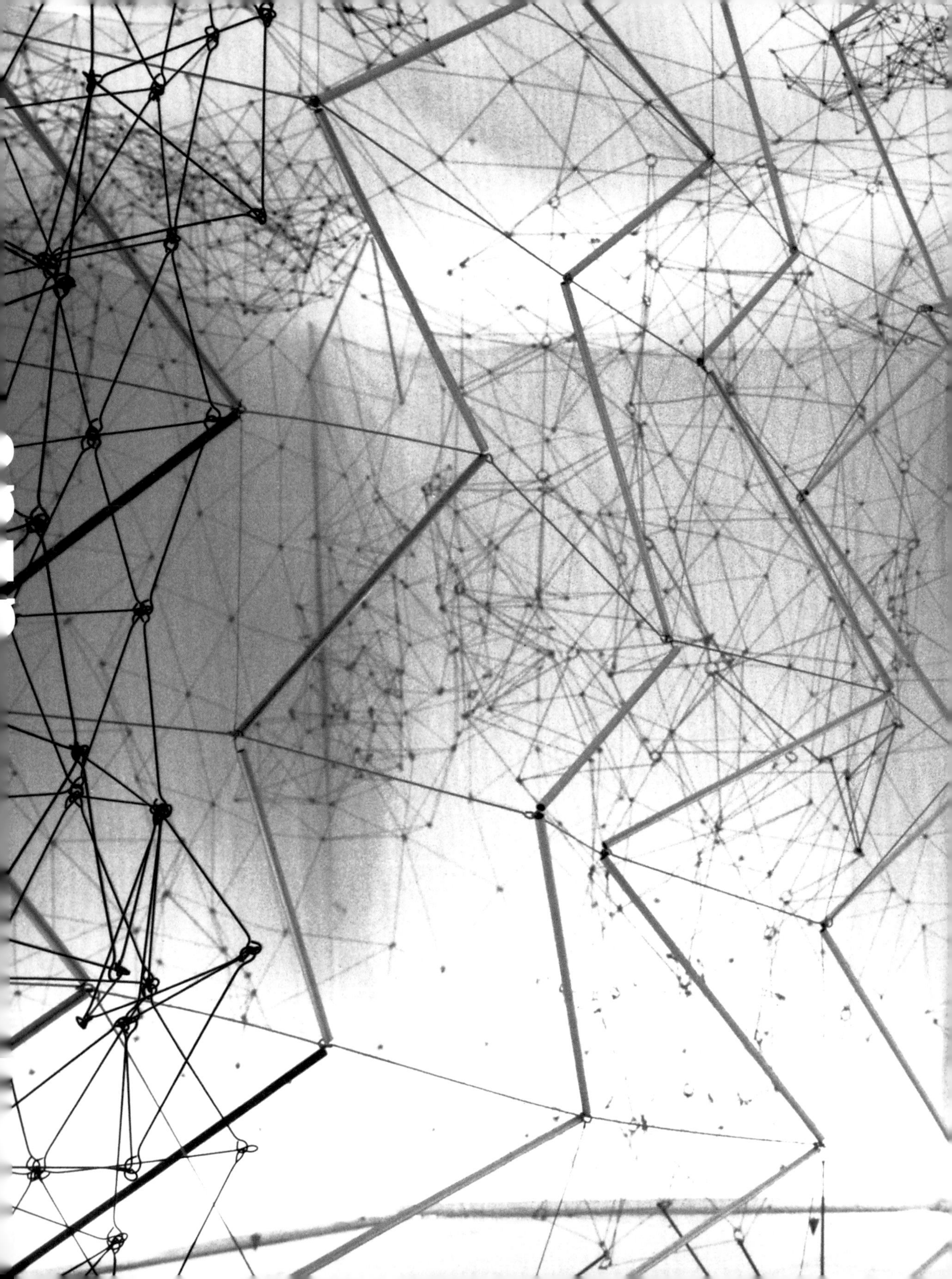

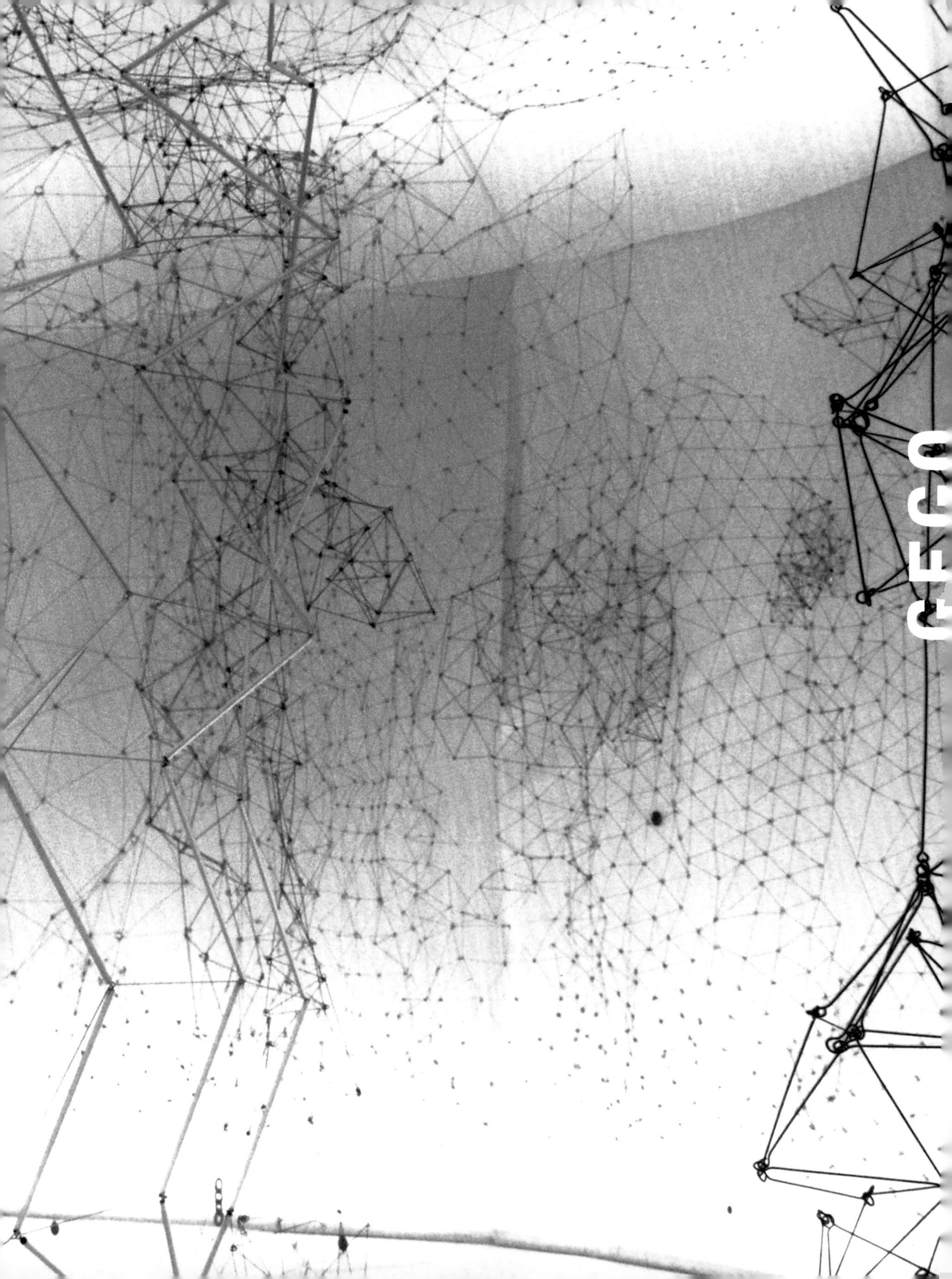
GEGO

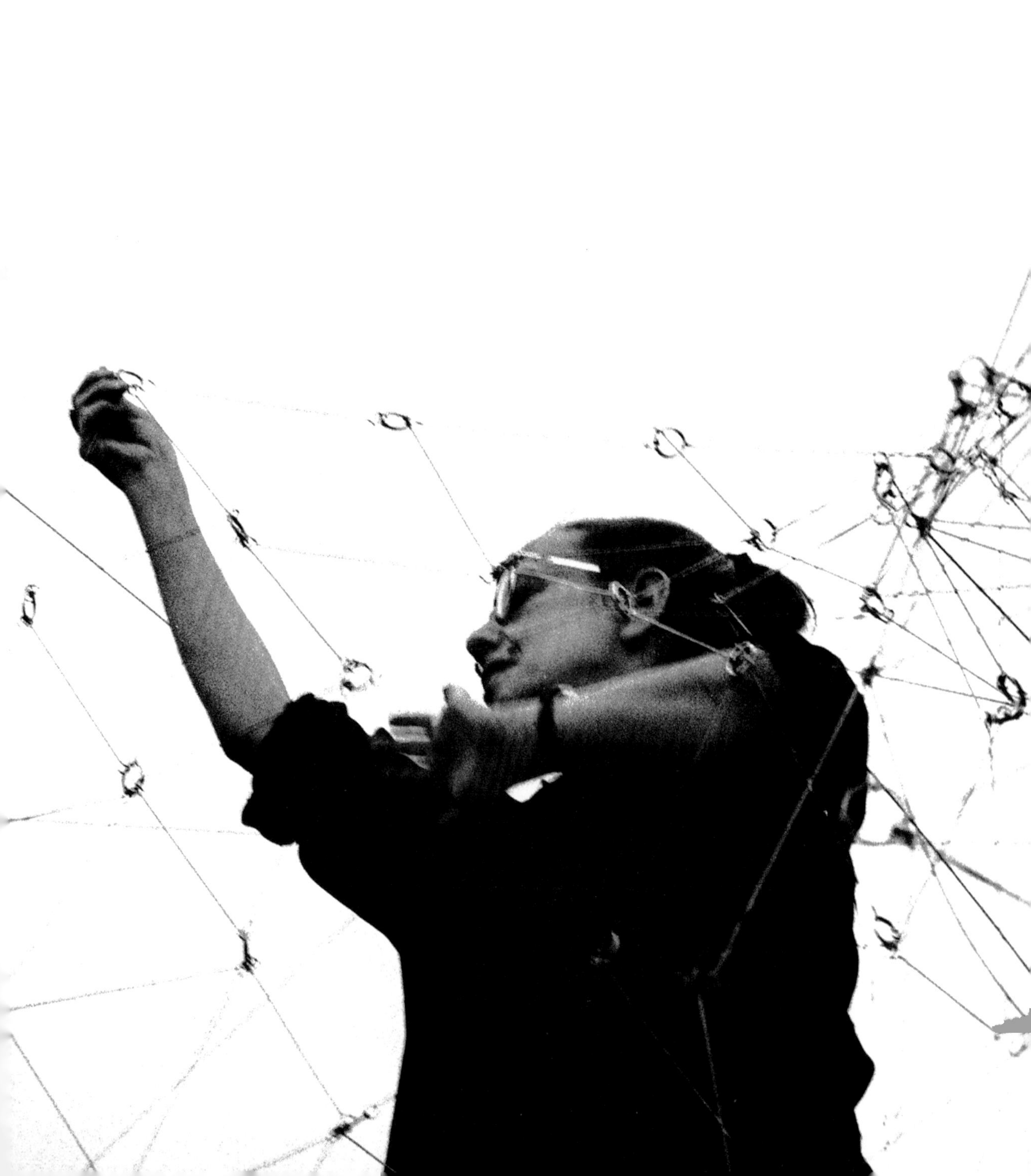

My thoughts are all sensations.

—FERNANDO PESSOA[1]

GEGO:

Outside In, Inside Out

Rina Carvajal

PRECEDING PAGES: ***Reticulárea***, Americas Society, New York 1969

Gego working on ***Reticulárea*** 1968

Chorros (Detail) 1970

With the creation of her *Reticuláreas* in the late 1960s, Gego opened new possibilities for reinventing a constructivist language, incorporating into the logical space of geometry the organic quality of life and a vital experience of the subject.[2] Her mature experiments gradually destabilized the scientific objectivity of geometric abstraction, marking the passage toward an existential subjectivity. They express the "concrete" through a state of constant transience, disintegration, and reconfiguration, articulating an ever more flexible and open identity for form. In Gego's work, form creates and recreates itself at its very limits through a permanent process of flux and dislocation, constituting itself in the pulse of two distinct notions of order—one logical and rational, the other vulnerable and indeterminate—coexisting and interpenetrating in continuous movement.

Born Gertrude Goldschmidt into a liberal Jewish family in Hamburg in 1912, Gego fled Germany at the outset of World War II. She left shortly after completing her studies in architecture and engineering at the Technische Hochschule, now the Universität Stuttgart (University of Stuttgart), a conservative institution based on historicist principles which taught the methods of traditional German craftsmanship and which was opposed to functionalism.[3] She immigrated to Venezuela in 1939, bringing with her the memories of dislocation and instability inherent in the experience of war, a will to survive, and an unyielding affirmation of life that years later would permeate the very methods of her art. Even though Gego always avoided discussing her personal life, she nevertheless inscribed a dimension of the self into her work by way of its processes and apparently formal terms. Her art gradually established the notion of an organic space, incomplete and endlessly in motion, potentializing itself at the very surface of form. This space operated like a dynamic field, an intensified flux of forces, energies, and perceptive possibilities marking the fragility and dislocation of a constructive order and incorporating, in a process of integration with the world, everything that circulates around it. In form's trajectory are registered the outlines of experience, the body, and thought.

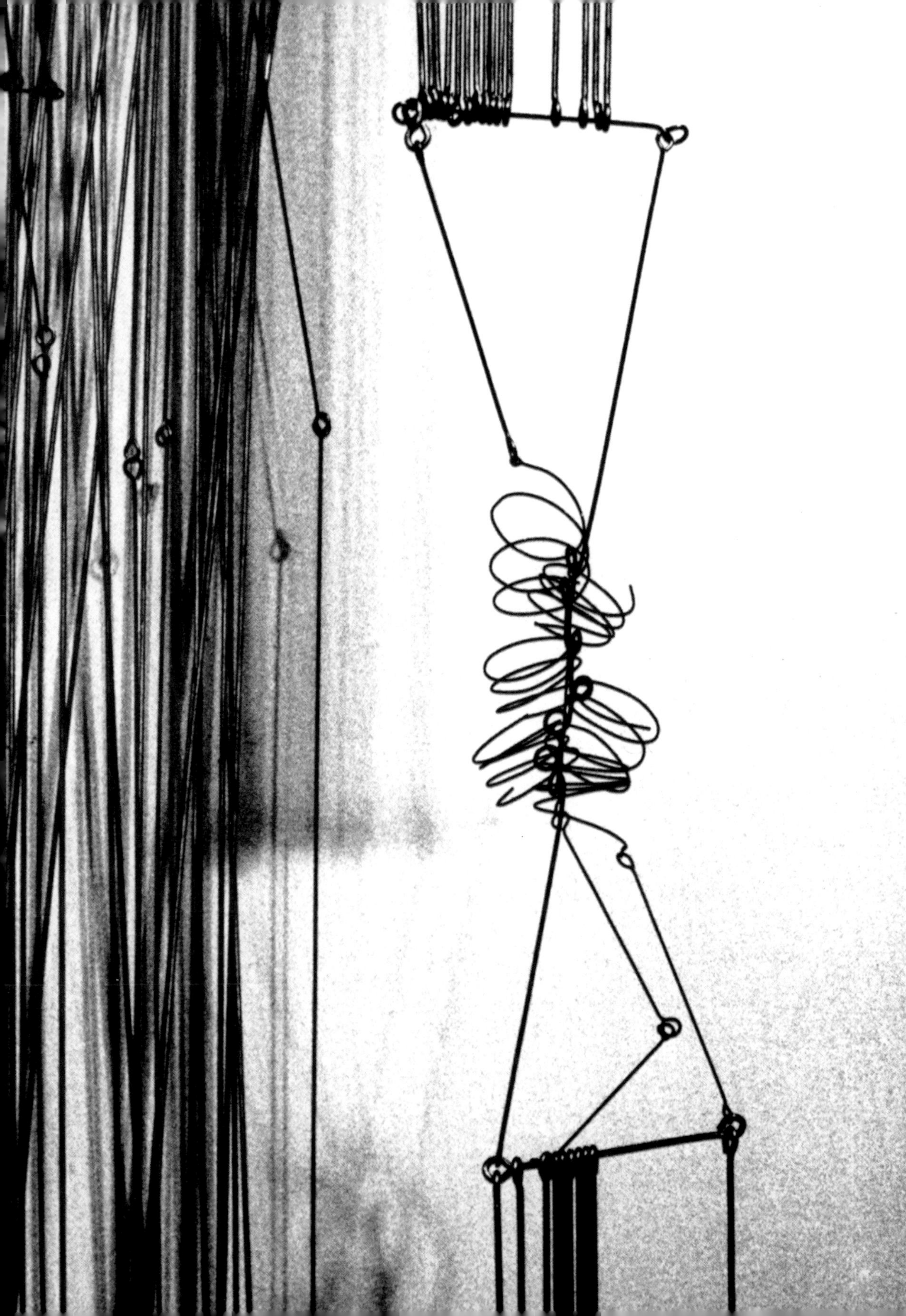

Gego began her artistic activity in Caracas in the mid-1950s, during a period of great transformation and artistic fervor in Venezuela. The country was at the peak of an oil boom, anxiously pursuing modernity and urbanizing rapidly in the midst of great social contradictions. Constructivist tendencies (geometric abstraction and kinetic art)—which proposed to integrate the arts with architecture and aspired to find a rational model for exploring form and creating a new culture, free of the weight of tradition—moved into the vanguard of the Venezuelan art world. This cultural project, animated by a utopian vision for the construction of a technological and industrialized society, translated universalist principles, without critical debate, to the local situation in Venezuela, distancing the project from the social reality of the

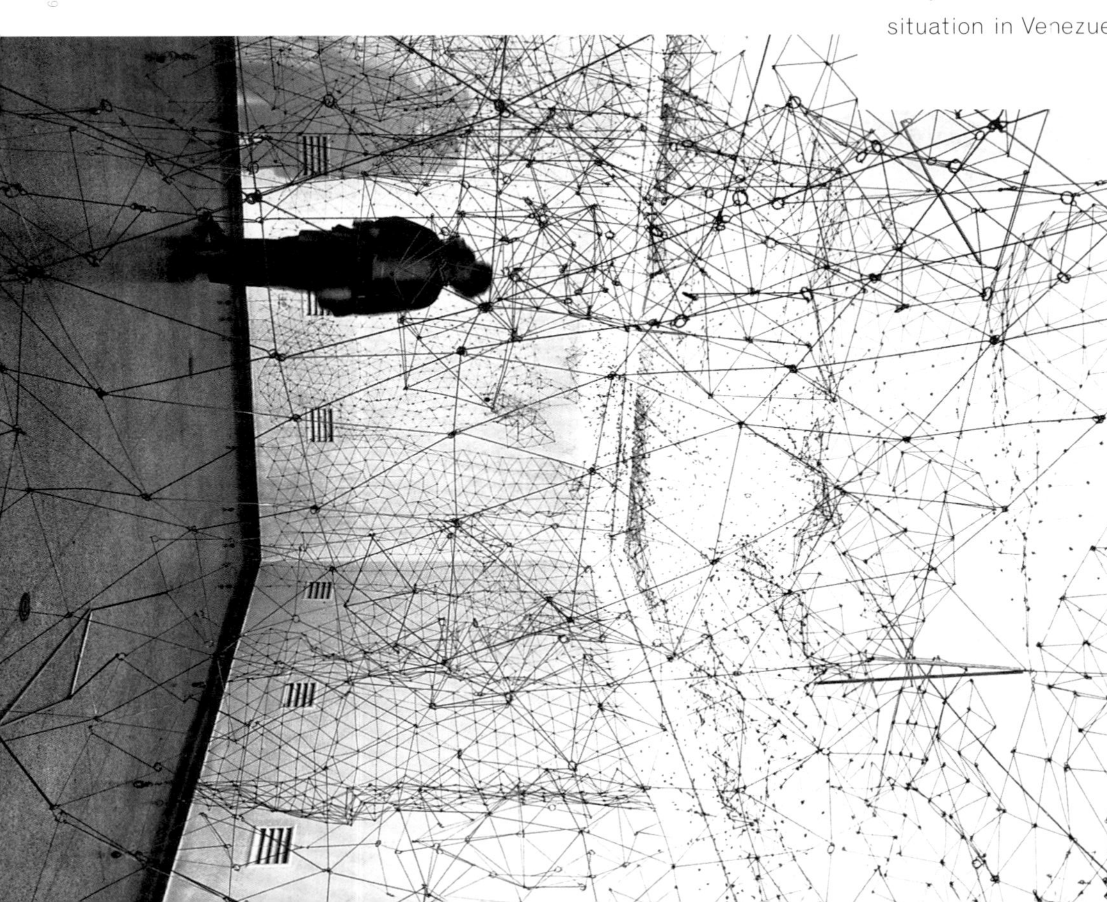

Reticulárea, Museo de Bellas Artes, Caracas 1969

country. It ultimately ended up serving the *desarrollista* (developmentalist) interests of the economic elite and the government. The kinetic artists in particular came to occupy a hegemonic role in Venezuelan cultural life, eventually becoming the purveyors of an official art and an emblem of the country's apparently progressive vision. Gego, by contrast, worked in a modest and solitary way, seeking to establish a dialogue with the local cultural environment and to incorporate into the methods and materials of her work the instability and contradictions marking the process of the country's modernization.

The Venezuelan abstract-geometric movement—resuming a debate begun in the 1940s between a nationalist, conservative, local tradition and a new generation seeking to participate in the language of international modernism—found an especially propitious moment in the 1950s. Many members of this new generation had been expelled from the Escuela de Artes Plásticas (School of Visual Arts) in Caracas in 1945 for protesting against its retrograde methods of teaching. Several left to study in Paris, often on government fellowships (a number also went to Mexico).[4] After absorbing the legacy of European constructivism in Paris, these young artists returned to Venezuela, optimistic and combative, ready to participate actively in the process of modernization. In 1952 they were invited to collaborate on a project to integrate the arts at the new Universidad Central (Central University) in Caracas designed by the architect Carlos Raúl Villanueva, a project that became a great catalyst for the new constructivist tendencies in Venezuela. Villanueva placed their work among the numerous buildings and open spaces of the campus in direct dialogue with pieces created by important international artists working in a constructivist vein (among them, Antoine Pevsner, Jean Arp, Henri Laurens, Fernand Léger, Sophie Tauber-Arp, Alexander Calder, and Victor Vasarely).

Over the next two decades, urban and public art projects, in which the abstract-geometric and especially the kinetic artists actively participated, were created in Venezuela on a monumental scale. Concerned with producing works of great refinement—on both material and optical-perceptual levels—which would reflect a new image of scientific and technological progress and allow them to deprovincialize the culture and take part in the artistic currents of the industrialized world, the kinetic artists neglected to integrate the individual and the social fabric of the country into their production.[5] Their epic works, resonating with the anonymous beauty of industrial materials, used serial repetition and the layering of elements to produce vibrations and explore the possibilities of movement as an enveloping optical whole affecting perception, which led viewers to experience the gradual disappearance of their own bodies. While some of the kinetic artists carried out important and original research, their urban projects rarely established an organic relationship or dialogue with public space.

Even though Gego arrived in Venezuela with the rigor of a conservative and traditionalist European education, quite remote from any constructivist substratum, she came nonetheless with a predisposition toward the speculative and the experimental, which helped her shape, after years of work in several disciplines, her own artistic practice.[6] That practice would reflect her response to the tensions and vitality she found in Venezuela and to the unfoldings of a local constructivist visual culture that was already hybridized and adapted to the particular circumstances of the country (at a moment of euphoria and at the height of its *desarrollista* project), rather than any influence of European constructivist ideas on her early formation. In the singularity of its configurations, Gego's work would manage to account for the enormous complexity and the rich process of hybridization involving the dynamic fusion of the local and the international at particular moments in the artistic production of Latin America, moments when the constructivist idioms of the prewar European avant-garde were absorbed and transformed in completely idiosyncratic and innovative terms to be reinserted into new expressive and subjectifying contexts.

Gego always resisted categorization, working independently and introspectively, deliberately remaining on the margin of the kinetic and abstract-geometric movements. She found her own path to reinvent a constructivist language, gradually deemphasizing the rational, objective aspects of her work, intuitively shifting them toward more expressive and experimental contexts. Although she conducted her research alone, in her own way Gego participated in the artistic system of the moment. She benefited from the favorable conditions Venezuela offered artists, particularly its grand urban and architectural projects, and she relied on the support of important public and private commissions. Her work, which grew out of the skepticism and disenchantment of her wartime experiences, significantly dissented from the optimistic and apologetic vision of the kinetic artists who were trying to emulate European rationalist and technological models.

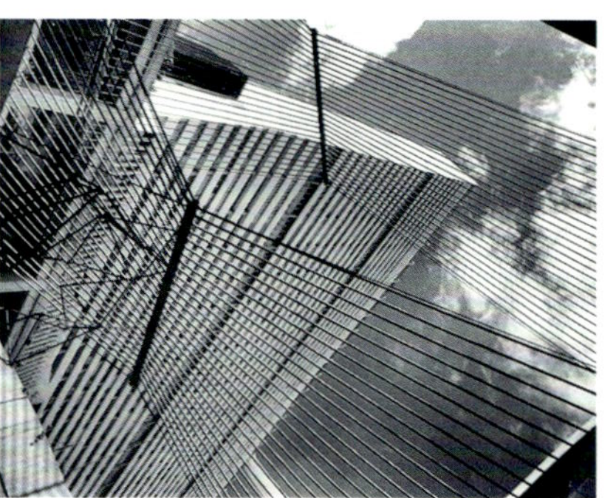

Cuerdas, Parque Central, Caracas 1972

Although Gego was not looking to assimilate the scientific and technological lessons of European modernism, science and technology nonetheless had a mediating role in her work, helping her to manage in a rigorous and efficient way techniques, measures, and materials that would allow her to connect abstract and rational planes with others of a more perceptual and organic character. Her projects integrating architecture—quite different in nature from the monumentality and opulence of the kinetic public works—use humble materials and establish increasingly freer and organic ties with space. Light, flexible, and full of transparencies, these sculptures incorporate the vital flux of the city and combine great delicacy with powerful structural force. They also express an ambiguous notion of equilibrium, simultaneously interweaving instances of tension and movement, energy and materiality. In *Cuerdas* (Strings, 1972), an environmental aerial sculpture, Gego used intersecting planes of faint lines to weave an immense weft between an open space and the dense structure of a building. Imperceptibly diluting the severity of the structure, this weft expands and contracts with great dynamism, multiplying itself in an uninterrupted rhythm of spatial forces, articulations, and tensions.

Gego began sculpting, engraving, and drawing in the mid-1950s, producing virtual planes and volumes with parallel lines. This rational structure would always serve as the path toward her most intuitive and subjective sources (a structure which, as she matured, became increasingly complex, taking shape in a state of constant transition, existing—through its transparency—at the edge of coming together or falling apart). All of her work grew out of experimentation with different structural systems of vertical and parallel lines and the figures derived from them (triangles, squares, polygons, polyhedrons), which are combined and transformed through different types of links. These systems in turn generate specific forms of work: *Líneas* (Lines), *Cuerdas* (Strings), *Chorros* (Streams), *Reticuláreas*, *Troncos* (Trunks), *Esferas* (Spheres), *Mallas* (Meshes), or *Dibujos sin papel* (Drawings without Paper).[7] Line and structure are the unifying and connective elements (the lexicon) of her anguage and the instruments for her attempts at the articulation and resolution of spatial problems, whether in her graphic output or her sculpture, genres that continually converge in her work. Gego ended up creating new forms of coexistence for her media (sculpture, drawing, and architecture), in which each is experienced as if in constant transmutation.

The rigorous technical and scientific precision Gego acquired in her early training as an architect and engineer and the skilled craftsmanship she developed over the course of her career allowed her to explore deeply the possibilities for structural systems and materials, spatial and modular organization, and the processes of manual labor. She managed to create innovative systems for manipulating aluminum, iron, and stainless steel which allowed her to work independently of welders. Later in her career, she incorporated discarded materials and leftovers from her larger sculptures, humanizing the technical elements of her work and subtly connecting gesture to geometry, arriving eventually at a working model much closer to weaving than to engineering.

In her mature work of the late 1960s Gego favored notions of process, flux, and temporality, giving greater value to the importance of expressiveness and the subjective. She created grand architectural pieces, as well as individual and environmental sculptures of great complexity, in which the intersection of planes suggests a dynamic reorganization of the space, a rupture of balance, and a constant mobility expressed through the line and its folds. She began to experiment with the grid and repetitive modules, destabilizing the objectivity of these forms to create a fluid and organic space that would allow her to restore a relationship to the body and introduce a presence—of herself and others—into the work. From the mid-1970s until a few years before her death in 1994, Gego simplified her techniques and formats, incorporating and recycling—with a playful, subtle irony—residual and humble materials that emphasized the ambiguous, the unstable, and the impermanent. The output from these years, intimate and personal, does not pursue the goal of earlier pieces to resolve complex structural problems; rather, it values the fragile and the precarious, emphasizing the gesture and the importance of the act over the stable and imperishable.

By the late 1960s Gego's sculptures had left behind any formal or constructive rigidity. The pieces reflected the increasingly malleable nature of her materials and the freedom that working by hand gave her. Her work came to shape spaces incorporating asymmetry, irregularity, and imbalance, as well as the rationality of calculations and measurements. These structures, which grew out of the use and bearing of the line and its modulations, are at once strong and delicate, logical and irrational, expressing, by way of the intense repetition and multiplication of planes and forms, a resistance to totalization and an open relation to the space. It was during this period, through the rituals of her working methods, that Gego gradually introduced—though not deliberately—an ontological dimension into her art: out of the intertwining of lines, the rhythms and repetitions used to shape grids and modules, the constant linking of forms, the folding and unfolding of the work beneath the repeated superimpositions of layers and planes, the very existence of the space, as well as the body in the space, emerges from her forms. Resistant and malleable, porous yet consistent, these sculptures seem to take part in a process of the permanent reelaboration of meaning.

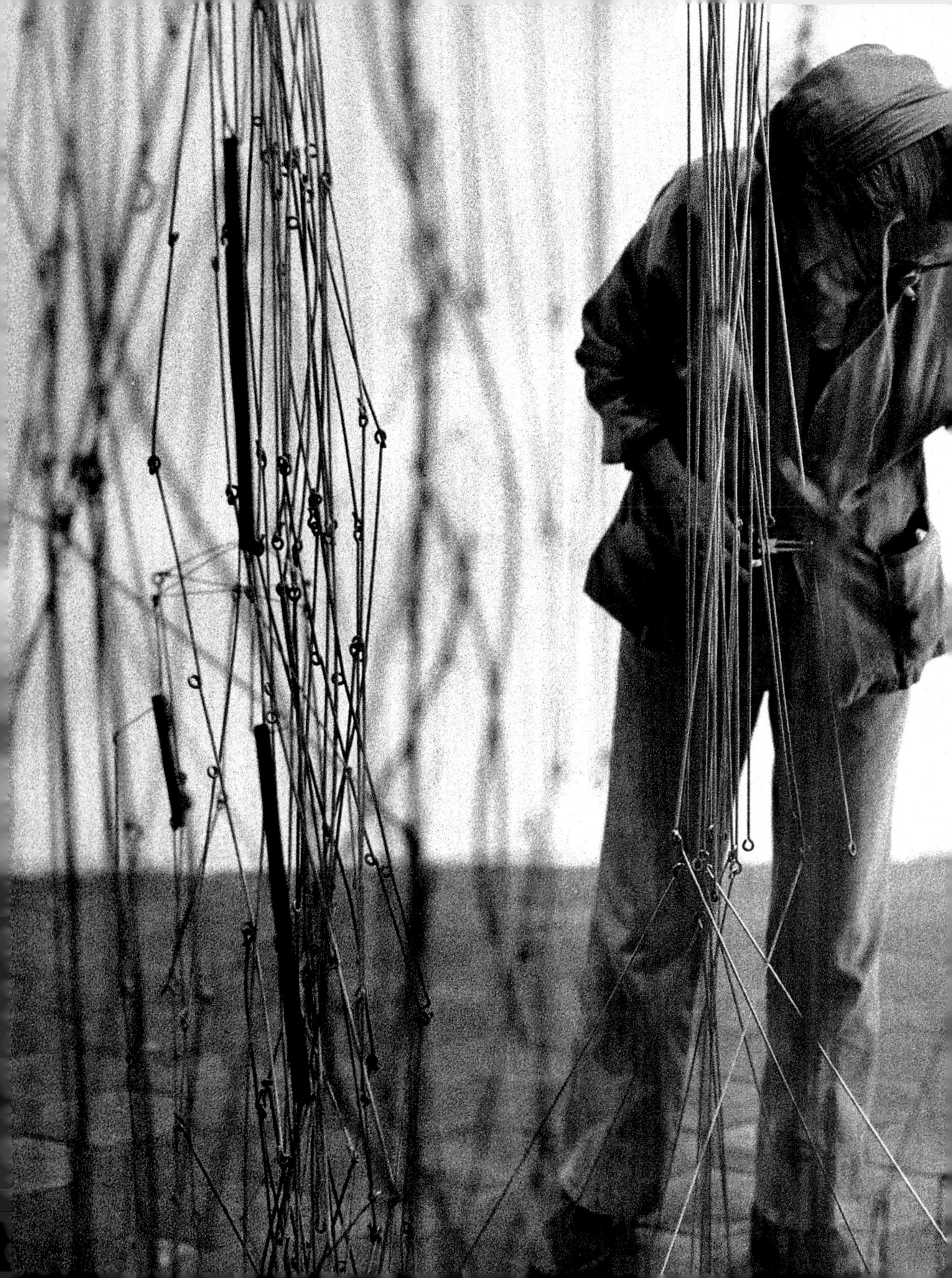

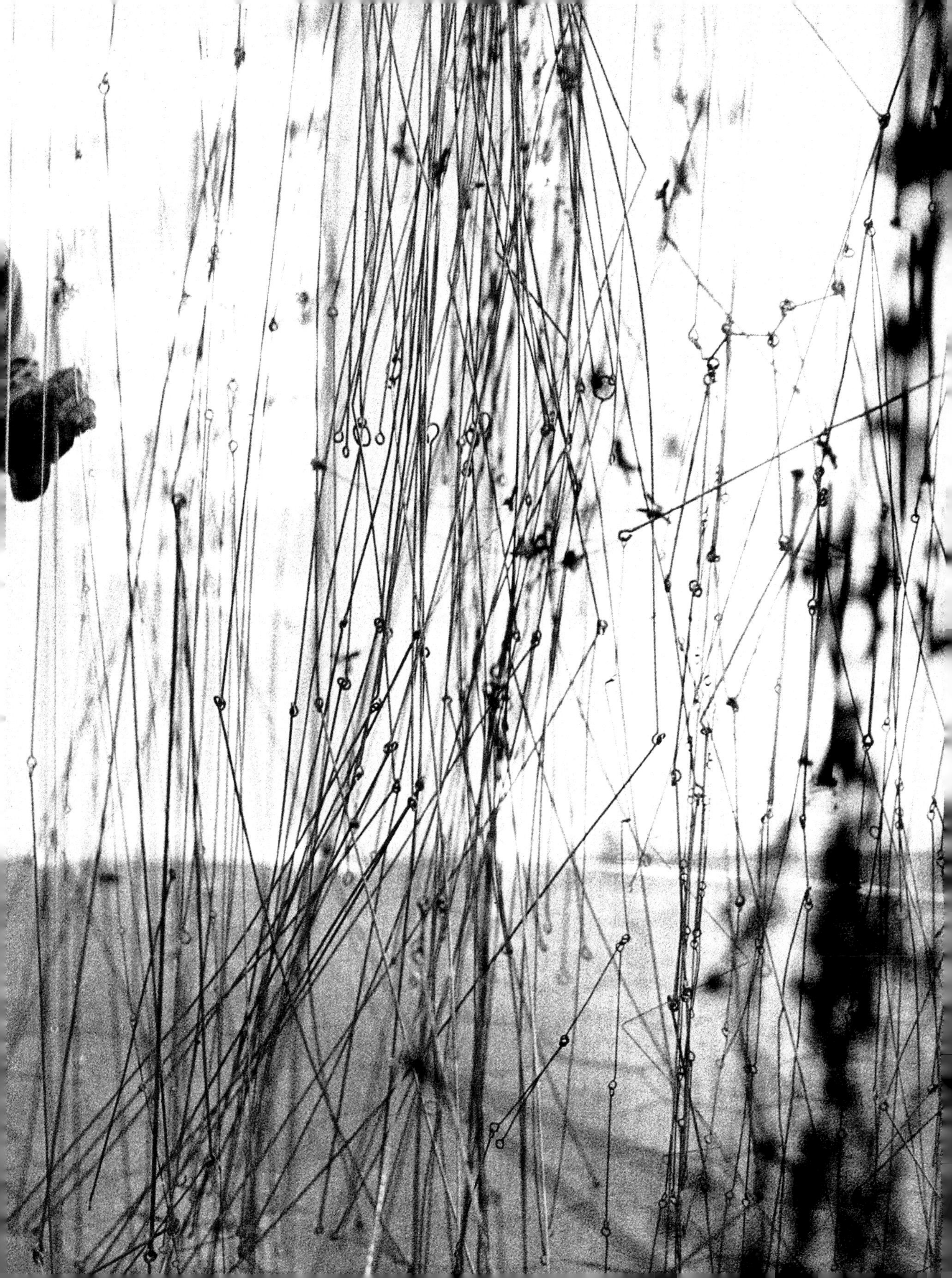

The line is also Gego's expressive scale for shaping space and for harnessing forces and energies in form. This scale is a measure of the imperceptible and the minimal, as much in the infinite unwinding of the ever more intricate webs as in the residual unwinding of her drawings without paper. Exceeding any technical and structural precision in the work, the line, with its folds and thicknesses, like a weave of converging trajectories, continually transforms itself, assuming subtle expressive registers that reveal a feeling for space and a dimension of the self in the work. With the line, its constant interweavings, tensions, and ruptures of balance, Gego not only draws but gives a body, a movement, and an architectural form to space.

In work from her mature period—the *Chorros, Reticuláreas, Mallas*, and *Dibujos sin papel*—Gego introduced a new fluidity into her methods and the dynamic coexistence of heterogeneous orders which from then on restructure and intensify her perceptive and expressive range. Line breathes, becoming intentionally unstable in its connections and orientations, indicating unforeseeable events that suddenly break with the linear, provoking discontinuities and revealing forces that generate a life energy in the form. The *Chorros* (1970), made up of disordered accumulations of hanging vertical lines of aluminum of different thicknesses arranged in a parallel fashion, present elements that—thanks to an ingenious system of ends folded into hoops that allow for variable links and directions—introduce unexpected conjunctions, folds, and curves that extend irregularly in several directions, falling lightly, apparently weightlessly, on the floor. In the activity and energy that these configurations express through the mobility and elusive balance emerging at the surface of her forms and in the displacements of her sight lines, Gego incorporated the idea of the work as a living field in constant transit between planes of subjectivity and flux.

In 1969 Gego created her first series of *Reticuláreas*, sculptures reflecting a new structural system based on repetitive modules and the triangle. The series included an immense weblike environmental sculpture constructed from

PRECEDING PAGES: Gego with ***Chorros***, Museo de Barquisimeto 1971 lines of anodized aluminum and stainless steel of different thicknesses connected by extremely subtle joints. In a dynamic interweaving of tensions, rhythms, and overlapping planes, the lines create discrete geometric modules of various sizes which together, in their layering, give form to a complex structure that—though apparently weightless and without any means of support—comes to occupy an entire room. This flexible and variable web, like a matrix or a living architecture, seems to expand infinitely until it can no longer be apprehended: it rejects any notion of totality in order to create an increasingly open relation with the space.

In its multiplication of virtual spaces and unstable constellations of simultaneously occurring triangles and planes, always showing different sides and angles depending on the perspective from which it is seen, the *Reticulárea* encourages a direct encounter with its space and introduces the idea of the

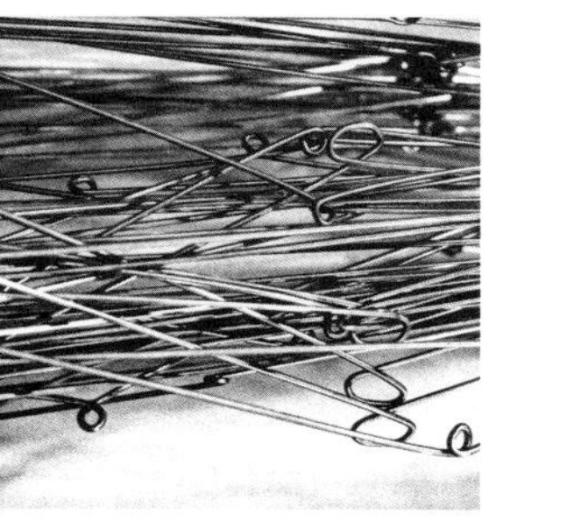

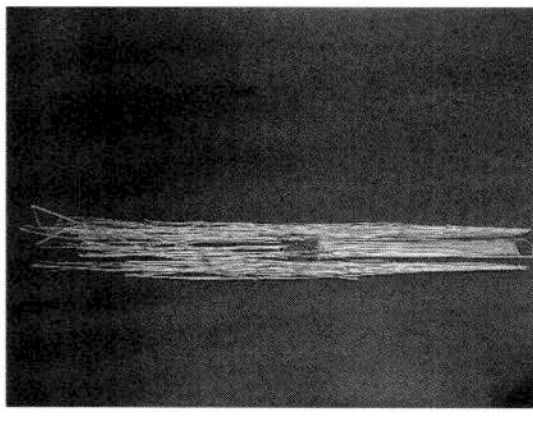

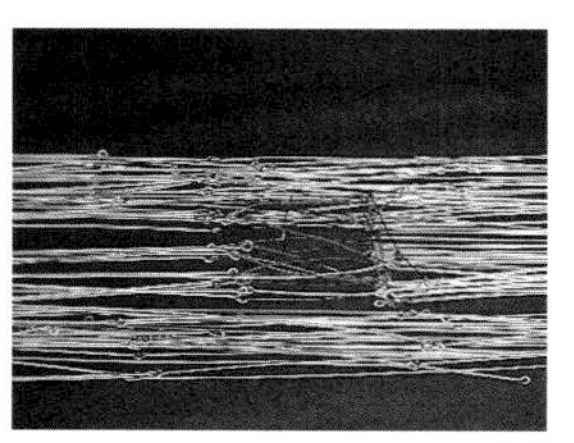

Chorros (Detail) 1970

Chorro: Group of Three ca. 1970–71

Chorro: Group of Three (Detail) ca. 1970–71

FOLLOWING PAGES: ***Reticulárea***, Museo de Bellas Artes, Caracas 1969

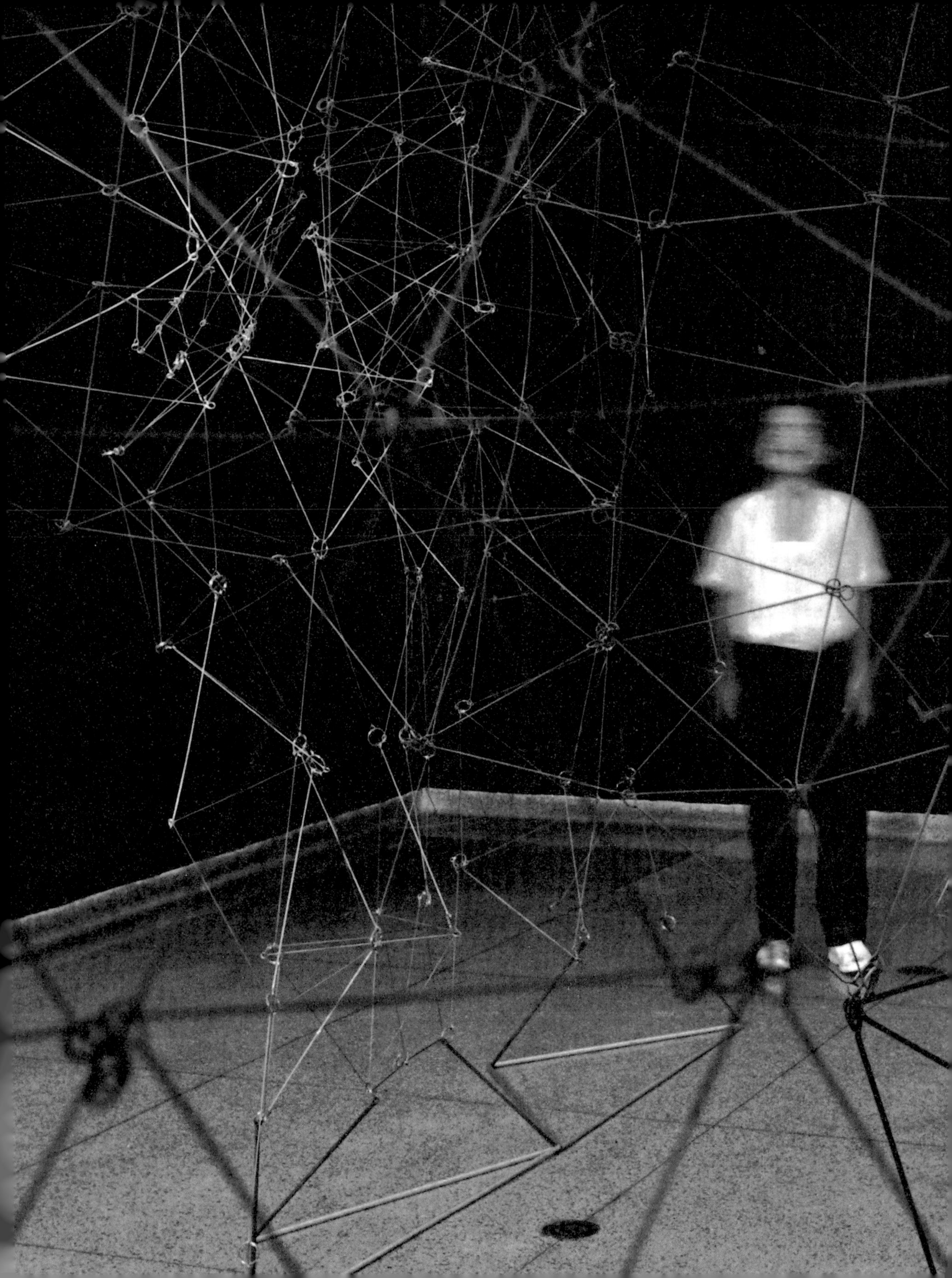

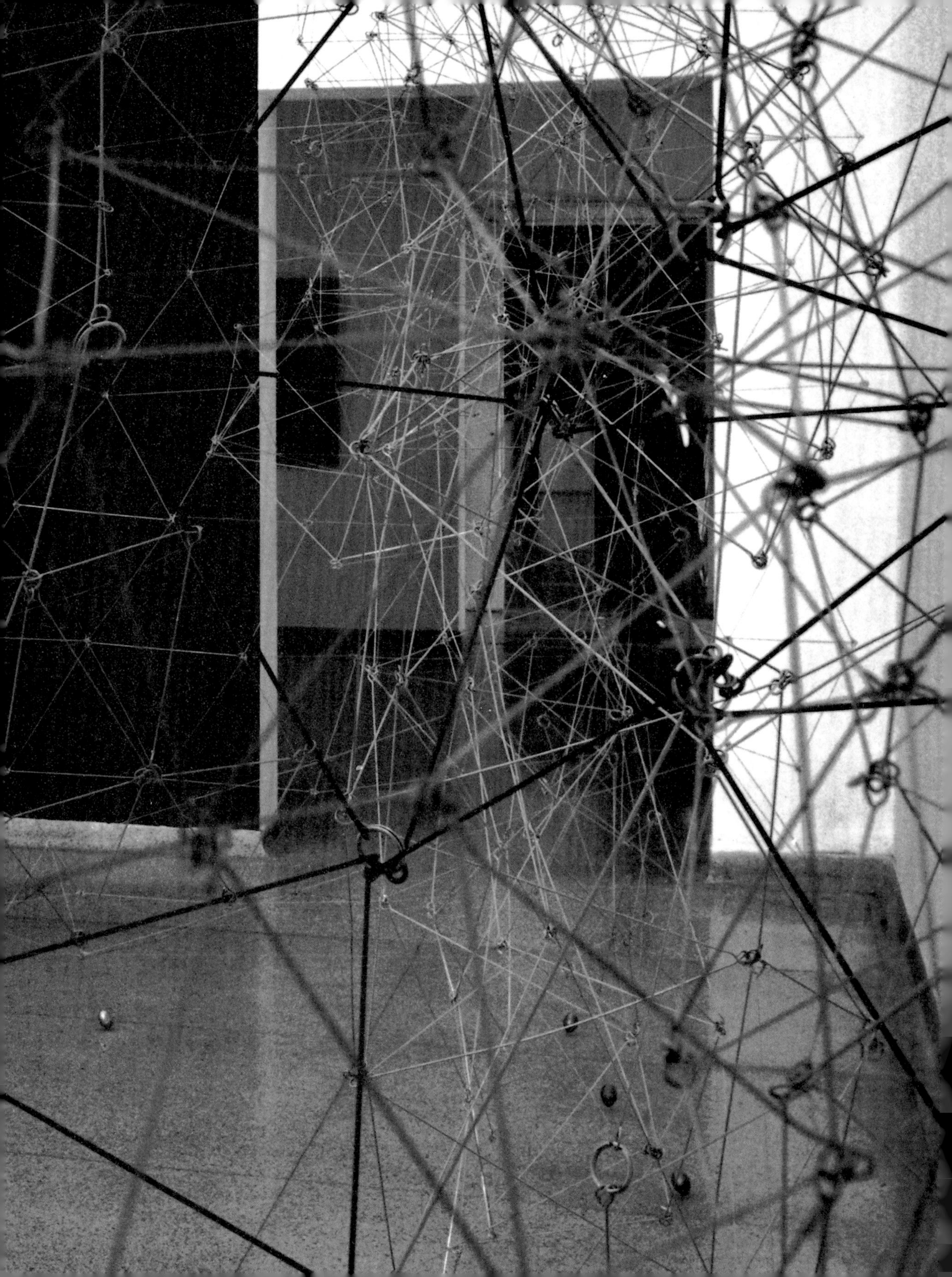

work as an open-ended field of perception, constantly creating and re-creating itself out of the participant's experience. It presents itself as a field that must be penetrated and explored by the participant and which functions as a vehicle for his or her own subjectivation. Subject to the perceptive contingencies that modify its configurations, the sculpture establishes itself in a territory of paradoxes, in the convergence of extremely varied spaces that rapidly contaminate each other. Light and yet charged with a great force, the *Reticulárea* incorporates the void out of which emerges the energy that constitutes immaterial space as expressive matter.[8] Thus Gego incites a relationship with the body and the idea of an interiority projected outward.

Moreover, she breaks with the idea of a fixed space or genre through a constant displacement of media and planes: sculpture becomes drawing which, in turn, becomes architecture; the three-dimensional becomes two-dimensional; and so on. Successive displacements eclipse each other, metamorphosing again and again, carrying structure to the edge of its own imperceptibility. Thus the *Reticulárea* fulfills the idea of the artwork as a practice of movement in which the transcendent dissolves in the immanence of the experience of things, impregnating thought in life and life in thought.

In the *Dibujos sin papel*, first created in 1976, Gego continued to emphasize the enigmatic relation between movement and stasis. (Even when static in

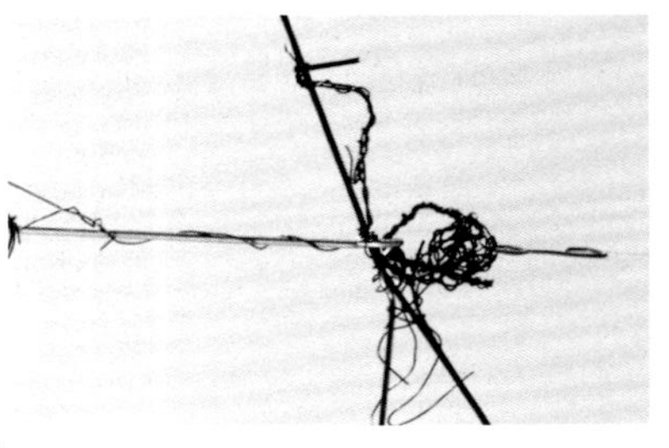

Untitled: Drawing without Paper No. 5 1985

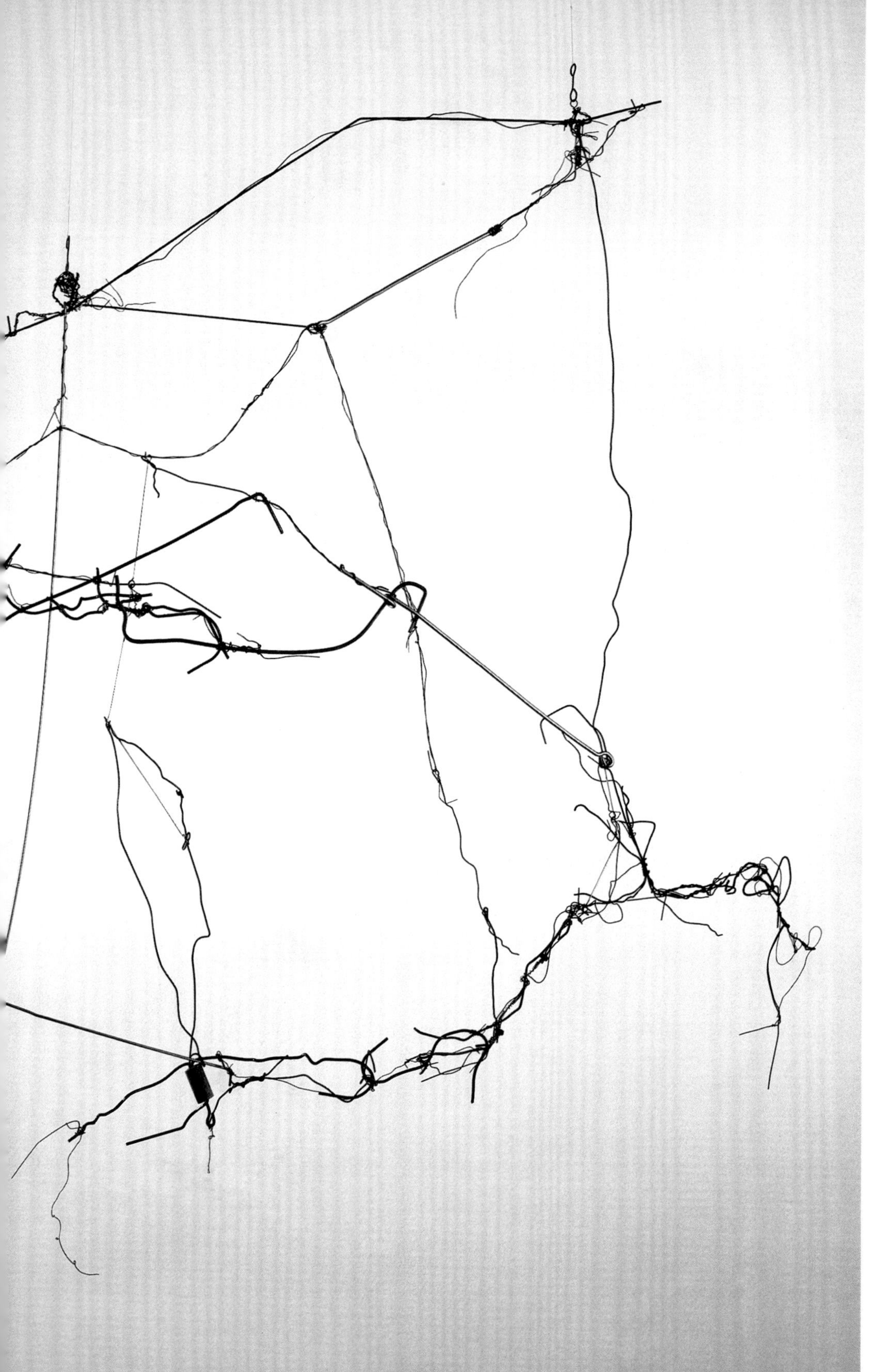

appearance, her work registers an intense movement through the tension and juxtaposition of its forms and the directions of its linear bodies.) Now, however, having overcome the resistance of her materials, she leaves behind the structural complexity of her large pieces and finds a new vitality in the manipulation of the material, allowing her to enter a freer, more expressive space, one evoking the elusive and transitory nature of the object and the action of movement in the smallest things, capturing the experience of the act as a way of thinking.

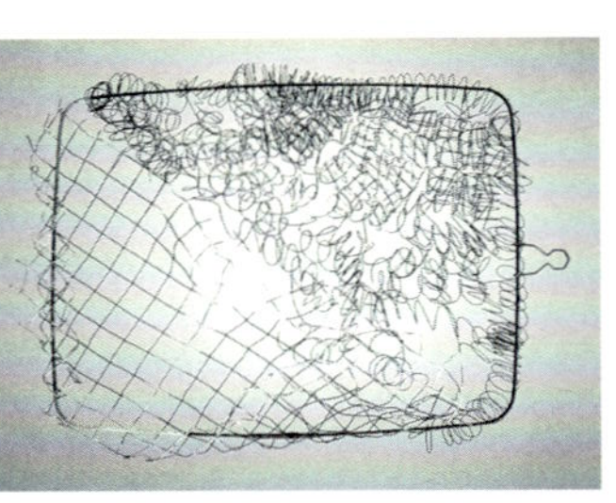

Untitled: Drawing without Paper 83/5A 1983

In these subtle and minute exercises in which she humorously and irreverently embraces the intimate and the precarious, the minimal stands out with amplified force. She works now with metal wires, leftovers, discarded materials. They hold the meditative reflexivity of weaving, encompassing the ephemeral and discontinuous time of the quotidian. In the opacity and imbalance reflected by these objects as a result of the processes that produced them and the modesty of their materials, they make visible something beyond the gaze and the forms, something that pertains to the time and the particular sociocultural milieu in which they were created. Counteracting the formal purity and the careful industrial refinement of kinetic artworks, these fragile *Dibujos sin papel* refer to the disorder that Venezuelan reality introduced into the expressive conditions of individual and collective subjectivity.

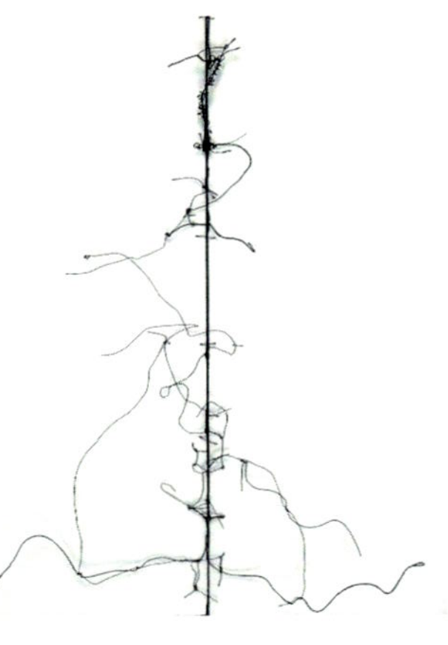

Untitled: Drawing without Paper 85/2 1985

In her mature work—informed by experiences of destabilization, uprootedness, and the paradoxes of the sociocultural environment of Venezuela—Gego intuitively made visible the latent imbalance underlying constructivism. She was able to create a new form of space and movement which counteracted the material purism and the heroic dimension of kinetic art with its human scale, meditative and craftsmanlike work processes, and flexible and modest materials. This was a space and a movement that considered the object as something alive, existing and expanding in a fragile balance, registering the coexistence of quite different orders—orders that took into account the oscillation between the internal and the external, the mathematical and the

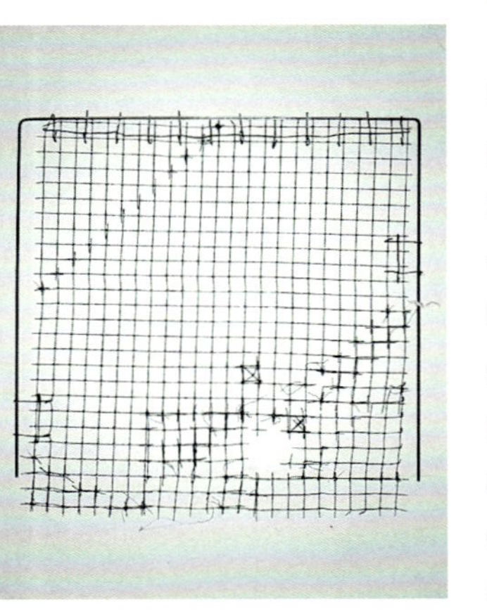

Untitled: Drawing without Paper 88/36 1988

organic, the stable and the unstable—making visible as well, from the very activity manifested in the forms, the contradictions and ambiguities of that moment in Venezuela. In this way, paradoxically, Gego's work inscribes itself in the experimental line of modern art, favoring process over form and exploring the precarious, the fragmentary, and the idea of space as an active field, registering architectural, corporeal, and sensory perceptions.

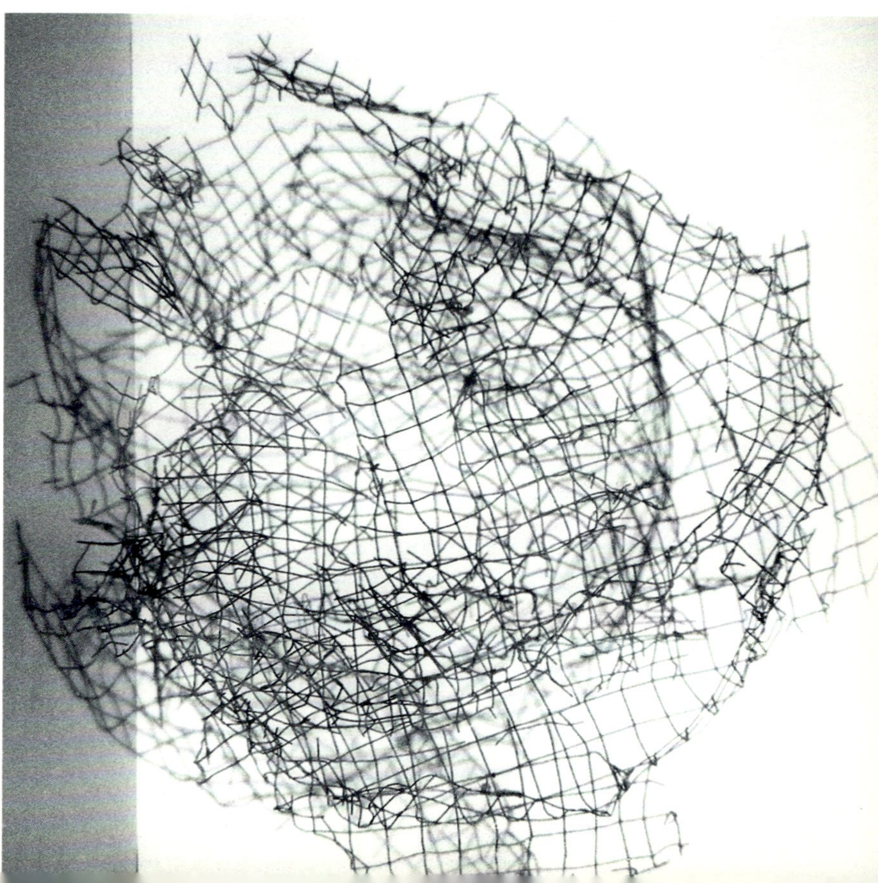

Untitled 87/9 1987

FOLLOWING PAGE: Gego with ***Drawings without Paper*** 1987

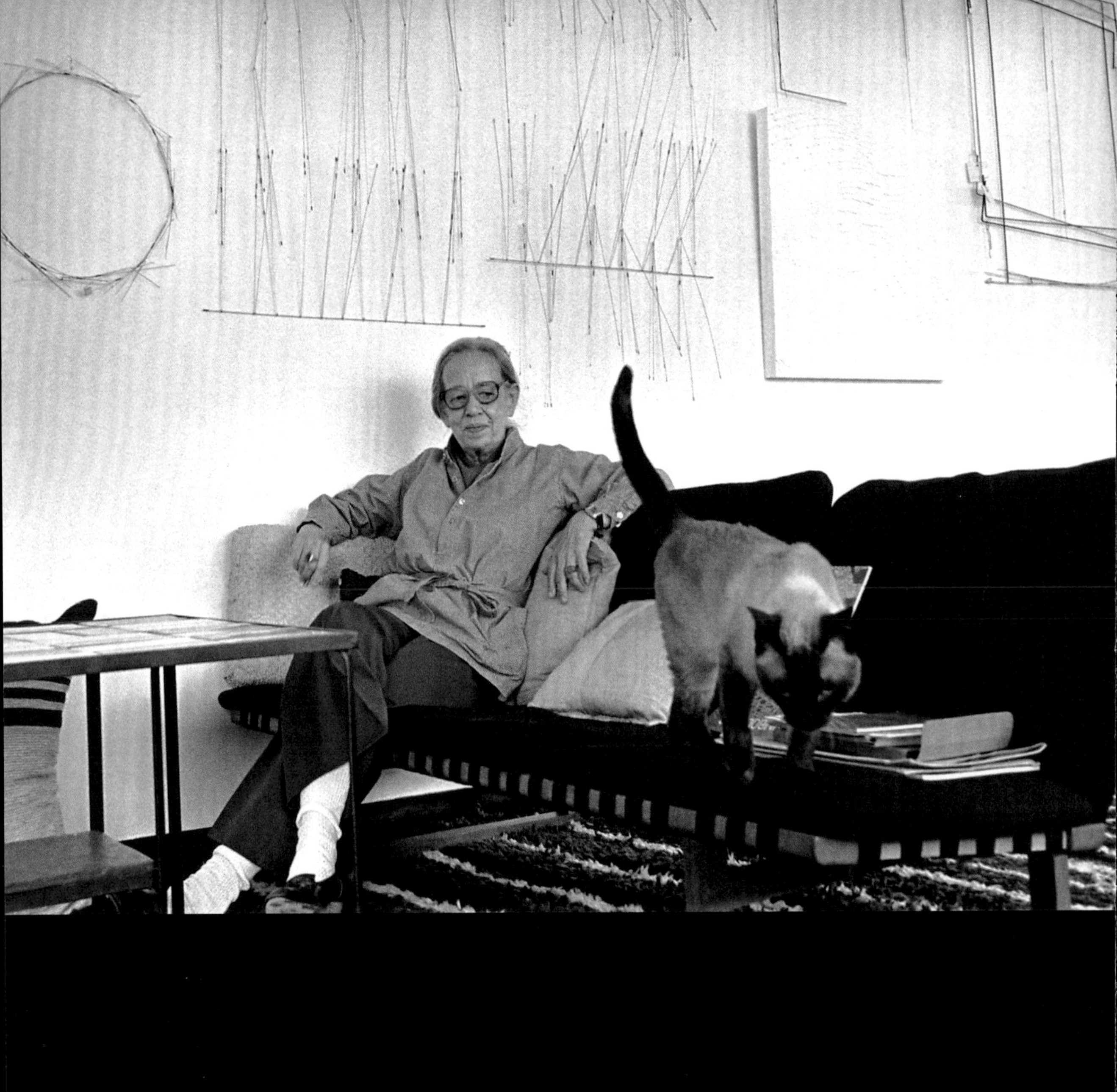

In the end, Gego reconciled widely differing perspectives, affirming through her methods not only the idea of the object as a flexible materiality, the focus of "immaterial" forces and perceptions, but also the experience of subjectivity emerging from form itself and its movement, leading to destabilization and to the passage of energies between opposite categories. The preeminence of a vitalism and a freedom of experimentation upon the aesthetic act, the object and space as planes of immanence and flux dissolving the body-mind dialectic, the idea of a new movement between the visible and the invisible in the form, and space as a source of intensities that continue to compose their vital configurations: these are some of the principles that guided Gego in a work in which life affirms its potency, always renewing itself in the repetitive deconstruction and reconstruction of the limits of the art object.

Translated by Jason Weiss

Notes

1 Fernando Pessoa, "Poemas de Alberto Caeiro: O guardador de rebanhos, IX," in *Poética* (Rio de Janeiro: Nova Aguilar, 1986), 212.

2 *Reticuláreas*: *retícula* means "web design"; the *reticuláreas* are a series of environmental and single sculptures made by Gego from these webs.

3 Since Gego never spoke about her past in relation to her work, assessments about early constructivist influences have been based on assumptions about the nature of her university training. In my previous essay, "Gego: Weaving the Margins," in *Inside the Visible: An Elliptical Traverse of Twentieth-Century Art in, of, and from the Feminine*, ed. M. Catherine de Zegher, exh. cat. (Cambridge, Mass.: MIT Press, 1996), 342, I stated that the Universitat Stuttgart "offered an education with interdisciplinary and constructivist bases close to that of the Bauhaus." In my initial research on Gego in Venezuela, I was unable to find any documentation on her early formation. I interviewed Gert Leufert, an artist and Gego's companion for forty-one years, who provided me with the information that I quote in the aforementioned essay. Publications produced in Caracas during the artist's lifetime also mention that her early education started from a constructivist basis close to that of the Bauhaus (Hanni Ossott, Ruth Auerbach). Thanks to the generous collaboration of two historians of modern architecture in Stuttgart, Dietrich W. Schmidt of the Institut für Architekturgeschichte, Universitat Stuttgart (Institute of Architecture, University of Stuttgart) and Karin Kirsch of the Universität Fachhochschule, Stuttgart, Hochschule für Technik (University of Applied Sciences, Stuttgart), I am able to reformulate Gego's formative context from a new perspective in this essay and to confirm that the artistic vocabulary she created in Venezuela represented her response to the hybridized constructivist visual culture that she found in her adopted country. It was not influenced by a European constructivism absorbed during her university education.

Gego studied at the Technische Hochschule, later the Universitat Stuttgart. During her stay there, its educational focus was traditional German craftsmanship, and the philosophy of its architectural program was diametrically opposed to that of the Bauhaus. Architectural functionalism (expressed in projects like Stuttgart's Weissenhof housing complex of 1927) was stigmatized as "cultural Bolshevism" (Paul Schmitthenner). The school had rejected international modernism and adopted the Nazi vocabulary by the time Gego was concluding her studies. Although the buildings designed by Paul Bonatz, her main advisor, reflected conventional, if not traditional forms, he was more liberal than most of his colleagues, accepting modern architecture that expressed the values of the machine age. Nevertheless, it is clear that Gego's constructivist base did not come from her training at the Universität Stuttgart. Any influence from the city likely came from the architecture of the Weissenhof estates, which had been constructed in the face of polemical resistance from the professors at her school. A number of the Weissenhof architects—Ludwig Mies van der Rohe, Walter Gropius, and Ludwig Hilberseimer—were architects at the Bauhaus; all of the houses they designed were later destroyed. The influence of the Bauhaus on architectural education at the Universität Stuttgart emerged only after the war.

4 For more than a decade after her arrival in Venezuela, Gego undertook pioneering work in the field of design and the production of furniture and objects. She also established a practice as an architect. Her artistic work took shape gradually, over many years, through an interaction with various disciplines, particularly architecture. Speaking of the way she saw interdisciplinary influences in the development of her own work in

the visual arts, she stated that "the different fields of labor are connected, there are bridges going from the craftsman to the designer and ultimately to the artist"; see María Fernanda Palacios, "Conversación con Gego," *Ideas* (Caracas), no. 3 (May 1971).

5 For a critical discussion of the relationship of Gego and the kinetic artists to the Venezuelan sociocultural milieu, see Marta Traba, *Mirar en Caracas: Crítica de Arte* (Caracas: Monte Avila Editores, 1974), 123–33, and Luis Pérez Oramas, *La invención de la continuidad* (Caracas: Fundación Galería de Arte Nacional, 1997), 16–19.

6 The young artists who remained in the country were grouped together for a while as the Barraca de Mariperez (Shack of Mariperez), and a bit later in the Taller Libre de Arte (Free Art Studio, 1948), an association dedicated to the confrontation of ideas and the experimentation of new artistic proposals. The artists associated with the Taller Libre explored a wide range of styles and tendencies and organized important national and international exhibitions. In 1948 they presented the Grupo Concreto-Invención (Concrete-Invention Group) from Buenos Aires (the first show of constructivist art mounted in Venezuela), and a little later Alejandro Otero and Jesús Soto, two central figures in Venezuelan abstract-geometric art who lived in Paris. While in Caracas the members of the Taller were laying the foundations for the modernization of the local culture, in Paris a group of young Venezuelans who had settled there after the conflict at the Escuela in 1945, led by Otero, found in geometric abstraction a way to both dissent against official Venezuelan teaching and insert themselves into the international currents of the time. They formed the group Los Disidentes (The Dissidents) and published a magazine in Paris and Caracas which disseminated their views, particularly their vehement critique of the conservatism of Venezuela's cultural environment. Los Disidentes' most effective contribution, resulting in the consolidation of the abstract-geometric movement in the country, came after they returned to Caracas (beginning in 1952).

7 These structural systems, as well as Gego's methods of construction and assemblage, are discussed by Hanni Ossott, in collaboration with Gego and Alvaro Sotillo, in Ossott's *Gego* (Caracas: Ediciones Museo de Arte Contemporáneo, 1977).

8 Referring to her practice, Gego said that her intention was not to make artworks but "to make visible" something that did not exist in reality; see Palacios.

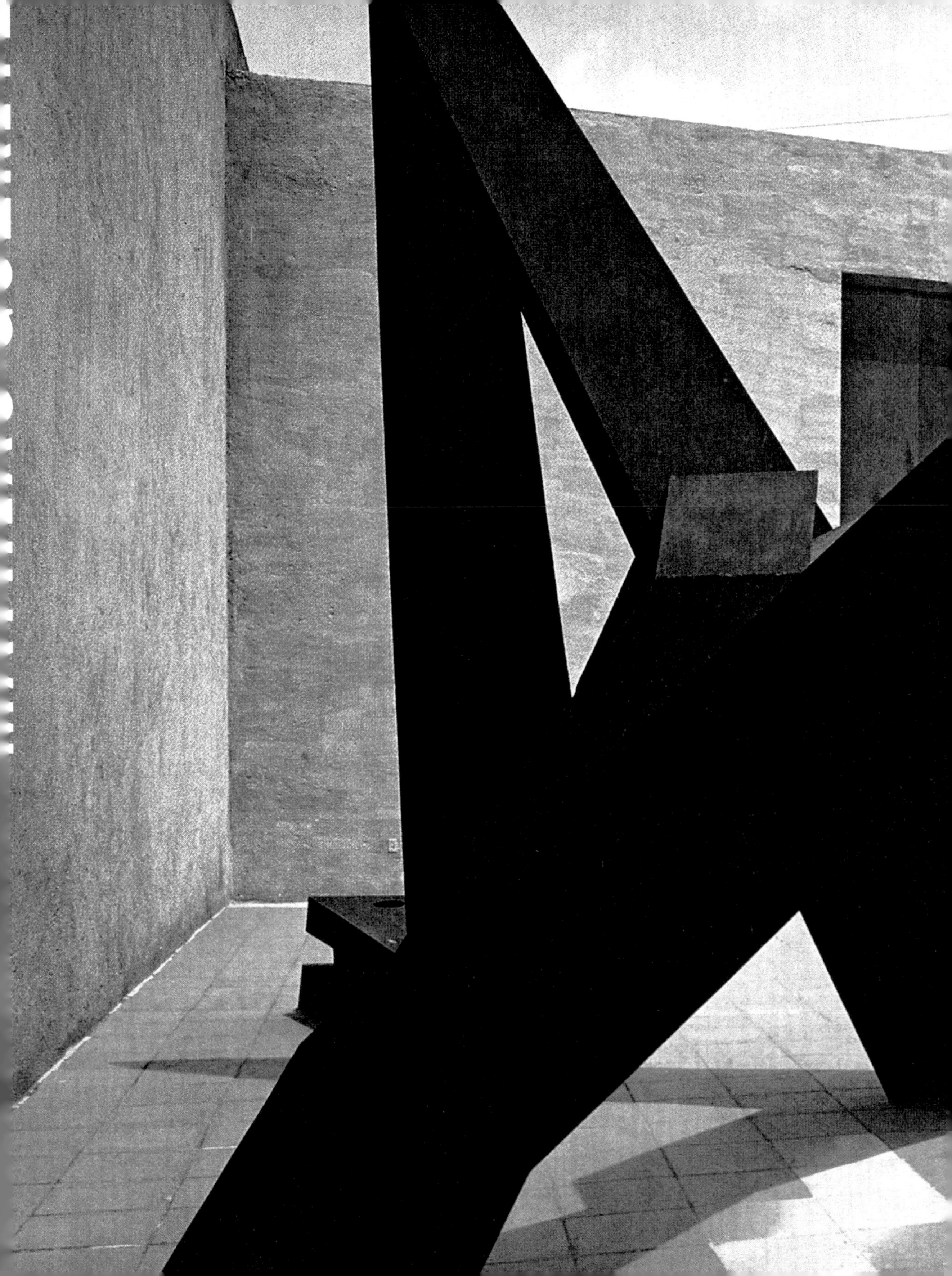

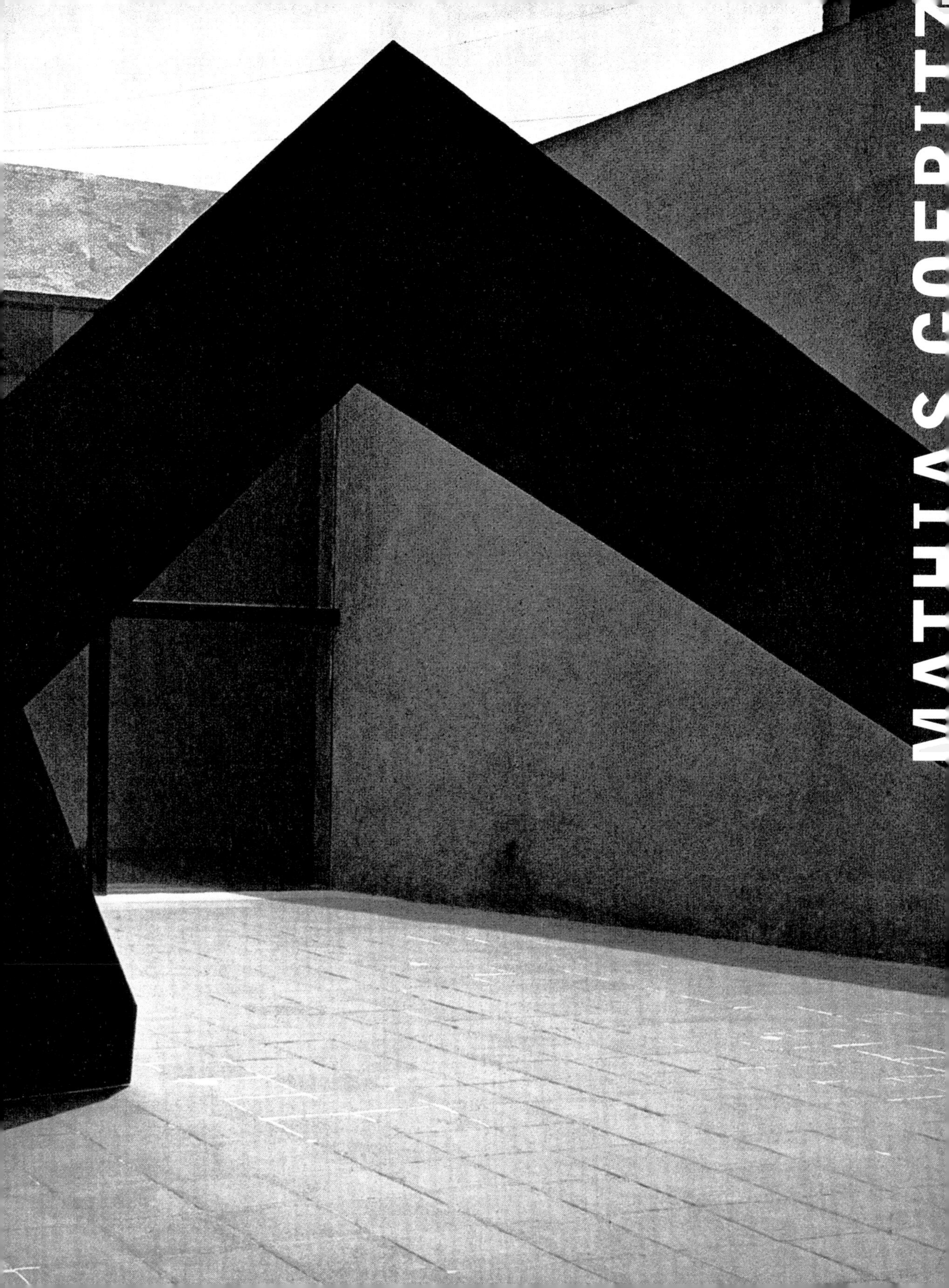
MATHIAS GOERITZ

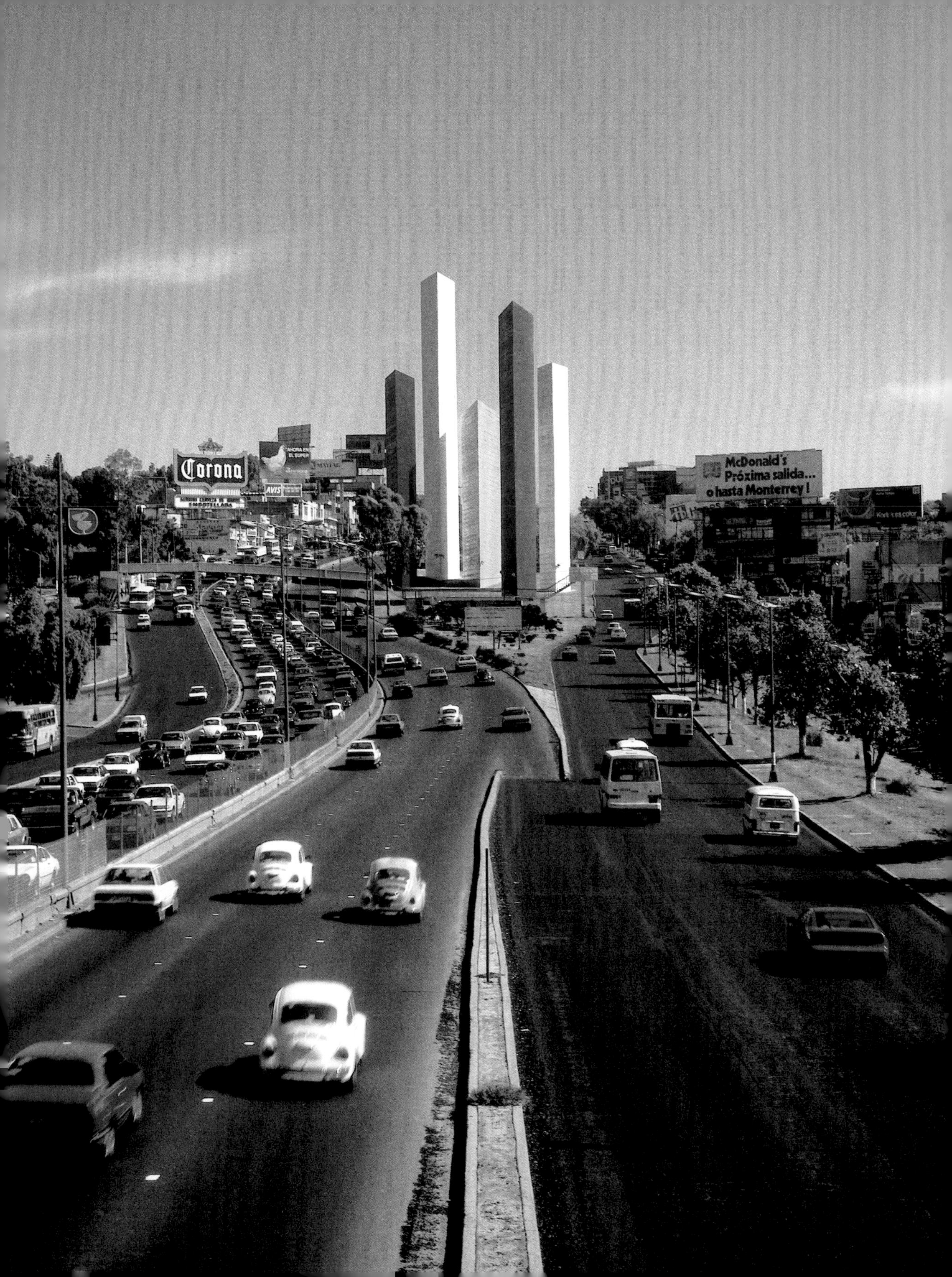
Corona
AVIS
McDonald's
Próxima salida...
o hasta Monterrey !

Soon we will have to learn to fly, to swim in the ether. If we really want to reorient our daily lives, we will soon need to change our bearings, to shift our sights "upwards."

—PAUL VIRILIO, "OPEN SKY"[1]

I understood architecture as immense sculpture.

—MATHIAS GOERITZ, letter to Jorge Romero Brest (4 April 1954)[2]

MATHIAS GOERITZ:

The Ministries of Space

Osvaldo Sánchez

In 1965 the Solomon R. Guggenheim Museum and Cornell University presented the exhibition "The Emergent Decade: Latin American Painters and Painting in the 60's," organized by the Guggenheim's director Thomas M. Messer.[3] It was one of many exhibitions of modern Latin American art organized by major museums in the United States from the 1930s onward (The Museum of Modern Art alone organized eight such exhibitions between 1940 and 1945). By presenting a certain tradition of painting as representative of Latin American art in general, these exhibitions perpetuated stereotypes about the nature of Latin American modernity as primitivist, exotic, naïve, and Other. Within this tradition, the work of the Muralists, who exalted a national identity fabricated from a cultural myth consumable by the illiterate masses and exportable as a postcolonial fantasy, became hegemonic.

When it became apparent that the Mexican selection for "The Emergent Decade" would include the figurative painters Rufino Tamayo, Ricardo Martínez, Pedro Coronel, and José Luis Cuevas, it was not surprising that Mathias Goeritz would assume the role of the curator's interlocutor (correspondence between Goeritz and Messer is published in the catalogue). Goeritz insisted on a new reading of Mexican modernity. First, he maintained that a purely aesthetic reading of the work of the Mexican Muralists extricated it from its social context, which predetermined its rise and initial value as an essentially political practice. Even more significantly, he stressed that the intellectual effervescence in Mexico at that time lay in the relationship between art and architecture—not in the work of the painters associated with the Ruptura.[4] He cited the achievements of architects like Luis Barragán, Félix Candela, Ricardo Legorreta, Mario Pani, and Ricardo de Robina in this regard. But he characteristically did not include himself among this group. Nevertheless, in his own synthesis of architecture and sculpture in monuments such as the Museo Experimental *El Eco*, *Las Torres de Ciudad Satélite*, and *El Espacio Escultórico*, Goeritz developed a language of monumentality, expressed through his concept of emotional architecture, which offered a powerful alternative to the Muralist tradition.

PRECEDING PAGES: Serpent in the Experimental Museum ***El Eco*** 1953 ***Towers of Satellite City*** 1957–58 ***Temixco Towers*** 1957–58

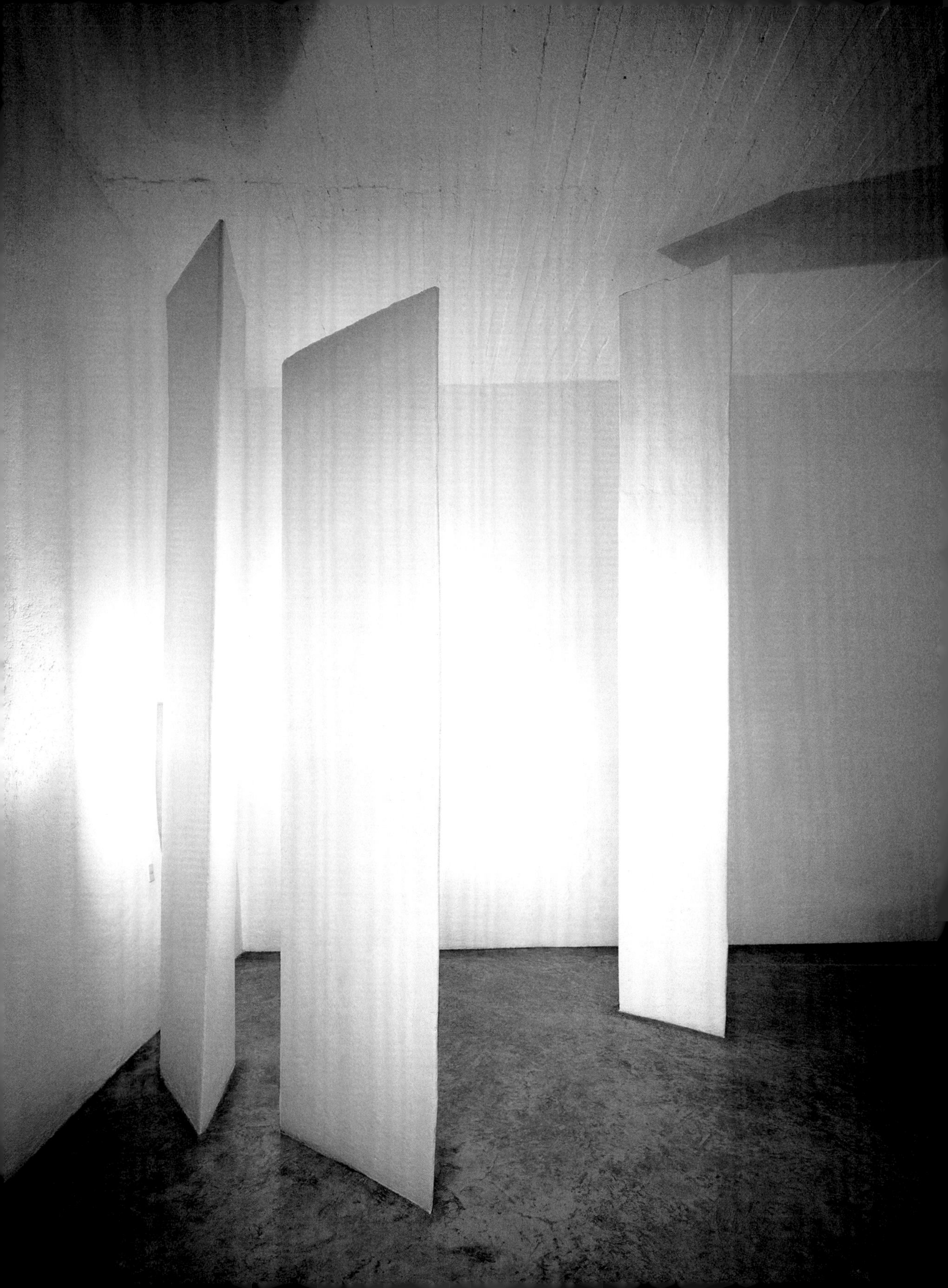

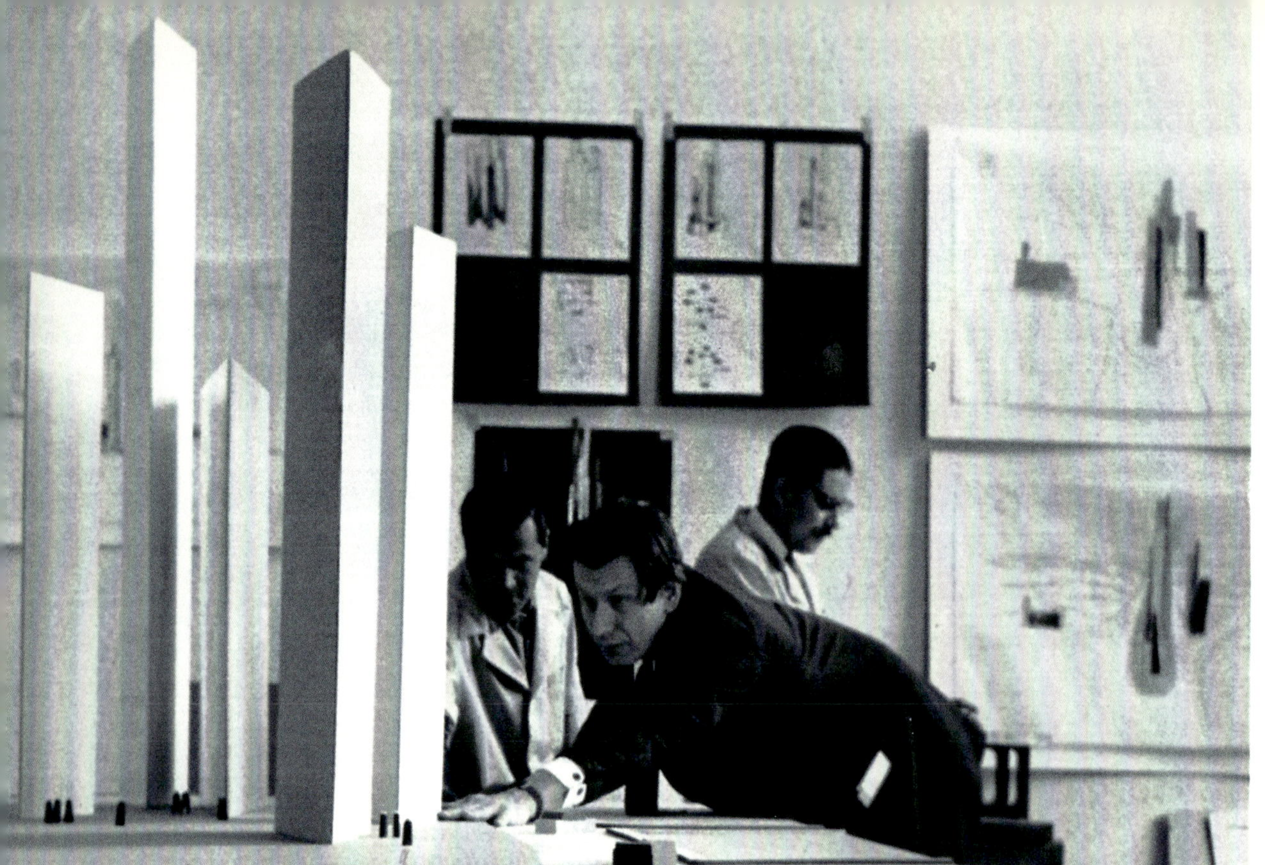

Goeritz designing ***Towers of Satellite City*** 1957–58

Toward Mexico

On October 2, 1949, Goeritz and his wife, the photographer Marianne Gast, reached the port of Veracruz after a journey from Spain, where they had been living; at the same time, the Palacio de Bellas Artes (Palace of Fine Arts) in Mexico City was presenting the major exhibition "Diego Rivera: 50 años de labor artística" (Diego Rivera: 50 Years of Art Work). During the 1940s, Goeritz had traveled from the lavish Berlin of Paul Ludwig Troost and of Leni Riefenstahl (1941), to the colonial enclave of the German Institute in Tetuan (1943), to the Granada of General Francisco Franco and the late writer Federico García Lorca (1945), to a Madrid haunted by the absence of its numerous exiles, to the faded elegance of the palace of the Marquis of Santillana. In 1948, in Santillana del Mar, Spain, he conceived the Escuela de Altamira (School of Altamira), his first utopian project.[5]

Goeritz left Spain for Mexico shortly after art critics in Madrid had expelled him from the elite Academia Breve (Breve Academy), directed by Eugenio D'Ors, in retaliation for his avant-garde ideas and zealous criticism. The Mexican architect Ignacio Díaz Morales had invited him to lecture in a recently opened school of architecture in the latter country. To travel to Mexico signified a new attempt on Goeritz's part to escape an imprecise sense of historical guilt that he, like many Germans of his generation, felt in response to the rise of Nazism—a confusion that would forever mark his life and work.

Goeritz's story might have been much like that of other European artists who had emigrated to Mexico before, during, and after World War II. However, his case was different from that of such figures as Leonora Carrington, Katy and José Horna, Wolfgang Paalen, Alice Rahon, and Remedios Varo, who experienced a certain ostracism (to some extent self-imposed) after they had emigrated. This ostracism was intensified by their eccentric differences from the artists, critics, and others who dominated local artistic circles, by their inability to articulate the radicalness of their idiosyncratic interpretations of modernism, and by their intellectual positions in the polemical debates that were then raging. Nevertheless, all of them, including Goeritz, lived hounded by the jealousy of a mediocre nationalism institutionalized by the Muralists and blessed by a demagogic state.[6]

Goeritz soon became the favorite target of the domesticated "revolutionary" thought of those years championed by Diego Rivera and David Alfaro Siqueiros, who were drunk with power and debased by bourgeois commissions and official engagements. For example, he survived repeated public accusations of being a parvenu and a Nazi, an imitator and an artist corrupted by abstractionism. His response to such accusations demonstrated that he was one of the most energetic activists against the dominant discourse of Mexican visual modernity (even during those years when the influence of the Muralists fueled the expressions of resistance of black and Chicano activist artists in the United States). He also resisted the growing influence of Functionalism in architectural circles, which was premised on the principle that a building's function should determine its form and which privileged an extreme rationalism. In fact, Goeritz not only brilliantly mapped the convergence of Functionalism with the formal reductionism associated with many artists of the Ruptura, but also, through his collaborative projects, catalyzed alliances, debates, and currents of thought key to the discourse of Mexican art during the second half of the century. This dissidence against the Muralist establishment brought to the Mexican artistic milieu a new, demystifying conception of the author and the viewer, of style and the nature of visual experience, of the relationship between architecture and painting, and of religiosity as a legitimate spiritual basis for a supreme collective aim.

Goeritz's anti-Muralist militancy—preceded by the lucid criticism of the architect Juan O'Gorman and the obsessions of the artist Carlos Mérida—was propelled by a broadly ethical and social motivation rather than a narrowly artistic one. If we assume modernity, as the art historian Rosalind Krauss has suggested, to be "a parable of self-creation," it is easy to understand how art critics not attached to the Muralists attempted to redefine the iden-

The Experimental Museum *El Eco* (Detail: Hallway) 1953

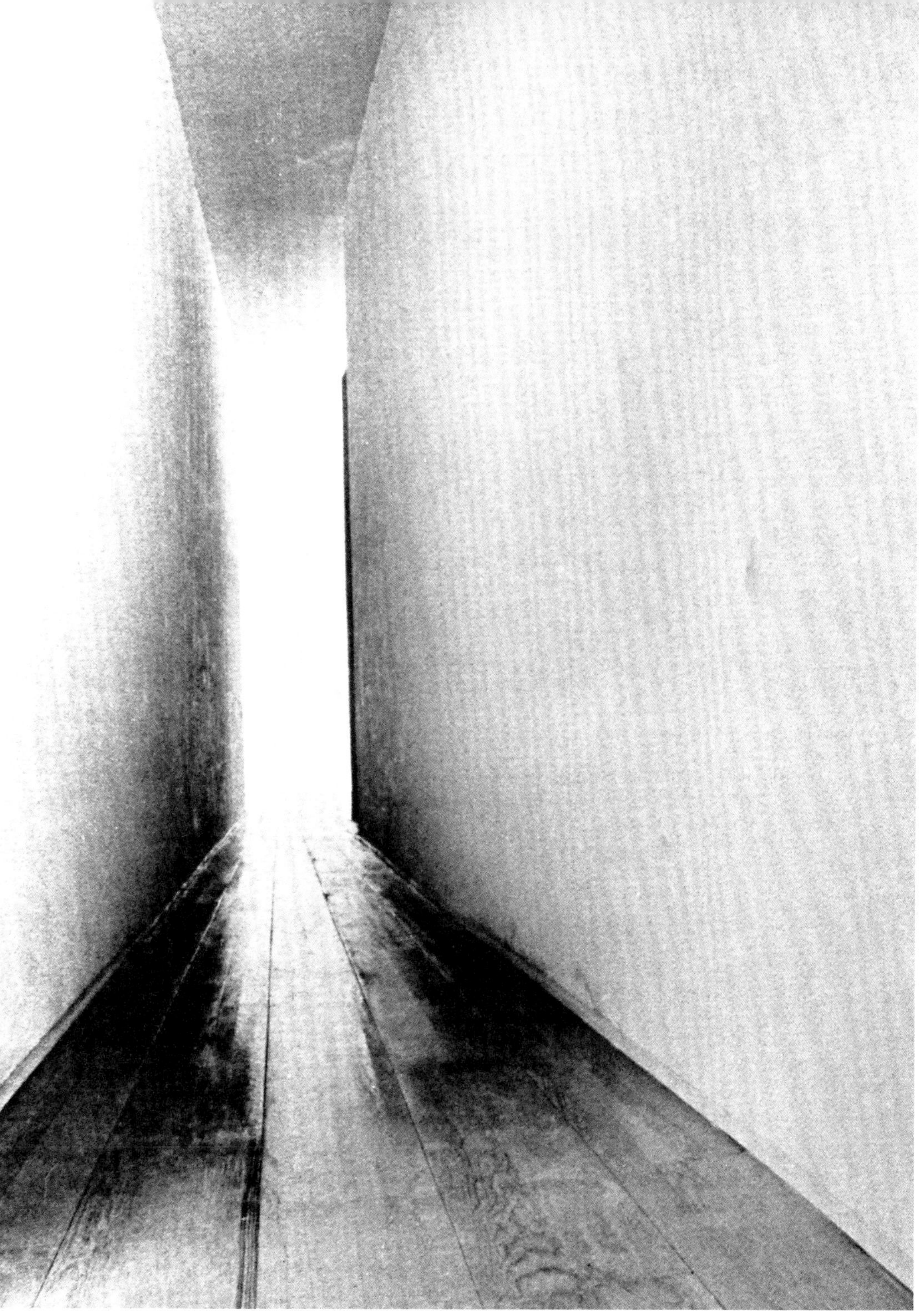

tity of Mexico after World War II in the context of new models of economic development and hemispheric integration. In the light of a desired "progress," this process constituted a second period of modernity in Mexican art, which was articulated as antimodernity and was opposed to the nationalist discourse of exotic self-construction. This new modernity, as some critics in Mexico have termed it, was in consonance with models of hemispheric integration which assumed that construction, architecture, industry, urbanization, and technology were the agents of a possible utopian future. Paradoxically, Goeritz also apostatized this new modernity, symbolized by mass culture, the triumph of machinery, and the nihilist ideology that nurtured the new avant-gardes.

Course on Visual Education

Escuela de Arquitectura de la Universidad de Guadalajara

Guadalajara, 1949

In 1949 Goeritz became a professor at the Escuela de Arquitectura de la Universidad de Guadalajara (School of Architecture of the University of Guadalajara) in the state of Jalisco. In a letter to the critic Jorge Romero Brest, he called this Jalisco laboratory "a type of Mexican Bauhaus." Undoubtedly, he was a student of his own Bauhaus. His lessons, like his art, followed an itinerary of precise teachings. These ranged from the structural exercises of Josef Albers's preliminary course, to Wassily Kandinsky's concepts of compositional rhythm, to De Stijl's visions of utopia, which served as a militant platform for many German intellectuals between the wars. And in Guadalajara numerous local influences were formative: the intimate religiosity of Jalisco; the monastic asceticism of Luis Barragán, who was fascinated by Nazarite gardens and the belfries of Umbria and who reduced the figurative paraphernalia of Muralism to one sole plane of color; the exotic erudition of the painter Jesús (Chucho) Reyes and his astonishment at the ingenuousness of certain folk toys, his scandalous palette of pink, magenta, orange, emerald green, gold, violet, and royal blue, and his perverse obsession for stylistic slips. And perhaps Goeritz came across the German philosopher Alexander Dorner's book *The Way Beyond Art: The Work of Herbert Bayer*, published in New York in 1947.[7]

During Goeritz's brief tenure in Guadalajara, he developed a pedagogical philosophy that stood in opposition to the prevailing Muralist ideology of the time. His experience in Spain with the Escuela de Altamira had given him a more open understanding of the concept of the collective authorship, as well as indifference to that of personal style, interest in ordinary materials of strong telluric charge, and a commitment to the primacy of the natural environment as the ideal context for all aesthetic experiences.[8] With his Course on Visual Education, he promulgated a more complex network of relationships among architecture, design, painting, sculpture, and drawing which surpassed the Muralists' demagogic use of the wall support.

Goeritz's understanding of architecture as the container of a generational *Gesamtkunstwerk* stemmed not only from his debt to the Bauhaus, but also resulted from the influence of those artists and architects in Jalisco who became his first friends. During this stage of experimentation, he discovered his vocation for three-dimensional space and his commitment to the principle that art could be a quest for spiritual experience. Also, the Catholic atmosphere in Guadalajara during those years fostered in Goeritz the beginning of an anguishing process of multiple religious conversions, like that experienced by many European artists of his generation who found in faith an antidote to the moral crisis instigated by the traumas of World War II. Even when he seemed to shield himself in a personal interpretation of Judaism, it is easier to understand his ecumenical and contradictory religiosity from the words of his later companion, Ana Cecilia Trebiño. As she stated, "His spiritual obsession concentrated on Moses, Ramakrishna, and the late rabbi Amran Blau of Jerusalem, which did not prevent him from

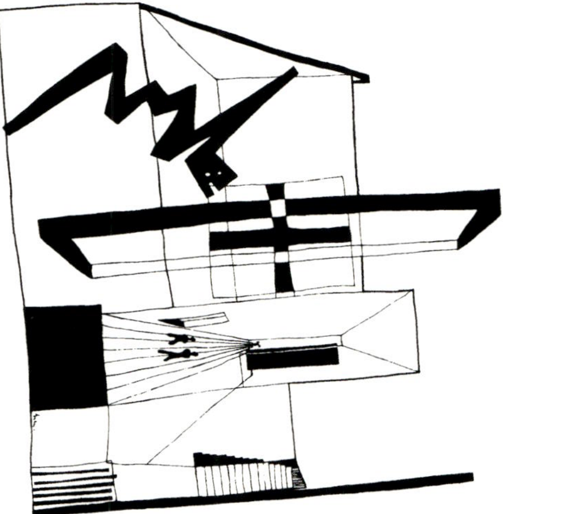

Ideographic Drawing for the Experimental Museum ***El Eco*** 1952

worshipping the Virgin of Guadalupe and insisting on his Lutheran roots."[9] Such mystic eclecticism braces the transcendental mood that his work emits.

The Experimental Museum *El Eco*

Mexico City, 1953

In the early 1950s, the Guadalajara entrepreneurs Daniel Mont and Gabriel Orendáin offered Goeritz a plot of land in Mexico City, located at Calle Sullivan, 43, on which he was given the freedom to construct whatever he wished. He was still living in Guadalajara when he conceived the Museo Experimental *El Eco* (*The Echo* Experimental Museum), a project that in principle represented the search for a *Gesamtkunstwerk* in Mexico, even though the critics of the time understood it as "something antifunctional, a great sculpture which must not be judged as architecture in an orthodox way."[10] *El Eco* would be, as he later stated, "a meeting point to experience artistic creation freely and convivially. It would be an open and transformable space: experimental museum, art gallery, theater, dance space . . . which, under its roof, would integrate art, artists, visitors, and work. It would be a museum, a living museum."[11]

Inaugurated on September 7, 1953, *El Eco* is a reductionist work that demanded to be read on its own terms—as abstract space not subjected to the national inertia of a historicist model. Its construction brought together many of the generation's key artists. The inauguration alone featured "a ballet to end all ballets" directed by the filmmaker Luis Buñuel, who at the time was living in Mexico. Lan Adomian composed the ballet's music (*La Tamayana*, in honor of Tamayo), and Walter Nicks danced it. The building featured a mural painted by Alfonso Soto Soria based on a sketch by Henry Moore, as well as the participation of Barragán, Carrington, Germán Cueto, Mérida, Felipe Orlando, and Rahon. Even though Goeritz strove to orchestrate

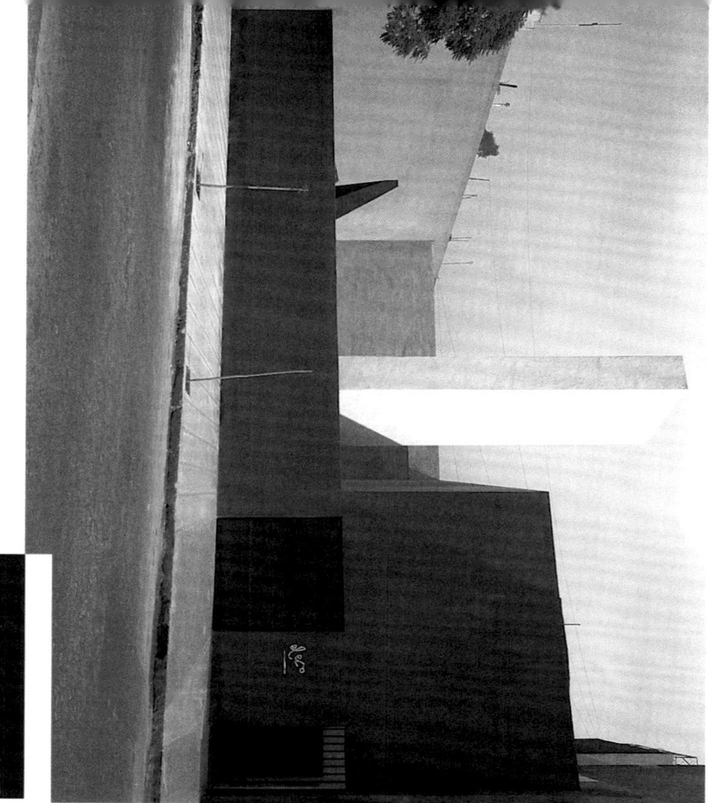

The Experimental Museum *El Eco* (Detail: Facade) 1953

a variety of expressions in this performative and experimental work, it was above all a spatial proposal, with tall walls that he defined as sculptural elements. Years later he described it as a modeling of the void: "It was total void. . . . and the void speaks more than words."[12] Alejandro Zohn, his student, confessed his surprise at the time: "There, all the planes were against the other planes, and all the elements were against the others."

Goeritz developed *El Eco* during a new era of modernization in Mexico. In the 1940s, Mexico City's population had increased by 43 percent, and Mexico began to experience a construction boom. Many of the major buildings constructed during the administration of President Miguel Alemán (1946–52)

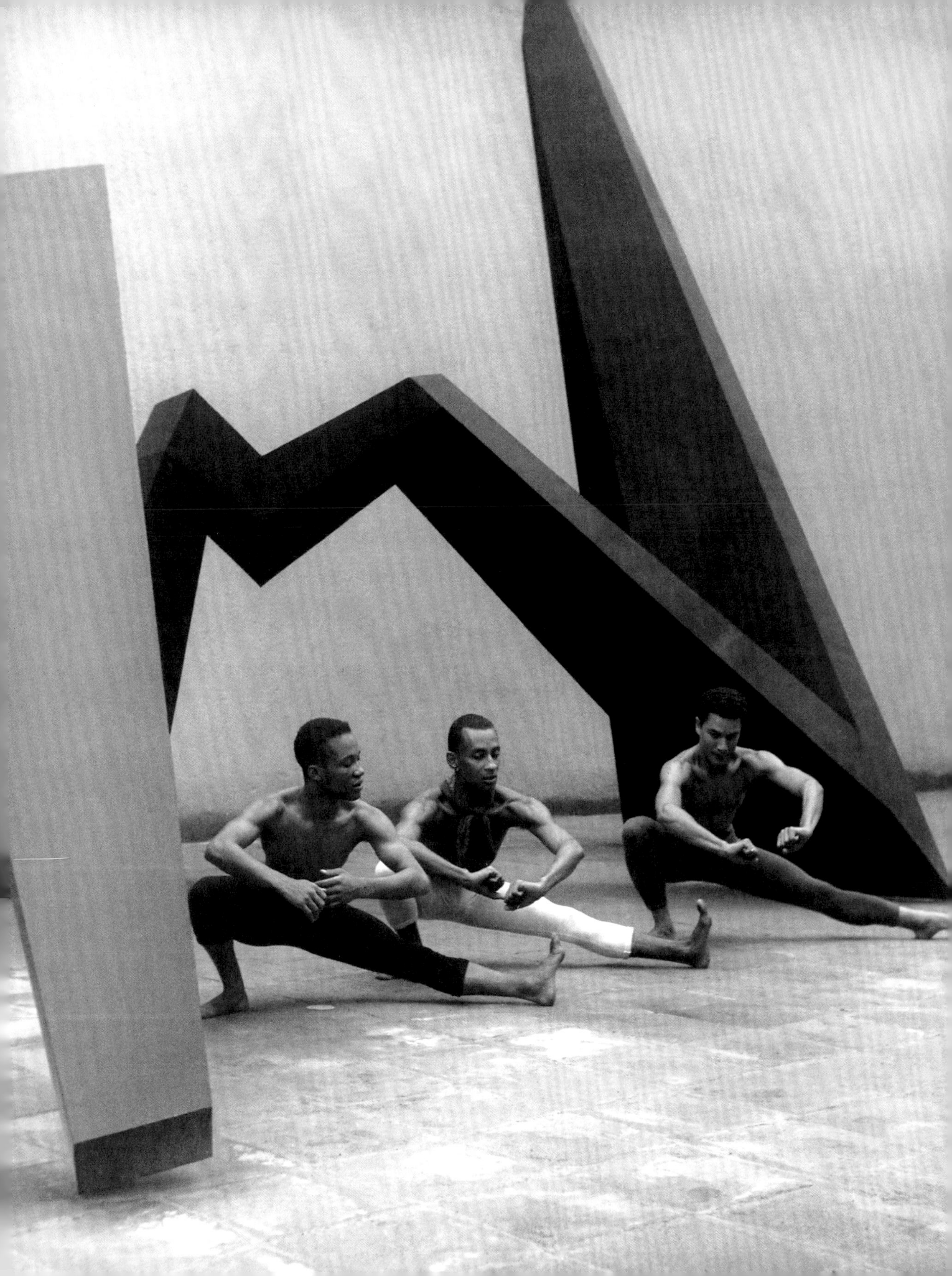

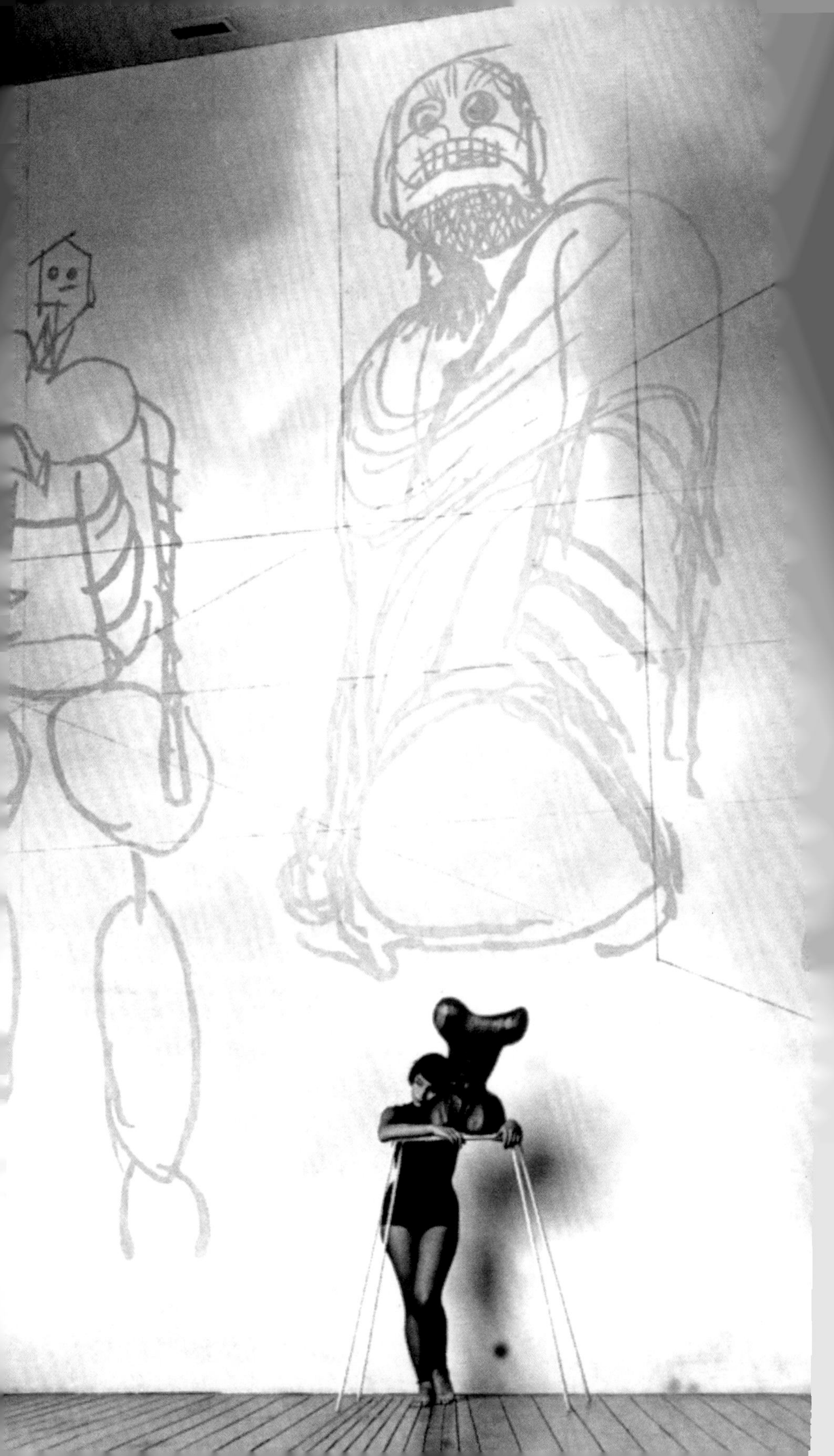

symbolized the newly created institutions of the modern state, perhaps as a smokescreen intended to obscure the nation's accelerated integration into the U.S. economy. One of the effects of this construction boom was the entrance of Functionalism into Mexican architecture, and with it the tacit legitimation of an "international style" in art—a trend that Siqueiros and Rivera vigorously opposed. O'Gorman, one of Goeritz's allies in the defense of modern Mexican architecture,[13] also condemned this uncritical embrace of Functionalism, though at the same time he ridiculed the Muralists' support of an architecture of decorative and rhetorical muraled facades lacking in architectural identity.

Although in practical terms *El Eco* implies an extraordinary shift in the architectural conception of space and its use, formally it betrays its constructivist roots and the utopian dimension of the Neoplasticist school. Both of these movements, as well as class works from Albers's preliminary courses or van Doesberg's and Walter Gropius's structural exercises, seem to have been the driving force for Goeritz in his quest for a new spatial dynamics, closely linked to Piet Mondrian's ideas concerning spiritual emotion and pure form. He conceived of space as an enormous negative sculpture (the corporeality of the void) and marked its containing walls in a manner similar to that in which van Doesberg had used planes of color to define countless angles, depths, and illusionistic spaces. *El Eco* also explicitly unveiled two key influences that Goeritz had repeatedly alluded to in his conception of space: German Expressionist cinema and Maghreb architecture.

In the middle of the public debate on the meaning of *El Eco*, Goeritz published his "Manifiesto de arquitectura emocional" (Manifesto on Emotional Architecture). The relevance of this text transcends the polemics surrounding architectural modernity in Mexico and the rest of Latin America at the time. It is the first text by Goeritz in which he articulates his complex artistic position from an ethical standpoint in the context of contemporary Mexican art, before the initial impact of the New York mainstream. Along with *El Eco*,

Pilar Pellicer Next to ***El Eco Torso*** 1953

PRECEDING PAGES: The Walter Nicks Ballet in the Experimental Museum ***El Eco*** 1953

the manifesto constituted the basis for a critique of the Mexican School represented by the Muralists, but also against the literal appropriation of European modernist styles by the Ruptura artists, many of whom did not understand the reductionist precepts of contemporary U.S. Abstract Expressionism. The utopian dimension of Goeritz's aesthetic formation, stranded in a German modernism cut short by the rise of Nazism, prevented him from disconnecting a conception of modern subjectivity that privileged collective experimentation from the philosophical supports of the Neoplasticists and Constructivists concerning space and perception. Hence, he did not recognize the Ruptura as a related investigation. On the other hand, he did not identify his studies of space, scale, and technology with the reductive and rational skepticism of the new avant-garde objectualists or Minimalists who were his contemporaries.

Goeritz lucidly described his conception of emotional architecture in the manifesto:

> Art in general, and naturally also architecture, is a reflection of the spiritual state of man in his time. But there is the impression that the modern architect, individualistic and intellectual, is sometimes exaggerating—perhaps for having lost close contact with his community—in wanting to emphasize the rational part of architecture too much, the result being that man in the twentieth century feels crushed or overwhelmed by so much Functionalism, by so much logic or utility within modern architecture.
>
> He looks for a way out, but neither exterior aestheticism, understood as formalism, nor organic regionalism, nor dogmatic Confucianism has deeply confronted the problem that the man—creator or recipient—of our time aspires to something more than a beautiful, agreeable, and appropriate house. He asks—or will have to ask one day—from architecture and its modern mediums and materials a spiritual elevation; simply put: an emotion, just as in his time the architecture of the pyramid gave it to him, as did the Greek temple, the Romantic or Gothic cathedral, the Baroque palace. Only by receiving true emotion from architecture will man be able to consider it an art.[14]

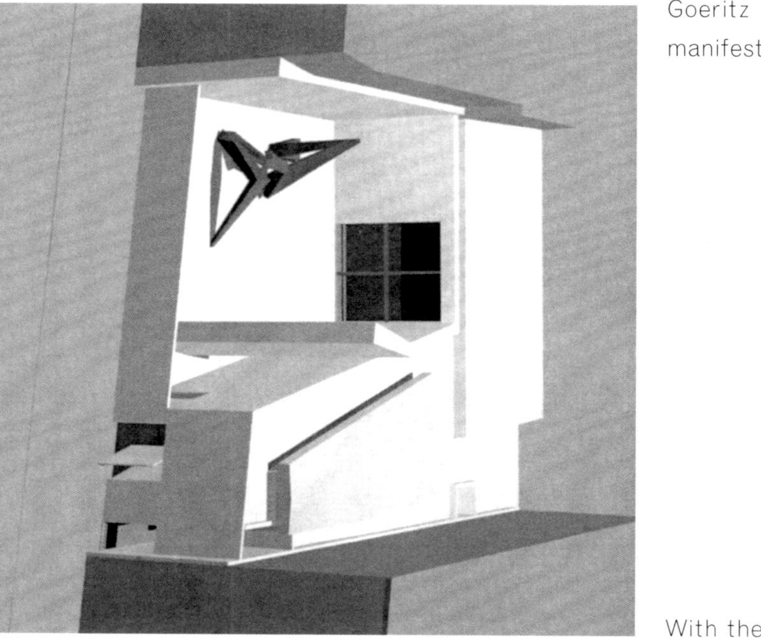

The Experimental Museum ***El Eco*** (Detail: Patio) 1953

With the partially completed project *Laberinto de Jerusalén* (Labyrinth of Jerusalem, 1974–80), Goeritz gave a mature form to his thesis of emotional architecture. By taking the angular flows of vision to the limit, he constantly broke expectations and conceived space as both organic and intellectually structured. This six-floor construction, with terraces, four mezzanines, and unexpected bays, was totally articulated to provoke unexpected, intriguing feelings, as Goeritz himself stated. Its plan suggests multiple radial axes, which open up and concentrate in irregular polygons. Goeritz's intention was for the composition to consist of two buildings of very different scales. In the end, the second construction, the smaller one, was never built, thus truncating his idea of falsifying perspectives of scale and creating a simulacrum of a skyline.

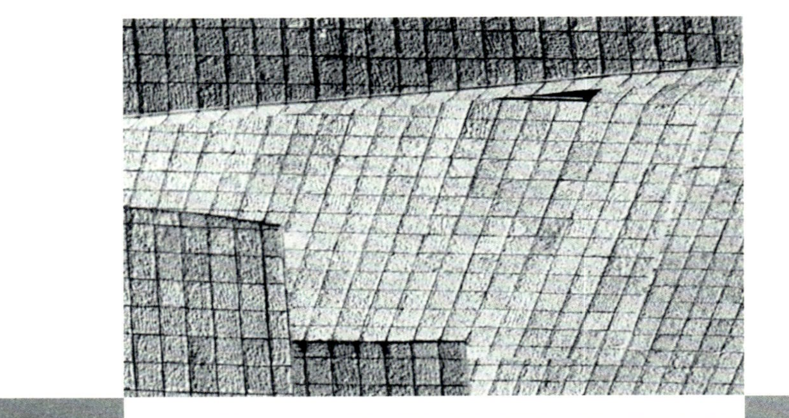

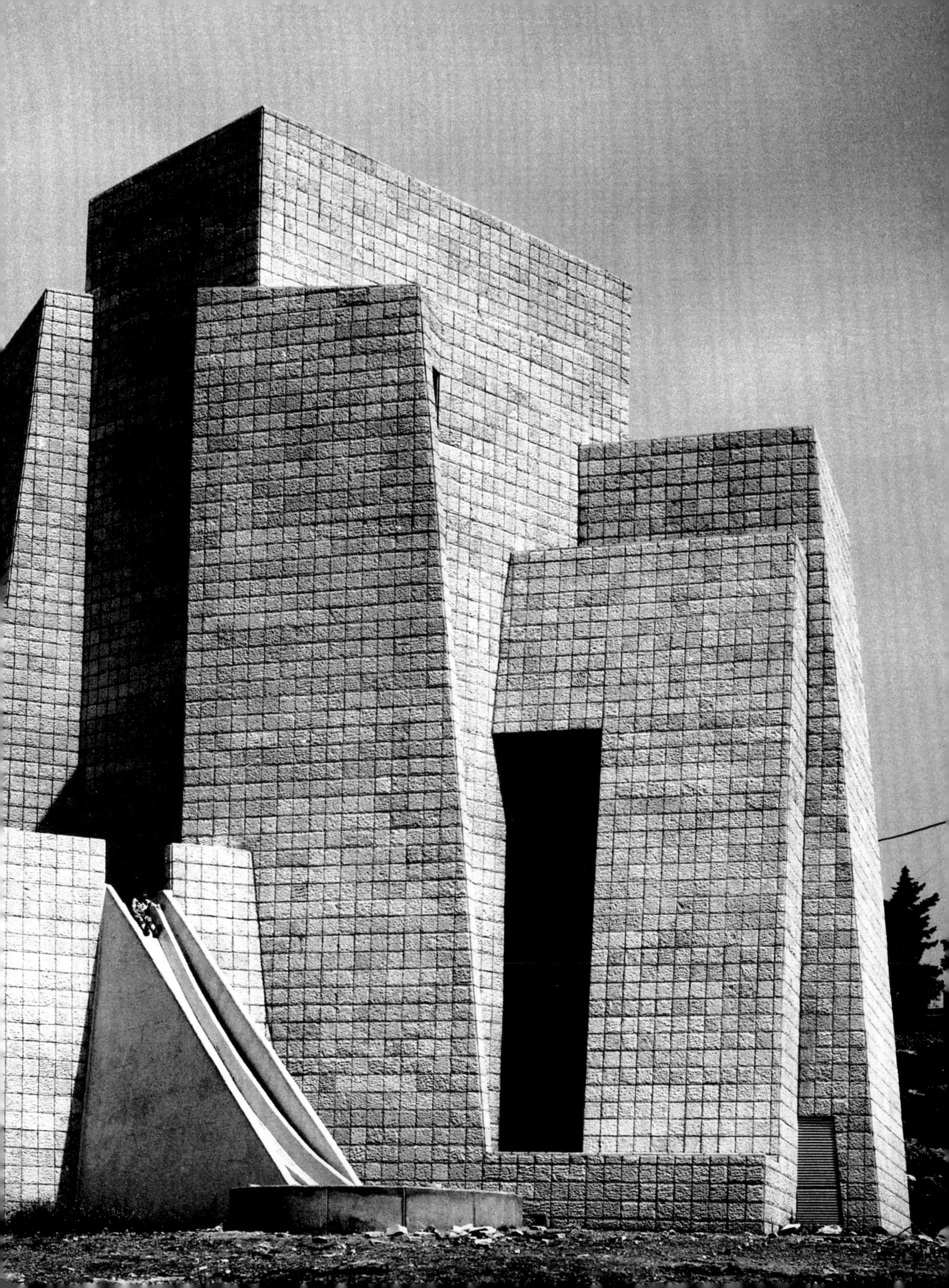

Towers of Satellite City

In collaboration with Luis Barragán

Mexico City, 1957–58

In the late 1950s, Mario Pani and Barragán invited Goeritz to propose a design for a structure that would serve the same function as a fountain at the entrance to a residential complex. In collaboration with Barragán, he developed *Torres de Ciudad Satélite* (Towers of Satellite City); nevertheless, the two disputed final authorship of the Towers, publicized to international audiences by the magazine *Architecture 58*, and a voluminous correspondence documenting the dispute survives.[15] The structure itself, situated on a plaza in the middle of a heavily used highway, consists of five isosceles prisms of reinforced concrete which vary in height from 121 to 187 feet. Initially, three of the prisms were painted white, one yellow, and the other orange; however,

Towers of Satellite City (Detail) 1957–58

some years later, the original proposal was recovered, and some of the prisms were repainted red and the others shades of orange. Overall, they reveal the difficulty of harmonizing mass and color—that is, of avoiding the dominance of the pigmented surface over the visual weight of the form. In addition to the color, one intimately feels the expressive charge of the rough texture of the monumental walls.

In a description of a visit to Barragán's home, the architect Felipe Leal cited a compendium of sources that influenced his conception of the Towers. He mentions a book open to etchings of the towers of San Gimignano, a screen with a reproduction of a monochromatic Cubist composition by José Clemente Orozco, and a painting by Albers. He also stresses Barragán's insistence on choosing colors directly from the paintings of his friend, the painter Jesús (Chucho) Reyes.

In his own discussions of the Towers, Goeritz suggested references to Manhattan skyscrapers—specifically, to the idea of creating a sculptural mass that would simulate a colossal urban skyline but that would function as a monument to faith rather than as a symbol of industrial power. As he wrote in the catalogue of his exhibition at the Carstairs Gallery in New York in 1956, "I would like to have my blocks upright, enormous, as buildings, in a desert landscape, for people to see them from afar." In fact, small-scale works that he had created before the Towers, such as *Aquí y allá* (Here and There, 1955), anticipate this group of prisms of different heights, oriented without angularity but articulated from a complex dynamics of mass, height, and profile. If Barragán speaks of the viewer's "memory," Goeritz speaks of "emotion."

Although the Towers perhaps best embody Mexico's intellectual leadership of architecture during the 1950s, a period in which many still believed in the possibility of the perfect marriage between art and progress, Goeritz was not entirely happy with the result. As he wrote:

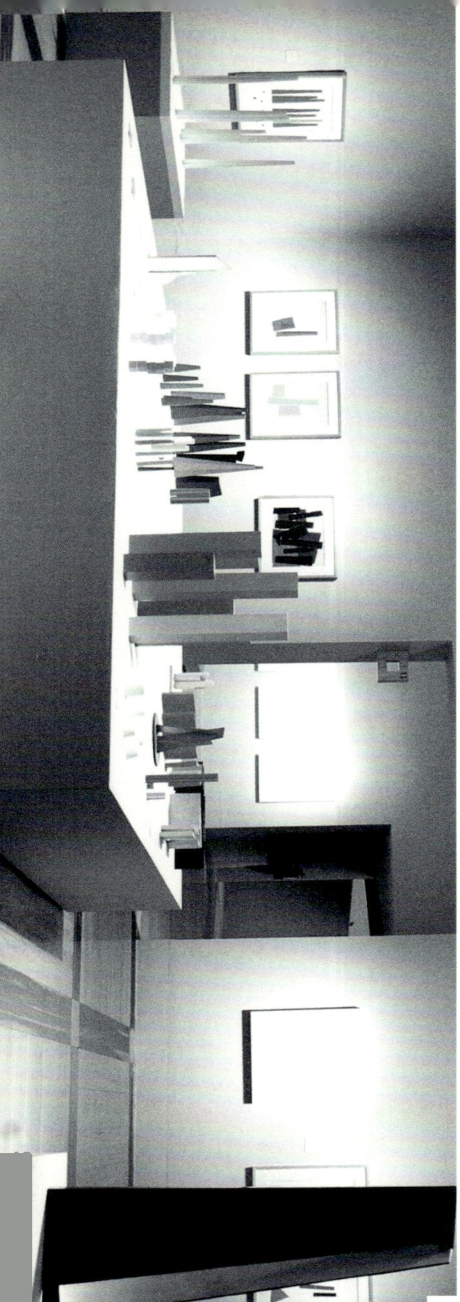

> Naturally, they are not as tall as I had imagined them at first. Also there are only five, instead of seven; the square itself is different and narrower than I would have liked, and even the color of one of the towers was changed. But here it was, at last, a monumental work the sole function of which should be emotion. . . . Architects insist that the towers are nothing but a large sculpture, and they are right. But what does it matter. For me they are painting, sculpture, emotional architecture. And I would have liked to have placed small flutes in the corners so the traveler on the road would hear a strange song caused by a million sounds in the wind.[16]

The significance of the Towers obviously exceeds the issue of scale, as well as their dubious status as a precursor of Minimalism. They are perfectly postmodern, even though they are inspired in part by Goeritz's transcendental and mystifying modernism. Like *El Eco*, they broke the boundaries between sculpture and architecture—in this case, as a work of art conceived from the position of a viewer in an automobile (a motorized viewer, if you will) and understood in formal terms as an intervention into the built environment.

Although it may be inaccurate to define the Towers as a precursor of Minimalism, they do share certain features with works associated with that movement. For example, they imply "the death of the author" by positioning the viewer as an active constructor of meaning. The viewer's perceptual experience as he or she approaches and then speeds past the site is an intrinsically mobile one—it is the perspective of the moving vehicle, the automobile, the airplane. This experience would have been different had Goeritz accepted Barragán's proposal to create a mirror of water at the foot of the Towers. In fact, their location—in the middle of the Querétaro highway—emphasizes Mexico City as a modern city planned for vehicular traffic, thus breaking with its colonial past and the modes of social interaction it fostered. A kinetic power pulses through the Towers. Their very shape was designed to accelerate the perspective of approaching a monumental mass at high speed,[17] and there is nothing like these towers in the referential perimeter of Minimalism.

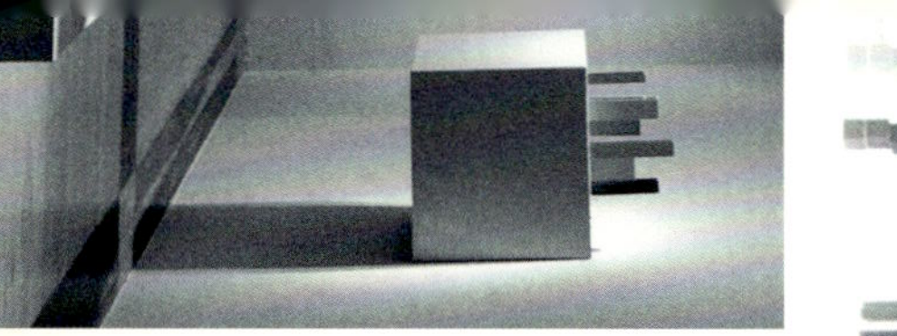

Models of Tower Prototypes 1955–82

After Goeritz completed the Towers he created numerous works in which he further explored the formal issues that they raised. These works include maquettes in several versions, such as *Do It Yourself* (1960–61), as well as architectural constructions, including his house in Temixco, a town in the state of Morelos (1957). In this house, he incorporated under a roof seven tower-obelisks, twenty-three feet tall, arranged in a random order. He also made other towers inspired by polygonal stars, such as *Osa Mayor* (Big Dipper, 1968) in Mexico City, and silos, such as *Torres de Automex* (Towers of Automex, 1963–64) in Toluca, in collaboration with Ricardo Legorreta.

The Sculptural Space

In collaboration with Helen Escobedo, Manuel Felguérez, Hersúa, Sebastián, and Federico Silva

Mexico City, 1978–79

El Espacio Escultórico (The Sculptural Space) is one of the most ambitious collaborative works that Goeritz conceived and coordinated. Constructed on the campus of the Centro Cultural Universitario (University Cultural Center) in Mexico City on a terrain of craggy volcanic rock, it is a circular band with an outer diameter of 394 feet and an inner diameter of 321 feet. On top of the band are sixty-four triangular prisms of reinforced concrete, each thirteen feet high. It is impressive not only because of its colossal size and its strange presence in the landscape, but also because it defines a complex spatial experience that cannot be understood within the categories of Land art, Minimalist sculpture, or public art.

It is impossible to speak of *The Sculptural Space* without referencing another major collaborative project that Goeritz coordinated, *La ruta de la amistad* (The Road of Friendship, 1968).[18] If *The Road of Friendship* used the city as an exhibition space and its thoroughfares as visual corridors, *The Sculptural*

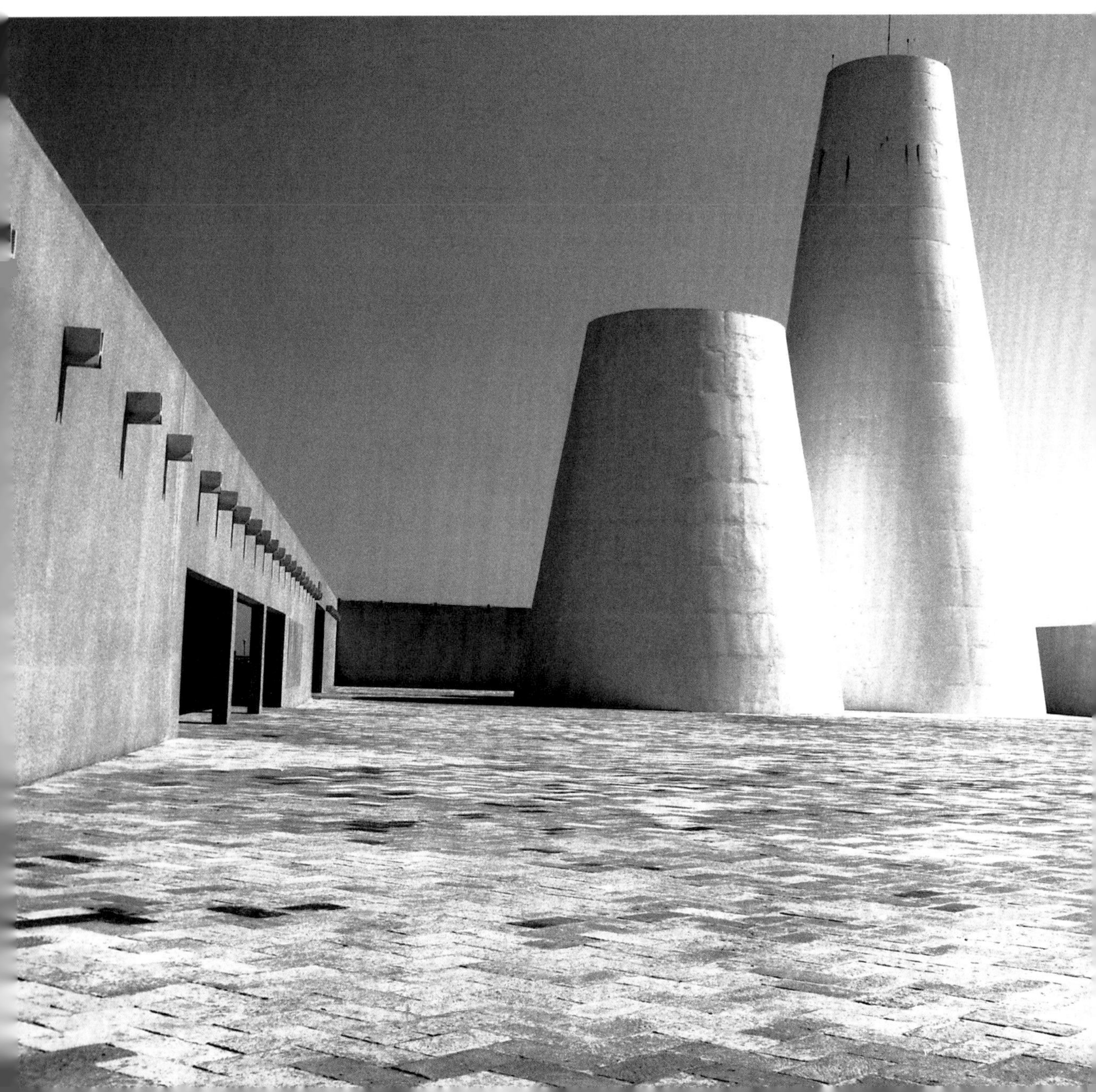

Space, for the first time in the history of the avant-garde in Mexico, questioned on a large scale the relationship between nature and culture through a transcendent architectural-sculptural expression.

Like many of Goeritz's most important works, *The Sculptural Space* stands in relationship to the legacy of Muralism, that tyrannical paradigm of Mexican modernity. Jorge Carpizo, then Coordinator of Humanities of the Universidad National Autónoma de México (National Autonomous University of Mexico) had proposed, at the suggestion of the sculptor Federico Silva, "a project comparable to Muralism" that would express the significance of the monumental geometric sculptural movement in Mexico "as an example of modernization."[19] The project needed to be "monumental" in order to demonstrate that Mexico was still an artistic powerhouse and to legitimate that generation of sculptors, deriving from the Ruptura, obsessed with industrial materials and varnishes, abstract forms, modularity, and heroic proportions. Both symbolically and conceptually, *The Sculptural Space* was the tomb of Muralism, the end of Mexico's modernity.

Rather miraculously, Goeritz assembled a group of very different artistic figures to develop *The Sculptural Space*, which in formal terms could be understood as the decalogue of Minimalism. It was perhaps his last lesson to a generation fascinated by the less analytical aspects of reductionist aesthetics. Helen Escobedo, the pioneer of Land art in Mexico, was interested in intervening in the landscape. Manuel Felguérez contributed the silence of his own sculptural aesthetic. Hersúa had a taste for the grandeur of pre-Columbian urban design. Sebastián brought an enthusiasm for monumentality. And Federico Silva brought an esoteric inclination and a cosmic vision. Yet, in spite of the scale of the project, the fact that it is experienced as a journey, and its location in the landscape, it lies very far from the Minimalist perimeter.[20]

To travel *The Sculptural Space* is to activate, through the physical experience of interacting with it, the underlying anthropological, ecological, and

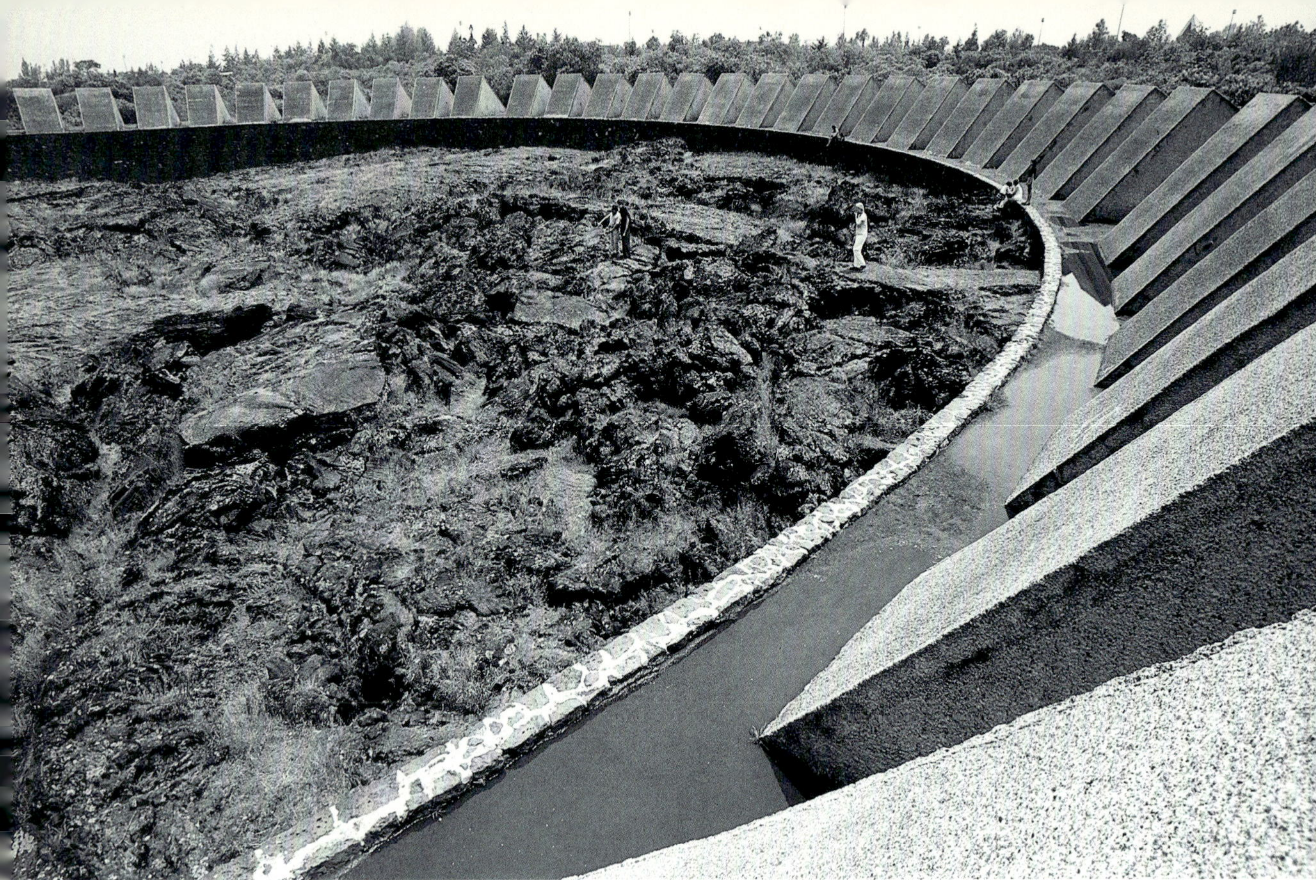

Two views of ***The Sculptural Space*** 1979

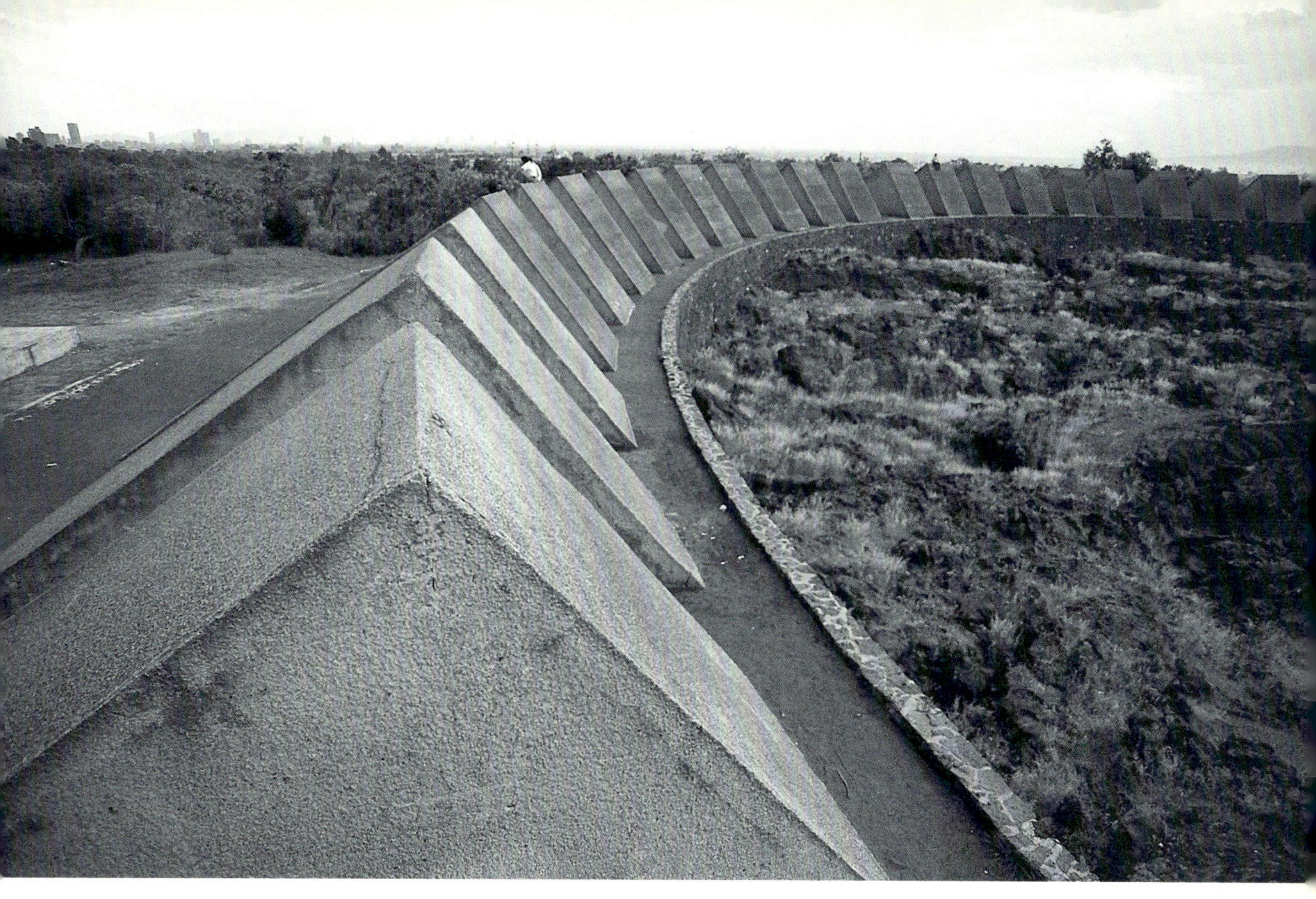

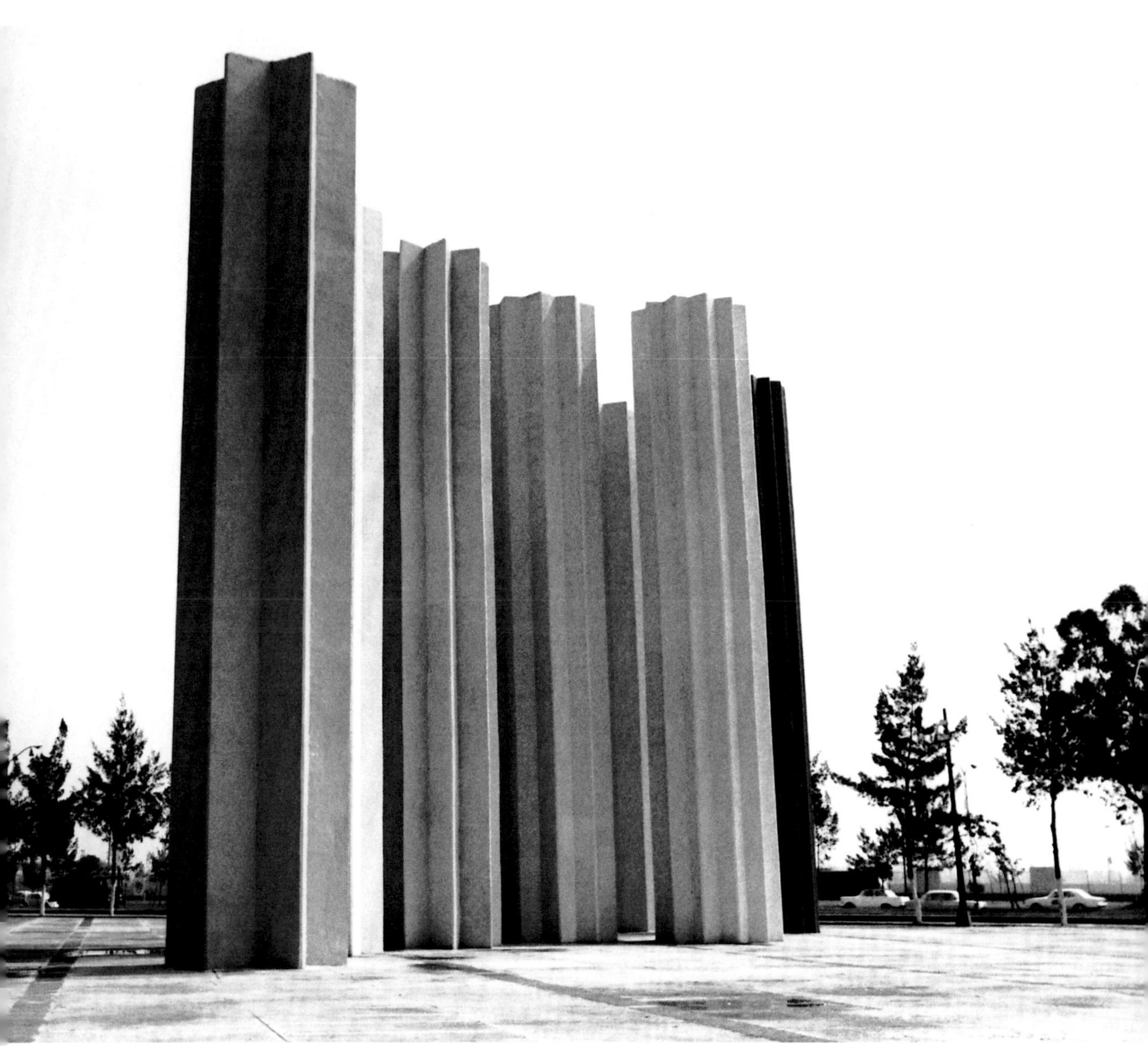

La Osa Mayor 1968

psychological dimensions of a tectonic articulation in the landscape, which is confronted not only by the viewer's social and cultural context but also by the skyline of one of the largest and most polluted cities in the world. Its location on the university's campus, in an area of desert volcanic rock that is presently an ecological reserve, connected the project to the ancient pyramids of Mexico, many of which incorporate rock of similar weight, texture, and color (monuments that revealed to Goeritz mystical emotion on a new scale), as well to more modern monuments such as Barragán's Jardines del Pedregal (Gardens of Pedregal). To see *The Sculptural Space* from above, with the city behind wrapped in a mist of ozone, is a moving and apocalyptic vision. To be in the middle of the circle is an atavistic experience of uncontrolled telluric flow, an experience of disembodiment of the sort produced by the hallucinogen peyote. Goeritz materialized the concept of an emotional architecture as a concrete physical experience with *The Sculptural Space*—a place from which it is perhaps still possible to learn to fly, or at least to shift our sight upwards.

Translated by Isabelle Marmasse

Notes

1 Paul Virilio, "Open Sky," in *La Vitesse de libération* (Paris: Ed. Galileé, 1995), 13.

2 Andrea Giunta, "Correspondencia entre Mathias Goeritz y Jorge Romero Brest," in *Los ecos de Mathias Goeritz: Ensayos y testimonios*, ed. Ida Rodríguez Prampolini and Ferruccio Asta (Mexico City: Instituto de Investigaciones Estéticas, UNAM, 1997), 223.

3 Thomas M. Messer, *The Emergent Decade: Latin American Painters and Painting in the 60's*, exh. cat. (New York: Solomon R. Guggenheim Museum, 1966). This exhibition included eighty paintings by fifty-five artists from eight countries. Its precedent was the exhibition "Latinoamérica: Nuevos puntos de partida," presented at the Institute of Contemporary Art in Boston in 1960.

4 The *Ruptura* (Rupture) refers to the break with the Muralist tradition that emerged in Mexican art in the 1950s and 1960s in the work of artists such as Carlos Mérida, Vicente Rojo, Rufino Tamayo, and others.

5 The Escuela de Altamira was a loose association of artists inspired by the example of the cave paintings of Altamira and the work of artists such as Joan Miro and Paul Klee. It organized the Primer Semana de Arte Moderno (First Week of Modern Art) in Santillana del Mar and produced a publication entitled *Los nuevos prehistóricos*. See Hilda Urréchaga Hernández, "Mathias Goeritz, promotor de la renovación artística en España: La Escuela de Altamira," in *Los ecos de Mathias Goeritz: Ensayos y testimonios*, 46–55.

6 Many other Mexican artists were not properly recognized because they did not participate in the nationalistic aesthetics of Muralism. This was the case not only with Frida Kahlo, but also Agustín Lazo, Carlos Mérida, Alfonso Michel, and Germán Cueto, among others.

7 Fernando González Gortázar observes that Goeritz consciously applied Herbert Bayer's contributions to typographical design in the Escuela de Arquitectura de la Universidad de Guadalajara. Examining later works by Goeritz, one can calibrate the extent of this influence. For example, there are similarities between parts of Bayer's *El jardín de mármol* (1955) and *Towers of Satellite City*. On the other hand, Bayer was deeply marked by Goeritz's work; his *Pirámides inclinadas* (1967), *La carretera de pirámides reclinadas* (1972), and *Levantamiento gentil* (1972), as well as many other plans for highways, are a pristine secretion of Goeritz's work. Finally, it would have been difficult for Goeritz to venture into concrete poetry had he not had the precedent of Bayer and his study of new alphabets.

8 "The School of Altamira mobilizes against the mechanization of art, against the elaborate encouragement of difficulty as a forced primitivism and affected simplicity." Ricardo Gullón, quoted in Lily Kassner, *Mathias Goeritz: Una biografía* (Mexico: Instituto de Investigaciones Estéticas, UNAM, 1998), 253 (Appendix II, "Anotaciones sobre la Escuela de Altamira").

9 Quoted in ibid., 239.

10 Mauricio Gómez Margoya, "Sobre la libertad de creación," *Arquitectura/México* (Mexico City), no. 45 (1954).

11 Mathias Goeritz, quoted in Natalia Carriazo, "El eco: Una ecuación del movimiento," in *Los ecos de Mathias Goeritz: Catálogo de la exposición*, exh. cat. (Mexico City: Instituto Nacional de Bellas Artes, Antiguo Colegio de San Ildefonso, Instituto de Investigaciones Estéticas, 1997), 98.

12 Interview with Enrique de Anda, 2 July 1987, quoted in *Los ecos*, 95.

13 Juan O'Gorman was one of Goeritz's allies in the defense of a modern Mexican architecture, and his texts characterizing the basis for this new architecture could serve as statements for Goeritz himself regarding *El Eco*. In *La palabra de Juan O'Gorman* (Mexico: UNAM, 1983), 188, O'Gorman claims that this new Mexican architecture "is characterized by pyramidal shapes in the compositions, by the three-dimensional exaggeration of volume, by the movement of its faces, in many cases inclined, which give architecture a further dimension in space; by the dynamic asymmetry of its axes, by the complexity and variety of its decoration, by the profuseness and richness of its shape and color, and by the supreme manner in which, as a whole, it harmonizes with the land where it is built."

14 Mathias Goeritz, quoted in Ferruccio Asta, "Arte urbano y arquitectura emocional," in *Los ecos*, 110.

15 This dispute did not discourage Goeritz from participating in other collaborative projects, which constitute the most extraordinary contribution of his career.

16 Ida Rodríguez Prampolini, "Mi encuentro con Mathias," *Revista de la Escuela Nacional de Artes* (Mexico City) 3, no. 13–14 (1991–92): 68.

17 Juan Acha, in Kassner, 107.

18 Ten years after completing *Towers of Satellite City*, Goeritz insisted on the idea of building unusual monuments for viewers in automobiles. For the 29th Olympic Games, held in Mexico City in 1968, he was appointed Artistic Counselor of the Organizing Committee. Before inaugurating the project *The Road of Friendship*, he organized an International Symposium on Sculpture, from which emerged numerous proposals that would be installed along a ten-mile stretch of the southern part of the peripheral ring road. The project consisted of eighteen sculptures made by fifteen artists from five continents; the size of the sculptures varied from approximately eighteen to sixty-four feet. Today, the supposed monumentality of the sculptures is barely a third of the size of the porticos of the large corporate buildings that have recently turned the south of the city into a financial, business, and middle-class residential area. In "Escultura y urbanismo: *La Ruta de la Amistad* en la Ciudad de México," *Excelsior* (Mexico City), 18 August 1968, sec. Urbe., 7B), Goeritz stated that the route "departs from the concept of art for art's sake and can make contact with the masses." Years later he recognized in the project "a rachitic result," as he observed in "Opinión sobre arte urbano," *Artes Visuales* (Mexico City), no. 8 (1975).

19 Elda Maceda, "Carpizo narró la historia del *Espacio Escultórico*," *El Universal* (Mexico City), 19 June 1991.

20 During that time the galleries and public parks of Mexico City were filled with hundreds of ornamental horrors deriving from this 1950s-style fantasy of progress and encouraged by the political figure of the "official commission."

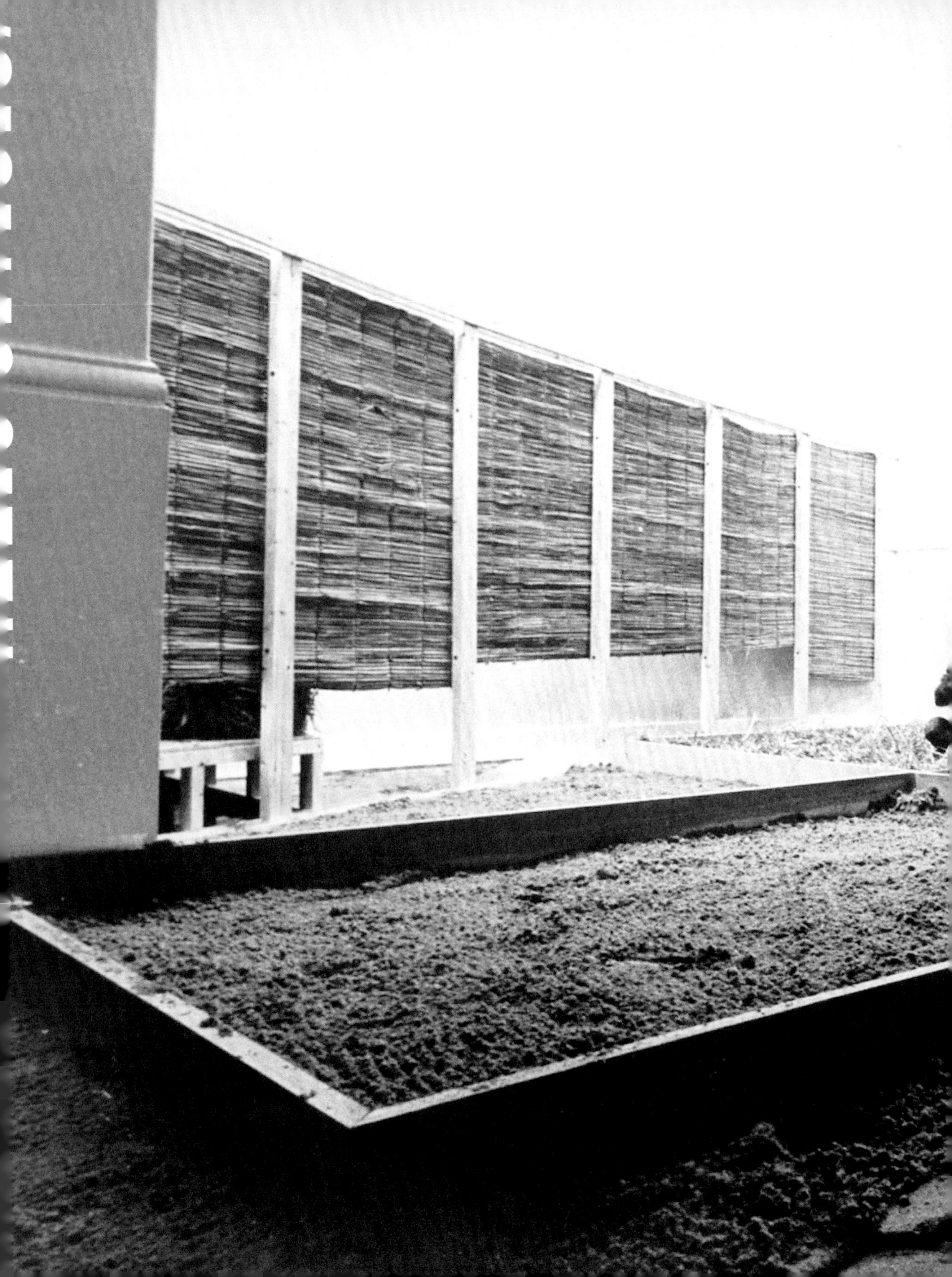

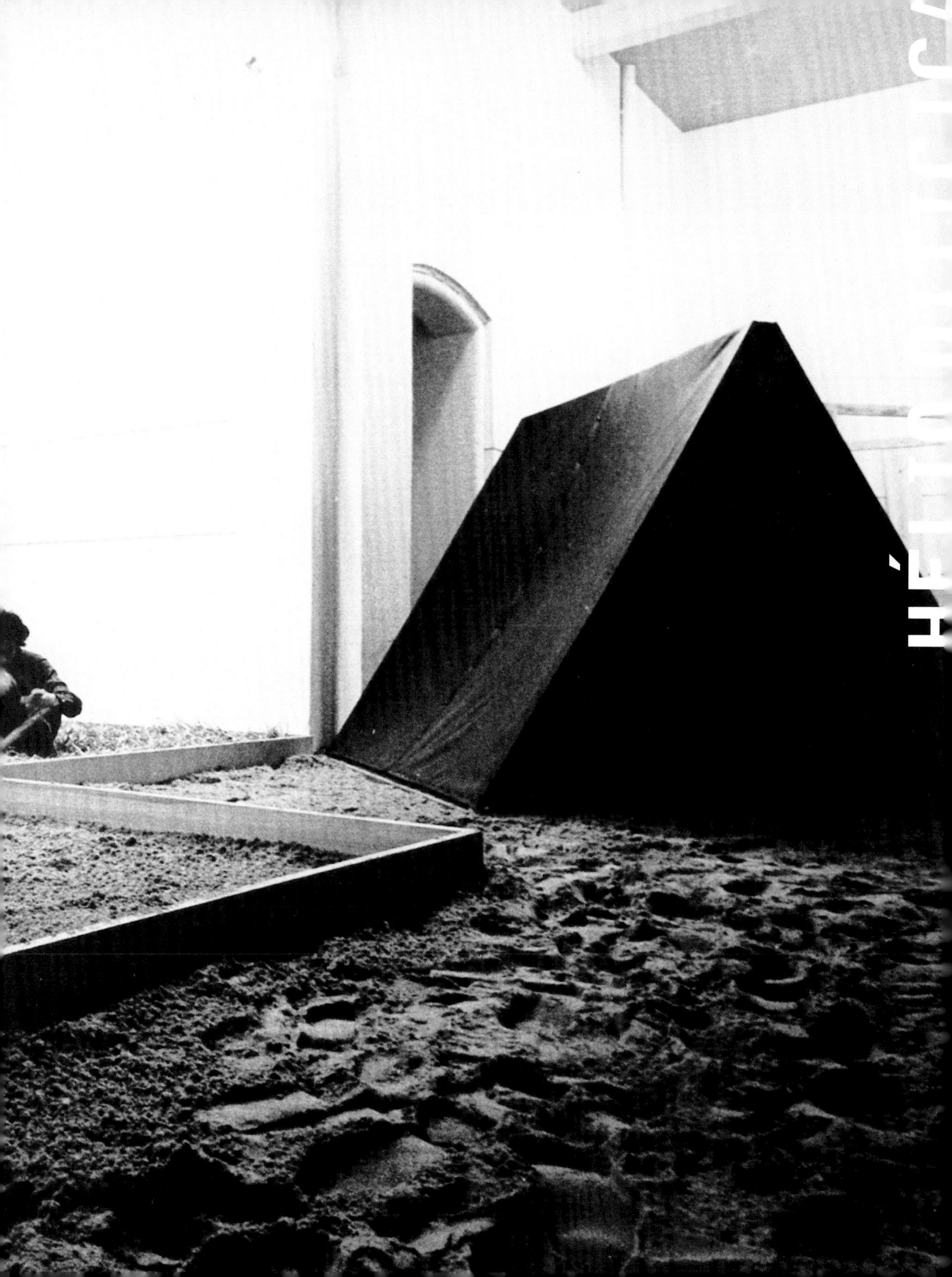

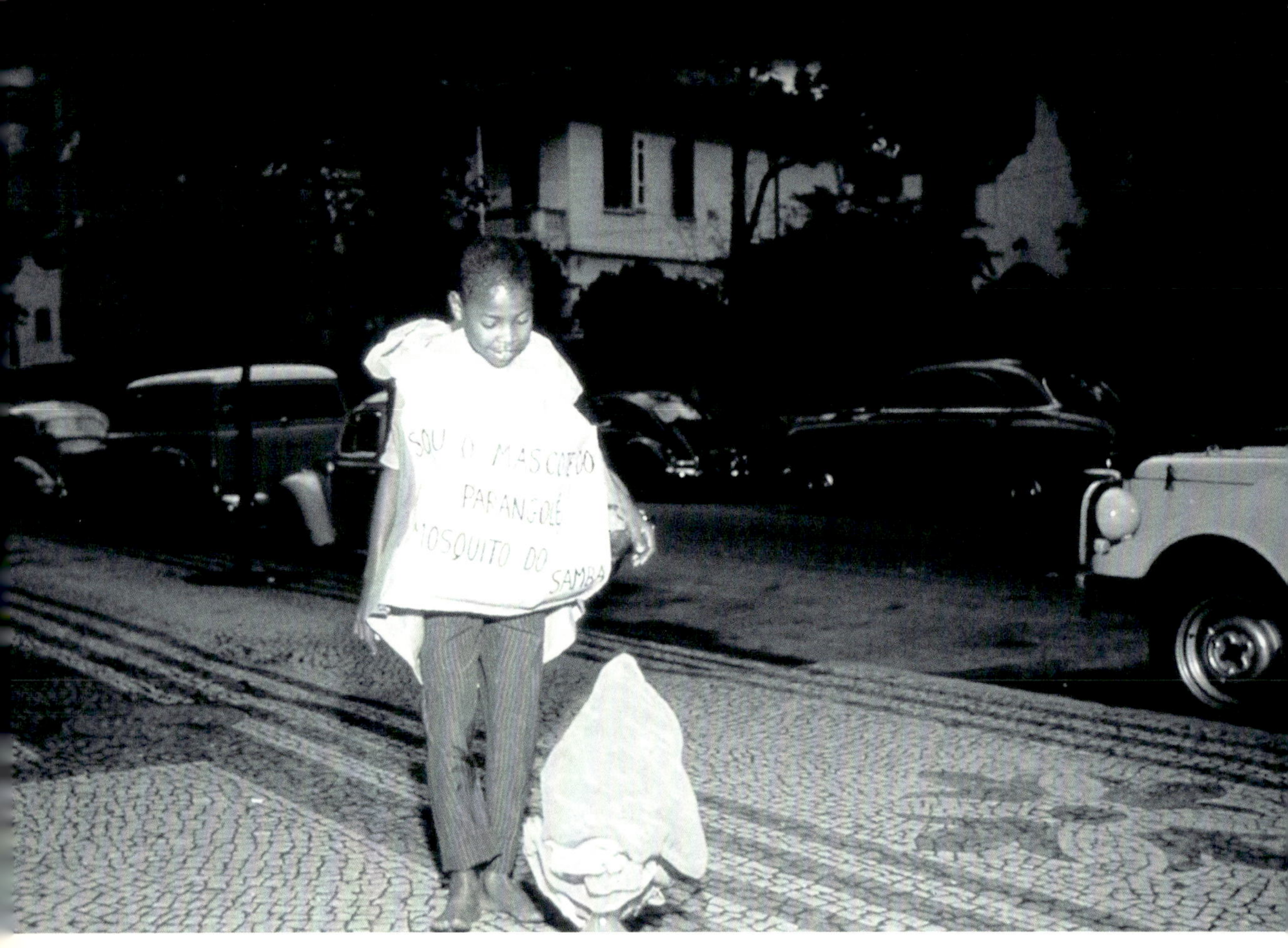

PRECEDING PAGE: ***Bólide área 1*** and ***2***, ***Penetrable PN5 Caetano-Gil Tent*** in ***Eden*** 1969

Mosquito of Mangueira dancing with ***Parangolé P10 Cape 6*** with ***Glass Bólide 5 (Homage to Mondrian)*** 1965

HÉLIO OITICICA:

Brazil Experiment

Catherine David

Despite the fact that it has been almost twenty years since Hélio Oiticica's untimely death—he was forty-three when he died in Rio de Janeiro in 1980—his work has only recently begun to receive worldwide recognition. Following the first international retrospective of his work, which was presented in Rotterdam, Paris, Barcelona, Lisbon, and Minneapolis in 1992 and 1993, there have been many individual and group shows of Oiticica's work in Brazil, of course, but primarily in Europe and in the United States, where a new audience has been introduced to his artwork. In the late fifties he had garnered the interest and respect of many artists and intellectuals connected to the *Concretismo* (Concretism) and *Neoconcretismo* (Neoconcretism) groups in São Paulo and Rio; he was, in fact, a major figure in the Brazilian avant-garde, and he largely inspired the *Tropicalismo* Movement in the sixties and seventies. Oiticica was so influential in Brazilian cultural life, that, along with his contemporary Glauber Rocha (1939–1981)—whose brief, intense life and creative trajectory are remarkably close to Oiticica's[1]—he was one of the most inspired and turbulent "seismographs"[2] of Brazilian culture. In addition, his work was quickly embraced by London's avant-garde community after Guy Brett organized the 1969 exhibition "Whitechapel Experience" around *Eden* (1969) at the Whitechapel Gallery. In New York, where the artist lived from the end of 1970 to the beginning of 1978, except for his part in the rock-music scene and his involvement with a certain kind of experimental cinema, he conspicuously kept to the margins of the art world, participating officially only in the Museum of Modern Art's "Information" exhibition, which was organized by Kynaston McShine in 1970.

Nevertheless, it seems that if current and future shows of Oiticica's work (including reconstructions of such works as *Eden*, as well as unedited constructions from plans and projects such as *Cosmococas* [1973]) are to grasp the scope of the ambitions of an exceptional body of work which for a long time has remained on the margins of the hegemonic axis of U.S.–European legitimation, these exhibitions must serve as the occasion for a new reading of the work's strategies and its radical cultural and political

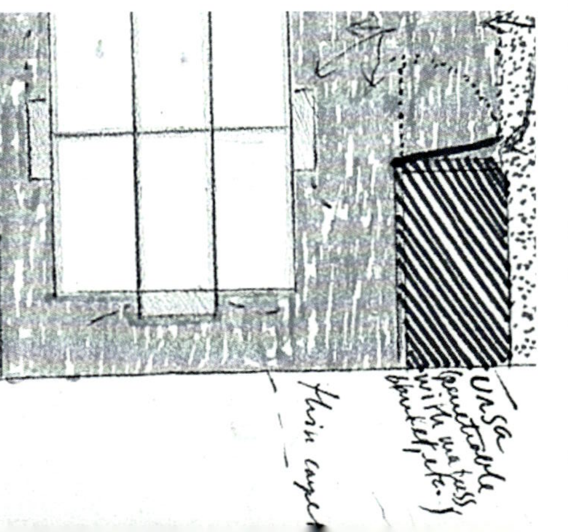

Drawing of ***The Eden Plan, Whitechapel Experience***, Whitechapel Gallery, London 196

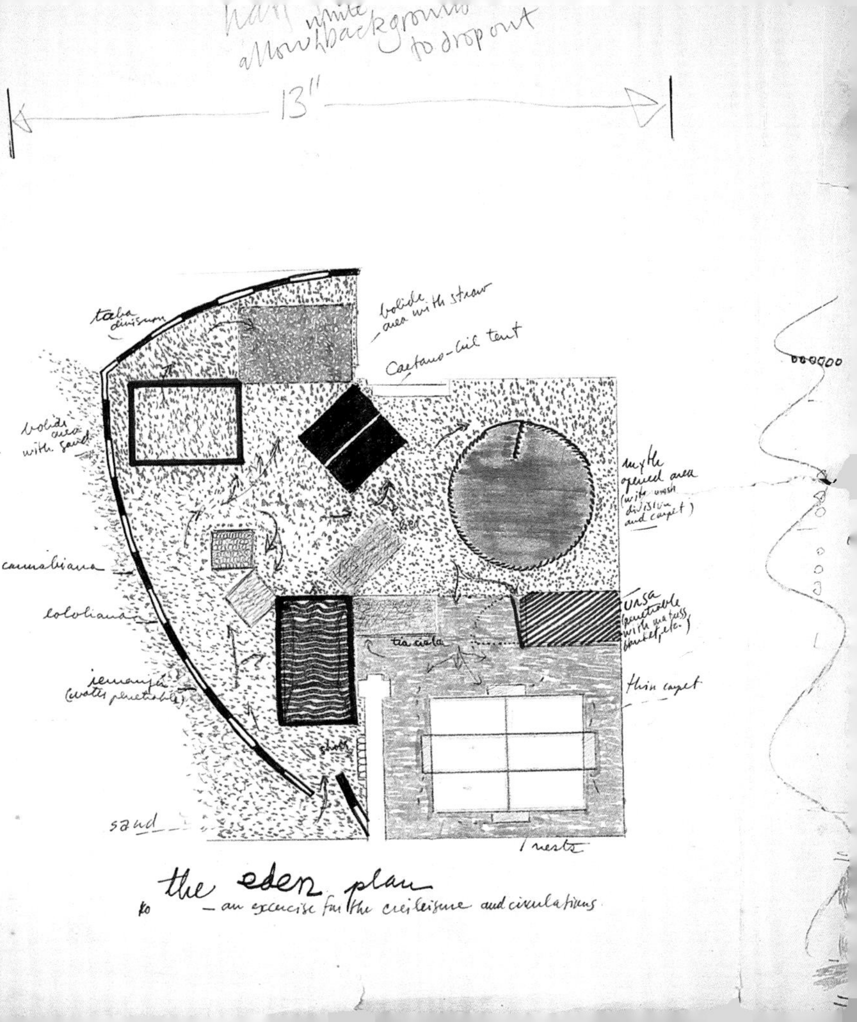

allow background to drop out
13"
taba division
bolide area with straw
Caetano-Gil tent
bolide area with sand
myth opened area (with wash division and carpet)
cannabiana
lololiana
tia ciata
ursa (penetrable with matress, blanket, etc.)
iemanjá (water penetrable)
thin carpet
sand
nests
the eden plan
— an exercise for the creleisure and circulations

project. Such a reading must take into account the recent remarkable analyses of Oiticica's work by Brazilian authors interested in its anthropological dimensions and its original inscription within the anthropophagic antitradition discussed by Celso Favaretto and Suely Rolnik. Oiticica's aim was to enact, in Brazil and elsewhere, "a transformative perspective, on the triple plane of ethics, society, and politics"[3] by problematizing the individual, social, cultural, and political conditions and the alienated culture and aesthetic experience in an economically underdeveloped country; at the same time, by displacing the aesthetic experience of the world and of art and extending it out toward the quotidian, contingent, and accidental aspects of lived experience—"*vivência*," to borrow one of the key words of the Brazilian lexicon during those years—he hoped to give a *participating* subject, who would no longer be a more or less passive spectator, the freedom to invent "his" world.

Above and beyond the works, plans, documents, and archives kept today almost in their entirety by the Projeto Hélio Oiticica in Rio de Janeiro, it is most certainly Oiticica's original and complex critical practice, developed within the "adversity"[4] and specific context of Brazilian culture and the countercultures of the sixties and seventies, which still needs to be clarified. Extending beyond the scope of the somewhat narrow field of the plastic arts, Oiticica's oeuvre can be properly understood only from the standpoint of current discussions of cultural criticism and aesthetic anthropology which it anticipates.

It is not irrelevant that Hélio Oiticica's work developed amidst the cultural effervescence of Brazil in the late 1950s. It would be checked forcibly by the toughening of the military regime in 1968 and the enforced repression of the Medici government's "black years," during which time constitutional rights were suspended by Institutional Act No. 5 (AI5), the number of kidnappings increased, and torture was practiced systematically. The 1960 inauguration of Brasília, the new federal capital relocated to the very heart of the country, marked the height of dreams of futuristic development and the possible self-rule of a nation of vast size at a time when the people's will to social and

Nests in ***Eden, Whitechapel Experience***, Whitechapel Gallery, London 1969

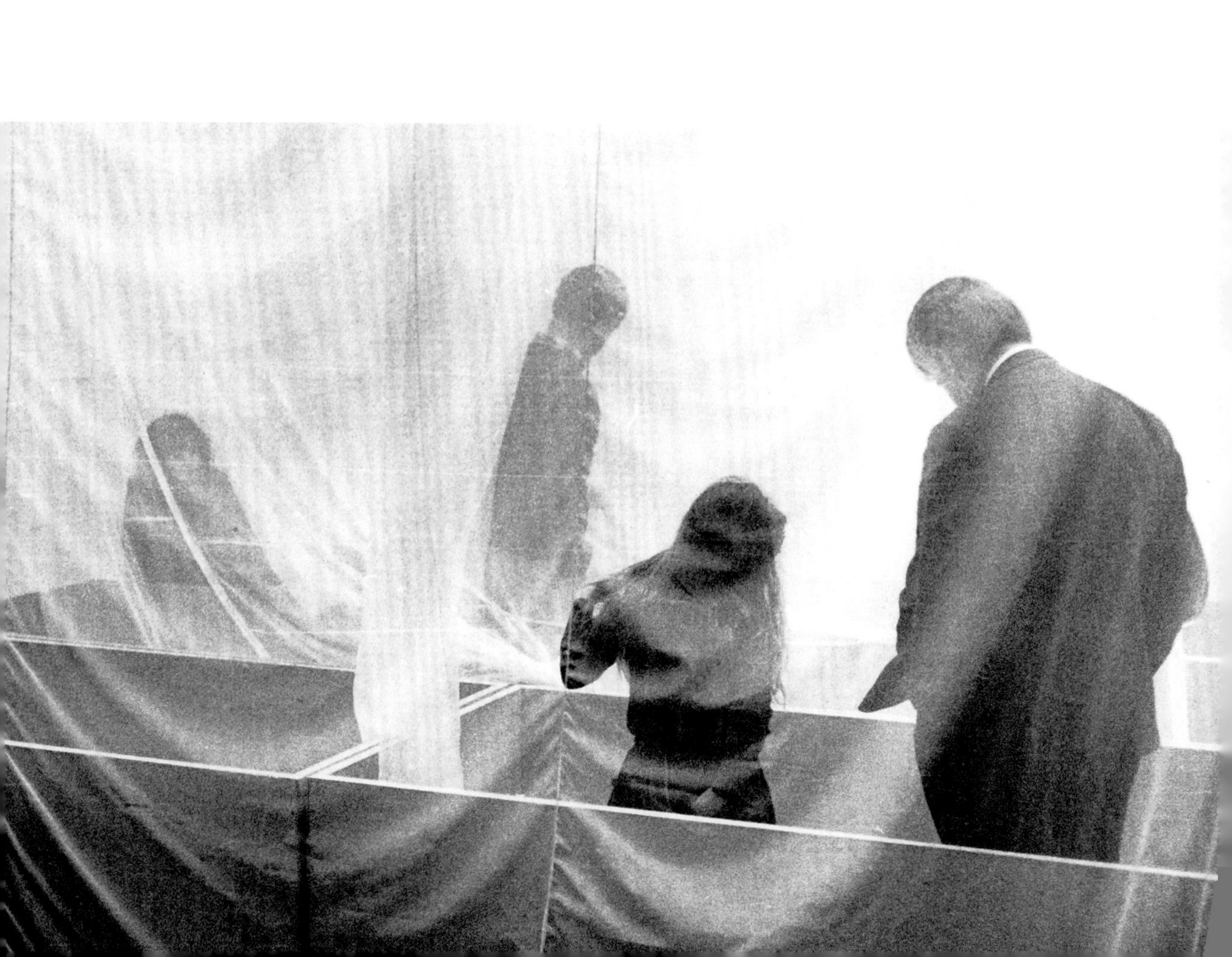

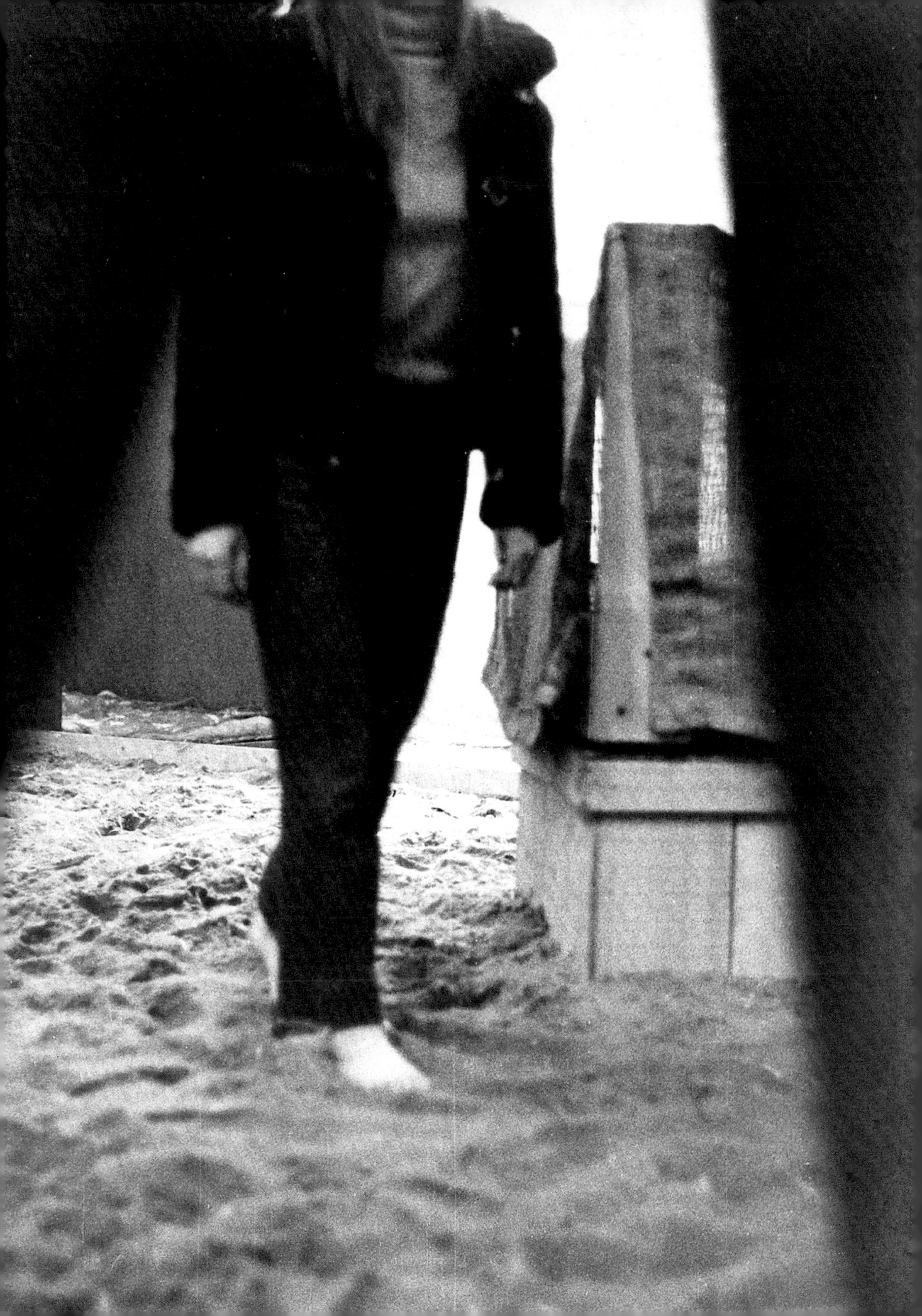

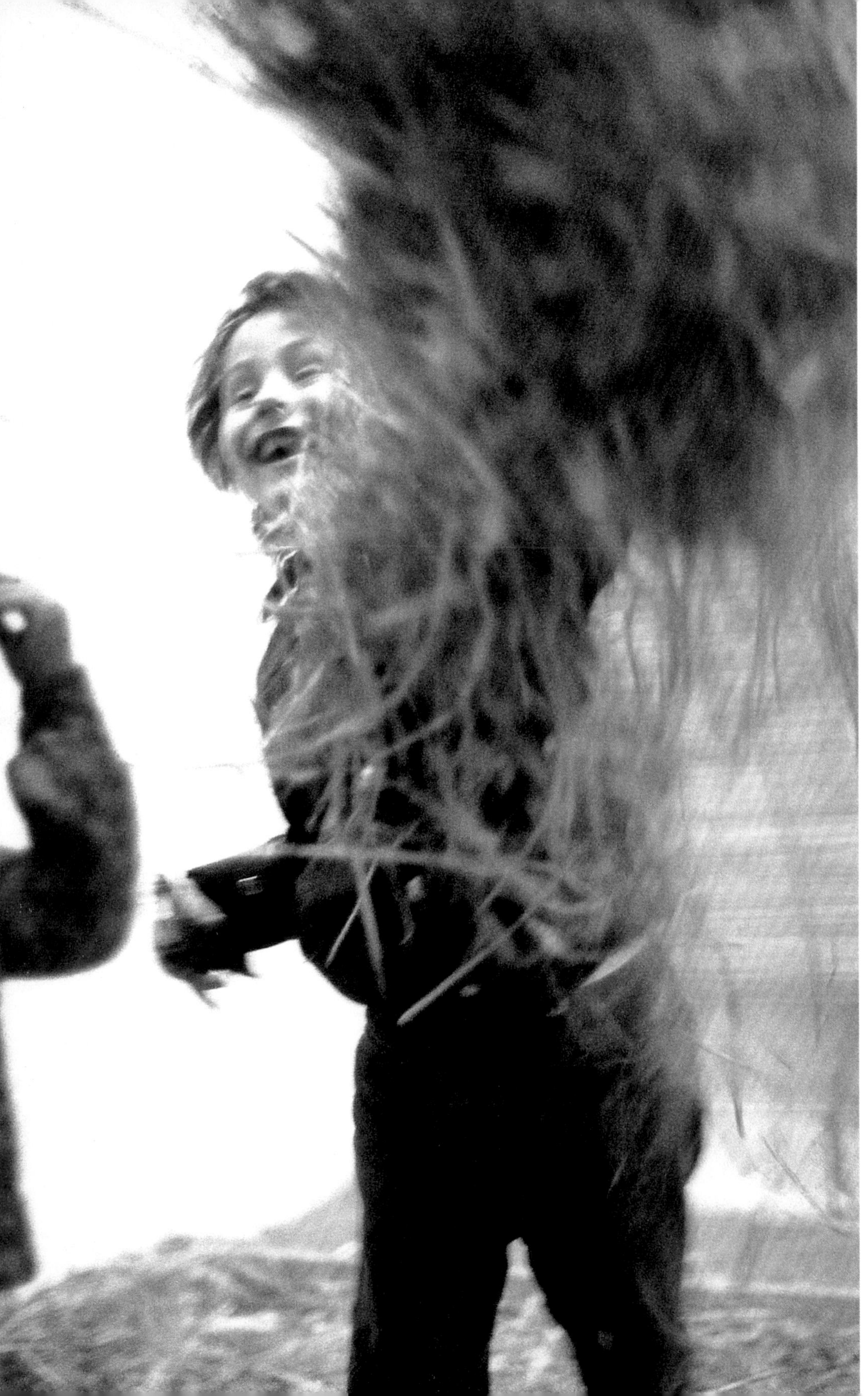

cultural reform was just beginning to assert itself. To change culture so as to transform society, to rethink the function of art and the conditions of its experience—these were the ambitions of an entire generation of artists and intellectuals, a generation in search of images and an idiom capable of translating the complex processes of identification at work within Brazilian culture and society in order to create the conditions for a living culture and community. The *Neoconcretismo* movement developing in poetry and the plastic arts "simultaneously marked the apogee of a constructive mentality in Brazil along with its explosion"[5] in experimental practices that more directly involved the spectator's body and subjectivity and their interactions within social space.

Oiticica explicitly laid claim to and rigorously assumed the complexity of these scenes of intervention, as well as the marginality of the conditions of production and distribution of his work within the national and international artistic context of this period. In this way, Oiticica, whose work Favaretto described as "a free circulation between diverse determinations of artistic practice,"[6] risked relative "invisibility" within the offical institutional contemporary art scene, but he also bet on the permanent inscription of a radically critical thought and action within Brazilian culture and modern art. This specific dimension of his work appears more and more clearly upon reading his many texts—various programs, articles, interviews, letters, notes, and drafts—which investigate, accompany, and comment on an incessant and plural artistic activity. This corpus, which unfortunately is thus far only partially published and translated, reconstructs the development and complexity of an ethical-aesthetic activity and discourse of which the "object [of art]" was not the ultimate aim and in which the museum did not function as the privileged destination; today, even in the best cases, museums will simply preserve an incomplete and easily fallacious memory if they are not able to activate and reinvent the conditions of the encounter between the "works" and the contemporary public.

THIS AND PRECEDING PAGE: ***Eden, Whitechapel Experience***, Whitechapel Gallery, London 1969

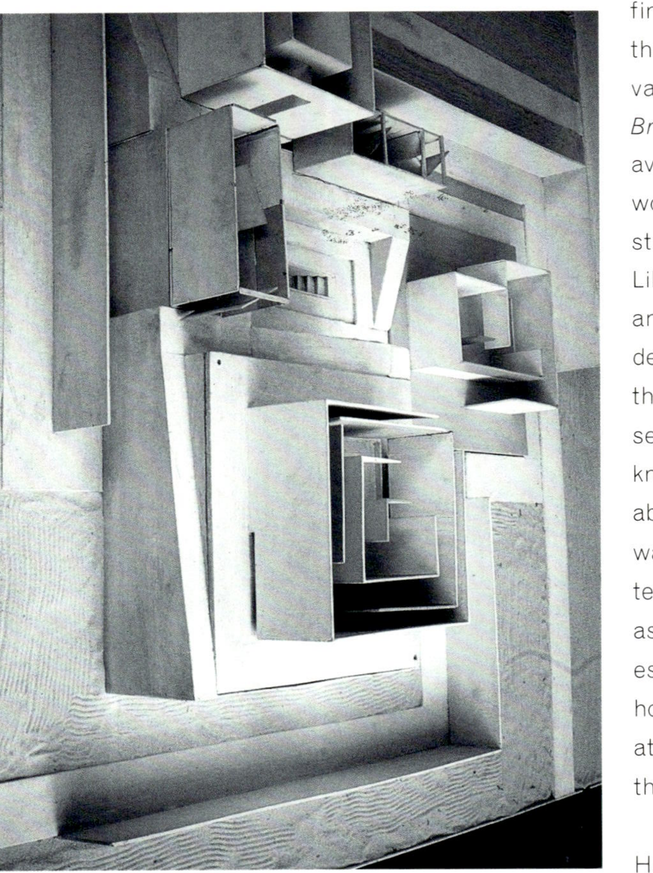

Model for ***Hunting Dogs Project*** (Detail) 1961

This theoretical and polemical body of work was also consciously and systematically archived. All the texts, including the letters and private exchanges, were copied several times using carbon paper and were then carefully organized in files, the titles and overall configuration of which transformed along with the evolution of Oiticica's work. Even though he didn't finish the collection of notes and texts he was working on in New York under the general title *Conglomerado* or *New Yorkaises*—which would have included various chapters concerning, notably, the *Block Experiments in Cosmococa*, *Brazil Experiment* (texts devoted to contemporary works of the Brazilian avant-garde), *Bodywise*, and *Nostalgia do corpo* (Nostalgia of the Body, on the work of Lygia Clark), he was still perfectly aware of the radical nature and the stakes of the rupture produced by his work within the fields of art and culture. Like the contemporary writings of Lygia Clark, Oiticica's texts serve an auto-analytic function: they are a notation and comprehension of the complex developments of a certain artistic and methodological procedure. In addition, they have a pedagogical dimension, both for himself and others, and they also serve as testimony for posterity, describing as they do an experience that he knew would not find immediate reception and in fact would remain unacceptable within the art and culture of his period for some time to come. Clark, who was seventeen years older than Oiticica, was a close friend and privileged interlocutor with whom he shared the experience of art as trangression as well as a rare sense of ethical and aesthetic exigency; they exchanged many letters essential to the definition and development of both their projects.[7] He also hoped that this testimony would protect him from present and future attempts at "mystifying the innovative character of [his] experiences by compromising them within inappropriate contexts."[8]

He summed up this project in his introduction to *subterranean* TROPICÁLIA PROJECTS, written in English in New York in September 1971 (by which time almost all of the work that was still "showable" in the more or less traditional conditions of the museum—and which has been shown in exhibitions organized in recent years—was complete):

> This series of projects relate to my former work from 1959 on; they are a consequence of the invention of what I call Penetrables (1960 on); all my work from that period on has been a development of the disintegration of formal concepts (starting with that of "painting" itself) of art, ultimately questioning the nature of the work of art, and looking for a form of non-contemplative contact; the participation of the spectator (or participator) touching, dressing, penetrating the actual pieces, developed towards actual propositions (propose to propose): something similar to practices of the spontaneous self, non-ritualistic, as an actual anti-art permanent position; the denial of the artist as a creator of objects, but turned into a proposer of practices in which ideas and discoveries are opened and nakedly suggested, and realize themselves in the course of such practices. This shows why the propositions in these projects are simple and general, not yet completed . . . shown as situations to be lived.[9]

A few years later in 1979, shortly before his death, he was interviewed for the last time by filmmaker Ivan Cardoso (who in making his documentary short *H.O.* was asking about the genesis and developments of Oiticica's work): "These things have led me forward; they're preludes. For me all these works have been the prelude of what I call the new, that which has to come. The new would arise when the inventive state I've attained emerges, and becomes a world, a solid and collective edifice. These things are a prelude to a collective state of invention."[10]

After twenty-five years of intense activity and a stay in New York devoted essentially to reflection, writing, and the conception of experimental projects with the many friends who visited or stayed in the Babylonests,[11] this provisional and paradoxical assessment in the form of "prelude," this inaugural sentiment of Oiticica's upon analyzing certain moments of his work and imagining other "situations" to come, is exemplary of the radical nature of his project; with the new spaces opened up by the environmental manifestations and the comportmental propositions resulting from his invention of the *Parangolé* in 1964, this project extended and displaced an aesthetic experience conditioned by the dominant culture and the system of art toward an individual and collective project of knowledge and transformation of oneself and the world.

From the first abstract-geometric paintings shown with the Grupo Frente in 1955 to the individual and collective "state of invention" (re)gained through an experimental work of exemplary rigor and precision, Oiticica's approach maintains a strict coherence. He was concerned with reactivating (or questioning) and actualizing the utopic, formal, and ethical project of the historical avant-gardes—namely, that which proposed forms and ideas capable of both transforming our relationship to the world and reconciling art and life. More specifically, he was interested in enacting this project within the cultural and political context of Brazil in the years between 1950 and 1970, in a country "condemned to modernity," in Mário Pedrosa's words.

Oiticica's visionary, emancipatory, and libertarian project is very clearly inscribed within the modern tradition of a radical critique of the traditional mediums and categories of art and the idea that aesthetics is "not the 'theory of art,' but the confrontation with the sensible which establishes a community."[12] Drawing upon the propositions of suprematism, constructivism, and Neoplasticism revisited and discussed by the *Concretismo* and *Neoconcretismo* groups with which he was involved at the end of the fifties, Oiticica retained the idea of "surpassing" painting and leaving behind the tableau in order to occupy real space; his specific aim was to more directly confront art and life, the works, and the spectators' bodies. From the beginning, his "experimental program" very closely associates production with theoretical, pedagogical, and polemical discourse, in an "organic whole" developed by "degrees." This concern with engaging the experimental, and indeed, its ethics—which he constantly emphasized by his use of the phrase "*experimentar o experimental*"—reflects a conception of aesthetic practice as the activity, process, and transformation both of culture and within culture: "There is no such thing as 'experimental art'; there is only 'the experimental,' and the experimental assumes not only the very idea of modern art and of the avant-garde, but also a radical transformation within the domain of current concept-values: it proposes transformations within the context of behavior, thereby swallowing up and dissolving *convi-convivência*."[13]

This important concept—the behavioral aspect of experimental art—is a forgotten (and often neglected) dimension of the work of the historical avant-gardes, whose "works" "museums of modern art" (appearing late on the scene) have preserved only in the form of "objects," forgetting or neglecting their performative and often participatory dimensions; Oiticica reactivates this dimension within the specific historical and cultural circumstances of the "nonmuseum culture" in Brazil at a time when few of the people had access to education and cultural institutions and when there was a relative absence or weakness of a "system" of established art institutions, galleries, and collectors. These specific cultural and social conditions undoubtedly provided Oiticica with a paradoxical freedom of intervention in terms of the places he presented his work, his modes of representation, and his encounter with and convocation of participating audiences.

In his work and in his life Oiticica combined a rigorous method and strict discipline with a "dissolution of the senses" via the samba trance, use of drugs, "delirium," or "ecstasy" through which he experienced, in a secular and programmed way, certain archaic rituals of initiation, as well as Eastern spiritual belief systems such as Zen (for example, in his concepts *Suprasensorial* and *Crelazer*). As his friend and occasional collaborator Haroldo de Campos remarked:

> He had an extremely complex intellectual side; this was someone who, remarkably, and in his personal life as well, made an extreme, meticulous, almost Cartesian concern with organization—(just look at his files, his way of structuring the entire production)—coexist with another side of his life which was intensely free, almost Rimbaudian: he put himself through all sorts of trials, bringing his body to the limits of vital experience; order and chaos coexisted in him, and he succeeded in a certain way, as Pierre Boulez would say, at organizing delirium.[14]

Oiticica's work and life partake in one and the same process of emancipation from all subjective, cultural, and social conditionings. Even the articulation of the terms that describe the successive concepts and sequences of his

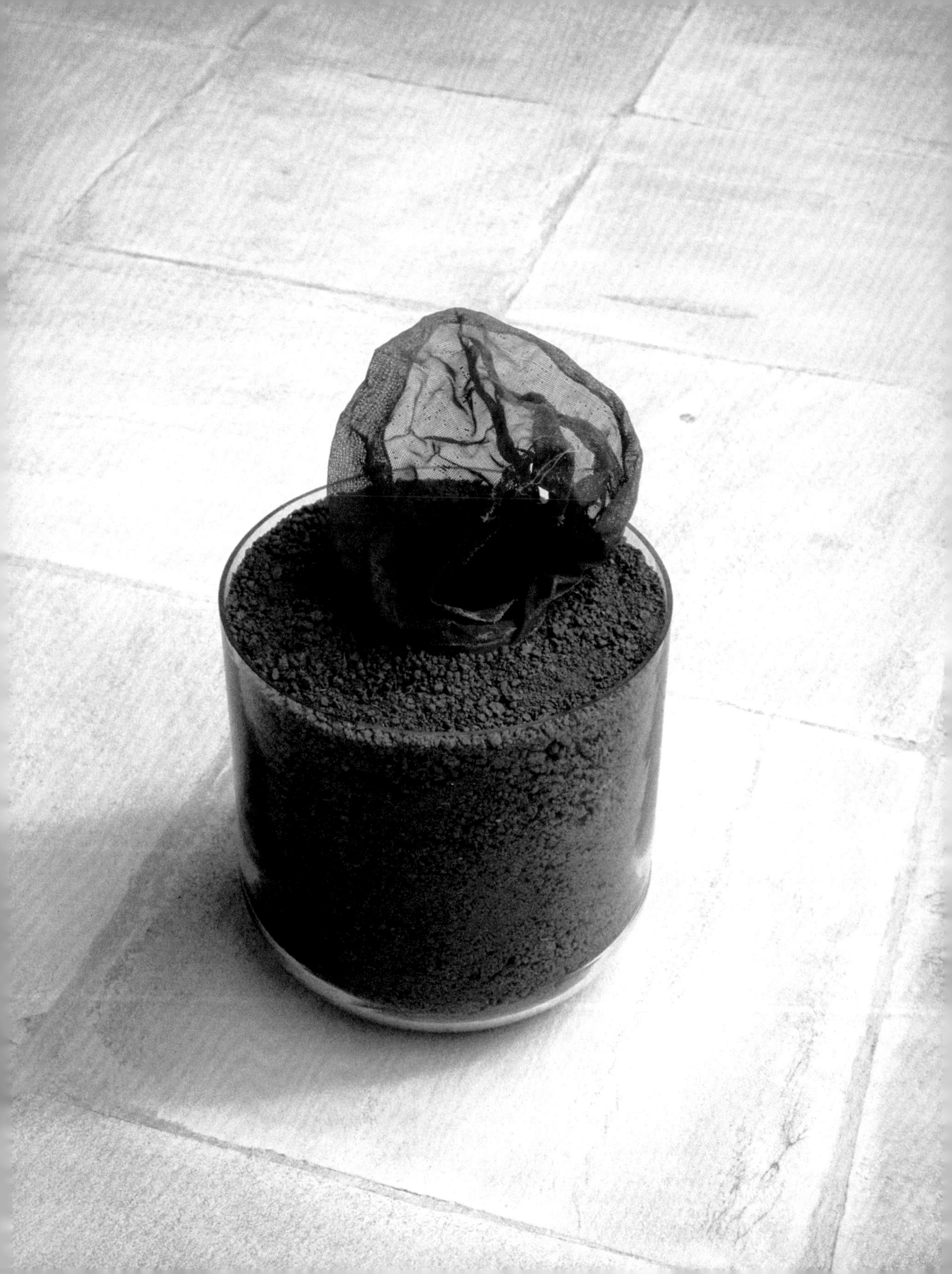

"program in progress" reflects the organic nature of its development, as well as the intellectual and sensible "new orders" or new territories that he wanted to see arise in the aesthetic act and experience: *Metaesquemas*, *Invenções* (Inventions), *Bilaterais* (Bilaterals), *Relêvos espaciais* (Spatial Reliefs), *Núcleos* (Nucleus), *Penetráveis* (Penetrables), *Bólides (Caixa* [Box], *Vidro* [Glass], *Cama* [Bed]), *Transobjetos* (Transobjects), *Parangolés (Capas* [Capes], *Tendas* [Tents], *Estandartes* [Banners], *Bandeiras* [Flags], *Faixas/Parangolé poetico* [Bands, strips, ribbons/Poetic *Parangolé*], *Parangolé social o de protesto* [Social/Protest *Parangolé*], *Parangolé lúdico* [Playful *Parangolé*]), *Manifestações ambientais* (Environmental Manifestations), *Apropriações* (Appropriations), *Tropicália, Suprasensorial, Crelazer, Projeto* (Project), *Apocalipopótese, Eden, Ninhos* (Nests), *Barracão* (Tent/Shed), *Não-narrativas*, (Non-narratives) *Cosmococa, Quase cinema, Subterrânia* (Subterranean), *Delirio ambulatorio* (Ambulatory Delirium), *Contrabólides.*

It is not within the scope of this essay to analyze systematically the various stages of the development of an "environmental anti-art" from the end of painting and the depiction of real space to the individual and collective "state of invention" and the establishment of certain radical forms of cultural intervention. I would simply like to emphasize some of the operations and displacements effected by that development within the sphere of the aesthetic act and aesthetic experience and what they inaugurate in their active relationship to a culture and to specific subjects.

"My pre-'59 production should not be taken seriously," Oiticica wrote in 1972[15]; he described *Metaesquemas* (gouache on cardboard, 1957–58) as "an obsessive dissection of space, of space without time: cracks on a mute plane, an infinitized Mondrian structure."[16] On the other hand, in the *Invenções*, the last monochrome paintings of intense pinks, reds, yellows, and oranges (which will show up in almost all of the later works), "the painting hangs behind the frame, which is slightly detached from the wall"; this series constitutes his "first discovery of invention"[17] and the beginning of his

PRECEDING PAGE: **Glass Bólide 4 Earth** 1964

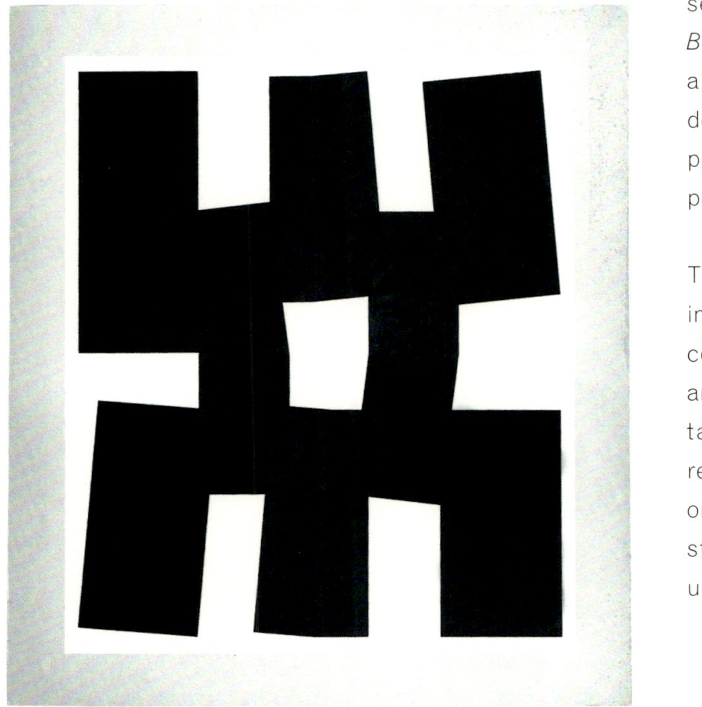

Metaesquema 1958

search for a "structure-color in space and time," a search developed in *Bilaterais* and *Relêvos espaciais*, painted structures displayed in space (actually hung from the ceiling) which served as the beginning of his "nuclear development of color." In being multiplied, they form *Núcleos*, structures penetrable by the spectator's body as one moves between painted wood panels hung from an orthogonal structure fixed to the ceiling.

This experience of color, movement, and time, and of a visual but also more immediately sensual relation to the materials, will lead to the generic concept of penetrable art, applied from that time on to Oiticica's entire program and to the complex constructions of cabins or labyrinths that invite the spectator-participant into an exploratory perambulation along corners and recesses, steps, sliding panels, curtains, or partitions made of plastic, cloth, or straw, all to be traversed and discovered. Penetrable art thus deconstructs the space and materials of the everyday by installing them in an unresolved tension with a more abstract, nonimmediate space.

> For me the invention of the *Penetrable* . . . opens the field onto a completely unexplored region of the art of color, introducing a *collective* and cosmic element, as well as rendering more clear the intention behind this experience of transforming the immediacy of everyday life into the non-immediate, of eliminating any representative or conceptual relation which the artwork might have accidentally preserved.[18]

In an interview with Guy Brett, Oiticica was more explicit:

> The idea for the *Penetrables* arose in part from my fondness for two rooms in the house where I grew up. They were bathrooms, one painted orange, the other blue. It was very pleasant to take a bath in these rooms. I think it's pathetic that in modern homes the bathroom is the only place set aside, the only place where the individual might feel free from oppression. I'm sure primitive peoples are more conscious of the need for privacy.[19]

This memory is not simply anecdotal, but exemplary of the way in which Oiticica abstracted concepts from the more immediate and concrete elements of reality, from its colors, materials, and structures. It is as if he objectivized the words of Oswald de Andrade: "Poetry exists in facts. The saffron and ochre cabana in the greenery of the *favela*, under the Cabralian blue; these are aesthetic facts."[20] The *Penetrable* thus opens an active, temporal, living space, which lies in contiguous (and ambiguous) relation to the space of the everyday. As Favaretto points out, "This redimensioning of space avoids concrete serialism and the illusionism of 'representative' painting: the space becomes literally architectural, open to the virtual inclusion of the organic time of the *vivências*; it "draws aesthetic activity toward a generalized urbanism (nherited from the constructivist utopias),"[21] an urbanism extending to the informal architecture of the *favelas* (slums) and opening up multivalent readings between aesthetics, anthropology, and architecture.

The *Bólides (Caixas, Vidros, Camas)* are "transobjects," "structures of inspection," or "transcendent immanent structures" that come to be only through the intervention of a "participant" who opens, touches, and lifts to discover basic structures and materials such as sand, pigments, shells, colored water, gauze, plastic, and so on, or in one instance, a newspaper clipping with a photo of the bullet-riddled body of Cara de Cavalo, a friend of Oiticica who was a well-known outlaw gunned down by the police (*Box-Bólide 18*, *Box-Poem 2*, *Homage to Cara de Cavalo,* 1966). These structures propose experiences "which are not limited to vision, but cover the entire sensorial gamut, and plunge the subject into an unexpected renewal, into a search for the roots of a collective or simply individual, existential behavior."[22] Later, Lygia Clark radicalized this type of experience with her invention of *Objetos relacionais* (Relational Objects), which she explored in her *Estruturação do self* (Structuring of the Self) séances organized in her home with individual "patients":

> [The relational object] does not have any specificity in itself. As the name suggests, it is defined in its relation to the subject's imagination. . . . Formally, the relational object is not analogous to the body (i.e., it is not illustrative); rather, it creates relations with the body through texture, weight, size, temperature, sound, and movement (produced by the displacement of its various materials).[23]

Clark and Oiticica share a conception of art as "transgression and not repression," even if "Clark's work is marked by a phenomenological and psychological orientation, and a focus on the phantasmic production of an intersubjectivity arising out of regions of interiority, while Oiticica's phenomenological and anthropological orientation (working as he does with the carnival, the *favela*, and social marginality), leads him to approach subjectivity by way of its social fabric." In fact, both approaches develop an "êpistemé of *vivência* as a process of knowledge" and emancipation,[24] with Lygia Clark concentrating on the process of subjectivization itself and Oiticica focusing more on the imaginative-perceptive constructions of a subject that is always social and historical.

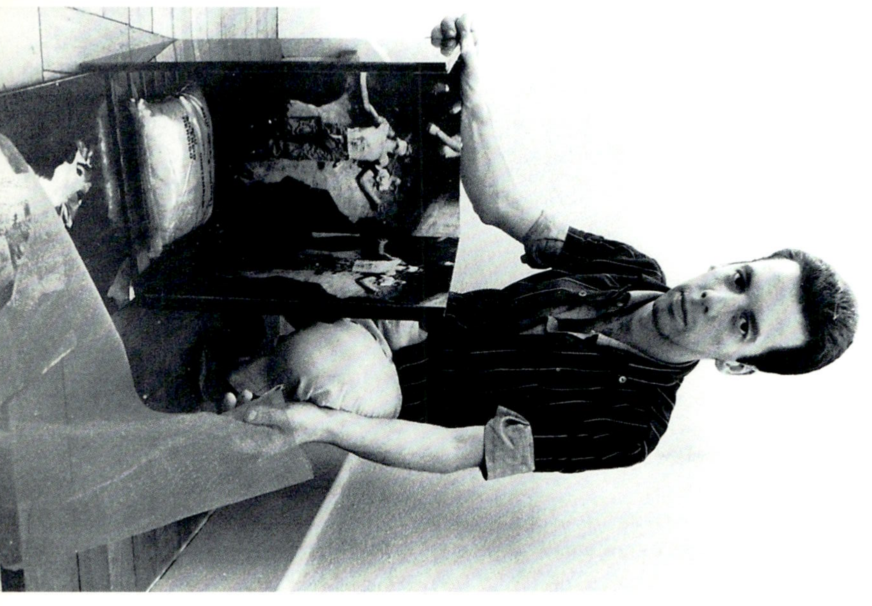

Oiticica with ***Bólide Box 18, Poem Box 2 (Homage to Cara de Cavalo)*** 1966

The final stage of Oiticica's development of a "structure-color" within space came with his invention of the *Parangolé*, which also served as an opening onto other "orders of manifestation"; the *Parangolé*, in his words, constitutes the "definition of a specific experimental position, fundamental for the theoretical understanding of my entire work."[25]

> [It] is the definitive formulation of environmental anti-art, precisely because in these works I have had the opportunity and idea of blending color, structures, poetic meaning, dance, speech, and photography—this was the definitive engagement with what I have called totality-work. In fact, from now on I will call *Parangolé* all the definitive principles formulated here, including that of the nonformulation of concepts, which is the most important. I neither want nor pretend to create a "new aesthetic of anti-art," which would be an outmoded and conformist position anyway.[26]

The *Capas, Tendas, Estandartes, Faixas,* and *Bandeiras* are realized with materials "uninfected by artistic rank"[27]—nylon, burlap, various kinds of fabrics, string, gauze, political or poetic texts, photographs or printed images, bags full of pebbles, sand, straw, shells, etc.—which are carried, used, and displayed by carnival-goers and the participants of samba processions in Mangueira, or in other collective manifestations. *Parangolé* unveils "*environmental totalities* which would be created and exploited each according to its own order, from the infinitely small, to architectural space, urban space, and so on."[28] These totalities in fact radicalize the experience of the penetrable by proposing structures that are open to the participant's imagination, "receptacles open to significations"[29] along with a "poetics of the instant and of the gesture, of the precarious and the ephemeral."[30] These are "structures which propose a non-theatre, a non-ritual, a non-object of art, a non-myth . . . the material aspect of imagination . . . the incorporation of the body in the work and of the work in the body."[31] Their "temporality" is that of "actions without rules, either foreseeable or improvised, a temporality of invention and surprise."[32] The revelation of the *estar* (the "Being-there") and the expressive immanence of moving bodies leads to a "disinterest with respect to structures" and implicit significations:

Nildo of Mangueira with ***Parangolé P15 Cape 11*** 1967

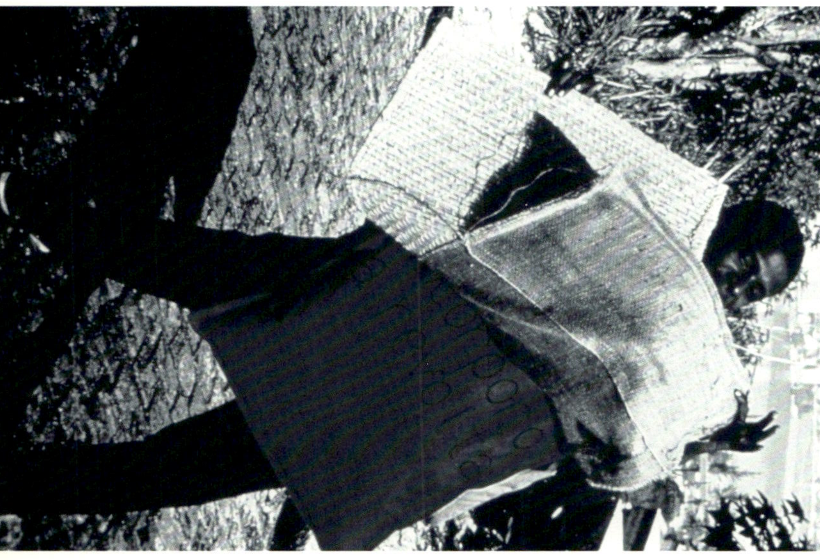

Interpretation, the attempt to search for signifieds and experiment with signifying structures, all of that is overcome, and in reality what remains is simply the proposal of a great invention, a proposal which mobilizes the participant, the ex-spectator who is now also a participant, into a state of invention; that's why the artist doesn't exist here . . . the role of the artist is simply to set off this state of invention. . . .[33]

This transfer of the active role, the "perceptive-imaginative-structuring" act of the artist over to the participant, echoes the radical gesture of immediate and direct communication with the participant introduced by Lygia Clark in her *Caminhando* (Walking, 1963), a Moebius strip made out of paper or other flexible material which the participant follows lengthwise and which can be infinitely manipulated and transformed. Clark repeated this gesture in her séances, in the collective works organized within the framework of her instruction at the Sorbonne in Paris, and later in her invention of the *Objetos relacionais*: "The spectator of before takes the place of the artist. In dissolving into the world and merging with the collectivity, the artist loses his singularity and expressive power. He simply suggests to others ways of being themselves and of attaining *the singular state of art without art*."[34]

For Oiticica the aesthetic experience progressively expands to an awareness of the "Being-there" of things and the world, which the artist can then "appropriate" without any other form of mediation or any kind of "remainder":

> . . . I would like to extend the meaning of "appropriation" to include those things which I encounter every day in the streets, in the city's wastelands, in its gardens, in short, in the environs of my world—things which I would not transform, but in which I would invite the public to participate—this would be a fatal blow to the concept of the museum, the art gallery, and so on . . . and to the very concept of exhibition—as long as we don't modify this concept we carry on in the same old way. Because the Museum is the world; it is everyday experience. . . .[35]

Like epiphany, appropriation is not restricted to the privilege of the artist; any form or event can be arbitrarily aestheticized, for example, the *lata-fogo* (barrel-torches) that light up the nonelectrified Rio neighborhoods at night:

> . . . [S]omeone who saw the barrel-torch isolated as a work would not be able to forget that it is a "work" when he sees, in the silence of the night, others scattered throughout the city like cosmic, symbolic signals. I swear with my hand over my heart that there is nothing more moving than those abandoned barrels, lighting up the night, like a fire that never goes out—they are an illustration of life: the fire lasts and suddenly one day it goes out, but as long as it lasts it's eternal.[36]

These urban epiphanic experiences inspired the *Delirio ambulatorio* (1968), a series of experiences of *estranhamento*, or estrangement, which synthesize all the polysemous impressions and associations suggested to Oiticica in his wanderings around the cities of Rio and São Paulo: "For me all the spots in Rio have a concrete and living meaning which incites what I call a 'concrete delirium': the Sugarloaf, the famous Central Station, the neighborhood streets, the shantytowns of Rio: São Carlos, Mangueira, Juramento. . . ."[37] Though less explicit, this memory/invention of the city evokes James Joyce's epiphanies as well as Robert Smithson's 1967 *Tour of the Monument of Passaic, New Jersey*, or the urban drifts of the Situationists.

But the "collective state of invention" is not and would never be a kind of pure presence reconciled to the world; rather, it is a perception that is both poetic and critical, active and transformative. Oiticica's practice and environmental-comportmental propositions occur, in a way, as an active, creative, cultural critique; his aesthetic and semantic operations set free qualities within immediate cultural references and practices which have become dormant in everyday life by displacing and deconstructing them in heterogeneous, momentary arrangements. These deterritorializations are also akin to Foucault's notion of heterotopia, "that which, right next to the known, the proper, in light ripples hollows out the different very nearby, introducing a movement, a disturbance, a fissure, which to be maintained, alters no less definitively the identity, the order thus separated in some way from themselves."[38]

Oiticica's story of how he came up with the word *Parangolé* and its concept in the streets of Rio is in this respect exemplary of the complex operations that determine in his work the search for an "objective grounding of the object" and a nonillustrative and nontotalizing "objectivization of a Brazilian image":

> I discovered this magic word in the street. I was working on a bibliography with my father at the National Museum de la Quinta, and one day when I was on the bus I saw a beggar in the Plaza de la Bandeira making one of the most beautiful things in the world: it was a kind of structure. By the next day he had disappeared. There were four panels made of wood planks one or two meters high, which he had arranged as the walls of a rectangle on the ground. It was in an overgrown, destitute landscape, and there was this clearing he had made in front of a barbed-wire fence. It was all very well done. And there was a piece of cloth hung from the barbed wire which read "here . . ." and the only word I could make out was "Parangolé," and I said to myself, "That's the word."[39]

Elsewhere Oiticica emphasizes the radical difference between the critical dimension of the *Parangolé*'s experimental-behavioral aspects and an aestheticization of folklore and forms of precariousness: "That *Parangolé* is derived from folkloric slang might lead one to suppose—mistakenly—that it indicates a melding of folklore within my experience, or other similar kinds of identifications, which, transformed or not, would be completely useless and superficial."[40] The sensible and cognitive experience engendered by the

Parangolé frees the imagination and desire of the participant, who finds him- or herself in an extremely mobile and heterotopic relation to the most immediate and familiar kind of environment, in a situation of distantiation capable of transforming behavior through a "corrosion of the assignments and positions of subjects."[41]

> To say that one "finds" elements of *Parangolé* within an urban, rural, or other kind of landscape also means that one actually "establishes perceptive-structural relations" between what develops in the structural framework of the *Parangolé* on the one hand (*Parangolé* referring here to the general character of structure-color within environmental space), and what is "found" in the spatial world on the other. In the architecture of the *favela*, for example, one implicitly finds the character of *Parangolé* in the organic nature of its constituent elements, in the internal circulation and external development of the buildings: instead of there being abrupt passageways from the "bedroom" to the "living room" or to the "kitchen," each part is defined as connected to the others within an essential continuity.
>
> This also exists, on another level, in the fences of construction sites, or in all those usually improvised shelters and constructions of ordinary people which we see every day. Or the markets, the shacks of beggars, the populist decorations of the June holidays or of religious holidays, of the carnival, and so on. All of these relations could be called "imaginative-structural": they are superelastic in their possibilities and in their allowance for a multidimensional relation between what Kant called "perception" and "creative imagination," understood as inseparable from each other and mutually sustaining.[42]

Parangolé thus establishes "environmental-comportmental totalities," a circularity between individual, collective, and aesthetic experiences which displaces and transforms idioms, images, meanings, and behaviors. It is inscribed within what can be considered a cultural and political strategy of opposition to the traditional forces and forms of oppression within Brazilian culture and society: cynicism, hypocrisy, ignorance, and the widespread and effective dilution of constructive energies by the "typical sickness" Oiticica denounced with the term "*convi-convivência*" in *Brasil diarréia* (Brazil Diarrhea, 1973), one of his most polemical texts. To fight against the "abstract purity" of a "paternalistic and reactionary" culture, one must "understand

and take up the multivalence of immediate cultural elements, from the most superficial to the most profound"; one must "take on and assimilate the superficiality and mobility of that culture. . . . In contrast to a conformist position, which always relies upon absolute, generally accepted values, this constructive position arises from a state of critical ambivalence."

In this context *Parangolé* opens a new poetic and critical space by moving the aesthetic act to the field of cultural anthropology; as Favaretto writes, the *Parangolé* "articulates body and materials, references and images, music and dance" within an experience "conjoining experimental propositions with cultural practices."[43] After 1965 Mário Pedrosa had observed a certain decline of the visual for the sake of haptic or tactile impressions, as well as the displacement of the artistic toward the cultural; he considered these to be characteristic of an art he was already defining as "postmodern," an art in which "the properly plastic values tend to be absorbed by the plasticity of perceptive and situational structures."[44] The simultaneous displacement and transformation of the field and forms of "art" and of the modes of cultural intervention is indeed noticeable in a number of works from the sixties, the critical dimension of which is manifest in a radical questioning of the "fine arts" and a subversion of the hierarchies and traditional categories of knowledge which were then being redistributed. In retrospect, this process also seems essential to the analysis and comprehension, "against a simple teleology of the evolution of cultural significances,"[45] of the critical practices developed within non-European and non-Occidental areas of modernity, areas not reducible to simplistic notions of "periphery" or the "culturalist euphoria" of postmodern theories.[46]

Within the adverse political, social, and cultural conditions in Brazil in the sixties and seventies, Hélio Oiticica proposed a modern and alternative model of cultural intervention capable of surpassing and subverting social and historical determinations. The progressive and utopic suppression of all mediation within the aesthetic experience which was at the heart of his work

FOLLOWING PAGES: ***Tropicália*, *Penetrables PN2* and *PN3*** 1967 (LEFT)

The shantytown on Mangueira Hill, Rio de Janeiro 1965 (RIGHT)

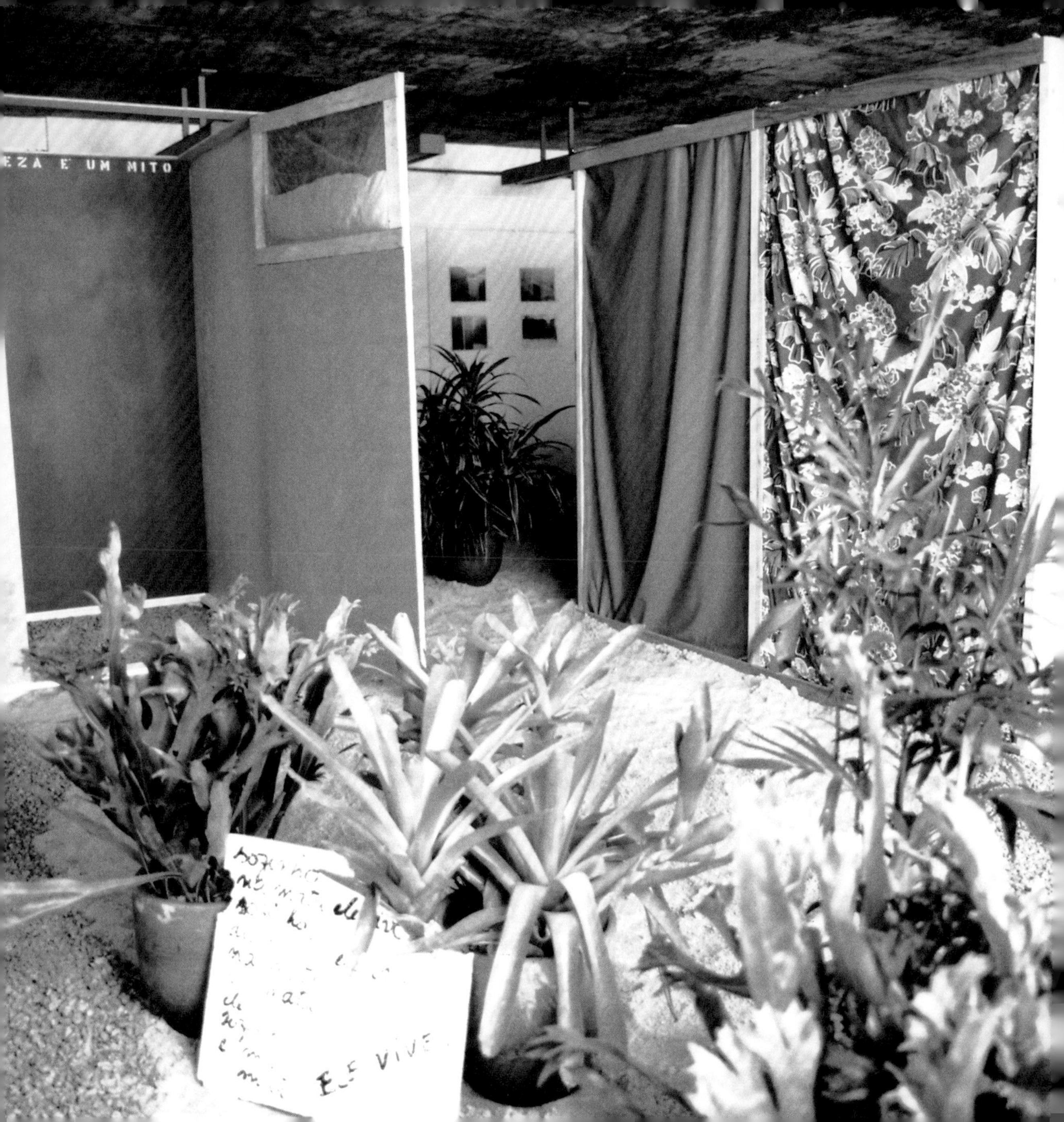
EZA E UM MITO
VIVE

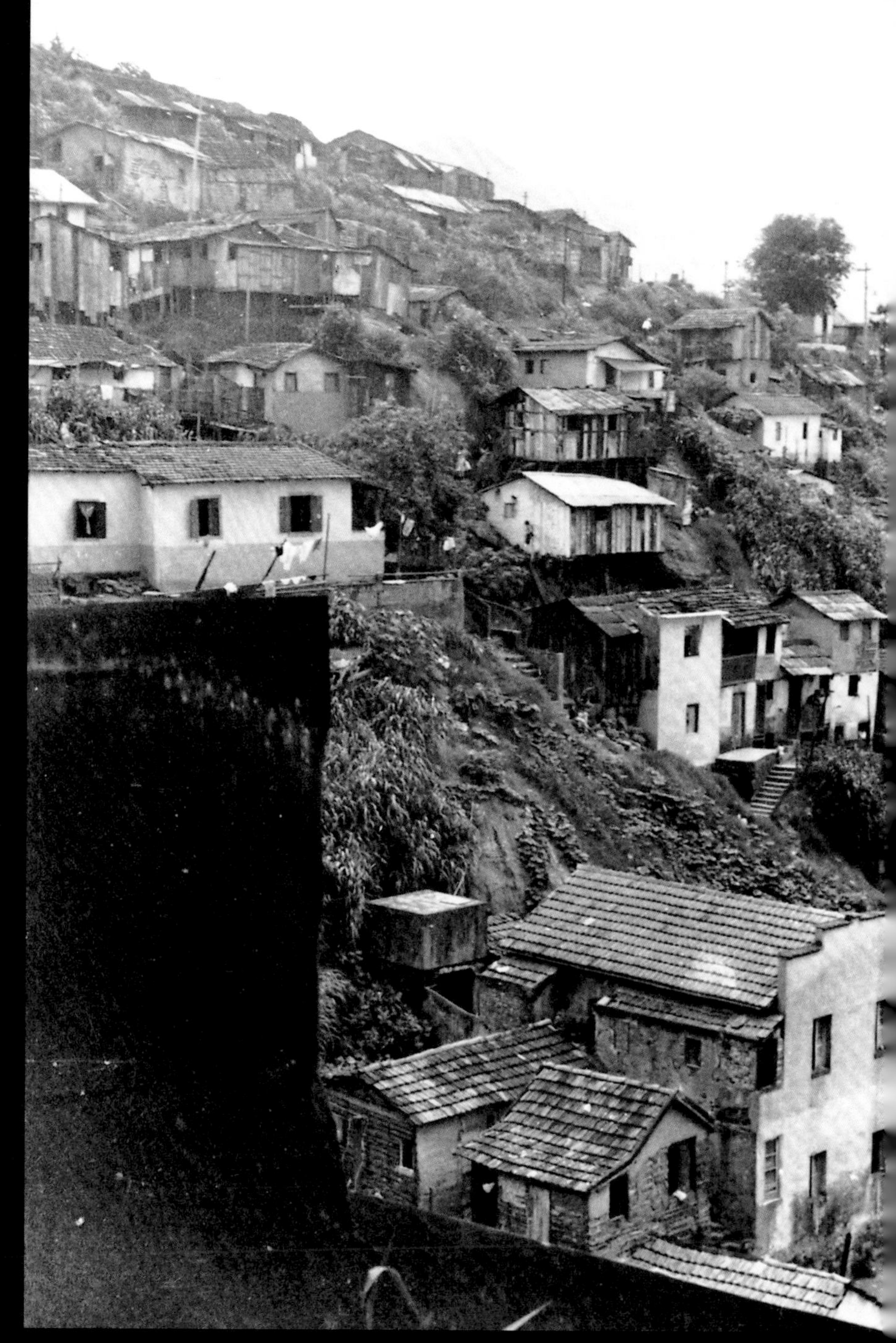

corresponded to his revolt against the inequality of subjects of history and society. Neither a romantic nor a tourist of exclusion, he lucidly described the ethical and aesthetic implications of his experience of marginality and of his "displacement" in the Mangueira *favela* in 1964:

> The overturning of social prejudices, of the barriers of groups, class, and so on, was inevitable and essential to that vital experience. That was how I discovered the relationship between collectivity and individual expression, and the most important step in that discovery was ignoring abstract levels and social "layers" so as to gain an understanding of the whole. The bourgeois conditioning I'd undergone since my birth was undone as if by magic, though I should add that the process had already been underway without my being aware of it. This social displacement and continual rejection of the rules governing our lives in society, and especially in Brazilian society, inevitably led to a state of disequilibrium and to many problems which, far from being totally resolved, are renewed each day. I believe it was the fact of ignoring so-called social "layers" that enabled me to see the dynamics of social structures in all their crudeness, in their most immediate expression; they became schematic and artificial, as if I were suddenly viewing their map or schema from a higher altitude, as if I were "outside" them. Marginalization, which already exists naturally for the artist, became fundamental for me; I understand it now as the total "absence of social place" at the same time as the discovery of my "individual place" as a man in the world, as a "social" being in the fullest sense of the term and not as a member of a class or predetermined "elite," not even of a marginal artistic elite (by which I mean real artists, and not the habitués of the art scene). . . . What matters for me is the "total act of being" I experience in myself, not through partial acts, but through an irreversible "total act of living—a disequilibrium in order to attain the equilibrium of being."[47]

This approach to art as a total experience of life and as a transgression of all preestablished social and cultural models obviously raises questions about the subjects of this experience. The radicalization of Oiticica's work in the proposals for situations that are more and more open (*supraberto*)—as in *Suprasensorial* and *Crelazer*—is related to the limits of an effective intervention within culture and a real transformation of its objective conditions. Just as Lygia Clark's work became more and more directly concentrated on subjectivity and the procedures of subjectivization at play within experiences, so too did Oiticica's work. Again, his work reveals a coherence and radicalism foreign to the pervasive and sometimes naive permissiveness of the period.

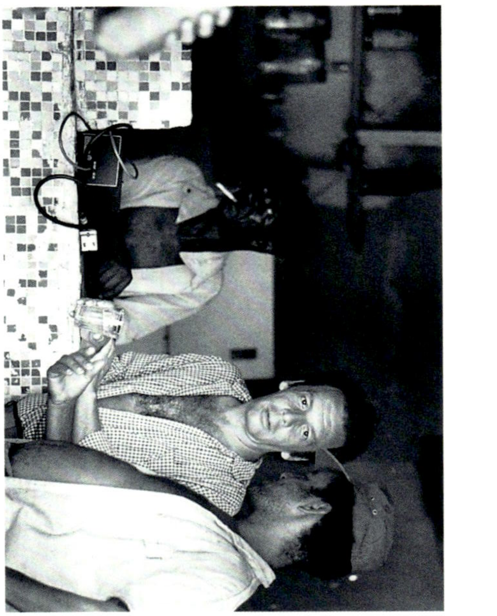

Oiticica in Mangueira, Rio de Janeiro 1978

In *Mundo-abrigo* (World Shelter, 1973) he explicates a state of nonalienated leisure which would permit a total and liberating experience of the world: "'[T]he experimental sphere of the 'WORLD' refers to the experimental as the exercise of a type of comportment-plenitude which tends at the very least toward a structure of *leisure as pleasure as opposed to that leisure of today which is the programmed desublimation maintained by the hour-periods of alienated work-production*."[48] Favaretto points out that what is at play in the state of *Suprasensorial* is an opening onto complex processes of subjectivization (and identification):

> To destroy and replace individual and social repressive forces, one has to produce actions which, in suspending regulated time, its efficacity and calculation of the future, leap into a kind of pure intransitivity which would reject the trappings of repressive desublimation. This is how the displacement effected by *Suprasensorial* avoids falling back into mere spontaneism or solipsism: it proceeds rather from a mytho-poetics, and is derived from the experience of a plural subject.[49]

With her concept of the "anthropophagic process of subjectivization," Suely Rolnik sheds light on the political and cultural implications of this direct intervention in the process of subjectivization; this concept points up the underlying relation of Oiticica's work to *antropofagia* (antropophagy), the major antitraditional critique of Brazilian culture: "[T]he question is precisely of shaking the feeling of subjective identity, of getting rid of the identic-figurative principle in the construction of a 'self'—that is the anthropophagic principle of our time." This conclusion in favor of a plural, open subjectivity always in movement sounds like a contemporary echo of Oiticica's always-in-progress program, his *Brazil Experiment*, which anticipates that subjectivity "made of partial, singular, provisional, fluctuating totalities in a state of becoming, which everyone (as a group or as an individual), constructs from the flux touching the body and its selective filtering operated by desire."[50]

Translated by Patience Mohl

Notes

1 "Hélio and Glauber are what one might call short wicks, which burn out very quickly, 'tropical flowers.' They were never moderate. . . . It was not by chance that they died. I think they died because they gave so much of themselves in an adverse situation." Paulo Sergio Duarte, *Lygia Clark e Hélio Oiticica* (Rio de Janeiro: FUNARTE, 1987).

2 Arnaldo Carrilho, "De la faim à la déraison: Le discours (géo)politique de Glauber Rocha," in Sylvie Pierre, *Glauber Rocha* (Paris: Cahiers du Cinéma, 1987).

3 Hélio Oiticica, *Aspiro ao grande labirinto*, ed. Luciano Figueiredo, Lygia Pape, and Waly Salomão (Rio de Janeiro: Editora Rocco, 1986). Most of the Oiticica texts cited in this essay have been taken from this collection; many have already been published in English in *Hélio Oiticica* (Paris: Galerie National du Jeu de Paume; Rio de Janeiro: Projeto Hélio Oiticica; Rotterdam: Witte de With Center for Contemporary Art; Barcelona: Fundació Antoni Tàpies, 1992).

4 "Da adversidade vivemos," in ibid.

5 Ronaldo Brito, *Neoconcretismo: Vértice e ruptura do projeto construtivo brasileiro* (Rio de Janeiro: Edição FUNARTE/Instituto Nacional Artes Plásticas, 1985).

6 Celso Favaretto, "Oiticica e a música Tropicalista," in *Arte Contemporânea Brasileira: Um e/entre outro/s, XXIV Bienal de São Paulo* (São Paulo: Fundação Bienal de São Paulo, 1998).

7 *Lygia Clark–Hélio Oiticica: Cartas, 1964–74*, ed. Luciano Figueiredo (Rio de Janeiro: Editora da UFRJ, 1996).

8 *H.O./NY Sept. 1971*, text published in Torquato Neto's column "Geleia geral," *Ultima Hora*, 9 September 1971; republished in the *O q faço é música* (São Paulo: Galeria de Arte São Paulo, 1986).

9 *Hélio Oiticica*.

10 Hélio Oiticica–Ivan Cardoso interview (1979), published in *A Folha de São Paulo*, 16 November 1985.

11 The writer Silvano Santiago has described the mixture of secrecy and poetry, the dreamlike atmosphere of these constructions, tropical *Merzbau* in the middle of Manhattan, built in the lofts on Second Avenue and Christopher Street which Oiticica successively occupied from the end of 1970 to 1977: ". . . It was a kind of boat cabin, with a veil which gave the impression at the same time of a maternal shelter and of seeing the outside world through a mist. At that time Hélio Oiticica was almost electronic. He spent entire days in the nests with his indispensable television, camera, slide projector, cassette recorder, cassettes and telephone. Which was forever ringing. . . ." Quoted by Frederico Morais in *Pequeno roteiro das invenções de Hélio Oiticica*, in *O q faço é música*.

12 Jacques Rancière, *Mallarmé et la politique de la sirène* (Paris: Hachette, 1996).

13 *Aspiro ao grande labirinto*.

14 Haroldo de Campos, "Asa delta para o extase," in *Hélio Oiticica*.

15 ho nyk, 12 February 1972, in *Hélio Oiticica: Grupo Frente e Metaesquemas* (São Paulo: Galeria de Arte São Paulo, 1989).

16 Ibid.

17 Ibid.

18 *Aspiro ao grande labirinto.*

19 "Oiticica Talks to Guy Brett." *Studio International* (London), no. 909 (March 1969).

20 Oswald de Andrade, *Manifesto da poesia pau Brasil* (1924).

21 Celso Favaretto, *A invenção de Hélio Oiticica* (São Paulo: Editora da Universidade de São Paulo, 1992).

22 *Aspiro ao grande labirinto.*

23 Lygia Clark, "L'objet relationnel," in *Lygia Clark* (Rio de Janeiro: FUNARTE, 1980); reprinted in *Lygia Clark* (Barcelona: Fundació Antoni Tàpies), the catalogue for an exhibition also presented during 1997–98 at MAC, Galeries Contemporaines des Musées de Marseille; Fundação de Serralves, Porto; and Société des Expositions du Palais des Beaux-Arts, Brussels.

24 Paulo Herkenhoff, "Lygia Clark," in *Lygia Clark.*

25 *Aspiro ao grande labirinto.*

26 Ibid.

27 Oiticica–Cardoso interview.

28 *Aspiro ao grande labirinto.*

29 Favaretto, *A invenção de Hélio Oiticica.*

30 Ibid.

31 Ibid.

32 Ibid.

33 Oiticica–Cardoso interview.

34 Lygia Clark, *Livro-obra*, quoted in *Lygia Clark.*

35 *Aspiro ao grande labirinto.*

36 Ibid.

37 Ibid.

38 Sabine Prokhoris, "Troubles," in *Revue Européenne des Sciences Sociales* 37, no. 113 (1999).

39 Interview with Jorge Guinle Filho (1980), quoted in Favaretto, *A invenção de Hélio Oiticica.*

40 *Aspiro ao grande labirinto.*

41 Favaretto, *A invenção de Hélio Oiticica.*

42 *Aspiro ao grande labirinto.*

43 Favaretto, *A invenção de Hélio Oiticica.*

44 Mário Pedrosa, "Arte ambiental, arte pos-moderna: Hélio Oiticica" (1965), reprinted in *O q faço é música.*

45 Geeta Kapur, "Crackle in the Code: How to Interrupt the Clean Course of Critical Transcendence," lecture at Documenta X, Kassel (1997).

46 Ibid.

47 *Aspiro ao grande labirinto.*

48 Hélio Oiticica, MUNDO-ABRIGO, ho nyk, 21 July 1973, reprinted in *Hélio Oiticica: Mundo-abrigo* (Rio de Janeiro: Galeria 110 Arte Contemporânea, 1989).

49 Favaretto, *A invenção de Hélio Oiticica.*

50 Suely Rolnik, "Beyond the Identity Principle: Antropophagy Formula," *Parkett*, no. 55 (1999).

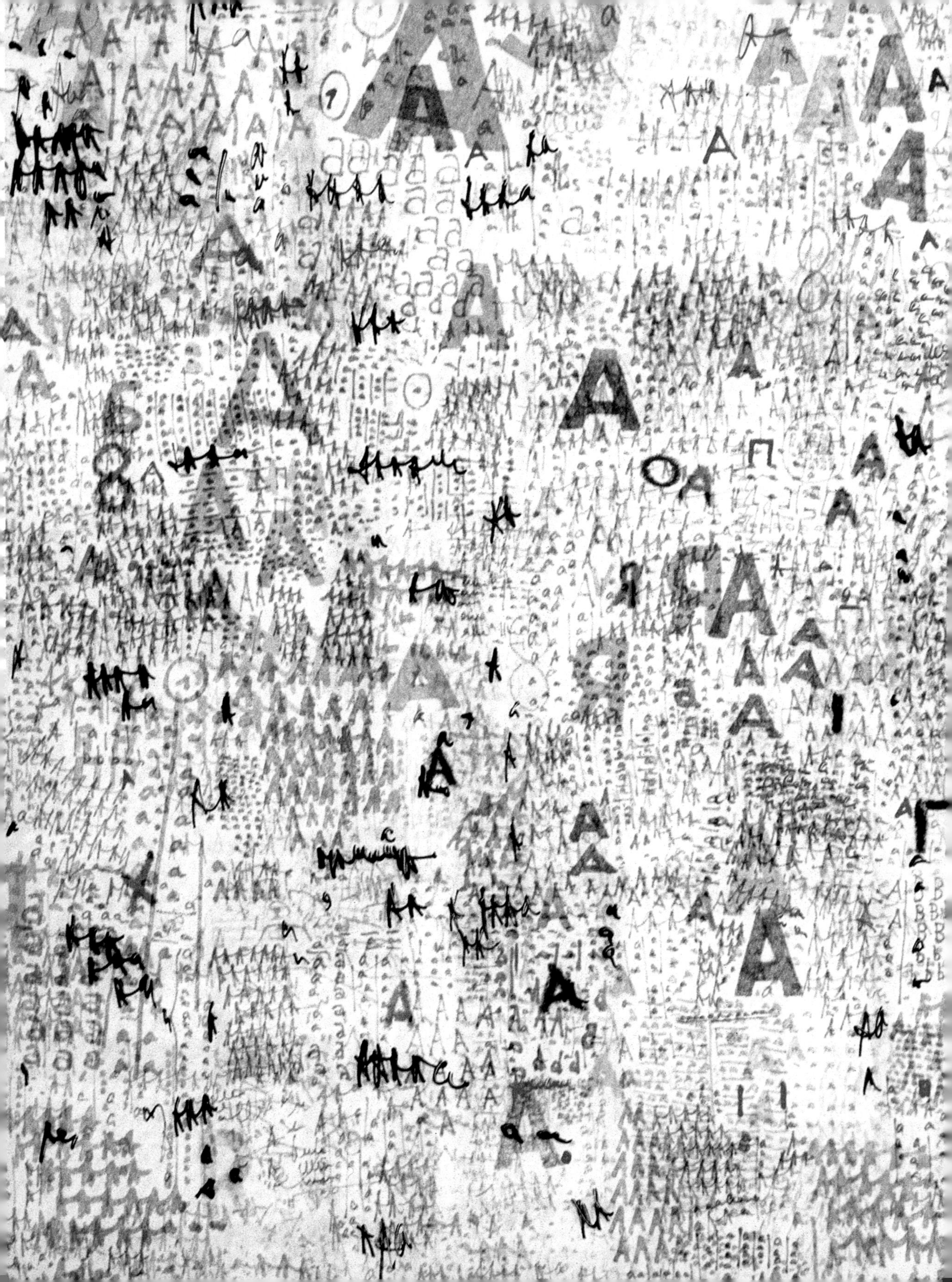

MIRA SCHENDEL

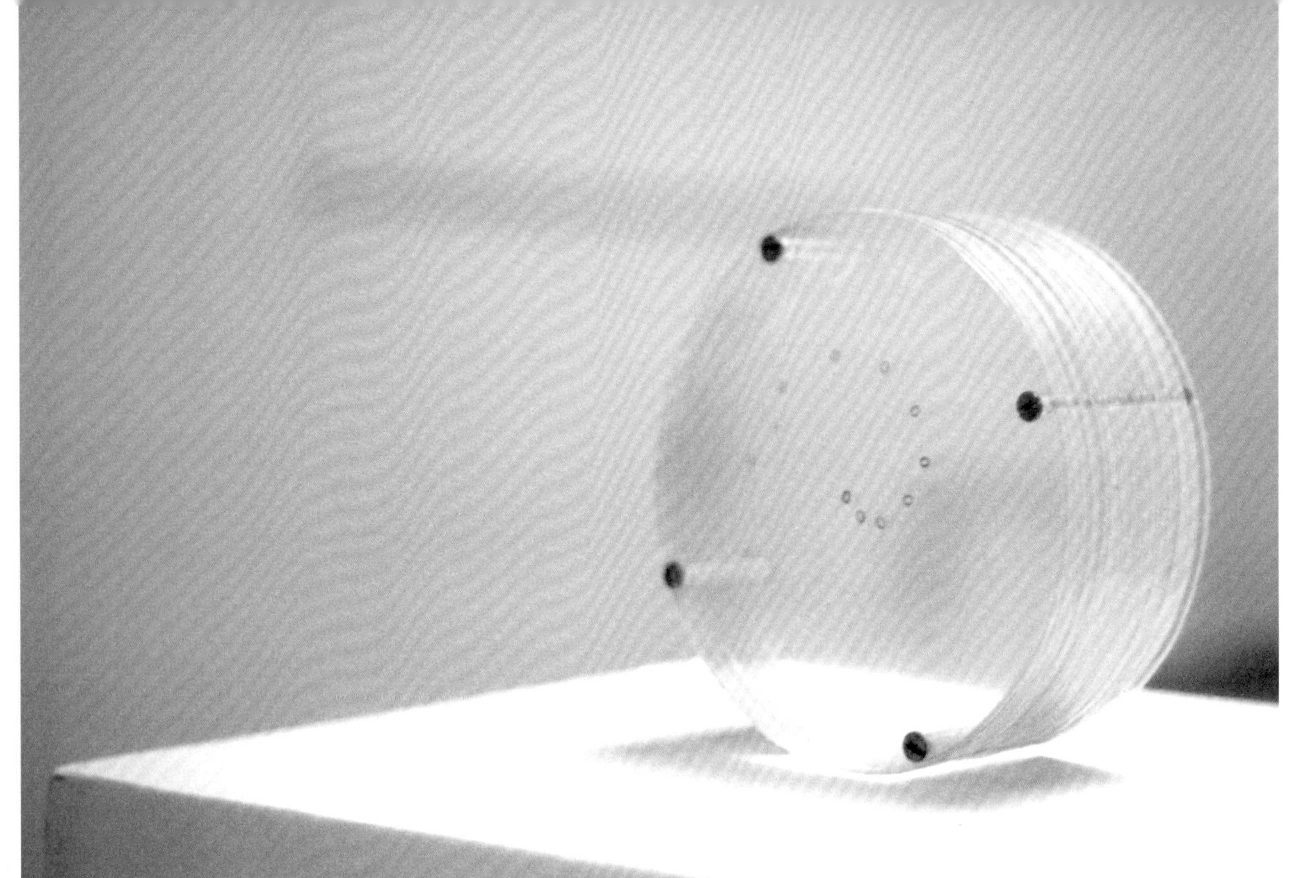

PRECEDING PAGES: ***Red Graphic Object*** 1967–68

Three-dimensional I Ching 1972

MIRA SCHENDEL:

The Immersion of the Body in Thought

Sônia Salzstein

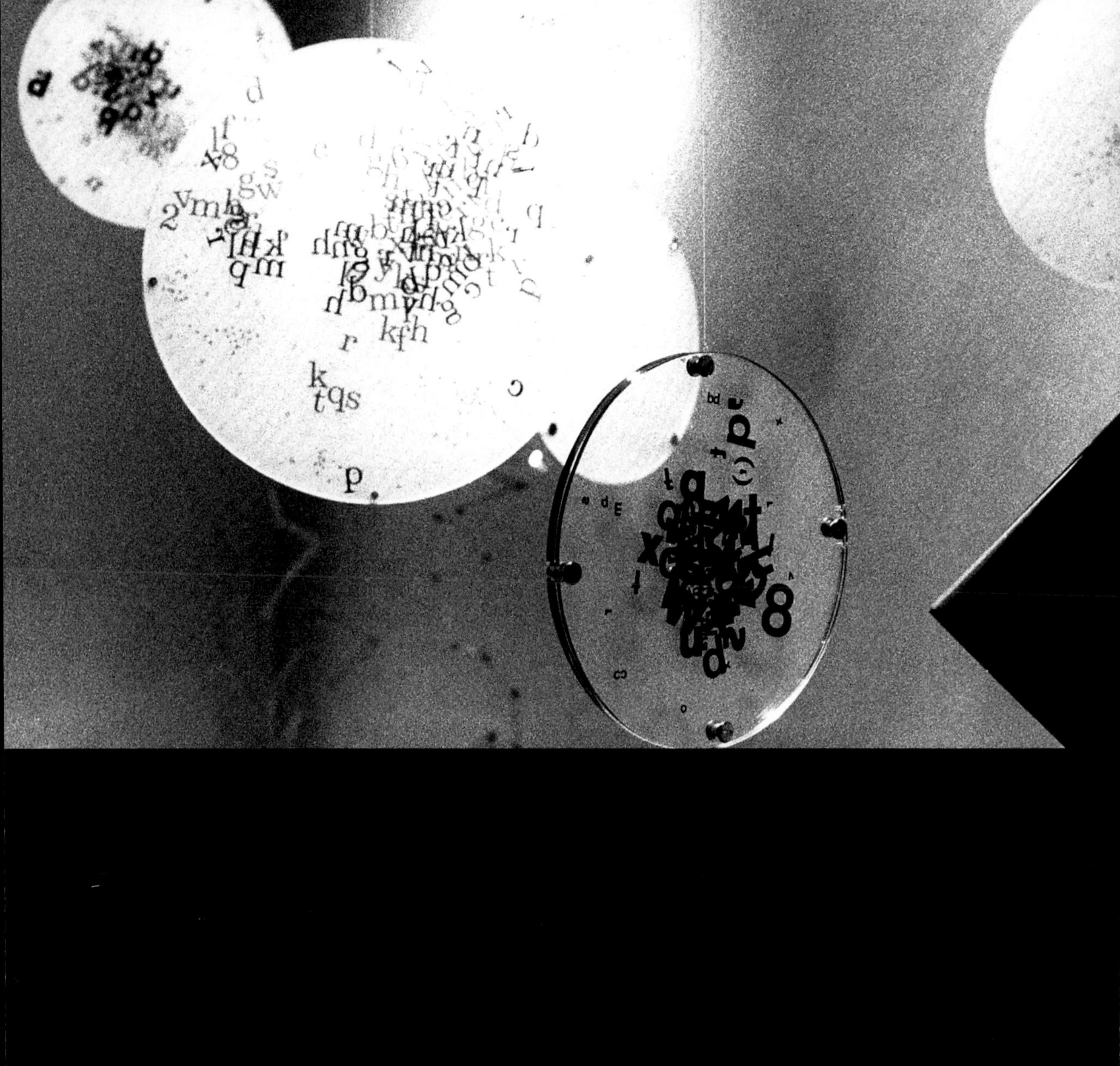

Disks, **Ralph Camargo Gallery, São Paulo** 1972

When she arrived in Brazil in 1949, Mira Schendel[1] ended a tortuous journey, begun in 1941, of flight from the forces of Nazism. Born in Zurich, she came from a German-speaking Czech father and an Italian mother, both Jewish. She had been baptized and received a Catholic education; for a time she even took an interest in theological questions. Such a significant sequence of background events perhaps explains something of the philosophical and aesthetic bent that was to reveal itself in all her work: the emancipation from the body/mind dialectic and the surmounting of a metaphysics of art toward *experience* in which the urgings of body and thought, fully immanent in themselves, would coincide.

Schendel resided in Italy for many years, always maintaining her family's double linguistic universe—German and Italian—to which she would later add Portuguese. Leaving Naples and initially settling in the south of Brazil in the city of Porto Alegre (she would later move to São Paulo), the artist was accompanied by a Yugoslavian acquaintance whom she had married to facilitate permission to emigrate. She was one of the many people "displaced by war"[2] then entering Brazil, and she brought with her an immigrant's background marked by the confluence of deeply ingrained cultural traditions but deracinated by the uncertainties and instability of the present. Her background, spread among so many places, surely awakened in Schendel the willingness to launch herself into the "void of the world," a recurring issue in the artist's work and a phrase found in one of her monotypes from circa 1964, in which can be read "*Nel vuoto del mondo*." Despite the solitude and skepticism that the words may suggest, coming from one who had survived the vertiginous abyss of humanism that had been the war "the void of the world" was to inspire in all of Schendel's work ideas of empowerment and renewal—something like a Spinozan enthusiasm before the constructive power of thought.[3]

When she arrived in Brazil at the age of thirty, what she brought with her was not, in fact, a career as an artist, but a certain experimental and reflective attitude toward things—the combination of those two seemingly contradictory traits reveals itself in the path taken by her work—as well as the memory of her study of art and philosophy during her adolescence in Milan. Her cultured, albeit "nonspecialized," background presaged her work, in which philosophical curiosity and enthusiasm merged to create a broad aesthetic horizon removed from clashes with contemporary art practices of the time. With the energy of the self-taught, Schendel appeared to find in art propitious grounds for a reflective activity that did not involve objects but rather unfolded immediately around the sphere of personal behavior and the confrontations of daily life.

The rarefied and provincial cultural milieu of Brazil in the 1950s, certainly restricted by economic underdevelopment but for that very reason vulnerable to outside influences and more predisposed to change, provided an ideal soil for the germination of Schendel's work (in addition to suiting an uprooted person). Indeec, a little more than a decade after her arrival in Brazil, Schendel's separation from the dilemmas of postwar European modernism was already evident, as was her lack of interest in delving into the language of painting. At the same time, her work pointed in a more process-oriented direction, driven increasingly by the idea of action. It is no accident that during her first decades in Brazil Schendel rarely took part in the small local artistic scene; one of the few people from the artistic and intellectual circles with whom she would initiate a continuous dialogue in that period was the physicist and art critic Mário Schenberg, at the time an enthusiastic advocate of the possibility of establishing connections between scientific debate and contemporary artistic developments. It is also worth recalling, as testimony to Schendel's growing "extra-artistic" motivations, the engrossing theological and philosophical discussions with São Paulo Dominican clerics in which she participated from the sixties to the beginning of the following decade.[4]

In a more-or-less unprofessional artistic setting, then, Schendel must have felt more at ease in her speculative inclinations, free from the pressure of the hegemonic trends of international art circles. And in Brazil she found, above all, a cultural context predisposed to the new, immune to the marketing imperatives of highly institutionalized milieus, and removed from the ubiquitous repertoire of tradition and art history which culturally impregnates those milieus.[5] (Hadn't the country's celebrated modern architecture—peculiarly erected from a cultural starting point of zero rather than from a maturation of industrial rationality—been a typical product of this young nation without tradition?)

Despite the relative "amateurism" present at the root of her work, when Schendel began to paint on a regular basis at the beginning of the fifties her paintings betrayed the legacy of tradition. The first of these call to mind the somber European informalism of the final years of the forties. They are paintings with subdued tones, which seem to have their origin in a sort of instinctive reconstitution, in a Brazilian setting, of a modern tradition chilled by postwar nihilism and contained in the prudent intermediacy between abstraction and figurative art which had prolonged the evanescence of the School of Paris. Vestigially figurative, they oscillate ambiguously between the schematic, anonymous scale of a landscape and the intimacy of a still life.

Elemental forms emerge, sometimes compressed onto flat surfaces and saturated with material; at other times they are two-dimensional silhouettes of objects (pliers, weights, scissors) placed in series, which appear against a background covered in a thin substance as if to disclose their literal condition as signs. From these procedures springs a tense balance between the coldness of the scheme of representation and the expressiveness of the pictorial surface, between the representational field inescapably established by vision and the literality of signs of the objects represented. In addition, the paintings seem to suggest a shifting back and forth between two diametrically opposite points of view: an intimate psychological scale, toward which the "still lifes" incline, and an "external" and impersonal scale, toward which the "landscapes" incline. It is relevant to note how, in these early paintings, Schendel already brought into play these opposite registers by relativizing the field of representation. She subjected the intellectual space where objects can emerge only as discrete elements—denominated and quantified *a priori* and therefore separate from their surroundings—to a perceptive and "organic" space in which objects are glimpsed in the weave of smooth, indefinite depths.

Despite the formal sobriety that evokes a "European style," the structural lapses—the gaps between the order of representation and the materiality of the surface—which occur in these works produce discontinuities between the representation and the organic and phenomenological spatiality of objects (as well as calling into confrontation those two opposing points of view), and thus were an early indication of the corporeal nature that would emerge with impressive force in the artist's works beginning in the mid-1960s. In fact, with *Droguinhas* (Nothings) and *Trenzinhos* (Little Trains), Schendel was to abandon the artistic repertory of painting, with its presuppositions of visuality and frontality and its inevitable subsumption under the history of techniques and styles, and she began to brush against that broad aesthetic horizon that impelled her toward an encounter with the sphere of *experience*.

Before confronting the totally new set of problems revealed by these works, however, Schendel still had to radicalize her experiments with the corporeal dimension of painting. Thus, at the beginning of the sixties she exchanged the pictorial vocabulary rooted in the ambiguities between figure and field for a phenomenology of pictorial space, this time pulsing in all its intensity, emancipated as it was from compositional schemes. In the new paintings, surfaces, now freed from any vestiges of figuration, took on extraordinary physical density and came to establish themselves as experiments of space. The works executed mainly between 1962 and 1965 (a conjecture, as few of them are dated) display thick layers of paint to which Schendel added organic and mineral materials, with the result that they can be thought of as blind objects resistant to perceptual schemes or the pattern-seeking habits

Untitled 1964

of vision. They are highly expressive paintings, but they lack any authorial character. They thus display the nature of "things" and indicate, moreover, the drastic reduction of the distance between the entreaty of subject and object, interiority and exteriority.

In addition, the artist attempted to question any "optical" approach to these paintings. She grappled with this, making cuts in the surfaces, delimiting areas of differing luminosity, and varying textures and surface densities. These procedures came to replace the ideal of lines or forms "added" to a visual plane with physical intervention in the pictorial material itself, which produced differing levels and irregularities in the surface. The emphasis on materials did not result at that time in expressive undulation or in any kind of affective subordination of the canvas, which, on the contrary, demonstrated a certain impassibility and clearly affirmed its condition as surface. It is worth remembering, however, that these canvases do not invoke the Greenbergian *tabula rasa*, because in these works surfaces always permit a glimpse of a certain internal dynamic privileging the accidental or the singular event via a small deposit of material, a fragment of canvas left uncovered or even excised, a wrinkling of the surface. Such happenings, obviously, indicate the presence of a subjectivity irreducible to the order of the plane, an open-ended process of the forming of the subject, to speak in the terms of the duality that would prove to be as instigative for Schendel as it was problematic.

It is as if we could achieve knowledge of that subject, which adjoins the surface in a kind of insurmountable psychological recess, only from its exteriority, as if it has established itself just behind the surface, upholding the fragile, narrow limits of a private dimension—and here we return to the issue outlined in the earliest paintings, with their tense dynamism between the psychological recess of a subject that manifests itself only obliquely and the unreachable two-dimensionality/exteriority of the canvas. But in these new works Schendel seemed to have overcome the dichotomous relationships deriving from the subject-object/interiority-exteriority opposition, so that now the paintings come bathed in a diffuse subjectivity, powerful but yet not manifesting themselves in an impudent or demanding manner.

It should be noted that with these corporeal works, in which the issue was a tactile and sensual spatiality unattainable through idealist models of vision, Schendel in no way joined the trends that in the sixties were reviving the anarchical vanguard spirit of Dadaism and Surrealism, with its strategies to unleash liberating psychoanalytic elements and thus free materials to a primordial entropy and the pulse of the unconscious. Affirming a skin-deep materiality, Schendel's paintings unquestionably departed from the constructive ideals of classic visuality, but in no way did they approach contemporary nonconstructive trends linked to ideas of excess and to the notion of a subject permanently on the verge of disintegrating into the formless. These tendencies, in the end, would frequently redound, as was seen in *Arte Povera*, in a paradoxical (and narcissistic) perfectionism of the amorphous.

Here is the challenge that became ever more urgent and ubiquitous in the development of her work, for even as it was emerging like a body stuck to the heterogeneous surface of the real (and for that very reason immune to metaphysical depths), it must still radiate some constructive, normative strength. (The large "*Sim*" (Yes) that we see stamped on one of Schendel's drawings from the mid-sixties clearly demonstrates that constructive disposition even as it reveals itself to be accidental, sardonically promotional in the face of the new commercial culture that would assert its hegemony from that time on.) From this constructive, normative strength, perhaps, arose the artist's refusal to capitulate to a saga of materials, for despite the growing importance to her of the idea of corporeality, the works must always evince the mark of some formal intervention. It is through this discreet intervention—this preliminary gesture of formalization and dominion over the undifferentiated—that the public and suprapersonal aspect of these works is constituted, still preserving the psychological niche of an interiority that cannot be turned into spectacle but only inferred behind the surface.

Untitled mid-1960s

sim

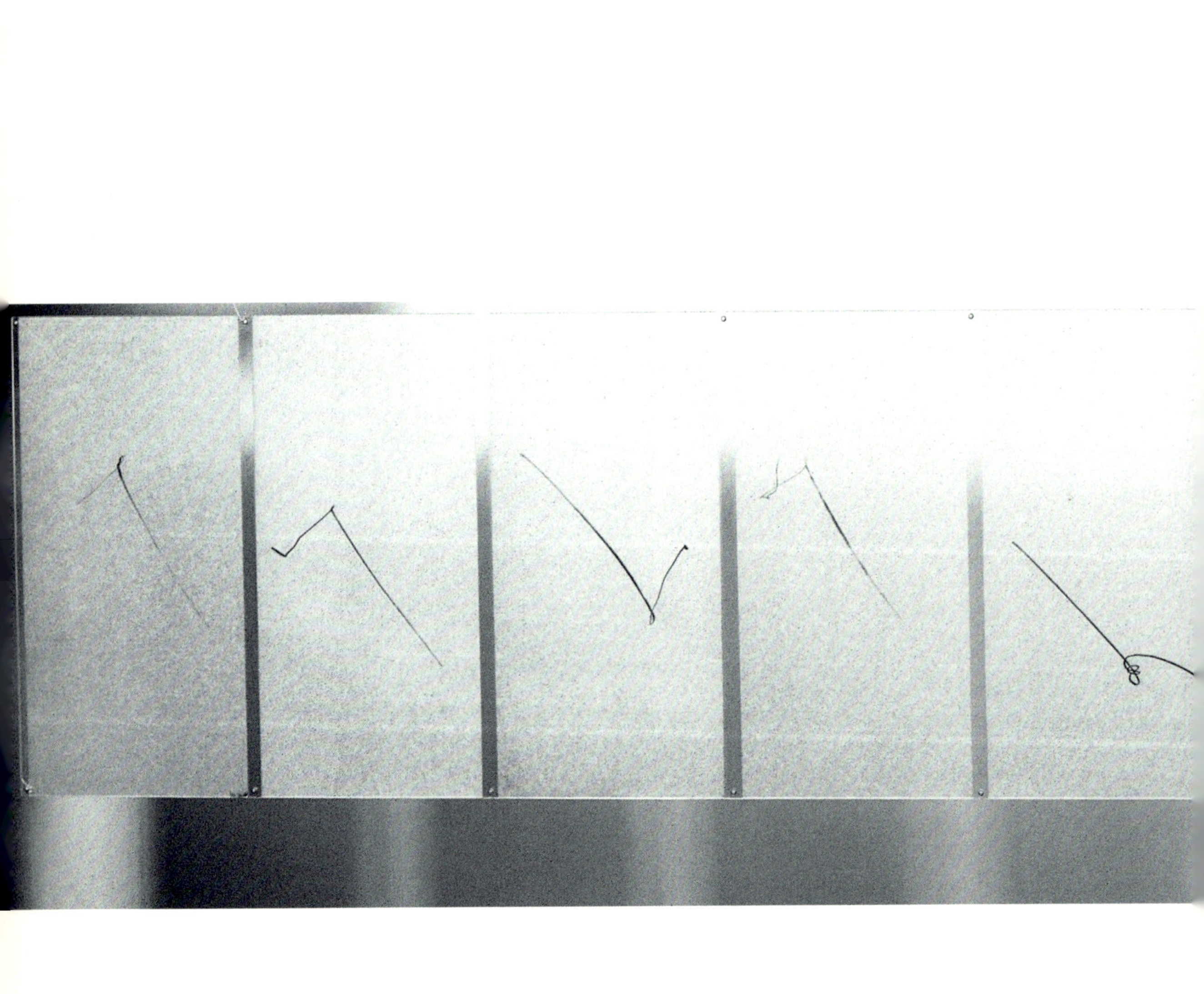

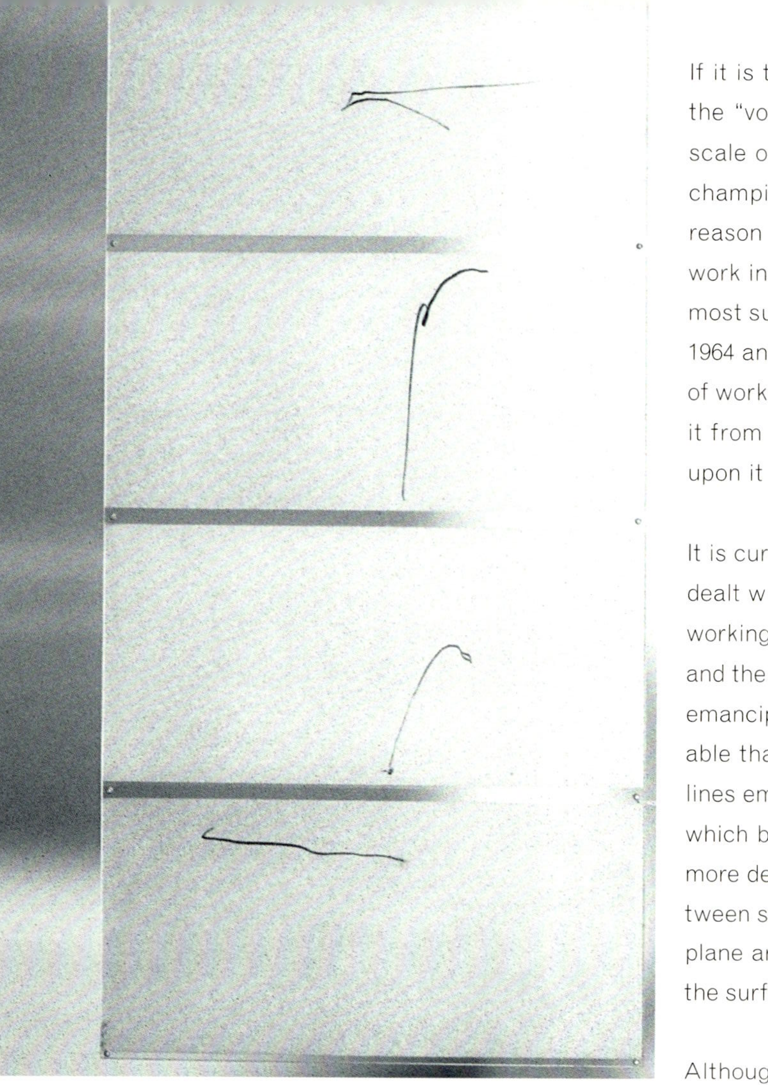

Linear Object 1965

If it is true, then, that her work would later culminate, as has been said, in the "void of the world," which obviously would submerge it in the intimate scale of daily life and exclude it from the selective field of autonomous art championed by the modern tradition, it can be seen that not even for this reason did Schendel totally reject the notion of subject. The immersion of the work into this sphere of the humblest (which for the artist would also be the most subjectively charged) would begin with the *Monotipias* (Monotypes, ca. 1964 and ca. 1970) and culminate in the *Droguinhas* (ca. 1965). In both series of works Schendel was seeking to dehierarchize the gesture and emancipate it from the tired and lackluster functionality of the quotidian by conferring upon it extraordinary assertive energy.

It is curious to note that the artist executed the vast set of *Monotipias*, which dealt with notions of void and transparency, in the same period that she was working on those paintings with thick materials; however, in both the former and the latter we find the same desire to seize the immediacy of experience, to emancipate the body and relate it to the vitality of its environment. It is undeniable that the drawings executed on a nearly transparent base, in which the lines emerge as if done on air, submerged Schendel into a "void of the world" which brought her close to the process-oriented dimension of experience in a more decisive way than did the paintings.[6] In the *Monotipias*, the distance between subject and object appears to dissolve completely. The virtualities of the plane are consumed because the real dimension of movement was attained; the surfaces vibrate with the synesthetic complexity of the body.

Although, *faute de mieux*, these works can be described as "drawings," they display nothing of the projectual character—the component of planning, measuring, articulating, and calculating—of a drawing; rather, they allude directly to the placement of the body, to its innate expressiveness. They isolate the gesture as the primordial, significant form of the body, and it is necessary to add that what is meant here is the significant gesture, the gesture that emerges into the material field of language, never as an obscure force or one alien to it. The gesture, therefore, that Schendel captured in her *Monotipias* always bore within itself the kind of historicity that from the beginning would project it into language. It was, in fact, with these works that Schendel began to probe the frontiers between gesture and writing and to become aware of a potential power in language, making it possible to capture a link to the materiality of the body even as language became a formalizing constructive principle.

The *Monotipias* can be grouped by "themes"—that is, according to the different ways in which they address the gesture/writing issue. We have already seen that in almost all of them what is at stake is primarily a process of deautomatizing the gesture (as will occur later in the *Droguinhas*). Each "drawing" records a unique movement, even though (or actually, because) such movement unfolds in an accelerated and unrestrained rhythm through countless *Monotipias*. Some groups carry inserted letters or fragments of writing combined with those gestural recordings, or even enigmatic tracings that suggest horizon lines, spaces in perspective, and other architectures. One large group of works is more intensely involved with writing, which appears not articulated in poetic form but opaque and disjointed, only phrases, words, and individual letters. It is as if it had been expanded into an emptiness in which the entire body is projected and spatialized.

In the *Monotipias* that associate gesture and writing, Schendel seems to be striving to dissolve the interpretive, ideological crust of language in order to reach its rough, constructive surface. Here it would offer itself without the polishing of technique, without hierarchies, without the dramas or intentions of a subject preexistent to it. It is clear in all these groups of *Monotipias* that Schendel was concerned with integral experience, not predicative and therefore immanent in that gesture/writing, an experience that could reveal itself in all its historicity, to be sure, but emancipated from the dramas and the ideological virtualities embedded in the subject/object duality. Let us note,

Untitled: Monotype from the series "Writings" 1965

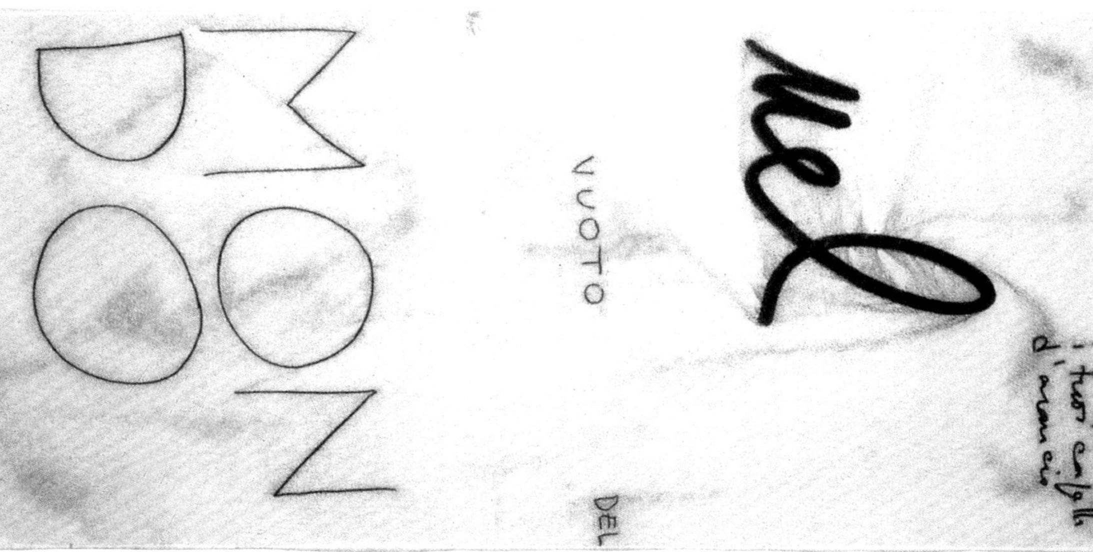

for example, the kind of compaction of subject and object expressed through the use of writing and symbols in a maximization of literality: in *Aqui* (Here), the word is reiterated by the drawing of an arrow; in *Isto é uma casa* (This Is a House), the text indicates a rudimentary drawing of a house; in *Oggi ho disegnato questa porta* (Today I Drew this Door), the text points to a sketchy structure of lines resembling a door or passageway; in *Zeit* (Time), the *Monotipia* bears only the inscription *Zeit*, with the letter T having an extended vertical axis as if to indicate duration; in *Un rien de temps et ce sera le jour entier* (A Nothing of Time and That Will Be a Whole Day), we see a text in which the real time of the duration of the writing is stretched through its semantic repercussion.

After the productive burst of the *Monotipias* (the artist executed close to two thousand of them in the mid-sixties, returning to them for a short time at the beginning of the seventies), Schendel found herself thrown more than ever into the midst of that turbulent "void of the world." The *Droguinhas* series

FOLLOWING PAGES: ***Untitled (Droguinha)*** 1964–65

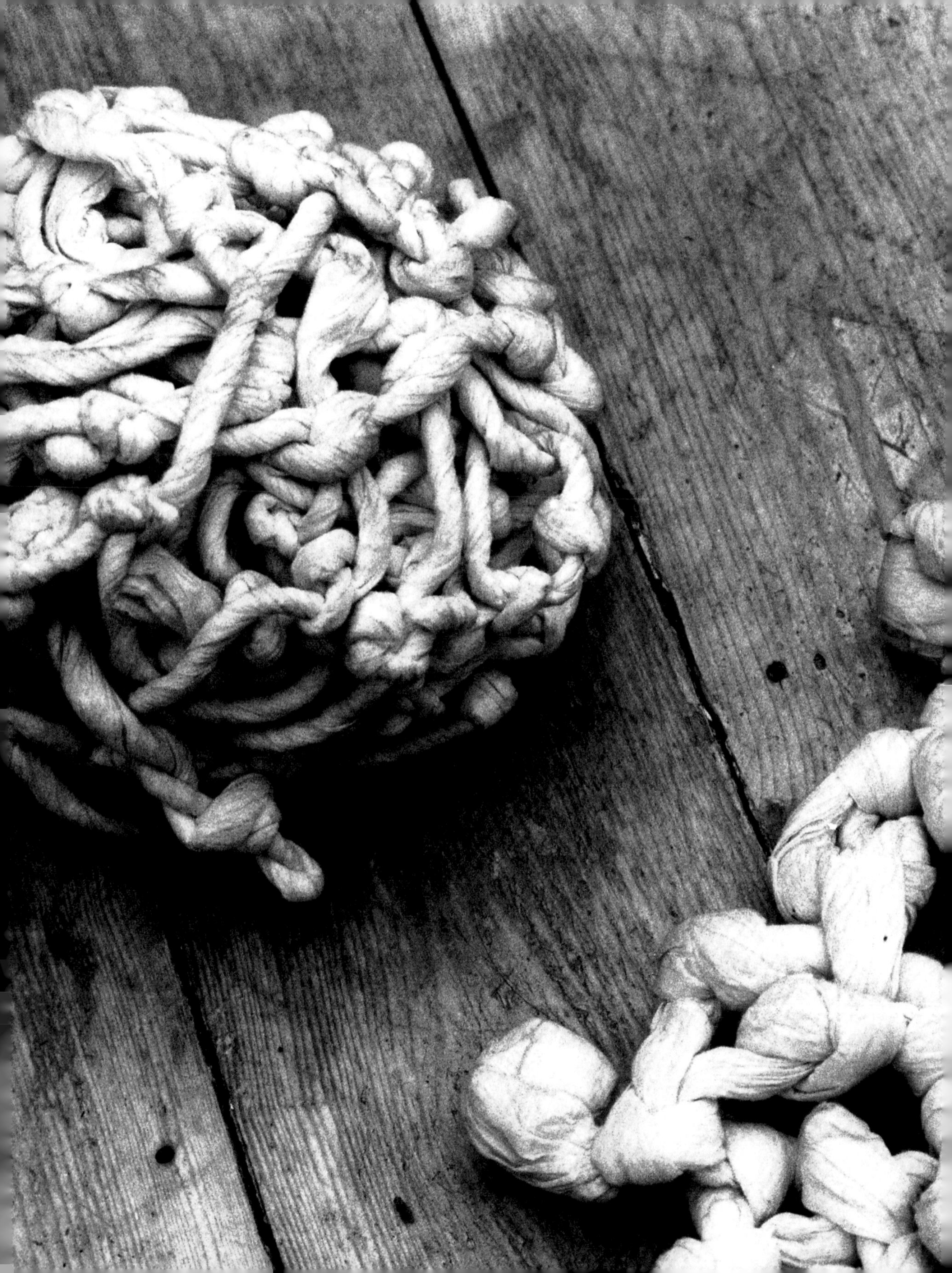

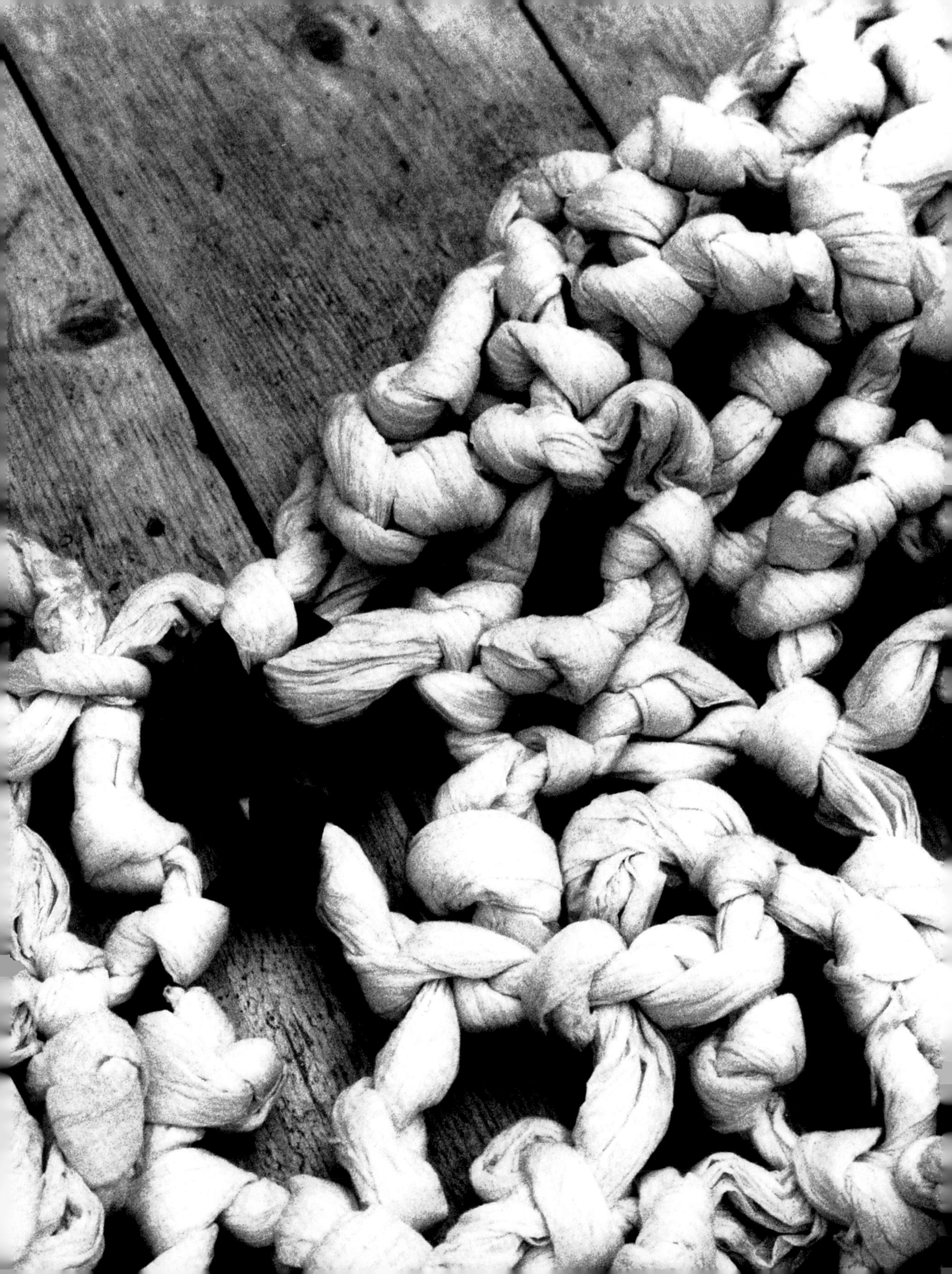

emerged, then, as a response to the imperative demand revealed in the process of producing those drawings on rice paper: having once experienced something of the adventure of a body completely immersed in thought, the work henceforth could only result in the very action of which it was both instrument and end.

As pure action, the *Droguinhas* do not convey an interiority to be examined or unveiled; they neither embody the differentiated action of a performance nor constitute a manifestation of conceptual art that could equally well be realized in another medium. On the contrary, the vitality of these works lies precisely in their rigor as action, in the intellectual humility that they affirm, in the fact that they "merely" reveal to the observer an action coming out of a strong gesture of self-determination and steadfastness in the real. In this sense, they are not an abstract model of action but rather the continuous and unpredictable unfolding of one action into another in an indefinite and regenerative succession of movements that configure the body as a bundle of psychic and biological energies in permanent renewal.[7]

The search for this self-cognitive dimension of the personal sphere was thus radicalized in the *Droguinhas*. They are made with soft sheets of rice paper twisted and interwoven with knots in such a way that at a certain point what remains is an amorphous mass revealing the movements of the hands. They are a kind of living record of all the gestures deposited in them, not an object or something separate from the body. But, however frankly contingent and incomplete they appear as form, they forever exist as the fruit of an action and therefore presuppose the constructive presence of a subject. Thus, even though they comprise some of the more "unformed" of Schendel's works, there is in the *Droguinhas* something of an ordering principle: it consists of the very force of self-determination with which the action unfolded in them imposes itself upon its environment. It is in the extreme example of these works, ultimately, that we were to see emerge the aforementioned volatile form whose unique and experimental character would have been fated to rigidify (and to become institutional) if not for the unleashing of a vital energy that permanently updated the productive élan of the action.

It is important to emphasize that the cognitive subject sought in the *Droguinhas* had nothing to do with an abstract ethic of freedom or some hollow paradigm of experimentalism which, at that period in the sixties, seemed to have absorbed the modern notion of subject. On the contrary, the work's strength lies precisely in the impossibility of generalizing the gesture that constituted it. Its strength comes from its uniqueness, its intrinsic fragility and incompleteness.

We should remember, moreover, that the title—or antititle—of these works already represented Schendel's taking a stand, along with the fact that one is able to use the word *droguinha* equally well in the singular or the plural. In Portuguese slang, *droguinha* is something that we attach no importance to, something disposable, something that declares itself almost as an absence. It is likely that Schendel conferred this title precisely because she wanted nothing to act as mediator, neither skill, technique, style, nor art history. The material impoverishment of *Droguinhas* expressed above all an accessible constructive power, despite everyday alienation; as has been said, it dealt with action, with the emergence of a gesture that recognized itself and cast itself into history.

The *Trenzinhos* series, which Schendel produced in the same period, was born from a similar attitude and, like *Droguinhas*, raised the issue of bodily scale. These works consisted of uniform sheets of rice paper suspended by a cotton thread and arranged as if on a clothesline, sufficiently extensive to go beyond the compass of the hands without surpassing the scale of the body. The artist seemed to confer upon both these series of works an organic and physiological pulse—in the case of *Droguinhas*, because of a mimetism of movement, and with *Trenzinhos* because by being suspended in the air they react to the surroundings, such as observers' breathing: it is as if the setting

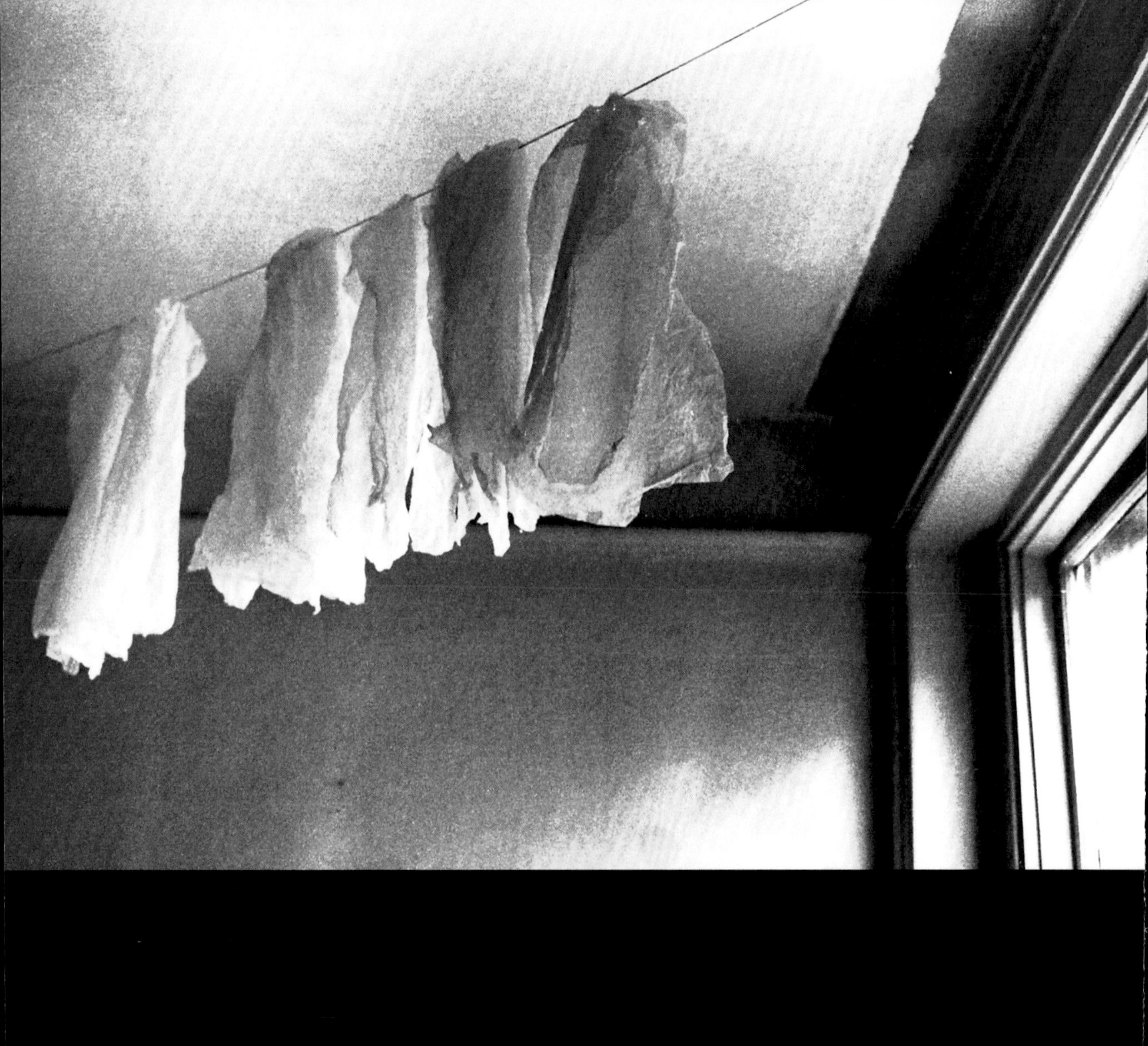

Untitled (Trenzinho) mid-1960s

itself suddenly begins to breathe, brought to life by the human movements passing through it.

So strong was the corporeal experience established by *Droguinhas* and *Trenzinhos* that today, more than ten years after Schendel's death, staff at museums and galleries often rack their brains as to how to properly exhibit them without betraying their original organic dynamism. They are simply there, in the superficial interface in which inside and outside, interior and exterior, public and private touch, in which areas of the psychic and the biological intermingle in a declarative movement. In that sense, everything indicates that the most correct way to show them is to leave them to their own seeming inertia by hanging them from a wall or some other place as is usually done with items of clothing or other things that must remain accessible.

After the route that would lead her to the *Droguinhas*, to the *Trenzinhos,* and to a work such as *Ondas paradas de probabilidade*[8] (Still Waves of Probability, 1968), at the end of the sixties Schendel seemed to have distanced herself from the idea of action, although she continued to be interested in working within the horizon of *experience*. She now involved herself more and more with writing, motivated always by the question that would bear fruit in so many works in later years: how to deautomate language and reconvey it to the condition of experience. From this period come her *Objetos gráficos* (Graphic Objects), *Discos* (Disks), and *Toquinhos* (Stubs), as well as the *Cadernos* (Notebooks) series that appeared at the beginning of the seventies.

This crop of works is rooted in the notion of transparency and immateriality—in other words, a drastic autonomizing of the body in space. "Here there is the problem of transparency," Schendel would say, referring to one of her acrylic disks, "of inside and outside, inside and outside at the same time; as object and subject they are the same, concave and convex are together, and this is how one feels the theme of transparency. The mirror is symmetrical and transparency isn't."[9] In these acrylic works Schendel addressed the same key ideas she had in her previous series: the immersion of the body in thought (and of the latter in the former, reciprocally), the body as the material substratum of thought—not thought as a vessel of ideas, but the dense thought of language.[10]

What draws our attention in Schendel's commentary is the mention of the mirror as a place of symmetry—and, therefore, the privileged place of the projection of a subject—and the conversely transparent quality of the acrylic as something that would make possible experiences of passage and transformation, a surface that would gather the subject/object polarity into a continuous wave of open and unstable relationships. In these works the word does indeed move about restlessly in the direction of immediate dispersion in the space, keeping in check the virtual representational background. Letters freed from the proselytizing of the word, degrammaticized, thus silence the "informative" loquacity of language; they shun the demand of social functionality and resist reduction to any explicative relation to things. It is no accident that these acrylic pieces were thought of as light objects without a fixed support point: in this way, they could lend themselves to varying spatial situations, creating a dynamic of passage when suspended in nonlinear fashion in groups of four or more, revealing themselves vulnerable

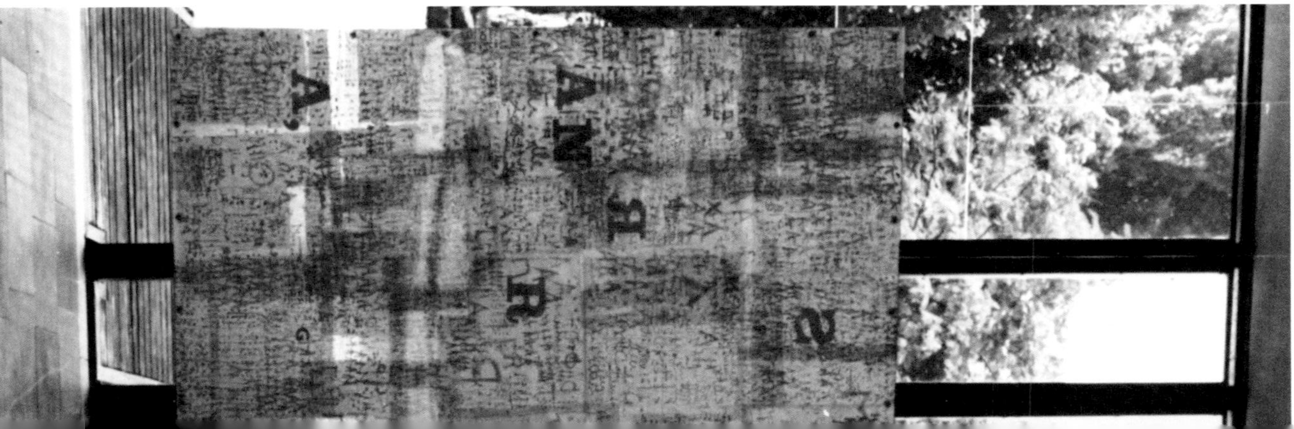

Graphic Objects, XXXIV Venice Biennale 1968

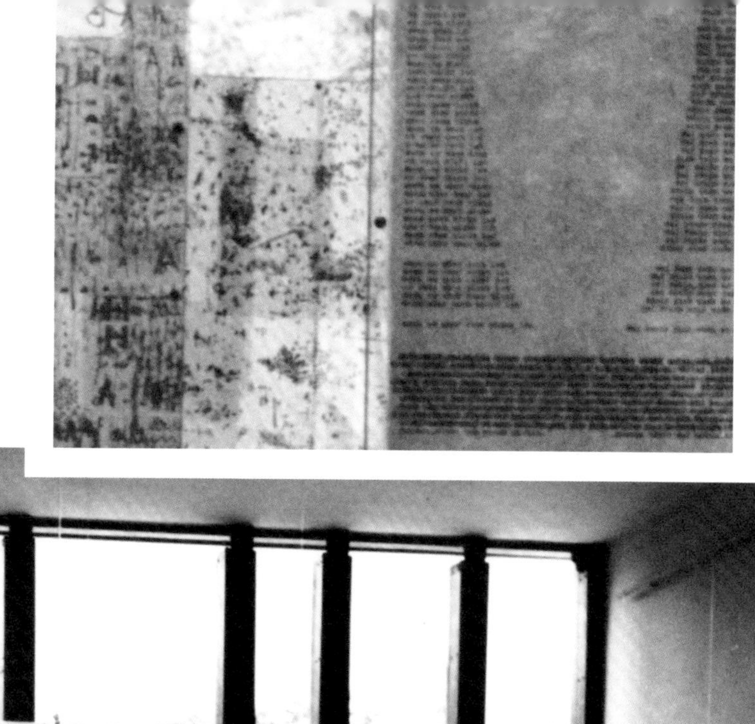

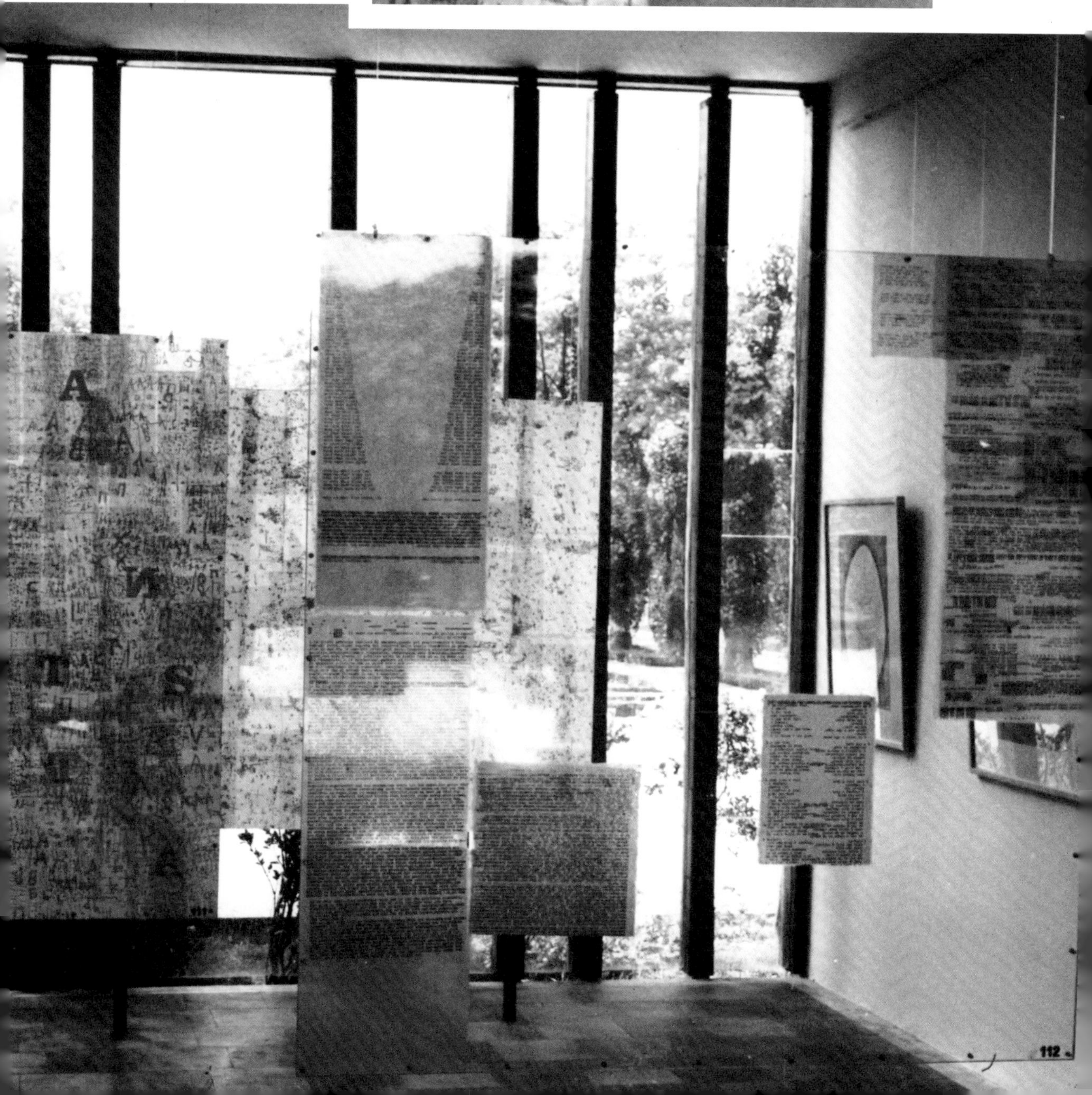

112

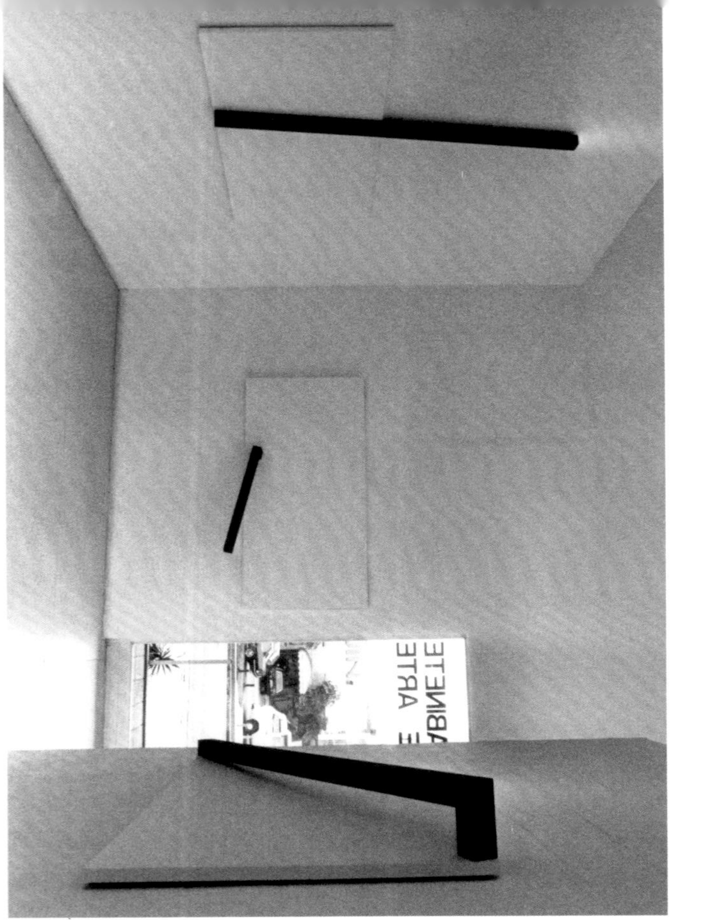

Sarrafos, Gabinete de Arte Raquel Arnaud, São Paulo 1987

to the slightest oscillations of air and to ambient light. They constituted, then, by means of the density acquired through the fluctuation of these letters, an empirical experience of space.

The radicalism that had dominated Schendel's production from the sixties to the beginning of the seventies would not resurface until the *Sarrafos* (Slats), a series of twelve works executed in 1987. In this interval of time the artist produced a vast and important set of monochromatic temperas, drawings, collages, and a numerous series of notebooks, which will not be examined here,[11] but it is important to note that only in the *Sarrafos* would the gesture reappear so acutely; it is now restrained, harsh, and laconic, without the resplendent lyricism and eroticism of the early period. Schendel's work had decidedly undergone a change in mood.

It is as if she had replaced the idea of liberation with an eminently political attitude, a skeptical attitude about the libertarian nature of private life and about the possibility of its stimulating the emergence of a personal creative sphere. The frozen and ultraformalized gestures of the *Sarrafos* sealed the exhausting of a certain utopia of action, given the ultraindividualistic pragmatism and the marketing hegemony that arose in the eighties—after all, contemporary "public" life was a confessional scenario par excellence in which unrestrained and spectacular flourishing of the personal, of that which, in the final analysis, we once considered the innermost and most painful levels that constitute subjective life, was not only permitted but even encouraged. Quite aptly, the *Sarrafos* consist of a closed series of just twelve works, an eloquent counterpoint to the prodigality of gesture in the *Monotipias* series, which, as we know, totaled nearly two thousand. This disenchantment, however, does not mean that the *Sarrafos* do not reveal the desire to rediscover a new potency of the gesture. The impossibility of the unrestrained, extroverted gesture which the sharp, angular movements of these objects appear to embody indicate after all the reservoir of an extraordinary *will* merely awaiting the right moment to burst forth. It is from the feeding of that will that they extract their political meaning.

The Modern Utopia Devoured by the Brazilian Environment

It was, then, the works executed between the mid-sixties and the beginning of the seventies which marked Schendel's definitive separation from the

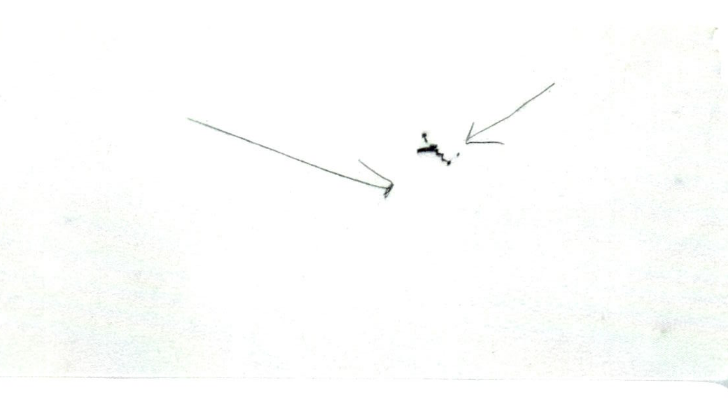

Untitled (Monotype) 1964–65

tacit framework of the European pictorial tradition of modernism and launched her intc the entanglements of contemporary art, at that time convulsively embroiled in the attempt to surmount the reification of the artistic object and to react to the guile of an art institution ever more inseparable from an autonomous field of art. In just a few years Schendel's work had matured vis-à-vis these dilemmas, and her élan, simultaneously deconstructive and lyrical, was an original and stimulating counterpoint to the cold pragmatism of Pop art, the most radical and incisive reaction to the cultural situation of the time.

We can very well imagine that, if it had continued in the wake of the modern tradition, exhausting the experimentation with material-laden surfaces, Schendel's work might have arrived at the melancholy elegance that dominated much of European painting in the transition from the fifties to the sixties, as evidenced in the gestural expressionism of such artists as Antoni Tàpies, Alberto Burri, or Lucio Fontana.[12] Surprisingly, however, she did not draw upon her European background but rather sought in the simplicity of the anxieties of daily life the central motivation for an experimental practice of art. It is reckless to speculate (at the risk of falling into the schematizing and generalizations that chronically characterize debates about a "Brazilian culture"), but it is equally irresistible to suppose that the cultural permissiveness of the Brazilian environment favored Schendel's boldness in quickly freeing herself from a pictorial tradition to which she had hitherto seemed inclined.

The *Monotipias* series, the *Droguinhas*, and the *Trenzinhos* are works of notable freedom; they declare their "nonartistic" nature as well as a corrosive, optimistic disrespect for the authority of style and the ethic of technique and skill. They were the perfect counterpoint to the discreet existential pathos nurtured by the informal abstraction that, along with constructive abstraction, had dominated the Brazilian artistic scene since the fifties, especially in the expanding nucleus of the São Paulo Bienal after 1951. And, if Schendel's works were far from allowing themselves to be moved by this pathos, they still did not address (at least directly) the constructive issues raised by the Rio de Janeiro Neoconcretist group, whose works nevertheless demonstrate some affinity to her own: although it can be said that we find in Schendel and in the Neoconcretists the same tension between construction

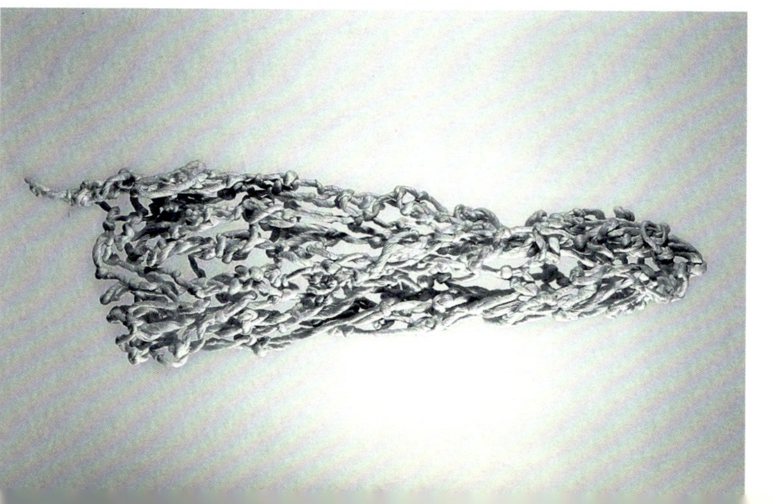

Untitled (Droguinha) 1966

and deconstruction, her work did not originate in the drive to revive and take to its ultimate consequences a misguided modern project, as desired by Rio artists. On the contrary, the *Monotipias*, *Droguinhas*, and *Trenzinhos*, as well as some of her drawings (e.g., *Que beleza* [How Beautiful] and the aforementioned *Sim*) and figurative paintings from the mid-sixties, allow a glimpse of a certain irony in Schendel's work revelatory of a cultural awareness of the new times, a cultural awareness to which the neoconcretist artists would remain to some degree remote or indifferent.

In any case, it is worthwhile to emphasize that this relatively short journey of Schendel's from European informalism to the *Droguinhas* testifies to the fluid and contradictory mobility with which Brazilian art in the fifties linked itself to a modern program (one should take into account that at this moment the local context was being swept by a truly modernizing wave, with the building of Brasília among its most defining examples). And when she appropriated this sense of the modern, fraught with impasse and disillusionment—a sense that the timid Modernist movement of 1922 had not succeeded in separating itself from the ideological pressures of nationalism and populism—Schendel's artistic production, paradoxically, surpassed it. Her work violated certain crucial presuppositions of modernism—notions of style, technique, and the modern notion of form itself—and plunged into the anguishing and objectless informalism of contemporary art. We know that Schendel, as well as Lygia Clark, Hélio Oiticica, and Lygia Pape, having begun from the same modern perspective (although, as has been said, Schendel did so by different routes than those taken by the Neoconcretists), achieved in a few years a resplendent historical experiment in which limits were tested and which collided with insurmountable cultural obstacles. This experiment, among other things, portrayed forcefully and tellingly the defeat of a utopian modern form, freeing itself, purified and omniscient, from its social substratum. Such a defeat, if precipitated in the developed countries by the advent of a well-nourished and omnipresent commercial culture that the world of art could not avoid, took on a very special meaning in Brazil.

Obviously, that commercial culture also replicated itself outside the countries of the center, and as the fifties became the sixties it impressed upon the Brazilian context a swirling trail of sociocultural contradictions, a phenomenon that would not go unnoticed by the more restive productions of the period—the Brazilian *Cinema Novo* and *Neoconcretismo* (already divided at the time by the deconstructive spirit of *Tropicalismo*)—which sharply criticized the explosive mixture of industrialization and underdevelopment. Still, it is necessary to admit that the modernizing wave that took over the country in that period was not fated to produce only timid and derivative fruits but actually involved the artistic debate in a generalized process of cultural deprovincialization. Unlike, for example, the pastoral images of entanglement between city and countryside and nature and technological progress which can be seen in the 1924–25 paintings of Tarsila do Amaral, the works that emerged at this time revealed an uneasy, demanding perception of the very idea of the modern not foreign to the political, historical, and cultural repercussions that the term held in the Brazilian context. It should be mentioned that this phenomenon was not a tardy mirroring of production based on the model of countries of the center, as seemed to be the fate of processes of modernization in so many peripheral regions; on the contrary, it was remarkable precisely because from this modern form was revealed an acute agent for questioning both Brazilian culture and the historical means of expansion of the modern program (for the conservative and destructive effects of modern expansion manifested themselves far more sharply in the periphery than in the center.)[13] As we have seen, in just a few years works such as those of Mira Schendel, Lygia Clark, Hélio Oiticica, and Lygia Pape caused the European heritage of an abstraction rooted in the old Cubist grid to age suddenly, pushing Brazilian art beyond the formal premises of modernism.

Translated by Clifford Landers

Notes

1 In this essay, the third I have devoted to the work of Mira Schendel, I have tried to limit myself to certain questions relating directly to works on display in the exhibition "The Experimental Exercise of Freedom: Lygia Clark, Gego, Mathias Goeritz, Hélio Oiticica, and Mira Schendel," in contrast to earlier ones in which I focused on her work more extensively. (They are: "Resisting the Present," in M. Catherine de Zegher, ed., *Inside the Visible: An Elliptical Traverse of Twentieth-Century Art in, of, and for the Feminine* [Cambridge, Mass.: MIT Press, 1996], 233–38, and "No vazio do mundo," in Sônia Salzstein, ed., *No vazio do mundo/Mira Schendel* [São Paulo: Galeria de Arte do Sesi, 1996], 15–29.) In this essay, therefore, not all of the important segments of Schendel's work are considered—for instance, her monochromatic temperas of the seventies and eighties—but these are discussed in a reasonable number of critical texts in Brazil, as are the mandalas and the series of quick spray drawings that she executed in the seventies; these works in fact have remained virtually absent from the debates about Schendel during the last two decades, and I still hope to be able to turn my attention to them in the future. In any case, although they are specific to works in this exhibition, questions raised in the text nonetheless explore key elements that concerned the artist throughout her career. Moreover, it is necessary to bear in mind that, despite the recognition that has come to her in the last decade, her work is still little known; broader and more systematic studies are needed to bring attention to her true contribution to the recent history of Brazilian art.

2 This phrase was used in the Porto Alegre newspaper *Correio do Povo*, 6 January 1950, in an article about the difficulties faced by recently arrived European immigrants. Cited in Célia Euvaldo, "Cronologia," in *No vazio do mundo*, 82.

3 In regard to the relevance that I attribute to the question of experience in Schendel's work, it strikes me as useful to evoke a key figure in the history of philosophy: Benedict de Spinoza, with his notion of immanence. Spinoza enters here through the commentary by Antonio Negri, a scholar of the Dutch philosopher, who brings to the contemporary debate the Spinozan notion of experience: "On those points where, in Spinoza, the destruction of transcendence and the recognition of the world are the rough affirmation of the consistency of experience and of its harshness, which only passion can reach and transform, in the postmodern, the ontological experience is spectral and spectacular. And where, in Spinoza, the destruction of all finalism and of every theological movement is compensated by the emergence of the creativity of desire, in the postmodern—accepted the death of teleology and of ideology—it is history itself that meets its end" (Antonio Negri, "Spinoza: Herói do povo pós-moderno," *Caderno Mais! Folha de São Paulo*, 28 February 1999, 5). In this commentary Negri responds (negatively) to the question of whether the revision of Spinoza carried out by such postmodern thinkers as Gilles Deleuze and Alexandre Matheron could reinforce certain topics of the postmodern argument which basically concern the affirmation of an intrinsic inconsistency of *experience* in the contemporary world. Although we do not know of any specific interest of Schendel's in the Dutch philosopher, her concern with the notion of immanence, her criticism of transcendence, and her esteem for corporeality (which can be traced back to the Spinozan recognition of the natural world) take us back to a philosophical tradition that points inevitably to Spinoza. If, furthermore, Schendel's work contains nothing of the postmodern, she did maintain the loose ties with the modern tradition and had a critical attitude vis-à-vis certain modern presuppositions, beginning with the figure of all-encompassing and transcendent subject.

4 Dominican clerics are known in Brazil for their historical position against the military regime that was in power from 1964 until 1984, for their unstinting intellectual activism in furtherance of freedom of expression, and for their support of sectors of the Catholic church in connection with social issues.

5 A self-understanding of the country as "predisposed toward the new," or, in the words of art critic Mário Pedrosa, "condemned to the modern," is frequent in Brazilian cultural history and is linked to the peculiar forms that Modernism would take on Brazilian soil beginning in the twenties—it eschewed the historical wedge of an industrial civilization and was instead an open horizon of possibilities for a culture that saw itself in the making and therefore was consecrated to the building of the present. In fact, the modernism of the twenties saw Brazilian art as a quintessential modern experiment inasmuch as it came forth in a young nation free from the burden of tradition. The modernist poet and writer Oswald de Andrade—who in the mid-twenties wrested Brazilian letters from the Parnassian universe and launched it into the unstable field of modern subjectivity with its syncopated speech and its hybrid, accelerated perception of the new industrial reality—hailed in his *Manifesto Antropófago* of 1928 the advent of the "technized primitive." In the very near future this would play a lead role in the vertiginous plunge of Brazilian culture into industrialization from which the "technized primitive" would be able better than anyone to reap the fruits, propelled by the power of the present and unshackled from the morality of culpability found in European civilization. We reencounter something of the sentiment of the new as a kind of Brazilian cultural atavism in a 1959 address by Mário Pedrosa, obviously now in a historical context very different from that of the primitive modernists: "Our past is not fatal, for we re-create it every day. And it has very little power over our destiny. We are, by the very inevitability of our background, *condemned to the modern* [emphasis mine]. Mário Pedrosa and Aracy Amaral, eds., *Dos murais de Portinari aos espaços de Brasília* (São Paulo: Editora Perspectiva, 1981), 347.

6 Schendel used glass plates to execute her *Monotipias*. When she was not employing some cutting instrument, she would crease with her nails or simply apply pressure with her arm to the back of the delicate sheets of rice paper placed on the glass plates, thus producing fleeting paint stains.

7 "One does not pass from a body to a thought but from one body to another body, successively," as we read in one of the innumerable typed texts by Hermann Schmitz that Schendel kept. Schmitz, with whom Schendel corresponded and in whose work she would find support for her ideas of corporeality and a relationship of reciprocal immanence between body and thought, was a specialist in philosophy and professor at the University of Kiel in the seventies.

8 *Ondas paradas de probabilidade*, shown in the São Paulo Bienal of 1968, is one of the transparency works that Schendel executed at the end of the sixties and the beginning of the following decade. It consisted of a perfect but evanescent environment in the form of a cube produced by thousands of extremely thin white threads hanging from the ceiling—an image of the dispersion of the subject into a multiplicity of surface vibrations.

9 Mira Schendel, "Mira Schendel pintora/o espaço vazio me comove profundamente" (interview with Jorge Guinle Filho), *Interview* (July 1981), 54.

10 "The art that completely covers this texture, this movement of the hand, is seriously mistaken. I place the greatest importance on its being manual, its being artisanal, its being experienced, on its coming from the belly. I think that's of the greatest importance. . . . Because even intellectual life . . . presupposes a specific corporeal disposition, that is, we can never abstract ourselves from corporeality" (Mira Schendel, ibid., 52).

11 As explained in Note 1.

12 Having, of course, to settle suspicions of derivativeness raised by fidelity to a tradition lacking roots in the peripheral country, and moreover at a time in which that tradition was beginning to show signs of exhaustion, as was presaged in the disenchanted and antimetaphysical performance of Pollock and in the lighthearted market-value conversions of Pop.

13 Otília Beatriz Fiori Arantes, *Urbanismo em fim de linha* (São Paulo: Editora da Universidade de São Paulo, 1998).

BIBLIOGRAPHY

General Works

Abstracionismo geométrico. Exhibition catalogue. São Paulo: Museu Banespa, 1996.

Ades, Dawn, ed. *Art in Latin America: The Modern Era, 1820–1980*. Exhibition catalogue. New Haven: Yale University Press; London: Hayward Gallery, 1989.

Amaral, Aracy. *Projeto construtivo brasileiro na arte: 1950–1962*. São Paulo: Pinacoteca do Estado; Rio de Janeiro: Museu de Arte Moderna, 1977.

Belluzzo, Ana Maria de Moraes, ed. *Modernidade: Vanguardas artísticas na América Latina*. São Paulo: Memorial, Editora UNESP, 1990.

Boulton, Alfredo. *Historia de la pintura en Venezuela*. Caracas: Editorial Arte, 1968.

Brett, Guy. "A Radical Leap." In *Art in Latin America: The Modern Era, 1820–1980*, ed. Dawn Ades. Exhibition catalogue. New Haven: Yale University Press; London: South Bank Centre, 1989.

———. *Transcontinental: An Investigation of Reality: Nine Latin American Artists*. London and New York: Verso, 1990.

Brito, Ronaldo. "Neoconcretismo." *Malasartes* (Rio de Janeiro), no. 3 (April–June 1976).

———. *Neoconcretismo: Vértice e ruptura do projeto construtivo brasileiro*. Rio de Janeiro: Edição FUNARTE, 1985.

Calzadilla, Juan, ed. *Movimientos y vanguardia en el arte contemporáneo en Venezuela*. Caracas, 1978.

Cardoza y Aragón, Luis. *Ruptura, 1952–1965*. Exhibition catalogue. Mexico City: Museo de Arte Alvar y Carmen T. Carrillo Gil and Museo Biblioteca Pape, 1988.

Carlos, Esther Emilio. *Grupo frente*. Retrospective catalogue. Rio de Janeiro: Instituto Brasil–Estados Unidos, 1994.

Cocchiarale, Fernando, and Anna Bella Geiger, eds. *Abstracionismo geométrico e informal: A vanguarda brasileira nos anos cinqüenta*. Exhibition catalogue. Rio de Janeiro: Edição FUNARTE, 1987.

"A divergència neoconcretista." Interview with Ferreira Gullar. *Fôlha de São Paulo* (São Paulo), 8 December 1996.

Elliott, David, ed. *Argentina 1920–1994: Art from Argentina*. Oxford: Museum of Modern Art, 1994.

García Canclini, Néstor. *Hybrid Cultures: Strategies for Entering and Leaving Modernity*. Trans. Christopher L. Chiappari and Silvia L. López. Minneapolis: University of Minnesota Press, 1995.

Goldman, Shifra M. *Contemporary Mexican Painting in a Time of Change*. 3rd ed. Austin: University of Texas Press, 1981.

Gradowczyk, Mario H. *Argentina: Arte concreto-invención 1945/Grupo Madí, 1946*. New York: Rachel Adler Gallery, 1990.

Guevara, Roberto. *Arte para una nueva escala*. Caracas, 1978.

Gullar, Ferreira. "Arte neoconcreta: Uma contribuição brasileira." *Crítica de Arte* (Rio de Janeiro), no. 1 (December 1961–March 1962).

———. "Da arte concreta à arte neoconcreta." *Módulo* (Rio de Janeiro), no. 13 (April 1959).

———. "Manifesto neoconcreto." *Jornal do Brasil: Suplemento Dominical* (Rio de Janeiro), 22 March 1959.

——. "Teoria do não-objeto." *Malasartes* (Rio de Janeiro), vol. 1 (1975): 26–27.

——. *Vanguarda e subdesenvolvimento.* Rio de Janeiro: Civilização Brasileira, 1965.

Manrique, Jorge Alberto, and Teresa del Conde et al. *El geometrismo mexicano.* Mexico City: Instituto de Investigaciones Estéticas, UNAM 1977.

Morais, Frederico. *Artes plásticas na América Latina: Do transe ao transitório.* Rio de Janeiro: Civilização Brasileira, 1979.

——. "Vocação construtiva na arte brasileira." *José* (Rio de Janeiro), no. 2 (August 1976).

Mosquera, Gerardo, ed. *Beyond the Fantastic: Contemporary Art Criticism from Latin America.* London: Institute of International Visual Arts, 1995.

Out of Actions: Between Performance and the Object 1949–1979. Los Angeles: The Museum of Contemporary Art, and New York: Thames and Hudson, 1998.

Pedrosa, Mário. *Mundo, homem, arte em crise.* São Paulo: Editora da Universidade de São Paulo/Editora Perspectiva, 1976.

——. *Arte/forma e personalidade.* São Paulo: Kairós Livraria e Editora, 1979.

——. *Forma e percepção estética escolhidos II.* São Paulo: Editora Perspectiva, 1981.

——. *Politica das artes.* São Paulo: Editora da Universidade de São Paulo, 1995.

Concretismo e neoconcretismo. Projeto arte brasileira: Abstração geométrica 1. Exhibition catalogue. Rio de Janeiro: FUNARTE, 1987.

Rasmussen, Waldo, with Fatima Bercht and Elizabeth Ferrer, eds. *Latin American Artists of the Twentieth Century.* Exhibition catalogue. New York: The Museum of Modern Art, 1993.

Rodríguez, Bélgica. "Arte geométrico, arte constructivo: Venezuela 1945–1965." In *Arte constructivo venezolano 1945–1965: Génesis y desarrollo.* Caracas: Maraven Editores, 1980.

Traba, Marta. *Mirar en Caracas: Crítica de arte.* Caracas: Monte Avila Editores, 1974.

Vandenbroeck, Paul, ed. *America, Bride of the Sun: 500 Years Latin America and the Low Countries.* Exhibition catalogue. Trans. Arte Belas et al. Antwerp: Royal Museum of Fine Arts, 1992.

Yúdice, George, Jean Franco, and Juan Flores, eds. *On Edge: The Crisis of Contemporary Latin American Culture.* Minneapolis: University of Minnesota Press, 1992.

Zanini, Walter, ed. *História geral da arte no Brasil.* 2 vols. São Paulo: Instituto Walther Moreira Salles, 1983.

Zilio, Carlos. "Da antropofagia á tropicália." In Carlos Zilio, João Luiz Lafetá, and Lígia Chiappini Moraes Leite, *Artes plásticas e literatura,* 11–56. São Paulo: Brasiliense, 1982.

Artists

Lygia Clark

Amaral, Aracy, ed. *Arte construtiva no Brasil: Coleção Adolpho Lerner*. São Paulo: DBA Dórea Books and Art, 1998.

Bense, Max. "Lygia Clark: Objetos variáveis." In *Pequena estética*, 219–21. São Paulo: Perspectiva, 1975.

Bois, Yve-Alain. "Lygia: L'art hors des enceintes." *Réforme* (Paris), 8 March 1969.

———. "Lygia Clark: Nostalgia of the Body." *October*, no. 69 (Summer 1994): 91–109.

———. "Lygia Clark, Palais des Beaux Arts, Paris." *Artforum* 27, no. 5 (January 1999): 116–17.

Brett, Guy. "Lygia Clark: In Search of the Body." *Art in America* 82, no. 7 (July 1994): 56–63, 108.

———. "Lygia Clark: The Borderline Between Art and Life." *Third Text* (London), no. 1 (Autumn 1987): 65–94.

———. "The Proposal of Lygia Clark." In *Inside the Visible: An Elliptical Traverse of Twentieth-Century Art in, of, and from the Feminine*, ed. M. Catherine de Zegher, 419–26. Exhibition catalogue. Cambridge: MIT Press, 1996.

Brito, Ronaldo. *Neoconcretismo: Vértice e ruptura do projeto construtivo brasileiro*. Rio de Janeiro: Edição FUNARTE, 1985.

———. "O moderno e o contemporâneo (o novo e o outro novo)." In *Arte brasileira contemporânea*. Rio de Janeiro: Edição FUNARTE, 1980.

Clark, Lygia. *Livro-obra*. Twenty-four copies published by Luciano Figueiredo and Ana Maria Aráujo. Rio de Janeiro, 1983.

Clay, Jean. "Lygia Clark: Fusion généralisée." *Robho* (Paris), no. 4 (1968): 12–14.

Fabbrini, Ricardo Nascimento. *O espaço de Lygia Clark*. São Paulo: Atlas, 1994.

Figueiredo, Luciano, ed. *Lygia Clark–Hélio Oiticica: Cartas, 1964–74*. Rio de Janeiro: Editora UFRJ, 1996.

Gullar, Ferreira. "Lygia Clark e a pintura brasileira." *Jornal do Brasil* (Rio de Janeiro), 7 September 1958.

Herkenhoff, Paulo. "A aventura planar de Lygia Clark: de caracóis, escadas e 'Caminhando.'" In *Apresentação da exposição Lygia Clark*. Exhibition catalogue. São Paulo: Museu de Arte Moderna, 1999.

Lygia Clark. Exhibition catalogue. Barcelona: Fundació Antoni Tàpies, 1998.

Medalla, David. "Participe présent: L'art de Lygia Clark." *Robho* (Paris), no. 4 (1968): 16–17.

Milliet, Maria Alice. *Lygia Clark: Obra-trajeto*. São Paulo: Editora de Universidade de São Paulo, 1992.

Rolnik, Suely. "Lygia Clark et la production d'un état d'art." In *L'art au corps*, 276–83. Exhibition catalogue. Marseilles: Musées de Marseille; Paris: Réunion des Musées Nationaux, 1996.

———. "The Hybrid of Lygia Clark." In *Lygia Clark*. Exhibition catalogue. Barcelona: Fundació Antoni Tàpies, 1997.

———. "Anthropophagic Subjectivity." In *Arte brasileira contemporânea*. Fundaçao Bienal de São Paulo, 1998

———. *O corpo vibrátil*. São Paulo: DBA Editora, 1999.

Sergio Duarte, Paulo. *Anos 60: Transformação da arte no Brasil*. Rio de Janeiro: Editora Campos Gerais, 1998.

Gego

Acuarelas de Gego. Exhibition catalogue. Caracas: Galería de Arte Nacional, 1982.

Amaral, Aracy. "Abstract Constructivist Trends in Argentina, Brazil, Venezuela, and Colombia." In *Latin American Artists of the Twentieth Century*, ed. Waldo Rasmussen with Fatima Bercht and Elizabeth Ferrer. Exhibition catalogue. New York: The Museum of Modern Art, 1993.

Amor, Mónica. "Gego: Desafiando estructuras." *Poliester* (Mexico City) 4, no. 14 (Winter 1995): 20–25.

Calzadilla, Juan. *El arte en Venezuela*. Caracas: Círculo Musical, 1967.

Carvajal, Rina. "Gego: Weaving the Margins." In *Inside the Visible: An Elliptical Traverse of Twentieth-Century Art in, of, and from the Feminine*, ed. M. Catherine de Zegher, 340–45. Exhibition catalogue. Cambridge: MIT Press, 1996.

Catálogo esculturas Gego. Exhibition catalogue. Bogotá: Biblioteca Luis Angel Arango del Banco de la República, 1967. Essay by Isaac Chocrón.

Chocrón, Isaac. "Viewpoint." *The Daily Journal* (Caracas), 18 May 1958.

Constantine, Mildred, and Jack Lenor Larsen. *Beyond Craft: The Art Fabric*. New York: Van Nostrand Reinhold Company, 1972.

Diament de Sujo, Clara. "Una mañana con Gego." *El Nacional: Papel Literario* (Caracas) (October 1960).

Espinoza, Eugenio. *Gego: Dibujos*. Exhibition catalogue. Caracas: Museo de Barquisimeto, Editorial Arte, 1985.

Figarella, Marianna. *Gego: Dibujos sin papel*. Exhibition catalogue. Caracas: Museo de Bellas Artes, 1984.

Gego: "Reticulárea." Exhibition catalogue. Caracas: Instituto Nacional de la Cultura y Bellas Artes y Museo de Bellas Artes, 1969.

Guevara, Roberto. "Gego." In *XXIII Bienal Internacional São Paulo: Sala especiais*, 150–69. Exhibition catalogue. São Paulo: Fundação Bienal de São Paulo, 1996.

———. *XXIV Bienal Internacional São Paulo*. Exhibition catalogue. São Paulo: Fundação Bienal de São Paulo, 1998.

———. "Gego: Sobre papel, sobre espacio." *El Nacional* (Caracas), 26 November 1968.

———. "'Reticulárea' de Gego." *El Nacional* (Caracas), 10 June 1969.

Introducción para "Reticulárea." Exhibition catalogue. Caracas: Galería Conkright, 1969. Essay by Lourdes Blanco.

Mahlow, Dietrich. "Los espacios de Gego." *Arte Armitano* (Caracas), no. 11 (October 1986): 65–76.

Oramas, Luis Pérez. *La invención de la continuidad*. Exhibition catalogue. Caracas: Fundación Galería de Arte Nacional, 1997.

Ossott, Hanni. *Gego*. Caracas: Ediciones Museo de Arte Contemporáneo, 1977.

Painting and Sculpture Acquisitions. Exhibition catalogue. New York: The Museum of Modern Art, 1960.

Palacios, María Fernanda. "Conversación con Gego." *Ideas* (Caracas), no. 3 (May 1971): 23–27.

Ramírez, Mari Carmen, ed. *Re-Aligning Vision: Alternative Currents in South American Drawing*. Exhibition catalogue. Austin: Archer M. Huntington Art Gallery, University of Texas at Austin, 1998.

Schön, Elizabeth. "Los trabajos de Gego." *Revista CAL* (Caracas) (1964).

Sierra, Eliseo. *Gego: Dibujos, grabados, tejeduras*. Caracas: Editorial Ex Libris, 1996.

Silva, Ludovico. "Lo nunca proyectado." *El Nacional* (Caracas), 29 January 1965.

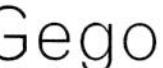

Tamarind: A Renaissance of Lithography. Baltimore, Md.: Garamond Pridemark Press, 1971. Introduction by E. Maurice Bloch.

Traba, Marta. "Gego." *Séptimo Día/11* (Caracas), 1 April 1973.

———. *Gego*. Exhibition catalogue. Caracas: Museo de Arte Contemporáneo de Caracas, 1973.

———. *Gego*. Exhibition catalogue. Caracas: Ediciones Museo de Arte Contemporáneo, 1977.

———. "Gego: Caracas tres mil." In *Mirar en Caracas: Crítica de Arte*, 51–60. Caracas: Monte Avila Editores, 1974.

Una visión del arte contemporáneo venezolano: Colección Ignacio y Valentina Oberto. Exhibition catalogue. Caracas: Fundación Noa Noa, 1995.

Mathias Goeritz

Angel Ferrant–Mathias Goeritz. Exhibition catalogue. Madrid: Galería Palma, 1949. Essay by Ricardo Gullón.

Auer, Gerhard. *Mathias Goeritz: El eco*. Bonn: Deutschen Forschungsgemeinschaft, 1995.

Ayfre, Amédée. "Mathias Goeritz: Misère, prière, lumière." *Art et Architecture: Aujourd'hui* (Paris), no. 33 (October 1961): 28–29.

Bayer, Herbert. "Reflections from One of the Sculptors Who Contributed to the 'Route of Friendship.'" In *Architecture: Formes fonctions*. Lausanne: Editions Anthony Krafft, 1969.

Bense, Max. "Mathias Goeritz: Nó solo en México." *Nivel* (Mexico City), no. 69 (25 September 1968).

Buchloh, Benjamin H. D., and M. Catherine de Zegher. "Ver América: A Written Exchange." In *America, Bride of the Sun: 500 Years Latin America and the Low Countries*, 223–49. Exhibition catalogue. Antwerp: Royal Museum of Fine Arts, 1992.

Damaz, Paul F. *Art in Latin American Architecture*. New York: Reinhold Publishing Corporation, 1963. Preface by Oscar Niemeyer.

Exposición de la Escuela de Altamira. Exhibition catalogue. Santillana del Mar: Fundación Santillana, 1981. Essay by Eduardo Westerdahl, "La Escuela de Altamira." Essay by Rafael Santos Torroella, "Breve historia de la Escuela de Altamira."

Ferrant, Angel. "Conocimiento de Mathias Goeritz." *Ver y Estimar* (Buenos Aires), no. 20 (October 1950): 43–46.

Gasch, Sebastián. "Mathias Goeritz y la Escuela de Altamira." *Destino* (Barcelona), 28 May 1949.

Goeritz, Mathias. "Las Torres de Satélite." *Plural* (Mexico City), no. 49 (October 1975).

———. "Manifesto: Arquitectura emocional." *Cuadernos de Arquitectura* (Guadalajara), no. 1 (March 1954).

———. "Manifesto: Estoy harto." In *Mathias Goeritz*. Exhibition catalogue. Mexico City: Galería Souza, 1960.

———. "'The Route of Friendship': Sculpture." *Leonardo* (Great Britain), vol. 3 (1970).

Gortázar, Fernando González. *Mathias Goeritz en Guadalajara*. Guadalajara: Editorial Universidad de Guadalajara, 1991.

Kassner, Lily. *Mathias Goeritz: Una biografía, 1915–1990*. Mexico City: Instituto Nacional de Bellas Artes, 1998.

Katzman, Israel. *La arquitectura contemporánea mexicana: Precedentes y desarrollo*. Mexico City: Instituto Nacional de Antropología e Historia, 1963.

Levin, Michael D. *Architectural Sculpture: Mathias Goeritz*. Exhibition catalogue. Jerusalem: The Israel Museum, 1980.

Los ecos de Mathias Goeritz: Catálogo de la exposición. Retrospective catalogue. Mexico City: Instituto Nacional de Bellas Artes, Antiguo Colegio de San Ildefonso, Instituto de Investigaciones Estéticas, UNAM, 1997.

Mathias Goeritz: Ein deutscher Kunstler in Mexiko. Marburg: Jonas Verlag. Kunst und Literatur GmbH, 1987. Foreword by Elke Werry.

Mathias Goeritz: Arquitectura emocional. Exhibition catalogue. Mexico City: Museo de Arte Moderno, 1984.

Mathias Goeritz, 1915–1990: El eco: Bilder, Skulpturen, Modelle. Exhibition catalogue. Berlin: Akademie der Kunste, 1992.

Morais, Frederico. *Mathias Goeritz*. Mexico City: UNAM, 1982.

Nesbit, G. "'The Towers of Satellite City.'" *Arts & Architecture* (Los Angeles) 75, no. 5 (May 1958): 22–23.

Platschek, Hanz. "Las direcciones formales de Mathias Goeritz." *Pro Arte* (Santiago de Chile) 4, no. 147 (8 November 1951).

Poniatowska, Elena. "Juicio de un arquitecto." *Excélsior* (Mexico City), 8 April 1954.

Preston, Stuart. "Rebel with Cause." *The New York Times: New Frontiers*, 2 March 1962.

Ragon, Michel. "Mathias Goeritz: Le pour et le contre." *Robho* (Paris), no. 4 (1968): 24–27.

Rodríguez Prampolini, Ida. "Mathias Goeritz: De la materia hacia Dios." *El Nacional* (Mexico City), no. 16 (9 September 1990): 4–7.

Rodríguez Prampolini, Ida, and Ferruccio Asta. *Los ecos de Mathias Goeritz: Ensayos y testimonios*. Mexico City: Instituto de Investigaciones Estéticas, UNAM, 1997.

Smith, Clive Bamford. *Builders in the Sun: Five Mexican Architects*. New York: Architectural Book Publishing, 1967. Foreword by Dr. José Villagrán García.

Toledo, Mario Monteforte. *Conversaciones con Mathias Goeritz*. Mexico City: Editorial Siglo XXI, 1994.

Westerdahl, Eduardo, and Ricardo Gullón. "Sobre Mathias Goeritz." *Ver y Estimar* (Buenos Aires), no. 20 (October 1950): 49–50.

Zúñiga, Olivia. *Mathias Goeritz*. Mexico City: Editorial Intercontinental, 1963.

Hélio Oiticica

Amaral, Aracy, ed. *Arte construtiva no Brasil: Coleção Adolpho Leirner*. São Paulo: DBA Dórea Books and Art, 1998.

———. *Projeto construtivo brasileiro na arte 1950–1962*. São Paulo: Pinacoteca do Estado; Rio de Janeiro: Museu de Arte Moderna, 1977.

———. "Fait sur le corps: Le 'Parangolé' de Hélio Oiticica." *Cahiers du Musée National d'Art Moderne* (Paris), no. 51 (Spring 1995): 32–45.

———. "Hélio Oiticica: Reverie and Revolt." *Art in America* 77, no. 1 (January 1989): 29–41.

———. "Lygia Clark and Hélio Oiticica." In *Latin American Artists of the Twentieth Century*, ed. Waldo Rasmussen with Fatima Bercht and Elizabeth Ferrer. Exhibition catalogue. New York: The Museum of Modern Art, 1993.

———. "Oiticica Talks to Guy Brett." *Studio International* (London), no. 909 (March 1969): 134.

Brito, Ronaldo. *Neoconcretismo: Vértice e ruptura do projeto construtivo brasileiro*. Rio de Janeiro: Edição FUNARTE, 1985.

Buchloh, Benjamin H. D., and M. Catherine de Zegher. "Ver América: A Written Exchange." In *America, Bride of the Sun: 500 Years Latin America and the Low Countries*. Exhibition catalogue. Antwerp: Royal Museum of Fine Arts, 1992.

Cocchiarale, Fernando. *Hélio Oiticica: Grupo frente 1955–1956, Metaesquemas 1957–1958*. Exhibition catalogue. Rio de Janeiro: Joel Edelstein Arte Contemporânea, 1996.

Duarte, Paulo Sergio. *Anos 60: Transformação da arte no Brasil*. Rio de Janeiro: Editora Campos Gerais, 1998.

Favaretto, Celso Fernando. *A invenção de Hélio Oiticica.* São Paulo: Editora da Universidade de São Paulo, 1992.

———. "A música nos labirintos de Hélio Oiticica." *Revista* (São Paulo) (December 1980–January/February 1981): 45–54.

Figueiredo, Luciano. *Hélio Oiticica.* Exhibition catalogue. Rio de Janeiro: Centro Hélio Oiticica, 1992.

Figueiredo, Luciano, ed. *Lygia Clark–Hélio Oiticica: Cartas, 1964–1974.* Rio de Janeiro: Editora da UFRJ, 1997.

Figueiredo, Luciano, Lygia Pape, and Waly Salomão, eds. *Aspiro ao grande labirinto: Textos de Hélio Oiticica.* Rio de Janeiro: Editora Rocco, 1986.

Gullar, Ferreira. "Diálogo sobre o não-objeto." *Jornal do Brasil: Suplemento Dominical* (Rio de Janeiro), 26 March 1960.

Hélio Mangueira Oiticica. Exhibition catalogue. Rio de Janeiro: Galeria Universidade Estadual do Rio de Janeiro, 1990. Essay by Waly Salomão.

Hélio Oiticica. Exhibition catalogue. London: Whitechapel Gallery, 1969. Essay by Guy Brett.

Hélio Oiticica. Retrospective catalogue. Paris: Galerie National du Jeu de Paume; Rio de Janeiro: Projeto Hélio Oiticica; and Rotterdam: Witte de With, Center for Contemporary Art, 1992. Essay by Guy Brett, "The Experimental Exercise of Liberty." Essay by Haroldo de Campos, "Hang-glider of Ecstasy." Essay by Waly Salomão, "Homage." Essay by Catherine David, "The Great Labyrinth."

Lygia Clark e Hélio Oiticica. Exhibition catalogue. Rio de Janeiro: IX Salão Nacional de Artes Plásticas da FUNARTE, 1986. Essay by Glória Ferreira, "Terreiro do paço: Cena para Lygia Clark e Hélio Oiticica." Essay by Hélio Oiticica, "Cartas a Lygia Clark."

Morais, Frederico. "Contra a arte afluente: O corpo é o motor da obra." In *Depoimento de uma geração, 1969–1970.* Exhibition catalogue. Rio de Janeiro: Galeria BANERJ, 1986.

Nova objetividade brasileira. Exhibition catalogue. Rio de Janeiro: Museu de Arte Moderna, 1967. Preface by Hélio Oiticica.

Os projetos de Hélio Oiticica. Exhibition catalogue. Rio de Janeiro: Museu de Arte Moderna, 1961.

Pedrosa, Mário. "Arte ambiental, arte pós-moderna: Hélio Oiticica." *Correio da Manhã* (Rio de Janeiro), 26 June 1966.

———. "Os projetos de Hélio Oiticica." *Jornal do Brasil: Suplemento Dominical* (Rio de Janeiro), 25 November 1961.

———. *Mundo, homen, arte em crise.* São Paulo: Perspectiva, 1975.

Pignatari, Decio. "Hélio Oiticica e a arte de agora." *Jornal da Tarde* (São Paulo), 4 April 1980, and *Código 4* (Salvador) (August 1980).

Salomão, Waly. *Hélio Oiticica: Qual é o "Parangolé"?* Rio de Janeiro: Relume-Dumará/Prefeitura do Município do Rio de Janeiro, 1996.

Zilio, Carlos. "Da 'Antropofagia' à 'Tropicália.'" In Carlos Zilio, João Luiz Lafetá, and Lígia Chiappini Moraes Leite. *Artes plásticas e literatura,* 11–56. São Paulo: Brasiliense, 1982.

Mira Schendel

Amaral, Aracy. "Mira Schendel: Os cadernos." *O Estado de São Paulo* (São Paulo), 7 November 1971, 1.

Bense, Max, ed. *Mira Schendel: Grafische Reduktionen.* Stuttgart: Universität Stuttgart, 1967.

Brett, Guy. *Kinetic Art: The Language of Movement.* London: Studio Vista, 1968.

Brito, Ronaldo. *Singular no plural.* Exhibition catalogue. Rio de Janeiro: FUNARTE/Galeria Sergio Milliet, 1988.

———. *Gesto e estrutura.* Exhibition catalogue. São Paulo: Gabinete de Arte Raquel Arnaud, 1989.

Campos, Haroldo de. *Mira Schendel.* Exhibition catalogue. Rio de Janeiro: Museu de Arte Moderna, 1966.

———. "Via Chuang-tsé 2." In *Mira Schendel: Desenhos de 1974–75: Datiloscritos, mandalas, paisagens*. Exhibition catalogue. São Paulo: Gabinete de Artes Gráficas, 1975.

Campos, Paulo Malta. *XXII Bienal Internacional de São Paulo: Salas especiais*, 74–82. Exhibition catalogue. São Paulo: Fundaçao Bienal de São Paulo, 1994.

Dias, Geraldo de Sousa. "Zwischen metaphysik und Leiblichkeit: Leben und Werk der Künstlerin Mira Schendel." Doctoral dissertation, Hochschule der Kunste, Berlin, 1999.

Duarte, Paulo Sergio. *Anos 60: Transformação da arte no Brasil*. Rio de Janeiro: Editora Campos Gerais, 1998.

Dwek, Lisette Lagnado. "Transparência e escritura nas monotipias de Mira Schendel." Master's thesis, Pontifícia Universidade Católica de São Paulo, 1999.

———. *Entre o desenho e a escultura*, 4–8. Exhibition catalogue. São Paulo: Museu de Arte Moderna de São Paulo, 1995.

Farias, Agnaldo. "Uma visão interna." *Jornal de Resenhas da Fôlha de São Paulo* (São Paulo), 10 January 1997.

———. "Mira Schendel: O movimento das margens." In *Mira Schendel*. Retrospective catalogue. São Paulo: Museu de Arte Contemporânea da Universidade de São Paulo, 1990.

Flusser, Vilém. "Indagações sobre a origem da língua." *O Estado de São Paulo* (São Paulo), 29 April 1967, 1.

———. "Fora do alcance da língua." *Arte em São Paulo* (São Paulo), no. 36 (1987): 44.

Herkenhoff, Paulo. "Mira Schendel and the Shaping of the Inexpressible." In *Mira Schendel: Art from Brazil in New York*. Exhibition catalogue. New York: The Drawing Center, 1995.

Medalla, David. "Mira Schendel." *Signals News Bulletin* (London) 1, no. 9 (1965).

Naves, Rodrigo. "Conceitos sensíveis." In *Mira Schendel: Pinturas recentes*. Exhibition catalogue. São Paulo: Paulo Figueiredo Galeria de Arte, 1985.

———. "Limite e determinação." In *Mira Schendel*. Exhibition catalogue. São Paulo: Galeria Camargo Vilaça, 1994.

———. "From Behind." In *No vazio do mundo: Mira Schendel*, 67–69. Exhibition catalogue. São Paulo: Galeria de Arte do SESI, 1996.

Resende, José. "Entre o desenho e a pintura." *Arte em São Paulo* (São Paulo), no. 36 (1987): 53.

Salzstein, Sônia, ed. *No vazio do mundo: Mira Schendel*. Exhibition catalogue. São Paulo: Galeria de Arte do SESI, 1996.

———. "Resistindo ao presente." In *Mira Schendel: A forma volátil*, 16–25. Exhibition catalogue. Rio de Janeiro: Centro de Arte Hélio Oiticica, 1997.

Schemberg, Mário. *Mira Schendel*. Exhibition catalogue. São Paulo: Galeria Selearte, 1962.

———. *Pensando a arte*. São Paulo: Nova Stella, 1988.

Schendel, Mira. *Deposition for the X Campinas Contemporary Art Salon*. Campinas: Museu de Arte Contemporânea de Campinas "José Pancetti," 1975.

Tassinari, Alberto. "Mais ou menos frutas." *A Fôlha de São Paulo* (São Paulo), 3 September 1984, 10–11.

"Um olhar Inglés sobre a arte Brasileira." Interview with Guy Brett. *Caderno de Cultura* (São Paulo), 30 August 1997.

Zegher, M. Catherine de, ed. *Inside the Visible: An Elliptical Traverse of Twentieth-Century Art in, of, and from the Feminine*. Exhibition catalogue. Cambridge, Mass: MIT Press, 1996.

BIBLIOGRAPHY

CHECKLIST

Dimensions are in feet and inches, height precedes width precedes depth. A bullet (•) indicates works in the exhibition. Page numbers correspond to the works illustrated in the catalogue.

Lygia Clark

1 *Sem título*
(Untitled), 1950–51
Ink on paper
Courtesy Coleção Família Clark/MAM–RJ
PAGE 62

2 *Descoberta da linha orgânica*
(Discovery of the Organic Line), 1954
Oil on canvas anc wood
35 [illegible] x 35 [illegible] inches
Courtesy Coleção Família Clark/MAM–RJ
PAGE 71

3 *Unidades (no. 1 e no. 7)*
(Units 1 and 7), 1958
Industrial paint or wood
11 [illegible] x 11 x [illegible] inches
Courtesy Coleção Família Clark/MAM–RJ
PAGE 72

4 *Casulo*
(Cocoon), 1959
Iron
16 [illegible] x 16 [illegible] x 2 [illegible] inches
Courtesy Coleção Família Clark/MAM–RJ
Photograph by Rômulo Fialdini
PAGE 74

5 • *Caminhando*
(Walking), 1963
Black-and-white photographs and text; set of 7
Coleção Família Clark/MAM–RJ
PAGES 64–66

6 *Trepantes (Obra mole)*
(Grubs [Soft work]), 1964
Rubber
Courtesy Coleção Família Clark/MAM–RJ
PAGE 78

7 • *Água e conchas*
(Water and Shells), 1966/1999
Plastic bag, rubber strings, shells, and water
11 [illegible]/4 x 7 [illegible]/2 inches
Coleção Família Clark/MAM–RJ

8 • *Desenhe com o dedo*
(Drawing with Your Finger), 1966/1999
Plastic bag and water
Coleção Família Clark/MAM–RJ

9 • *Livro sensorial*
(Sensorial Book), 1966/1999
Book with transparent plastic pages filled with different materials (shells, pebbles, elastic bands, etc.)
Approx. 7 x 7 inches
Coleçao Família Clark/MAM–RJ

10 • *Pedra e ar*
(Stone and Air), 1966/1999
Plastic bag and stones
Coleção Família Clark/MAM–RJ

11 • *Ping-pong*, 1966/1999
Plastic bag, water, and ping-pong balls
Coleção Família Clark/MAM–RJ

12 • *Respire comigo*
(Breathe with Me), 1966/1999
Rubber tube
$15\frac{7}{10} \times 1\frac{3}{5} \times 1\frac{3}{5}$ inches
Coleção Família Clark/MAM-RJ

13 • *Diálogo de mãos*
(Dialogue of Hands), 1966/1999
Elastic band
$4\frac{7}{10} \times 5\frac{9}{10}$ inches
Coleção Família Clark/MAM-RJ

14 • *O corpo coletivo*
(The Collective Body), 1966/1999
Fabric and cotton thread
Coleçao Família Clark/MAM-RJ

15 • *Cesariana: Série roupa-corpo-roupa*
(Caesarian: Clothing-Body-Clothing Series), 1967/1999
Plastic overalls, paper, and sponge flakes
$59\frac{9}{10} \times 27\frac{4}{5} \times 5\frac{9}{10}$ inches
Coleção Família Clark/MAM-RJ

16 *O eu e o tu: Série roupa-corpo-roupa*
(The I and the You: Clothing-Body-Clothing Series), 1967
Plastic overalls, plastic bag, water, and rubber
Courtesy Coleção Família Clark/MAM-RJ
PAGES 80-81

17 • *O eu e o tu: Série roupa-corpo-roupa*
(The I and the You: Clothing-Body-Clothing Series), 1967/1999
Plastic overalls, plastic bag, water, and rubber
$59\frac{9}{10} \times 27\frac{4}{5} \times 5\frac{9}{10}$ inches
Coleção Família Clark/MAM-RJ

18 • ***Máscaras sensoriais: Máscara azul, Máscara branca, Máscara cereja, Máscara côr-de-abóbora, Máscara verde, Máscara preta***
(Sensorial Masks: Blue Mask, White Mask, Cherry Mask, Pumpkin-colored Mask, Green Mask, Black Mask), 1967/1999
Cotton cloth with irregular cuts, objects, and fragrances
$25\frac{3}{5} \times 19\frac{7}{10} \times 2$ inches
Coleção Família Clark/MAM-RJ

19 *Máscara abismo*
(Abyss Mask), 1968
Photograph by Michael Desjardins
Courtesy Guy Brett
PAGES 26, 86

20 **Bienal de Veneza**
Installation view (Venice Biennale), 1968
Courtesy Coleção Família Clark/MAM-RJ
PAGE 71

21 • *Arquiteturas biológicas: Ovo mortalha*
(Biological Architectures: Egg-Shroud), 1968/1999
Plastic, nylon net, and cotton thread
Coleção Família Clark/MAM-RJ

22 • *Luvas sensoriais*
(Sensorial Gloves), 1968/1999
Gloves (two chamois leather pairs, two rubber pairs) and balls of various materials and sizes
$11\frac{3}{4} \times 7\frac{7}{8} \times$ inches
Coleção Família Clark/MAM-RJ

23 • *Máscara abismo*
(Abyss Mask), 1968/1999
Cotton net, pebbles, and plastic bags
Coleção Família Clark/MAM-RJ

24 • ***A casa é o corpo. Penetração, ovulação, germinação, expulsão***
(The House Is the Body: Penetration, Ovulation, Germination, Expulsion), 1968/1999
Wood, plastic, fabric, elastic bands, balloons, rubber balls, fibers, and incandescent light
Coleção Família Clark/MAM-RJ

25 • *Óculos*
(Goggles), 1968/1999
Diving goggles connected by folding metal parts to form a set that can be expanded and contracted
$1\frac{7}{10} \times 5\frac{9}{10}$ inches
Coleção Família Clark/MAM-RJ

26 • *Diálogo: Óculos*
(Dialogue: Goggles), 1968/1999
Diving goggles made to be used by two participants
$2\frac{1}{5} \times 5\frac{9}{10} \times 7\frac{2}{5}$ inches
Coleção Família Clark/MAM–RJ

27 *Arquiteturas biológicas I*
(Biological Architectures I), 1969
Plastic, nylon net, and cotton thread
Courtesy Coleção Família Clark/MAM–RJ
PAGE 83

28 *Arquiteturas biológicas II*
(Biological Architectures II), 1969
Plastic, nylon net, pebbles, and cotton thread
Courtesy Coleção Família Clark/MAM–RJ
PAGE 83

29 • *Casal*
(Couple), 1969/1999
Plastic and wire
$66\frac{9}{10} \times 17\frac{7}{10} \times 17\frac{7}{10}$ inches
Coleção Família Clark/MAM–RJ

30 • *Camisa-de-força*
(Straitjacket), 1969/1999
Nylon net, pebbles, and cotton thread
Coleção Família Clark/MAM–RJ

31 • *Estruturas vivas*
(Living Structures), 1969/1999
Rubber bands
Coleção Família Clark/MAM–RJ

32 *Arquiteturas biológicas I*
(Biological Architectures I), 1969/1998
Courtesy Fundació Antoni Tàpies, Barcelona
Photograph by Marc Corominas
PAGES 34–35

33 • *Arquiteturas biológicas II*
(Biological Architectures II), 1969/1999
Plastic, nylon net, pebbles, and cotton thread
Coleção Família Clark/MAM–RJ

34 • *Arquiteturas biológicas: Nascimento*
(Biological Architectures: Birth), 1969/1999
Plastic, nylon net, and cotton thread
Coleção Família Clark/MAM–RJ

35 *Baba antropofágica*
(Anthropophagic Slobber), 1973
String and saliva
Courtesy Coleção Família Clark/MAM
PAGE 90

36 • *O mundo de Lygia Clark*
(The World of Lygia Clark), 1973
Video
Coleçao Família Clark/MAM–RJ

37 • *Túnel*
(Tunnel), 1973/99
Fabric and cotton thread
Coleção Família Clark/MAM–RJ

38 *Rede de elástico*
(Elastic Net), 1973
Rubber
Courtesy Coleção Família Clark/MAM
PAGES 88–89

39 *Estruturação do self: Objetos relacionais*
(Structuring of the Self: Relational Objects), 1976
Light pillow, light-heavy pillow, heavy pillow, big mattress, blankets, pantyhose, plastic bag, seeds, stones, nylon net, rubber tube, water, sand, shells, and cardboard tube
Courtesy Coleção Família Clark/MAM
PAGES 56–58, 93–97

40 • *Memória do corpo*
(Memory of the Body), 1985
Video
Coleçao Família Clark/MAM–RJ

Gego

1 Gego working on *Reticulárea*, 1968
Courtesy Fundación Gego, Caracas
Photograph by Juan Santana
PAGE 112

2 *Reticulárea*
Installation at Museo de Bellas Artes, Caracas, 1969
Environmental wire sculpture
Collection Galería de Arte Nacional
Courtesy Americas Society, New York
Photograph by Paolo Gasparini
PAGES 47, 116, 126–27

3 *Reticulárea*
Installation at Americas Society, New York, 1969
Environmental wire sculpture
Size of room: 20 1/2 x 21 1/2 x 11 1/2 feet
Courtesy Americas Society, New York
Photograph by Charles Uht
PAGES 110–11

4 • *Sin título*
(Untitled), ca. 1969
Iron wire and lead pieces
25 3/16 x 13 1/8 x 15 1/4 inches
Private collection

5 *Chorros*
(Streams) (detail), 1970
Natural aluminum rods and steel
Dimensions variable
Courtesy Fundación Gego, Caracas
Photograph by A. M. Castillo
PAGE 115

6 *Chorros*
(Streams) (detail), 1970
Natural aluminum rods and steel
Dimensions variable
Courtesy Fundación Gego, Caracas
Photograph by A. M. Castillo
PAGE 125

7 • *Chorro*
(Stream), 1970
Three pieces: Aluminum rods
110 1/4 inches high
Private collection

8 • *Chorro #3*
(Stream #3), ca. 1970
Anodized aluminum and paint
135 4/5 x 19 1/5 x 19 3/5 inches
Museo de Barquisimeto

9 • *Chorro #8*
(Stream #8), ca. 1970
Anodized aluminum
143 7/10 x 15 1/10 x 15 7/10 inches
Museo de Barquisimeto

10 • *Chorro #9*
(Stream #9), ca. 1970
Anodized aluminum
279 1/5 x 27 1/5 x 19 3/5 inches
Museo de Barquisimeto

11 • *Chorro: Tres agrupaciones*
(Stream: Group of Three), ca. 1970–71
Natural aluminum rods, steel, and paint
Three parts: 94 1/2 x 3 1/8 x 2 1/4 inches;
11/16 x 4 11/16 x 7 7/8 inches; 11/16 x 7 7/8 x 5 7/8 inches
Private collection
Photograph by Ricardo Armas
PAGE 125

12 *Chorro: Tres agrupaciones*
(Stream: Group of Three) (detail), ca. 1970–71
Natural aluminum rods, steel, and paint
Three parts: 94 1/2 x 3 1/8 x 2 1/4 inches;
11/16 x 4 11/16 x 7 7/8 inches; 11/16 x 7 7/8 x 5 7/8 inches
Private collection
Photograph by Ricardo Armas
PAGE 125

13 • *Chorro # 7*
(Stream #7), 1971
Steel and aluminum rods
68 7/8 x 16 1/2 x 10 5/8 inches
Private collection

14 • *Reticulárea cuadrada*
(Square *Reticulárea*), 1971
Mixed media: Steel and stainless-steel construction
78 [illegible]/4 x 23 [illegible] x 23 [illegible] inches
BRONDESBURY HOLDINGS LTD.

15 Gego with *Chorros*
(Streams), 1971
Installation at Museo de Barquisimeto, 1985
Courtesy Fundación Gego, Caracas
Photograph by Vieri Tomaselli
PAGES 122–23

16 • *Columna: Reticulárea Cuadrada*
(Column: Square *Reticulárea*), 1971–72
Stainless-steel wire, metal tubes, iron washers, four pieces of lead, and nylon thread
138 x 51 x 51 inches
Private collection

17 *Cuerdas*
(Ropes)
Installation at Parque Central, Caracas, 1972
Nylon, aluminum, steel, and copper ropes
55 [illegible] x 65 [illegible] feet on four levels
Courtesy Fundación Gego, Caracas
Photograph by Maxim
PAGE 119

18 • *Columna: Reticulárea cuadrada*
(Column: Square *Reticulárea*), 1972
Stainless-steel wire, metal tubes, iron washers, four pieces of lead, and nylon thread
35 [illegible]/16 x 35 [illegible]/16 x 1 [illegible]/16 inches
Private collection

19 • *Reticulárea: Siete mallas*
(*Reticulárea*: Seven Wire Meshes), 1973
Stainless-steel rods and iron washers
90 [illegible]/16 x 47 [illegible]/4 x 35 [illegible]/16 inches
Courtesy Seka Severin, Caracas

20 • *Chorro*
(Stream), 1974
Aluminum rods
76 [illegible]/4 x 20 [illegible]/16 inches diameter
Universidad Central de Venezuela

21 • *Tronco #3*
(Trunk #3), 1975
Stainless-steel wire
70 x 11 [illegible] inches
Fundación Polar, Caracas

22 • *Sin título: Dibujo sin papel 78/11*
(Untitled: Drawing without Paper 78/11), 1978
Metal assemblage
14 [illegible]/16 x 15 [illegible]/16 x [illegible]/16 inches
Collection Fundación Gego, Caracas

23 • *Sin título: Dibujo sin papel 83/5A*
(Untitled: Drawing without Paper 83/5A), 1983
Iron, galvanized metal mesh, and wire
18 [illegible]/4 x 15 [illegible]/4 x 3 inches
Collection Fundación Gego, Caracas
Photograph by Ricardo Armas
PAGE 130

24 Gego with *Dibujos sin papel*
(Drawings without Paper), 1984
Courtesy Fundación Gego, Caracas
Photograph by Isidro Núñez
PAGE 132

25 • *Sin título: Dibujo sin papel 84/28B*
(Untitled: Drawing without Paper 84/28B), 1984
Plexiglas, steel, and thread
15 [illegible]/4 inches diameter
Collection Fundación Gego, Caracas

26 • *Sin título: Dibujo sin papel 85/2*
(Untitled: Drawing without Paper 85/2), 1985
Metal assemblage
15 x 19 x [illegible]/4 inches
Collection Fundación Gego, Caracas
Photograph by Ricardo Armas
PAGES 6–7, 130

27 • *Sin título: Dibujo sin papel no. 5*
(Untitled: Drawing without Paper No. 5), 1985
Stainless-steel wire, aluminum wire, red cable wire, and metallic rods
34 x 30 x 7 inches
Collection Fundación Gego
Photograph by Reinaldo Armas
PAGES 128–29

28 • *Dibujo sin papel*
(Drawing without Paper), 1985
Iron wire, aluminum rods, wire clothes hangers, and metal mesh
28 $^{5}/_{16}$ x 33 $^{[illegible]}/_{16}$ x 3 $^{[illegible]}/_{16}$ inches
Collection Ignacio and Valentina Oberto

29 • *Sin título 87/9*
(Untitled 87/9), 1987
Metal assemblage sculpture
16 x 25 $^{1}/_{2}$ x 21 $^{1}/_{2}$ inches
Collection Fundación Gego, Caracas
Photograph by Ester Crespín
PAGE 131

30 • *Sin título: De la series "Dibujos sin papel"*
(Untitled: From the series "Drawings without Paper"), 1988
Drill bits, aluminum, and steel wire assemblage
39 $^{[illegible]}/_{8}$ x 27 $^{[illegible]}/_{8}$ inches
Colección Patricia Phelps de Cisneros, Caracas

31 • *Sin título: Dibujo sin papel 88/33*
(Untitled: Drawing without Paper 88/33), 1988
Metal assemblage
9 $^{[illegible]}/_{16}$ x 8 $^{[illegible]}/_{16}$ x 1 $^{4}/_{5}$ inches
Collection Fundación Gego, Caracas

32 • *Sin título: Dibujo sin papel 88/36*
(Untitled: Drawing without Paper 88/36), 1988
Bronze rod and steel mesh
13 x 13 inches
Collection Fundación Gego, Caracas
Photograph by Ricardo Armas
PAGE 130

33 • *Chorro*
(Stream), 1988
Stainless-steel wire
67 $^{[illegible]}/_{8}$ x 32 $^{[illegible]}/_{4}$ x 29 $^{[illegible]}/_{8}$ inches
Collection Banco Mercantil
Photograph by Carlos Germán Rojas
PAGE 24

Mathias Goeritz

1 • *Poema plástico*
(Plastic Poem), 1952
Wrought-iron forms on *El Eco*'s yellow wall
16 $^{1}/_{2}$ x 23 feet
Collection Acervo del patrimonio artístico y cultural de la Facultad de Arquitectura, UNAM

2 *Dibujo ideográfico para el Museo Experimental El Eco*
(Ideographic Drawing for the Experimental Museum *El Eco*), 1952
Ink on paper
10 $^{[illegible]}/_{8}$ x 8 $^{1}/_{2}$ inches
Private collection
PAGE 147

3 • *Museo Experimental El Eco*
(The Experimental Museum *El Eco*), 1952/1999
Reconstructed model
Private collection

4 *Museo Experimental El Eco*
(The Experimental Museum *El Eco*) 1953
Detail: Facade
Courtesy CENIDIAP-INBA
Fondo Mathias Goeritz, Mexico
PAGE 149

5 *Museo Experimental El Eco*
(The Experimental Museum *El Eco*), 1953
Detail: Hallway
Courtesy CENIDIAP-INBA
Fondo Mathias Goeritz, Mexico
PAGES 48, 145

6 *Serpiente de El Eco*
(*Serpent* of *El Eco*), 1953
Courtesy CENIDIAP-INBA
Fondo Mathias Goeritz, Mexico
Photograph by Armando Salas Portugal
PAGES 136-37

7 **Pilar Pellicer next to *El Eco Torso*.** 1953
Courtesy CENIDIAP-INBA
Fondo Mathias Goeritz, Mexico
PAGE 151

8 **The Walter Nicks Ballet in the Experimental Museum *El Eco*.** 1953
Courtesy CENIDIAP-INBA,
Fondo Mathias Goeritz, Mexico
Photograph by Marianne Goeritz
PAGE 150

9 ***Museo Experimental El Eco***
(The Experimental Museum *El Eco*), 1953
Detail: Patio
Published by Gerhard Auer in *Mathias Goeritz El eco*. (Germany: Deutschen Forschungs-gemeinschaft, 1995)
PAGE 153

10 • ***Aquí y allá***
(Here and There), 1955
Carved and polychromed wood
27 1/2 x 27 1/2 x 27 1/2 inches
Private collection

11 • ***Torres de Ciudad Satélite***
(Towers of Satellite City), 1957
Assembled and polychromed cardboard
7 [illegible]/10 x 26 [illegible]/5 x 11 [illegible]/5
Collection Daniel Goeritz

12 ***Torres de Temixco***
(Temixco Towers), 1957–58
Painted brick
Five triangular columns: 14 feet 1 inch; 15 feet 8 inches; 12 feet; 13 feet 7 inches; 12 feet 5 inches
One square column: 13 feet 4 inches
One circular column: 13 feet 4 inches
Photograph by Luis Gordoa
PAGES 21, 141

13 • **Mathias Goeritz in collaboration with architect Luis Barragán *Torres de Ciudad Satélite***
(Towers of Satellite City), 1957–58
Painted concrete
Five towers ranging in size from 121 feet 3 inches to 187 feet high
Courtesy CENIDIAP-INBA
Fondo Mathias Goeritz, Mexico
Photograph by Yutaka Saito
PAGE 138

14 **Mathias Goeritz in collaboration with architect Luis Barragán *Torres de Ciudad Satélite***
(Towers of Satellite City) (Detail), 1957–58
Painted concrete
Five towers ranging in size from 121 feet 3 inches to 187 feet high
Photograph by Luis Gordoa
PAGE 156

15 **Mathias Goeritz designing *Torres de Ciudad Satélite***
(Towers of Satellite City), 1957–58
Courtesy CENIDIAP-INBA
Fondo Mathias Goeritz, Mexico
PAGE 142

16 • ***Torres de Temixco***
(Temixco Towers), 1957–58/1999
Full-scale reconstruction
Five triangular columns: 14 feet 1 inch; 15 feet 8 inches; 12 feet; 13 feet 7 inches; 12 feet 5 inches
One square column: 13 feet 4 inches
One circular column: 13 feet 4 inches
Collection Boris and Yolanda Gerson and Manuel González

17 **Mathias Goeritz in collaboration with architect Ricardo Legorreta *Torres de Automex***
(Automex Towers), 1963–64
Painted concrete
Two towers: 148 feet and 82 feet high
Courtesy CENIDIAP-INBA
Fondo Mathias Goeritz, Mexico
Photograph by Kati Horna
PAGE 160

18 • *Cinco conos*
(Five Cones), ca. 1963–70
Folded and polychromed cardboard
4 1/2 x 13 3/4 x 13 3/4 inches
Private collection

19 • *Cinco torres a base de cubos apilados*
(Five Towers Made of Piled Cubes), ca. 1963–70
Cut wood
8 [illegible]/16 x 2 [illegible]/16 x 2 [illegible]/16 inches
Private collection

20 • *Cinco torres cónicas*
(Five Conical Towers), ca. 1963–70
Folded and painted cardboard
12 [illegible]/16 x 88 [illegible]/16 x 9 7/8 inches
Private collection

21 • *Cinco torres miniaturas en forma de estrella*
(Five Star-shaped Miniature Towers), ca. 1963–70
Assembled and polychromed wood
1 1/8 x 1 15/16 x 1 15/16 inches
Private collection

22 • *Diez torres con punta de prisma*
(Ten Towers with a Prism Top), ca. 1963–70
Assembled and painted wood
8 1/2 x 4 5/16 x 6 5/16 inches
Private collection

23 • *Diez torres*
(Ten Towers), ca. 1963–70
Lathed and polychromed wood
11 13/16 x 11 13/16 x 11 13/16 inches
Private collection

24 • *Once torres cónicas*
(Eleven Conical Towers), ca. 1963–70
Cut, sandpapered, and painted wood
6 7/8 x 11 13/16 x 11 13/16 inches
Private collection

25 • *Once torres cuadradas*
(Eleven Square Towers), ca. 1963–70
Cut wood
6 11/16 x 6 11/16 x 6 11/16 inches
Private collection

26 • *Siete torres cuadradas*
(Seven Square Towers), ca. 1963–70
Cut wood
9 7/8 x 66 [illegible]/16 x 10 5/8 inches
Private collection

27 • *Siete torres cuadradas*
(Seven Square Towers), ca. 1963–70
Assembled and polychromed cardboard
29 15/16 x 27 [illegible]/16 x 27 9/16 inches
Private collection

28 • *Siete torres miniaturas en forma de estrella*
(Seven Star-shaped Miniature Towers),
ca. 1963–70
Assembled and painted wood
1 5/8 x 1 [illegible]/16 1 [illegible]/16 inches
Private collection

29 • *Cuatro torres*
(Four Towers), ca. 1963–70/1997
Assembled wood (exhibition copy)
10 7/8 x 9 [illegible]/4 x 9 7/8 inches
Private collection

30 • *Cuatro torres piramidales*
(Four Pyramidal Towers), ca. 1963–70/1997
Wood (exhibition copy)
18 1/2 x 15 3/4 x 15 3/4 inches
Private collection

31 • *Dos torres*
(Two Towers), ca. 1963–70/1997
Gilded and painted wood (exhibition copy)
11 13/16 x 10 [illegible]/8 x 10 5/8 inches
Private collection

32 • *Nueve torres*
(Nine Towers), ca. 1963–70/1997
Assembled cardboard (exhibition copy)
9 7/8 x 19 11/16 x 19 11/16 inches
Private collection

33 • *Siete torres poliangulares*
(Seven Multiangular Towers), ca. 1963–70/1997
Glued and polychromed wood (exhibition copy)
16 [illegible]/16 x 19 [illegible]/16 x 11 [illegible]/16 inches
Private collection

34 • *Siete torres puntiagudas*
(Seven Pointed Towers), ca. 1963–70/1997
Assembled and painted cardboard
(exhibition copy)
8 [illegible]/16 x 9 [illegible]/8 x 9 [illegible]/8 inches
Private collection

35 • *Siete estrellas*
(Seven Stars), 1967
Cut and polychromed sheet metal
3 [illegible]/16 x 3 [illegible]/16 x [illegible]/16 inches
Private collection

36 • *Torres en medio círculo*
(Towers in a Semicircle), 1967
Carved wood
17 [illegible]/16 x 6 [illegible]/16 x 2 [illegible]/8 inches
Private collection

37 • *La Osa Mayor*
(The Big Dipper), 1968
Assembled and painted cardboard
Seven columns: 11 [illegible]/16 x 2 [illegible]/16 inches each
Collection Helen Escobedo

38 **Mathias Goeritz in collaboration with architects Félix Candela, E. Castañeda Tamborell, and A. Peyrí** ***La Osa Mayor***
(The Big Dipper), 1968
Painted concrete 49 [illegible] feet
Photograph by C. Squcaret
PAGE 164

39 • *Torres*
(Towers), 1969
Cut and polychromed wood
7 [illegible]/16 x 4 [illegible]/16 x 9 [illegible]/8 inches
Private collection

40 **Mathias Goeritz in collaboration with architects A. Spector and M. Amisar**
Laberinto de Jerusalén
(Labyrinth of Jerusalem), 1974–80
Concrete covered with stone from Jerusalem
Photograph by Yoram Lehmann
PAGES 154–55

41 **Mathias Goeritz in collaboration with Helen Escobedo, Manuel Felguérez, Hersúa, Sebastián, and Federico Silva**
El espacio escultórico
(The Sculptural Space), 1979
Ciudad Universitaria, Mexico City
Courtesy Ferruccio Asta (two views)
PAGES 162–63

42 • *Torres ENEP Aragón*
(ENEP Aragón Towers), 1982
Polychromed wood
10 11/16 x 30 5/16 x 30 [illegible]/16 inches
Private collection

43 **Models of Tower Prototypes**
Installation at Museo de Arte Contemporáneo (MARCO), Monterrey, 1998
Courtesy MARCO, Monterrey, Mexico
PAGES 58–59

44 • *Escultura urbana*
(Urban Sculpture), n.d.
Assembled and polychromed wood
7 [illegible]/8 x 6 11/16 inches
Private collection

45 • *Tres torres*
(Three Towers), n.d.
Assembled and painted wood
13 [illegible]/8 x 9 [illegible]/8 x 2 [illegible]/4 inches
Private collection

Hélio Oiticica

1 ***Metaesquema***, 1958
Gouache on paper
22 x 25 inches
Courtesy Projeto Hélio Oiticica, Rio de Janeiro
Photograph by Andreas Valentin
PAGE 187

2 **Model for *Cães de Caça***
(Hunting Dogs Project) (Detail), 1961
Courtesy Projeto Hélio Oiticica, Rio de Janeiro
Photograph by Mustapha Barrat
PAGE 180

3 ***Bólide Vidro 4 Terra***
(Glass *Bólide* 4 Earth), 1964
Courtesy Projeto Hélio Oiticica, Rio de Janeiro
Photograph by Desdémone Bardin
PAGE 184

4 **Nildo of Mangueira with *Parangolé P4 Cape 1***, 1964
Courtesy Projeto Hélio Oiticica, Rio de Janeiro
Photograph by Cesar Oiticica Filho
PAGE 41

5 **The shantytown on Mangueira Hill, Rio de Janeiro**, 1965
Courtesy Guy Brett, London
Photograph by Desdémone Bardin
PAGES 42, 197

6 **Mosquito of Mangueira dancing with *Parangolé P10 Capa 6 com Bólide Vidro 5 (Homenagem a Mondrian)***
(*Parangolé* P10 Cape 6 with Glass *Bólide* 5 [Homage to Mondrian]), 1966
Courtesy Guy Brett
Photograph by Claudio Oiticica
PAGE 170

7 **Hélio Oiticica with *Bólide Caixa 18, Poema Caixa 2 (Homenagem a Cara de Cavalo)***
(*Bólide* Box 18, Poem Box 2 [Homage to Cara de Cavalo]), 1966
Collection Gilberto Chateaubriand, Rio de Janeiro
Courtesy Guy Brett
Photograph by Claudio Oiticica
PAGE 191

8 ***Tropicália* installation with *Penetráveis PN2 and PN3***
(Penetrables PN2 and PN3), 1967
Museu de Arte Moderna, Rio de Janeiro, 1967
Photograph by Carlos
PAGES 42, 196

9 **Nildo of Mangueira with *Parangolé P15 Cape 11***, 1967
Courtesy Guy Brett
PAGE 189

10 ***Parangolé P19 Capa 15, Gilease: A Gilberto Gil***
(*Parangolé* P19 Cape 15, Gilease: To Gilberto Gil), 1968
Courtesy Projeto Hélio Oiticica, Rio de Janeiro
Photograph by Desdémone Bardin
PAGE 18

11 **Drawing of *The Eden Plan, Whitechapel Experience***, Whitechapel Gallery, London, 1969
Courtesy Projeto Hélio Oiticica, Rio de Janeiro
Photograph by Angelo Fiorini
PAGES 172 73

12 ***Bólide área 1 e 2 e Penetrável PN5 Tenda Caetano-Gil em Eden, Whitechapel Experience***
(Area *Bólide* 1 and 2 and Penetrable PN5 Caetano-Gil Tent in *Eden, Whitechapel Experience*), 1969
Installation at Whitechapel Gallery, London
Courtesy Projeto Hélio Oiticica, Rio de Janeiro
Photograph by John Goldblatt
PAGES 168 69

13 *Bólide àrea*
(Area *Bólide*) in ***Eden, Whitechapel Experience***,
1969
Installation at Whitechapel Gallery, London
Courtesy Projeto Hélio Oiticica, Rio de Janeiro
Photograph by Hélio Oiticica

14 *Ninhos*
(Nests) in ***Eden, Whitechapel Experience***, 1969
Installation at Whitechapel Gallery, London
Courtesy Projeto Hélio Oiticica, Rio de Janeiro
Photograph by Guy Brett
PAGE 175

15 ***Whitechapel Experience***, 1969
Installation at Whitechapel Gallery, London
Photograph by Hélio Oiticica
Projeto Hélio Oiticica, Rio de Janeiro
PAGE 178

16 ***Whitechapel Experience***, 1969
Installation at Whitechapel Gallery, London
Photograph by Hélio Oiticica
Projeto Hélio Oiticica, Rio de Janeiro
PAGE 177

17 • ***Eden, Whitechapel Experience***, 1969/1999
Installation
Dimensions variable
Projeto Hélio Oiticica, Rio de Janeiro

18 **Hélio Oiticica in Mangueira, Rio de Janeiro**,
1978
Courtesy Projeto Hélio Oiticica, Rio de Janeiro
Photograph by Desdémone Bardin
PAGE 198

Mira Schendel

1 *Sem título*
(Untitled), 1964
Tempera on wood
20 x 18 inches
Private collection, São Paulo
PAGE 210

2 • *Sem título: Monotipia da série "Arquiteturas"*
(Untitled: Monotype from the series "Architectures"), 1964
Oil on rice paper
18 1/2 x 9 inches
Collection Ada Schendel

3 • *Sem título: Monotipia da série "Arquiteturas"*
(Untitled: Monotype from the series "Architectures"), 1964
Oil on rice paper
18 1/2 x 9 inches
Collection Ada Schendel

4 • *Sem título: Monotipia da série "Arquiteturas"*
(Untitled: Monotype from the series "Architectures"), 1964
Oil on rice paper
18 1/2 x 9 inches
Collection Ada Schendel

5 • *Sem título: Droguinha*
(Untitled: Little Scrap/Nothing), 1964–65
Twisted and knotted rice-paper sheets
14 15/16 inches diameter
Collection Guy Brett, London

6 • *Sem título: Droguinha*
(Untitled: Little Scrap/Nothing), 1964–65
Twisted and knotted rice-paper sheets
(LEFT) Approx. 11 1/16 inches diameter
Twisted and knotted rice-paper sheets
(RIGHT) Approx. 35 3/8 x 35 3/8 inches n.d.
Collection Guy Brett, London
Photograph by Guy Brett
PAGES 218–19

7 *Sem título: Monotipia da série "Escritas"*
(Untitled: Monotype from the series "Writings"), 1964–65
Oil on rice paper
18 x 9 inches
Collection Ada Schendel
PAGE 228

8 *Sem título*
(Untitled), mid-1960s
Mixed media on paper
19 x 15 inches
Collection Maria Lúcia Cacciola, São Paulo
PAGE 213

9 • *Sem título: Trenzinho*
(Untitled: Little Train), mid-1960s
Rice-paper sheets and cotton thread
18 x 9 x 6 inches
Collection Ada Schendel
PAGE 222

10 • *Sem título: Monotipia da série "Escritas" [Ah come mi diverto]*
(Untitled: Monotype from the series "Writings" [Ah, How Much Fun I'm Having]), 1965
Oil on rice paper
18 $^{1}/_{2}$ x 9 inches
Collection Ada Schendel

11 • *Sem título: Monotipia da série "Escritas" [Si al mondo]*
(Untitled: Monotype from the series "Writings" [Yes to the World]), 1965
Oil on rice paper
18 $^{1}/_{2}$ x 9 inches
Collection Ada Schendel

12 • *Sem título: Monotipia da série "Escritas" [Ce sera le jour]*
(Untitled: Monotype from the series "Writings" [That Will Be the Day]), 1965
Oil on rice paper between acrylic sheets
18 x 9 inches
Collection Ada Schendel

13 • *Sem título: Monotipia da série "Escritas" [Mit welt]*
(Untitled: Monotype from the series "Writings" [With World]), 1965
Oil on rice paper
18 $^{1}/_{2}$ x 9 inches
Collection Ada Schendel

14 • *Sem título: Monotipia da série "Escritas" [Nel vuoto del mondo]*
(Untitled: Monotype from the series "Writings" [In the Void of the World]), 1965
Oil on rice paper
18 $^{1}/_{16}$ x 9 inches
Collection Ada Schendel
Photograph by Rômulo Fialdini
PAGE 217

15 • *Objeto linear*
(Linear Object), 1965
Nine monotypes: Oil on rice paper between acrylic sheets
18 $^{1}/_{16}$ x 79 inches
Collection Monica Gutglass
PAGES 214–15

16 • *Sem título: Monotipia da série "Letras"*
(Untitled: Monotype from the series "Letters"), 1965
Oil on rice paper
18 $^{1}/_{2}$ x 9 inches
Collection Ada Schendel

17 • *Sem título: Monotipia da série "Letras"*
(Untitled: Monotype from the series "Letters"), 1965
Oil on rice paper
18 $^{1}/_{2}$ x 9 inches
Collection Ada Schendel

18 • *Sem título: Monotipia da série "Letras"*
(Untitled: Monotype from the series "Letters"), 1965
Oil on rice paper
18 $^{1}/_{2}$ x 9 inches
Collection Ada Schendel

19 Mira Schendel with *Droguinha*, London, 1966
Courtesy Ada Schendel
PAGE 45

20 • *Droguinha*
(Little Scrap/Nothing), 1966
Twisted and braided rice-paper sheets
$19\frac{11}{16}$ inches diameter
Colección Patricia Phelps de Cisneros, Caracas
PAGE 29

21 • *Sem título: Droguinha*
(Untitled: Little Scrap/Nothing), 1966
Twisted and braided rice-paper sheets
18 inches diameter
Collection Ada Schendel
Photograph by Rômulo Fialdini
PAGE 229

22 • *Sem título: Objeto gráfico*
(Untitled: Graphic Object), 1967
Graphite and letraset on rice-paper sheets set between transparent acrylic sheets
$39\frac{3}{8}$ x $39\frac{3}{8}$ inches
Collection Guilherme and Israel Furmanovich
Courtesy Ada Schendel

23 • *Sem título: Objeto gráfico*
(Untitled: Graphic Object), 1967
Oil on rice-paper sheet between two transparent acrylic sheets
$37\frac{7}{8}$ x $37\frac{7}{8}$ inches
Museo de Arte Contemporânea de Campinas "José Pancetti"

24 *Sem título: Objeto gráfico*
(Untitled: Graphic Object), 1967
Oil and letraset on rice-paper sheets set between transparent acrylic sheets
$39\frac{3}{8}$ x $39\frac{3}{8}$ inches
Collection Konrad Gromholt, Oslo
PAGES 260–61

25 • *Sem título: Objeto gráfico*
(Untitled: Graphic Object), late 1960s
Oil on rice-paper sheets set between transparent acrylic sheets
$39\frac{3}{8}$ x $39\frac{3}{8}$ inches
Collection Pedro Tassinari Filho

26 • *Sem título: Objeto gráfico vermelho*
(Untitled: Red Graphic Object), 1967–68
Oil and letraset on rice-paper sheets set between transparent acrylic sheets
36 x 38 inches
Collection Israel Issar Furmanovich
Photograph by Vicente de Mello
PAGES 202–03

27 *Objetos gráficos*
(Graphic Objects)
Installation at the XXXIV Venice Biennale, 1968
Courtesy Ada Schendel
PAGES 224–25

28 • *Sem título*
(Untitled), 1968
Oil and letraset on rice-paper sheets set between transparent acrylic sheets
$39\frac{3}{8}$ x $39\frac{3}{8}$ inches
Collection Ada Schendel

29 • *Sem título*
(Untitled), 1968
Oil and letraset on rice-paper sheets set between transparent acrylic sheets
$39\frac{3}{8}$ x $39\frac{3}{8}$ inches
Collection Ada Schendel

30 • *Sem título: Transformável*
(Untitled: Transformable), early 1970s
Riveted strips of transparent acrylic
$35\frac{7}{16}$ inches length
Collection Ada Schendel

31 • *Sem título: Transformável*
(Untitled: Transformable), early 1970s
Articulated transparent acrylic strips
$78\frac{3}{4}$ x $11\frac{7}{8}$ x $11\frac{7}{8}$ inches
Collection Aracy Amaral

CHECKLIST

32 • *Sem título: Monotipia da série "Letras"*
(Untitled: Monotype from the series "Letters"), 1971
Oil on rice paper
18 1/2 x 9 inches
Collection Ada Schendel

33 *Discos*
(Disks)
Installation at Ralph Camargo Gallery, São Paulo, 1972
Courtesy Ada Schendel
PAGE 206

34 • *Sem título: Disco*
(Untitled: Disk), 1972
Graphite and letraset between brushed acrylic sheets
10 [illegible]/8 x 1/4 inches diameter
Collection Ada Schendel

35 • *Sem título: Toquinho*
(Untitled: *Toquinho*), 1972
White letraset and acrylic over brushed acrylic sheet
17 x 11 1/8 x 1 1/10 inches
Collection Ada Schendel
Photograph by Carlito Carvalhosa

36 • *Sem título: Toquinho*
(Untitled: *Toquinho*), 1972
White letraset and acrylic over brushed acrylic sheet
18 1/8 x 8 x 1 1/4 inches
Collection Ada Schendel

37 • *I Ging*
(I Ching), 1972
Letraset between acrylic sheets
8 1/4 x 1/4 inches diameter
Collection Ada Schendel

38 • *I Ging Tridimensional*
(Three-dimensional I Ching), 1972
Letraset between twenty-five brushed acrylic sheets
7 [illegible]/8 x 3 [illegible]/8 inches diameter
Collection Ada Schendel
PAGE 204

39 • *Objeto gráfico circular*
(Circular Graphic Object), 1973
Letraset on acrylic
8 1/2 inches diameter
Collection Ricard Takeshi Akagawa

40 • *Sem título: Droguinha*
(Untitled: Little Scrap/Nothing), 1987
Twisted and braided rice-paper sheets
15 x 6 x 4 inches
Collection Rodrigo Naves

41 *Sarrafos*
(Slats)
Installation at Gabinete de Arte Raquel Arnaud, São Paulo, 1987
Courtesy Sergio Tomisaki/Fôlha Imagem
PAGE 226

FOLLOWING PAGE: MIRA SCHENDEL ***Untitled: Graphic Object*** 1967

EXERCISE OF FREEDOM

THE EXPERIMENTAL